Down the Road Less Traveled

Alcoholism to Shangri~La

by
Gerald M. Knowles

edited by
Marilyn von Qualen

Best wishes Stan!

Gerald Knowles

FRONT COVER

The picture on the front page portrays the author atop Hunt Mesa looking off in the distant buttes of Monument Valley and its hidden 'Back of Beyond' recesses and passages – much like the labyrinth of challenges facing one's journey down the road of life.

BACK COVER

The scene at the top left is one of the many artist depictions of the fantasies of what Shangri La could have looked like. With the right attitude one can travel there in the mind wherein "the happiness of the soul his lifted above all circumstances."

The portrait at the lower right is a painting of the author done in one hour at an artist contest at a Creede, Colorado festival in 2009.

COPYRIGHT

PUBLICATION DATE: JANUARY, 2018

FIRST PRINTING,   JANUARY, 2018

ISBN—9780578201283

Down the Road Less Traveled

Alcoholism to Shangri-La

$10.00
ISBN 978-0-578-20128-3
51000>

9 780578 201283

1. MEMOIRS/BIOGRAPHY—NONFICTION

2. ALCOHOLISM/ADDICTION

3. NAVAJO/SKINWALKER/WITCHCRAFT

4. CIVIL RIGHTS

5. HARVARD J F SCHOOL OF GOVERNMENT

6. LOCAL EMPOWERMENT

DEDICATION

To all those patient and wonderful people from Flagstaff, Champaign, Gary, Philadelphia, Dine', Navajo, Kiowa, Apache and Zuni for their kind tolerance, support and love - I will never forget you —Wilfred Killup, Emil Nasser, John Paul, Fredde Castleberry, Bill McCullough, Kenny Cogdill, Dr. Minnie Roseberry, Irene Momacita Chavez, Dr. Virgil Gillenwater, Dr. Carry Dawson, Dr. Fred Rodgers, Dr. Ted Uric, Bennie Mae Collins, Dr. Ted Manolakes, Dr. Jacob Curruthers, Dr. Harlan Shores, Pia Melody, Sister Joyce DeHann, Kathleen, Lorraine, Charlene, Velma, Bob, Tim, Maureen, Gregory, Jerrell, Dillon Platero, Alfred Yazzie, James Haungooah, Dr. Francis Becenti , Albert Bailey, Lynne McDonald and Betty Duryea.

Aho!

Acknowledgements

For the thousands of epiphanies shared by my bother and sister alcoholics that have become a composite of my spirit—especially, Rick Hyde, Ed and Betty Aston, David Stuart, and Dr. Robert Peirce.

To all those pioneers in recovery who never stopped looking for answers and found the means to rescue, repair and renew the spirit from out of the grips of despair and incomprehensible demoralization.

Table of Contents

Thrust into the great American Southwest life faced me with a road fraught between the challenges created by emergent social expectations on the one hand and the successive phases of my personal development on the other hand. My path was marked with breathtaking natural wonders, astonishing friends and inspiring experience and rich opportunity. The cumulative deficits of failures to obtain necessary shares of such virtues at each successsive stage made it tough to adequately perform at common standards of success. Alcohol became the substitute to provide escape and a sense of "feel good." At the brink of my dark abyss of self-destruction and despair groups of sober allies lifted me up. The intervention has blessed my life with service and creation for good.

From whence unknown my tiny being alighted aside Cleopatra Hill in the United Verde Hospital amid the raucous and roaring copper mining souls of Jerome, Arizona. Doting females infused deep trust and hope that was essential later to sail through dark clouds of anger and abuse. Power and purpose were forged as tools of survival.

Independence, wealth, romance and determination were discovered in Albuquerque. Fidelity and competence were captured on the football fields of the Winslow Bulldogs. Leadership and sportsmanship were bestowed by long time Flagstaff buddies. Strong identification with the life of Father Damien of the leper colony of Molokai flowered which led to the quest to become a Catholic priest.

Leaving a religious vocation positioned me as ripe for romance and commitment. I suffered a Gatsby romance and ultimately partnered with an idyllic movie star look-alike, married her and fathered four children. I committed to become a teacher instructing elementary children, administering a large school and attaining advanced professional status as a university lab school demonstration teacher. I was catapulted out of Arizona to the University of Illinois doctorate program the attainment of which became a Rubicon crossing and total change of life—exhilarating, prolific, yet leading ultimately to disaster and demoralization.

Tours of duty at three major universities afforded the opportunity to share and implement long held skills and values about education—good motives but faulted delivery. Finding 'no home' again in native Arizona State pushed me to Purdue, the streets of Gary, Indiana and my commitment to social change and civil rights. The wide-open opportunities and pressures accelerated to such a degree that alcohol was required as a substitute for feeling and action. Life became a downward spiral into a black abyss of 'pitiful and incomprehensible demoralization.'

The flight back to Arizona ended in a crash dive into another jail cell. Angels of sobriety appeared and pulled me back from the edge of catastrophe. Cleared of the demons and dysfunction I pledged service to Navajo Nation. I witnessed the creation of hundreds of Navajo teachers and a group of school administrators. I played the unwanted role as prosecutor to remove the president of Navajo Community College.
Refugee from a cancelled election I assisted the administrative capture and embrace of the first Apache controlled school. Then, I worked as a sheep dog for Kayenta in the establishment of the first autonomous Township within a Native American community— awarded high honors by Harvard. The magic carpet of 'Dances with Wolves' days lifted me up and through major challenges.

Now is a time of contemplating my accomplishments and developing a sense of integrity for having a successful life. Noting my gifts of achievements has led to the acquisition of the virtue of wisdom. Onset of wisdom enables me to look back on my life with a sense of closure and completeness, and acceptance death without fear. It is a time of releasing the loss of existing relationships and reuniting with former acquaintances.

The demons of terror, shame, rage and loneliness that had chased my spirit down roads and over passages had vanished. Joy, peace and freedom became irreplaceably bound to my being. The eagle now flies untouched over the storm. 'Happiness of the soul is lifted above all circumstances' and remains inside my personal Shangri La.

Gerald Milton Knowles

Alcoholism

To

Shangri-La

The Road Less Traveled

"Many nights we prayed
With no proof anyone could hear
In our hearts a hope for a song
We barely understood
Now we are not afraid
Although we know there's much to fear
We were moving mountains
Long before we knew we could, whoa,
yes. . ."

(WHEN YOU BELIEVE *by Stephen Schwartz sung*
by, Whitney Houston and Mariah Carey, PRINCE OF
EGYPT. 1998)

I. PASSAGES—Down the Road

I had been bailed out of the Flagstaff jail after my fourth DWI, following prior journeys though jails in Laguna Beach CA, Lafayette IN and Bucks County PA.

The morning sun came through the kitchen window and hit me in the face, piercing the alcoholic fog of denial and dissolution that held me the captive for most of my days. At that time I had no idea that my future passage would be infused with sunlight, that it would grace my spirit and light my way to Shangri La. My spiritual Sherpa – a character named Rick who looked like Mark Twain – began to lead me down a road toward the most exciting and productive aspects of my journey – to a life wherein one embodies the happiness of a being whose soul is lifted above all circumstance, the joy of one undaunted by the ever-present eight winds of change.

As a very young child I was thrilled by the magic of the '30's movie, "Lost Horizon," a magical tale of a mystical little city hidden deep in the Himalayan mountains – an enchanted place where time stood still and where peace, joy and kindness reigned. My life in a way was a set of metaphors not unlike that cinematic plane crash, so similar to the trek across the Himalayas in search of Shangri La, an idyllic valley sheltered from the bitter cold and offering to me protection from the bitter chill of alcoholism.

High mountain inaccessibility, dense blinding blizzards – a terrible isolation begetting a most certain death depicted the sheer hopelessness of encountering any essential to sustain life by the survivors. Sherpas appear out of the blinding snow to rescue the stranded crash victims, guiding them though treacherous mountain passes and icy terrain whereupon, finally, they reached a chasm overlooking a beautiful green valley, a place of eternal joy, freedom and hope where no one ever grew old. Shangri La.

It does seem that life takes one ever upward over mountain passes, through falling rains and snows of experience but like many an alcoholic, deep inside I held the notion that there was a place such as Shangri La, and I came to find that one could in fact soldier on through every storm, achieve more than ever imagined and ultimately sustain the virtues of Hope, Will Power, Purpose, Competence, Fidelity, Love, Caring and Wisdom.

This memoir attempts to describe my life as it happened – an honest story reporting scenes, actions, thoughts and feelings as I recall them— the good the bad and the ugly. It is the truth from my perspective, albeit not the truth in the absolute, nor does it report of what other people or institutions say or think about me and therefore provides no conscious whitewashing of either me or others who have crossed my path. When other individuals come into play I have changed their names or used only first names to protect their confidentiality. Most importantly I wished to avoid any harm that might accrue because of my errors in judging them or misinterpreting their behavior

When writing about oneself the decision has to be made as to what story one wants to tell. There is a strong conscious temptation, or perhaps an unconscious drive, to chronicle solely the good accompanied by rationales, explanations and excuses – in other words, a positive set of memories. However, the rigorously honest truth as one sees it is the only valuable resource that can be shared if one is to help others in their trek through often difficult lives.

The book is organized as an episodic chronicle of my life experiences from infancy to the present. Interpretations of the underlying significance of life's journey are based upon two powerful analyses of the dynamics that heavily influence each phase of life. One faces challenges imbedded with opportunities to gain essential and valuable capabilities on the one hand while avoiding the crippling effects of failure to acquire a significant measure of such competencies on the other. The consequence of being left with deficits of character at each stage cumulate and weaken the ability to meet the challenges in the successive phases of life. For example unless the deep mistrust experienced as an infant is identified and remedied such a shortcoming can act as a thread of over cautiousness and fearfulness throughout life impacting in turn each stage of development.

In the counseling and subsequent analyses of thousands of clients Erik Erickson identified those defects resulting from relative failure during each of those eight stages. The more in depth analyses of the elements, i.e., the causes and conditions of a dysfunctional personality have been chartered by The Meadows. That institution has identified the basis and nature of "Developmental Immaturity"– an innocent-sounding phrase for arrant misery, hopelessness and confusion, and they have worked out successful means of mitigating corresponding defects of character.

I tell my story from the frame of reference of Erickson's "Stages." The conflict of opposing potencies, the challenge being to prevail through each stage by acquiring a given positive attribute of character, e.g., engendering trust over mistrust. I identify with those defects of character – dysfunctions of my persona – and they are discussed in terms of their origin and their detailed play in my life depicting how the presence of each positive ability or absence of same was carried forward, and how they played out in resolving conflicts at each successive stage. There are a number of defined periods in human development – Piaget charts the intellectual; Maslow the quest toward self-actualization; Eckhart Tolle the play of the ego, and so on. I chose Erikson because it aptly describes the roles and challenges imposed by our culture and society at each level of our existence. The resolution of conflicts between the expectation and the response determine the positive and negative consequences of how conflicts are resolved.

However, I point out in these, my personal "Canterbury Tales," the degree to which I was able to cope with each life stage and emerge with positive abilities – or the lack thereof – and manage the dysfunctional consequences of numerous crises. Hopefully the descriptive nature of the dynamic played out in meeting those challenges will be relatively free of ego contamination and be of help to those who yet struggle with substance abuse.

I used the phrase Down the Road Less Followed to relate that all people do not have to follow a life quest ending in darkness and ill-motivated achievement. Sadly, many do go down the road into an abyss of detraction, never to return. If only they could have endured the storms to find their Shangri La.

As my trip through life will attest I feel I was driven by a gift of imagination of which Einstein speaks: "Imagination is more important than knowledge. For knowledge is limited to all we now know and understand, while imagination embraces the entire world, and all there ever will be to know and understand." I cannot claim nor identify the source of my motivation and drive but I did think "Yes!" when I heard Robert Kennedy's "Some men see things as they are, and ask why. I dream of things that never were, and ask why not."

I believe creativity and imagination were gifts bestowed on me by a Higher Power in the Universe. Unfortunately, only late in life was I able to own the reality of who I really was, finally grasping the competencies given to me. Certainly genetic and familial factors contributed a great deal to who I am and what I have done. My father, even though on the far right politically was a very kind, generous and significant leader in pharmacy and local government. He once gave up a chance to acquire a very rich and successful drugstore to avoid taking income away from the owner, Mr. Grager, and instead moved the family from Arizona to Denver.

Early years in Flagstaff and trips to Jerome are detailed in the narrative. I believed (subsequently affirmed by a psychologist) that my mother's mental instability and my father's 24/7 attention to the drug store conditioned me to become a loner who spent a lot of time calculating and maneuvering. I was tagged a "street child" by some.

Like many small communities of the West, Winslow provided a crucible of democracy in the formation of character, commitment and compassion – a cheerful vortex of factors providing a near perfect setting for a teenager's coming of age. World War II roared in its intensity and successes; Route 66 ran through the center of town; settings of geological wonderment provided endless menus of exploration; the culture was densely unified and spirited by the Santa Fe railroad operations; a renowned high school reigned, feared by sports teams and finally, the place was characterized by demonstrated equality to Hispanic, Black, Greek, Chinese and Native American individuals.

I believed I learned empathy from my struggles at St. Anthony's and St. Mary's and watched it play out at Lincoln Elementary in Winslow. One Marcus Barrett, the spitting image of the chubby star of Our Gang, lost his hat to a roving clique of fifth grade bullies and tears steaming down his face, he chased his tormentors in vain. As the boys stormed past I felt something stir deep within me. Most of my life, fear and shame had governed my response to challenge and conflict – I basically froze or went out the back door both mentally and physically. That day I sensed the grief that Marcus was experiencing and saw myself so I reached out, grabbed the hat out of the hand of the gang's leader and returned it to Marcus. Marcus became a close friend that first Winslow year at the Lincoln School fifth grade. The boys who had chased him later became members of the Tucker Flat Gang, a group of fellows who were to be my most cherished pals for the next 70-odd years, our free and carefree escapades contributing significantly to my persona.

It was not surprising that the concept of Therapeutic Empathy emerged as a major variable in my doctoral dissertation. My need for understanding was projected in my role as a teacher and had been identified as critical in any effective interface between individuals.

Grandiosity had to be substituted by true humility – not the same as "humiliation." True humility I have learned is to realize as Einstein believed that all we are and all we have become originates from a mysterious universal dynamic or "higher power," as my fellow alcoholics term it. Humility also requires that I recognize my capabilities as gifts not to be demeaned by false humility, but to be exercised in caring for my fellows.

I have often alluded to the difference between the motivation to achieve and the need to avoid failure. Achievers select and make practical decisions following their choices and their ascent within professional hierarchies. Visibility, prominence and financial gain are construed as expected and respected endeavors. Those driven to avoid failure choose either very simple tasks or very difficult projects wherein if defeat presented, there would be no onus of failure for one "dreaming the impossible dream" – a perfect setup for the ego combining altruism with the impossible. Pursuing an avenue requiring a professional modicum of performance as traditionally defined in an academe gave made me shudder with the fear of shame that might accrue at failing to live up to expectations.

Still, limping along with an inadequate self confidence and carrying the wounds accumulated from past missteps, I now feel that my professional colleagues who had placed me in a position as a department chairman at the University of New Mexico were devastated when I withdrew my name from consideration the very morning of my pending appointment. My Boss, Dillon Platero, Director of the Navajo Division of Education, had spoken to me the night before assuring me that staying with the Navajo Tribe would be much more exciting than an administrative tour in New Mexico. The perfect paradigm and cliché – "man turns down power and money to help native people." The colleagues would not speak to me and audiences later in life recoiled with revulsion when I shared my "gallant scenario."

As I look back in life I have identified the "fear of the pain of shame" to be at the core of my thoughts, words and deeds. I avoided any overt performance that would expose weakness or imperfection in my persona. I had to find a way to walk through the dark cloud of shame to reach the sunshine of my soul. I have been one of those blessed to make that trip and survive down the road less traveled.

How I was able to actualize myself academically and professionally is a mystery. All my life, though, I did seem to enjoy creating. I ran a model-building workshop out of my garage when I was eight, making tanks and teaching the neighborhood how to do it by putting together two by four pieces and painting them red. I had my own football and basketball teams. I spent hours gluing together Naval ship models and a spitfire airplane demanding an intricate balsawood skeletal structure.

Saul Alansky (RULES FOR RADICALS) notes that some people are motivated to organize and others to manage or administer. Steve Jobs of Apple repeatedly commented to NBC's Brian Williams that he was inspired to create and not to rest on his achievements, prominence or fortune. When I heard that comment it ignited a realization in me about my own life. Since I am name-dropping as regards achievement, I might as well mention Einstein who stated that "Logic will get you from A to B – imagination will take you everywhere."

"The most beautiful thing we can experience is the mysterious. It is the source of all true art and science. He to whom the emotion is a stranger, who can no longer pause to wonder and stand wrapped in awe, is as good as dead – his eyes are closed. The insight into the mystery of life, coupled though it is with fear, has also given rise to religion. To know what is impenetrable to us really exists, manifesting itself as the highest wisdom and the most radiant beauty, which our dull faculties can comprehend only in their most primitive forms – this knowledge, this feeling is at the center of true religiousness," (Albert Einstein, THE WORLD AS I SEE IT, 1949).

I once wrote to my academic advisor at Illinois to apologize for what I had done with my professional degree. My sponsor stated in my files that I had been "the best graduate student he had in twenty years." Overtures came in from all directions – Emory University, New Mexico University, Buffalo, Washington, Department Chair at Kent State, and the University of Florida. An official of UF quipped to a friend that I "had to produce." I found this frightening, as my understandings of my professional goals were non-existent. I was driven by a dysfunctional ego puffed with immature arrogance and grandiosity. I once turned down an invitation to interview for a position at New York University.

A cumulative deficit of ineffectiveness made it harder and harder for me to handle situations. Escape to isles of security available in high school had long disappeared. My entry into the seminary, random courtship events, roles as a teacher along with the graduate school society thrust me into university visibility, but professional activities provided little cover for my ineptness. My travels across the U.S. to New York, Washington, St. Louis and San Francisco became opportune times to exhibit arrogance and grandeur and continue the never-ending search for "Her." Chance encounters appeared at every corner, and my character faults were easily hidden, or so I thought, by Old Grand Dad 100 proof, gimlets or the pernod and vodka cocktail discovered in Laguna Beach.

The devastation of alcoholism is poignantly chronicled by my personal episodes – the comical, the perilous, the tragic and the pathetic – but know that this is not an attempt to excuse my behavior nor minimize and rationalize the impact of such behavior on my family, friends, associates and intimate acquaintances. What is often shared as a "drunken log" by my alcoholic friends is not an "excuse for sins" but an essential testimonial offering understanding and gratitude for being snatched from the abyss of hell itself.

Recovery from alcoholism requires full amends to anyone and everyone. Such amends may include processes and even institutions impacted by dysfunctional behavior. The Navajo people call making amends "hozho," which means action designed to restore beauty, order, and harmony "back to the way things were." Making up for the damage done by alcoholic antics can mean a prison term, paying out large sums of money, going to extreme lengths to contact injured people and more. Such a transformation of life also requires developing and acting out habits and attitudes which are the total opposite of the extreme negatives that drove one's alcoholic mind and behavior. My arrogance had to be eased and substituted by empathy and compassion for anyone and everyone in my past and present environment. My mindset had to express what Francis of Assisi suggested – "It is better to understand than to be understood."

Unfortunately many alcoholics going through the process of identifying their dysfunctions get stuck in a sea of negativity and stagnate from a point of view of worth-lessness, from denying their true qualities and from failing to use their gifts in service of their brothers and sisters. It's like a talented fullback who, in dismissing his own talents, underperforms out of false humility and causes his team to lose.

I relate the causes and conditions of my problem with alcohol neither for self-con-demnation nor for self-glorification, but to share the gifts of hope, strength and expe-rience with others, to perhaps show them a way out and up. Too, I identify the imperfections causing one to seek a short-lived balm through mood altering chemi-cals, substituting them for real joy and freedom. I talk about the nature and acquisi-tion of new habits, new outlooks that provide the manifestations of peace and of beauty available to all human beings.

My addiction to alcohol was combined with an addiction to nicotine, which seductive cigarettes taught me that the craving of a substance could be totally overwhelming. Once tasted, alcohol not only manifested an obsession but also played upon a con-flicted mind, one that chronically lacked a sense of wellbeing and was characterized by irritable discontent. Once introduced into the psyche and body, both alcohol and nicotine set up voices crying over and over again to be fed with more and more. Thus, substances by their very nature have the ability to become addictive.

As chronicled in this book, the first forty years of my life were burdened by heavy character deficits. But in spite of such handicaps, I was somehow able to produce. But once I crossed the Rubicon and abandoned alcohol and mood altering substances, I came to a belief in the efficacy of doing the right thing and in that process recaptured a sense of purpose and competence as a professional.

Saved from disasters on the dark roads, rescued from the certain destruction of my ca-reer, my life and any chance to generate the good just the sheer joy of helping others in my realm, of being able to create, have been their own rewards. Still, I do say qui-etly to myself "if I had it to do over I would have done it differently, and better."

If you dare to laugh, weep, and be awed come follow me over the mountains and pas-sages Down the Road Less Traveled ~ from Alcoholism to Shangri La.

The United Verde Hospital-1932

II. BEGINNINGS

Grand Entry—Cleopatra Hill

Mother Mabel had struggled with intense labor pains for several days prior to my birth. Certainly my fetal self was aware of severe changes occurring. I probably exited the womb with some visceral concerns about what was happening. However the arrays of new and unpleasant feelings were met with a plethora of comforting hugs, rocking, coos and visual administers to body, skin and tummy.

Heehaws, clucking and barking resounding off the steep streets of Cleopatra Hill in old Jerome were a fitting setting for the first stage of my life. Grand people, adoring aunts and Mabel's friends infused the warm Arizona air with joy and contentment –I met each encounter with the exuberance of a Labradoodle puppy to each new face, each new smile.

The broad and distant panorama of the Verde Valley stretching below Cleopatra, the crimson spires of Sedona and distant and mysterious Sycamore Canyon beyond punctuated by the San Francisco Peaks atop the

Doting Ladies Everywhere

Mongolian Rim infused sense of exploration, mystery and expectation among Jerome residents of the 1930's.

Even in 1932 the United Verde Hospital was being established as a haven for ghosts. Whether or not ghosts played any role in my mother Mabel's three excruciating days of labor to bring me onto my first the stage of life and out of the secure contentment of the womb is not known. Somehow I seemed to have known about the suffering that preceded my birth. The swat on my backside to give me the breath of life hurled me into stark reality. Hungry, wet and struggling with hands and feet to grapple with and adapt to a hostile world I was met with high voices of love, praise, warm hands rubbing and rocking me. All those ladies and my mother seemed to be doing what I needed to make me feel okay. Cold wet diapers; an empty tummy and the darkness of the night lying in the crib planted a chronic fear of abandonment deep down inside my little mind and heart. Such anxiety was soon mitigated with infantile knowledge that my plight would not last – Mom and the ladies would come —— and I trusted and knew the pain would not last.

Thus, hope was born that November of 1932 in the copper mining town of Jerome,

STAGE ONE–TRUST OVER MISTRUST TO ESTABLISH HOPE (0–1 YR.)
The newborn arrives into unpleasentries-a slap, wet diapers, aching tummy and the loss of warmth and closeness of the womb. His uncertainty requires stability and consistency and with that he develops a sense of trust that leads to the virtue of hope. Hope means others will be there for support; lack of hope leads to fear. If care is inconsistent, unpredictable and unreliable, then the infant will develop a sense of mistrust and will not have confidence in the world. The basic sense of mistrust is carried to other relationships coupled with anxiety and heightened insecurities. (Erik Erikson. 1950. Childhood and Society. W. W. Norton & Company: New York)

Arizona. It would be a guiding light through many dark days and challenges of my journey through life.

Years later I realized that I had been deposited into the milieu of a western mining town that rocked with activity, joy, fun and vast expectations for what life had to offer. Somehow this was imprinted in my psyche and remained there all throughout my life.

TRUST AND HOPE

I existed with a sense of infantile joyful transcendence—"the happiness of a soul which is 'lifted above every circumstance.'"(This is a quote reminiscent of theologian and existential philosopher Paul Tillich's description of Joy). Jerome contained a "House of Joy" during the period, but it represented a totally different notion. That first year of my existence in old Jerome was almost like paradise. I even had a throne and a palace that turned out to be a place of comfort and meaning during each period life's journey—the corner Drug Store Soda Fountain. Doting characters responded everywhere I went—Grandma Trudy, Aunt Betty, Uncles Dan and Jim, cousin Jackie and even uncle Art Esty whose presence was often signaled by strong whiffs of bourbon depending on whether or not he had made the daily trek from way down from the Gulch up to the bar in downtown Jerome. Little did I know at that time how the smell of alcohol would play a major part of my life.

The first time I heard Bix Beiderbecke playing the trumpet I thought, "Ah, Aunt Lillian"— a quintessential roaring twenty's girl. I began to think Lillian was my mother as I spent so much time with her – this was before she and Jim McCord adopted their only son, Jimmy. The fundamentalist Christian Baptist aura of Jim and Lillian had little impression or impact on me. The Jerome subculture of fun, love of life and the mutual loyalty and respect characteristic of residents of Arizona mining towns acted as a bond that created a community in which the people were lifted above their individual circumstances.

THE LADIES

Aunt Faye, my Dad's sister, was her whole life a beam of sweetness and acceptance for me even after I shed that rain of infantile adoration given by all the "mothering" females of my first weeks and months of life. Faye was the female counter part of my father, Jack—calm, serious yet kind and supportive.

Grandma Gertrude Reedy, (Trudy) Dad's mother, was not a major player during the early days of Jerome. She was always on the go – to Jerome, back to Ohio and then again back to Oregon to visit Jack's half brother, Gene, and half sister, Marge. Yet

Trudy was still a part of the troupe of my admirers, always projecting love and acceptance, but never to the extreme. Trudy was the only grandparent I knew as all other grand people had died under questionable circumstances.

In retrospect, the cadre of women vying to take care and mother me probably acted as a buffer to my mother Mabel's psychosis masked by the her jolly and vivacious outside demeanor. Such reservations about my "preciousness" surfaced years later when Mabel revealed a sudden belief held silently for so long surfaced— "you almost killed me, and sometimes I wish you had never been born." The statement only confirmed those fleeting fears I had had at certain times. Searching for reasons why my mother might have difficulty with her maternal role brought to mind the fact that she had already been a "mother" to her five brothers who had more or less been orphaned at a very early age by the accidental and tragic death of my grandmother, Maggie (Lynch) Mason of theatric fame.

NEAR FETAL FALL

Dwellings of Jerome perched high upon the cobbled streets had entrances level with the street, but back doors that dropped as steep as forty feet. Among the favorite tales of family life in Jerome was the evening in which I, newly empowered with crawling, had disappeared out of the living room.

"Oh my God, Lillian screamed where is he"? Faye, Lillian, Mabel and Mary Lee rushed into the back rooms on the Upper Hogback. Faye caught sight of my paunchy-diapered rear end moving out near the edge of the back porch. The house had a lower level room, which made it a twenty-seven foot drop off the porch to the ground below. Breathless with fear Faye bolted and reached me by my little leg just when I was about to plunge off into space. As a baby, somewhat fearless in my explorations with the infantile unawareness of danger, I could only giggle at the reaction of alarm expressed by my adoring bondmaids who expected to respond with joy to my every act. I once stuck my hand in an electric socket and, not being grounded avoided electrocution.

LIFE IN OLD JEROME

Certainly life in Jerome in the late 20's and early 30's was rich and varied. Deer, duck, turkey and quail hunting actually provided meat on the table for many. The legendary event wherein father Jack and friends buried a chicken covered in mud in the ground packed with burning coals always surfaced at family gatherings and garnered a big laugh.

The young neophytes to western cuisine were instructed to cover birds with mud and bury them in a pit of coals to bake. When the bird was roasted to perfection they were told you could remove the hard baked mud shell and the feathers would come off with it. Everything went well as planed until after removing the shell and feathers the bird was sliced open to eat. They had forgot to take out the entrails of the chicken.

All over the Verde Valley below Jerome was the playground for residents. The lighted entrance of hexagonal Dance Pavilion at Peck's Lake beckoned couples each Saturday night. Festivals and other forms of merrymaking included participants across all social classes, from mine administrators, clergymen as well as those "muckers" who worked in the bowels of the mines under the city of Jerome itself. My Uncle Dan and Uncle Jim both came to Jerome to play semi-pro baseball which was only one of the vibrant activities that made for a most exhilarating life.

An accidental explosion in the 20's caused a subsequent movement of buildings down Cleopatra Hill, notably the small jailhouse and Jack's pharmacy, which slid one block down to the next level.

Thus, my infant persona was nurtured in a crucible of the magnificence of Arizona beauty, adoring and attendant females and men who reflected Antarctic Explorer Ernest Shackleton's attitude of "Never the Lowered Banner, Never the Last Endeavor".

That first year of life in Jerome became a grand entry for me. I became glad to be held, fed and cooed-even separated from Mom without fear or loneliness. I could approach any and all of my peers and adults without suspicion about their character or motives- all was good. I had learned to love the looks and touches I got from all those adoring admirers. I had been infused into a network of vibrant and nurturing relationships.

As the family moved to Holbrook I retained a deep trust and hope in what awaited me. I would need all the trust I could muster to survive the next two years.

OVERFLOWING WITH TRUST AND HOPE

To this day entering the Jerome area fires deep and hidden joys about my existence those first months of life. Jerome is home and "my spot" as Don Juan the Yaqui sorcerer would note. The especially joyous milieu that engulfed life in Jerome, coupled with the incessant comfort and love of the legion of adoring ladies armed me with enormous trust and hope about life that I could carry into my next phase of existence. That paradise existed would be forever embedded in my soul.

Darkness—Holbrook

Which Mother?

It was over fifty years later that I learned that I had two mothers. This revelation explained the source of my life long confusion in my dreams about the contrasting characteristics of the two prominent women who alternately appeared, one to always support and the other always to let down; one an angel, the other an angry vixen. I discovered nearly fifty years later that I had an additional non-maternal mother who was present the second year of my life—Momacita Irene Chavez. I experienced what I now remember of strong memories of uncertainty, pain, fear and loneliness in those Holbrook Days that made me yearn to be back on Cleopatra

Momacita Irene Chavez

Hill in the arms of those excessively doting ladies. Something went wrong and I obsessed about being with a mother. Which one, I wasn't sure. I was beginning to meet strangers with disinterest and turning my head away. I would not look at them. Placed in the arms of someone I didn't know often caused me to cry out and reach for my mother. I would rather be left alone with my toys on the living room carpet and did not welcome other children to play, except cousin Jackie whom I adored then and the rest of my life.

Frontier Town

Also, Holbrook, Arizona, where father Jack had accepted a position as pharmacist at the Guttery Drug, was a drab high desert town known for violence and a hang out for

STAGE TWO—Autonomy over Shame and Doubt toward establishing Will Power (1–3 yrs.) From ages of 18 months and three a child is developing physically and becoming more mobile, asserting his independence, discovering that he or she has many skills and abilities. The child explores the limits of his or her abilities within an encouraging environment that tolerates failure. With a growing sense of independence and autonomy a child should not be criticized for failures and accidents (particularly when toilet training). The aim has to be "self control without a loss of self-esteem" supported in their increased independence, a child becomes more confident and secure in his or her own ability to survive in the world. Criticized, overly controlled, or not given the opportunity to assert themselves, they begin to feel inadequate in their ability to survive, and may then become overly dependent upon others, lack self-esteem, and feel a sense of shame or doubt in their own abilities.

the infamous Hash Knife Outfit cowboys of the late 1800's. The Blevins House was a stone's throw from momacita Irene Chavez's residence. Five sheep people had been murdered there by Navajo County Sheriff Commodore Perry Owens in the famous Sheep-Cattle feud.

The north of Holbrook lay a ridge of red sandstone which had functioned as an inscription board for the ancient Anasazi inhabitants, who had left their messages on the stones eight hundred years ago. Such petroglyphs can be seen etched upon the face of rocks clear across northern Arizona north of Interstate 40.

In addition to its ancient human inhabitants, Holbrook also lay in what was one of the largest fresh water prehistoric lakes, Lake Bitahochee, which reveled the great lakes in size. Various layers of sediment long morphed into stone, including petrified wood trees, can be found in nearby hills of the Painted Desert and on the Navajo Nation. Holbrook was also a major stopping point for travelers across America from Santa Monica to Chicago traversing the National Highway that was later to become Route 66. Lt Beal surveyed the route across Arizona to California by using Camels. His original route went right through downtown Holbrook.

Holbrook was also a stage stop for the trip down to the Valley of the Sun to Phoenix and on south to Tucson. It functioned as a Pony Express Station.

Holbrook acted as a stopping point for the Pacific Railroad, later to become the Santa Fe and today, the Braniff-Santa Fe. Passengers could disembark off the chair cars and eat oysters quaffed down with French wine in an eatery made up of four boxcars. That eatery had found a place in the old west and became the dawn of Fred Harvey's gourmet cuisine chronicled in "Arizona's Dark and Bloody Ground." Down the street from Irene was also the Bucket of Blood Saloon, formerly called the "Cottage" until someone renamed it because of the huge pool of blood left after a Hashknife gun battle.

Momacita

Irene Chavez in her early twenties had migrated from Spain to Hot Springs (Truth or Consequences), New Mexico to join sheepherder relatives who had come to the New Mexico-Arizona Territories to find new lives. She soon moved to Holbrook and lived a stone's throw from the Santa Fe Railroad in a small house set in a bosque of giant cottonwood trees that still line the ancient and original front street of Holbrook along the railroad along with the Bucket of Blood and other businesses of long ago.

GUTTERY DRUG

My mother Mabel and father Jack moved into the back of Guttery's Drug on the Alley next door to the Masonic Temple. Both of my parents worked from dawn to dusk to serve not only locals, but also the travelers pouring through town on the Old Trails Highway, newly named, "Route 66." It has never been determined in my mind as to whether Mabel simply found it overwhelming to nurture me solo without the supporting covey of the Jerome family and friends, or that her commitment to Jack's career demanded her full attention. For whatever reason, most likely Mabel's unconscious distain for the mother role based on some tough experience "raising" her five brothers, Irene Chavez was commissioned as my baby sitter. Fifty years later, while teaching Developmental Learning and Educational Psychology for the University of Arizona, I visited Irene to find out about my early second year of life in Holbrook. As years went by I had received cards for my birthday and Christmas from Irene that contained poignant and touching phases in broken English scrawled across the face of the cards. Questioning my mother about Irene only received vague and even what appeared to be guarded responses. Hence a mystery was born that lasted for fifty years only to be dispelled by a quirk of fortune.

THE LITTLE HOUSE

As I trod toward that little house behind Romo's Mexican food restaurant on Holbrook's main drag (old Route 66) in 1981, I expected a nice reception and even a reunion of sorts with Irene. Instead, the little women with the hazel blue eyes opened the door and screamed with tears in her eyes, "Mi bebé dónde has estado todos estos años !!!, (My baby, where have you been all these years!!!)" In the back of the small living room I could see a tall chest with two candles burning. There was a framed picture in the center. I looked and saw a young beautiful Hispanic Irene Chavez standing next to a young girl with her arm on the handle of a baby buggy. As I looked closely I could see the face of this little child. The faced matched pictures I had seen and I shockingly realized that was me in the picture – I was Irene's Boy!

That day I learned that I had lived with Irene day and night for seven months – the total time Mabel and Jack lived and worked in Holbrook. It seemed that Mabel and Jack frequently took me "home" to the back of the drug store, but for all practical purposes and for whatever reasons I was abandoned and was learning Spanish as my first language. "Dame aqua, dame leche, Momacita!!" I now had not a covey of women but one beautiful warm and loving Hispanic woman giving me attention all the time. Her persona kept the trust and hope alive while off in the distance I seemed to see darkness. Having no children of her own, I was Irene's only child and she was fiercely protective of me that second year of life and intense about my welfare until she died in the late 1990's.

SOURCE OF DARKNESS

On that reunion day in Holbrook with my "Momacita" I found out the source of my darkness that occurred that second year of life. Knowing the extreme and turbulent youth that my mother had experienced helped me understand and accept my mother's reticence to give me total support. At the same time parents in those days were extremely sensitive to the achievements and progress of their kids. Successful potty training had to be accomplished by a certain age or it cast doubts upon the character of the child and the family itself.

Irene revealed an episode affecting me that until that day had been hidden deep inside my mind. It was a powerful and hidden ghost operating unconsciously chipping away at how I valued myself and even dimming the lights of trust and hope that I had acquired my first year in those wonderful Jerome days.

Irene described a scene of this little baby sitting on a potty chair grimacing with fear and frustration. Mabel was screaming. "Go!Go!Go!" When nothing happened Mabel would swat me with a paddle fashioned from a cigar box lid. Each time this regimen was repeated, Irene would scream, "Dejar de golpear a mi niño, (Stop hitting my boy)!" Finally, after forty-five minutes of "potty training" Irene grabbed the paddle out of Mabel's hand who in turn grabbed at Irene's hand only to receive a blow on the side of her head!

EXITING HOLBROOK

What part if any my loss of Irene's sweet presence had to do with the family exit back to Jerome is hard to say. My frequent requests and comments in Spanish- "Dame agua,Dame leche"— infuriated Mabel. She had acquired a severe prejudice against the Latino character which she often cited was caused by the frijoles diet and emission of gas emitted in the Secret Heart Church Services in Jerome. She claimed this to be her exit from Catholicism in Jerome and which she carried on into Holbrook days. Irene had been OK until she stepped out of her place in support of me appearing to garner a significant maternal role.

Holbrook had casted a deep shadow over my *bon vivant* and joyful infancy of early Jerome days and I was now less open to other adults, suspicious to any new strangers and different environs. There was a loneliness and unhappiness inside. "Mine! My toys!" I screamed when other children played with my stuff.

Father Jack was given the chance to return to Jerome to work once again in the drug store on Main Street. He had left his junior year in high school to work on its soda fountain and gravitated as a sub to cover the absence of the alcoholic pharmacist. Self study of stacks of pharmacy volumes prepared him to pass the state certification requirement in New Mexico while living in Gallup, a site no doubt and the spot on the planet where I was conceived. Jack's job offer at his old Drug Store in Jerome was the prime cause for the families return to Jerome in 1934.

Although the same team of doting females and extended family members still lived in Jerome, I had changed and lost some of my infantile charm and the light heartedness and the warmth of Jerome could no longer reach deep inside the shadows of my heart and mind. The shame of my apparent failure to do potty correctly amid a major war between "two mothers" had been etched in my soul dampening my zest and expectations for life – my baby passion for exploration had been dulled with doubt and fear.

REMEMBERING JEROME—BACK AT THE START
CRITICAL CHARACTERS

It fascinated me all my life to hear the special names for parts of Jerome. Grandma Trudy and Aunt Betty had houses in "The Gulch," a canyon at the base of Cleopatra Hill with a small dirt road winding west up the canyon off of Highway 89. It later became the family get-together rendezvous site for holidays. Then there was my original home on "Upper Hogback" and the place of my near fatal fall off a back porch. As it happened the family inevitably returned to live on the Upper Hogback and it was a treasured asset to me for my cousin Jackie Bean took me under his wing as a friend and confidant. Jackie possessed the major equipment treasured by all kids- a BB gun. It was the prized possession that I

On Upper Hogback

went for upon immediate arrival in the Jerome visits. I forced my dad to go to Millers Department Store to get a package of BB's. I saw Jackie Bean as the closest thing to me as a "brother" for his caring and kindness toward me. He was my mentor for the secure exploration of the streets and mine shaft ridden hills around Jerome. But most of all he like me had also had a shock of flaming red hair. Jackie's little sister Carole, who later grew to be a doppelganger of Rosemary Clooney, also played an important peer and support for me. And for the first time a dog entered my life as an unshakable ally and chum. "Skippy " was a true pointer who unfortunately didn't know to his consternation that Arizona quail did not set, but would only scatter and run along the ground in their escape. Golden days with Skippy, Carole and Jackie in the enthralling environs of old Jerome began to ease some of my deep doubts about life and infuse some joy and confidence back into my soul.

There were other characters in the "Canterbury Tales" of old Jerome that had primary significance in my little universe. Uncle Art Esty, the archetypal plumber, was the quintessential and classic caricature of a true alcoholic. White waxy skin, piercing cobalt eyes and jet-black hair postured him as a mysterious figure out of Bella La Gosse movie. Little was commented about Art except that Rattlers and Scorpion who had bit him under Jerome houses had no effect on his alcoholic carcass – in fact the bites were often fatal to snakes and bugs. The sad and solemn face of Grandma Trudy's sister and my grand Aunt Betty told the story of Uncle Art's life. It was humored he had molested every female relative he could get his hands on. There was a silent acceptance that his death from salivary gland cancer was in fact a form of *karmic* justice.

Uncle Gene, my Dad's half brother born to Trudy's second marriage, was to be the perpetrator of a major disabling blow to my sense of security and confidence. For on a certain night while I was alone in a large living room in Flagstaff Uncle Gene turned out all the lights and began to howl and scream like a wolf. I could catch glimpses of the shadowy figure moving rapidly and popping up from behind furniture. I stood motionless paralyzed by terror. As a result a part of my mind seemed to be perpetually stuck in that darkness. The scene and terror diminished over time, but I could never seem to dispel the cloud that hung over me as I tread each new path and challenge. It was just one more dimension of mistrust that would stand as a lifelong hurdle and challenge to conquer.

UMBILICAL CORD

Navajo medicine men often informed me that wherever one's umbilical cord is buried is the spot on earth that becomes most favored by an individual. Warmth, love and security always seemed to reflect off the mountains, hills and streets of old Jerome at any time I found himself there, even during many decades later.

It was many years later when I discovered the legend about the United Verde Hospital being considered the most haunted place west of the Mississippi. When it became the Jerome Grand Hotel it became a prized site by ghost hunters. Deep in the darkness one night I found some evidence to confirm its mythology.

Becoming A Significant Member

A revitalizing sense of security and identity emerged during my third year of life in Jerome. I was immersed at a higher level into the meaning and support of being a significant member of an extended family. Jerome had become "home" and would al-

A Signifigant Member-Jerome, 1938

ways stimulate a sense of belonging and the "good life" throughout all of the years when I found myself rolling up its steep avenues or gazing up the canyon in the Gulch. Each family member had a script and costume with a story to tell little me. Faye's dependable smile and calmness was always there no matter what; Uncle Dan's semi-pro baseball confidence stood as a model to be incorporated in one's identity. Aunt Betty's sweet kindness perpetually glowed in spite of her pain as she persevered the tribulations foisted upon her by her mate's alcoholism. Uncle Art's plumbing business signaled the possibility of one's complete independence; Grandma Trudy's quiet and sane way of looking at all dimensions of life affirmed the possibility of stability in life. By far the deepest impact on my life came from cousin Jackie's mentoring with its unending care and affirmations of my being. He became the treasured gift of my extended family identity even to that day when I cast his ashes off an old hang glider site atop Mingus Mountain.

Countless Holidays

Countless upon countless holidays were spent in the house down in the Gulch. Oh what sense of well-being arose when the family gathered around the Christmas dining table! I escaped the long line of root foods being offered. "No, Grandma, I don't eat turnips, no, Grandma, I don't eat parsnips, no, Grandma, I don't eat beets, no, Grandma, I don't eat rutabaga or even dressing for that matter, just give me some light turkey with gravy and some mashed potatoes," was my consistent litany. Pumpkin and pecan pie and some mince meat topped off the holiday dinner. There was fruit cake in slabs which I, Jackie, Carole and Jimmy loved and could have without Dan's specials sauce concocted into a paste combining butter, powdered sugar and brandy. I tried all my life to replicate the "strawberry fudge" created by Aunt Faye which was basically the ingredients of standard chocolate fudge with strawberrys a substitute for the chocolate. I have always ended up with strawberry jam each time I attempted

Faye's concoction.

No substantial leftovers ever. Uncle Dan and Jackie would remain as the sole isolates who were left at the table slowing eating almost any leftovers of the holiday dinner. The family adults had no need for the children during the consumption of alcoholic beverages until the sun disappeared over Cleopatra. Carole, Jimmy and I were stuffed into the Buick and hauled up the winding road to Jerome's downtown theatre, "The Liberty" for a Charlie Chan serial and an Andy Hardy movie.

WHITE SPECTER

Even to this day the Jerome setting provides mystery, enchantment and stimulating scenes. Up on the hill above the Gulch house on those holidays Skippy would always initiate a barking binge while standing motionless with nose and tail pointed strait out toward some bushes. The quail he had identified never stayed, but took off in low flying sprints off up the hill to Skippy's consternation. "Go call him, " Uncle Dam would say. Arizona quail did not fly but would run along the ground under the bushes.

During my high school sophomore year I stayed with his Aunt Faye at the Gulch home. One night I slept out on the front porch surrounded on two sides by those ivy-covered lattices, the winds drifting down from Mingus Mountain periodically rattling leaves on the vine covered lattices. The west end of the porch was open and I could peer far up Gulch Canyon. I'd been reading Bram Stoker's "Dracula" and I had struggled over the years with the notion that I really saw a white specter cross the canyon floor, stop and peer directly at me. It seemed so real that night in the moonlight, but so improbable in retrospect.

Standing at midnight on my sixty-fifth birthday on the old United Verde Hospital balcony looking down into the Gulch an icy breeze crossed my neck. I once again absolutely make out the apparition in the Gulch. I recognized that my fear of the dark instilled one night at age three by my uncle Gene was still operable. Dashing out the lights in that empty house, making howling sounds as Gene's shadowy figure moved around the room was an unforgettable terror. In spite of the knowledge that helped me cope, in spite of my acceptance of the roots of this fear of darkness, that fear would always remain to some degree in my psyche—enough to leave the lights on when alone in a house years later.

ENDURANCE—FLAGSTAFF

DUPLEX DAYS—TETHERED AND ESCAPE

A dazzling sage green spot had been burned into the back of my eye as I peered into the skies above Flagstaff not realizing that I had briefly gazed directly into the sun. The sound of the noon whistle in the hot summer air shifted my gaze to focus on the giant clock in the courthouse tower rising to the northeast of the duplex back yard. I was angered and frustrated at being tethered by a harness to the cloths line and I would run back and forth coming to a sudden jerking stop as I reached the end of my "leash." Though I could neither form nor hear the words, my little muscular body saw the scene

In the Grips of Wrath

being acted out. "She has me bound again – I will escape and go see Dad at the drug store downtown." I finally ran so hard that I broke my harness into "freedom."

Escaping the clothesline tether the first year of those six spent in Flagstaff was only the first of the many challenges and conflicts I would face and overcome. I would grasp the need for self-assertion, enjoy as sense of freedom, experience intense pain, the fear of death and just barely escape the grim reaper. I discovered romance and sex, the depth of feelings of inferiority. I was gifted with life-long buddies, both canine and human. Yet it seemed that terror and utter humiliation would be my major fare in that segment of life's journey.

I met my first challenge to escape demons of control and confinement by loosing myself from that clothesline tether and finding my way down four city blocks and across several busy streets to the Flagstaff Pharmacy, to my Dad, Jack, and my new "throne"

STAGE THREE–Initiative over Guilt to establish PURPOSE (3–6 yrs.)
From three to five children become assertive and interact with other childen to play, create games and explore interpersonal skills through initiating activities. A sense of initiative, and feeling secure in ability to lead others and make decisions arises. Intense questioning, if treated as trivial, a nuisance or embarrassing or threatening feelings of guilt for "being a nuisance" can be generated. Aggressiveness often squelched by criticism or control can also develop guilt creating a feeling the same sense as nuisance to others, begetting followers who lack in self
Initiative. Guilt slows to interaction with others and may inhibit creativity and disable learning how to exercise self control or have a conscience. A balance between initiative and guilt leads to the virtue of purpose.

– the stool at the end of the Soda Fountain. The frantic and angered voice of mother Mabel at this success did not dampen my newly acquired self-confidence that fourth year of my existence in 1936. In fact it unleashed an assertiveness and independence that was rewarded with an exhilarating feeling. So much so that I latterly tried to wipe out that fear and shame of the potty training pogrom by smearing my excrement on the bathroom walls of the duplex. On discovery, Mabel to my astonishment calmly and silently stated "we must clean the walls up." Even at such an early age I knew that my mother was not an evil person, but was troubled and that something was terribly wrong with her. Having shared my experience in therapy sessions later in life I was informed by Dr. Robert P., "Your mother was mentally ill." My self-assertiveness and newly experienced independence was short lived and severely blunted with the onset of the restoration of Mabel's power and control. Those were the days I refer to as the "enema inquisition." "Hold it! Hold it! Hold it! Hold it!" I was thrust once again into a state of total powerlessness combined with intense feelings of shame and defeat— a total sea of desperation. Phase two of the potty training.

SLEDDING, THUNDER CLOUDS AND BUDDIES FOREVER

KENNY

My family moved up the hill on the west side of town under Mars Hill up on Grand Canyon Avenue. There I would meet my first and dearest life long friend, Kenny C, who always looked at me with a smile and complete acceptance. Kenny C had a persona that combined the wisdom and understanding of his Canadian mother with the happy and joyful demeanor of a Missouri Dad. Looking back I realized that "staying at Kenny's" overnight or being with Kenny always lit the lamp of hope and trust in what life had to offer in spite of the pitfalls. Breakfast at Kenny's was like a royal banquet— strawberry jam, Wheaties with cream, bacon, toast and orange juice.

Speed

Those special times in the secret room behind the woodpile in the shed or under the bed sheets tent reinforced the idea that safe places could exist. Graham crackers, slathered with peanut butter and real butter was the required cuisine for the secret room meeting. Most often these meeting were convened in mid July when huge thunderheads appeared spiraling up 60 thousand feet. Those deafening lighting strikes in the Arizona skies signaled a message that there would always be a cozy port amid the worst of storms.

Life on Grand Canyon Avenue added a new dimension of fun and independence to my life. Going up and down the hill sledding at high speeds provided bliss and thrills. My first hiking trip was through dense forest over Mars Hill west of town to Camp Kit Carson on Route 66. It wetted my passion to explore and be free to travel the streams and canyons of Arizona.

Life up on Grand Canyon Avenue offered a panoply of new and exciting experiences. The sled runs down the hill made available and reinforced the chances to gain confidence, freedom and power. Those wonderful associations – buddies – Kenny, Dickey, Wanda, Ethel and all the Mars Hill Gang –garnered acceptance and friendship that I needed so badly at that time of life.

Hope and safety became physically symbolized for me mid the darkest of nights. It was the golden light glowing within the windows of houses up on the hill and the distant sounds of the friendly barking that marked the existence a secure life.

Vulnerabilities in life and the existence of death were brought home to me late one night when I was suddenly awakened by the excited and loud voices of my mother and father expressing hand wringing regret and depressive comments about some terrible event. They, along with a group of young people had developed the habit of skiing at night on a hill east of Flagstaff. They would position their cars with the head lights pointed up the hill to illuminate the steep and narrow ski run. What had happened that night was that one Carl G had come speeding straight down the hill and hit the only tree on the run. He died only hours later in the hospital with a fractured skull. I picked up the intense emotions—sadness, shock and fear. I discovered those eerie hours of a January night that terrible things could happen without warning.

NIGHT EPISODE

Although I tried very hard to reach back in my memory to find a vision of how I got on the floor of that bedroom under a blanket, I could never find the pieces to the puzzle. I could only recall seeing the face of a young baby-sitter and my departure from my bed to the corner and floor of the bedroom. Once again I experienced an episode of threat from a house at night. Somehow, I associated this time in life with the sounds of the Grand Canyon suite- the part depicting the mules on the "Trail" down the Canyon. I could see the old time radio that looked like the frontage of a miniature Catholic church; there was the golden light from a fringe rimed lamp and the baby bed in a dark room beyond the living room and then nothing but darkness.

Neighborhood Gang

My introduction to the Gang up on Grand Canyon acted as a preparation for my entry into school – the world of "can do" vs. "can't do" that society sets up to test and develop the capabilities of the young. My third and most important mother appeared as the teacher at the Laboratory School at Arizona State Teacher College located south off of Route 66. It was Minnie Roseberry who seemed to pierce my mind and heart and knew the monsters and scars left there from my life's journey those first six years of my life. It was the first time anyone looked into my eyes with some sense of empathy and understanding. I gained unconscious comfort and confidence from Minnie that extended from kindergarten through graduate classes at the college. Since most of the college administrative people had political personas, the "in your face" raw-boned honesty of Roseberry empowered her literally to dominate the college and later the whole university for over 65 years. Even at such a young age I sensed Minnie had Mabel's number and was my loving ally to me though she always seemed to come off on the outside as the wicked witch from the Wizard of OZ. I needed allies badly and as I look back I realize that she could look at me and comment in a way that reached into the core of my being. I am absolutely sure that she got me the job as a teacher at the Lab School at Northern Arizona University by twisting the ear of Dr. Lawrence J Walkup. She may have even plucked me from a disastrous existence at Temple and life in New Jersey to return me home to Arizona.

Amid Geological and Cultural Wonders

Flagstaff, Arizona lay at the center of several national parks, some extraordinary canyons, mountains and exceptional spots on the planet. Oak Creek Canyon, Sedona and Grand Canyons were extremely stimulating for me each time I was there. Oak Creek's rushing waters and unique smell would lift me up me to a totally carefree mood. Tolerating the icy waters of the swimming pool and being calmed by the whispering and quiet rapids of the stream acted as a mother nature soothing salon and spa.

The Grand Canyon

The Grand Canyon never failed to strike awe in me from both the sight of its eternal depths to the architectural and human curiosities on its rim. I often felt an almost out of body experience while looking at the reflection of the Canyon depths in the smoky glass panels rimming the ceiling in the top of the South Tower. The Indian House manned by Hopi tribesmen contained a museum-like menagerie of curios. I always aquired those glass statues and objects filled with tiny bits of candy through the kindness of visiting relatives. Distant canyon offshoots and buttes in the gigantic panoply of the Canyon wetted my unending lifetime enthusiasm to explore the unknown.

Santa Fe Avenue

My father moved us near downtown on Santa Fe Avenue that was walking distance from the Drug store. Even in the 1930's there was constant traffic moving on Route 66 within a stones throw of our front door.

Appendicitis

Even though I had suffered the intense pain of a nearly burst appendix and the horrible soreness of a tonsillectomy, I had not envisioned what my insides or that of any human looked liked, that is, until I peered over the bridge at the running Rio de Flagstaff to see the streaming chunks of a cat's carcass leave its body and float down stream. It was once again a lesson in stark reality of the vulnerabilities of life. I once thought 'cowardness' motivated my resistance to entering dangerous waters, deciding at the time that wisdom was the better part of valor, except when it meant capturing the glory of football. I discoved later that my fear was actually a gift of wisdom.

Surgery and First Drink

And an intense storm came that July as a dark form to accompany the intense pain that appeared deep inside my right side. I thought, "What had I done wrong this time?" Despair started to pull me down when nobody or nothing seemed to ease the pain. The pain was so great that I doubled over and lay on the living room floor. It was only years later when I found out that my Dad, Jack, had insisted from a recalcitrant doctor to do another white blood count. He saved my life from an appendix that was on the verge of bursting within an hour that would have consigned me in those days to certain death. Years later I stood in front of the surgeon's namesake elementary school, (Sechrist), and cussed the long gone surgeon who had left a seven-inch long one-inch wide scar across my midsection. Not trusting the old cigar-smoking surgeon, my dad had insisted that the family doctor, Dr. Fronske, monitor the surgery. Although the sting and overpowering scent of the ether was a shock, the immediate effect and impact on me killed that horrible pain throbbing in my gut (and psyche). In those days, ether was poured through a metallic mechanism filled with gauze right into a patient's nostril. That instant and blissful feeling registered so deeply into my

FIRST DRINK

I cannot now recall the pain I must have felt at the approaching rupture of my appendix but I do remember the fierce, biting ether being poured through gauze into my nostrils – the primitive anesthesia of the 1930's. I must have also noticed the anxiety experienced by my father who had saved my life by demanding a white cell count contrary to the doctor's prognosis. Adding a forbidding cloud over the crisis, the only surgeon in town was known as a butcher. My father insisted that the family doctor monitor the operation. I came off the operating table as a five year old with an incision scar six inches long and one inch wide. The old pains of abuse in the years preceding were lodged deep inside but the presence of these concerns was suddenly extinguished with a few hits of ether. Ether was my first drink, my first escape from reality, never to leave, always residing in my psyche, telling me that alcohol would relieve any trouble or distress.

mind in such a way that alcohol would stand a source of instant gratification at many episodes throughout my life only to eventually bring me down to my knees.

THE FIRST DRUNK- INEVITABLE BENDER

Evidence of my early addition to the effects of alcohol was manifested by my quest and acquisition of the wonderful elixir the first chance that I had right after the appendicitis operation. Mom and Dad had hosted a party only days after I got out of the hospital. The party had disappeared somewhere and left their highball glasses with a fraction of an inch in each glass. I immediately and gleefully quaffed the dregs from each glass

My initiation to my new life on Santa Fe was to get drunk by emptying the dregs from the bottom of the glasses left from the party. What made me decide to go across the street and climb up on the porch roof of that house is still a mystery. But I did somehow climb up there and then fell off that porch roof, experiencing a crush of air out of my lungs and my first exposure to the dire consequences of alcohol. My mother, dad and friends rushed across the street to see if my stitches were still intact and that my intestines were not spread out in the dirt. As a monstrous train engine rolled nearby belching dense black smoke, the adult rescue crew found my stomach to be whole and undamaged.

SCHOOL DAYS

KINDERGARTEN

The glowing light of a "Can Do" belief was ignited in my soul in the following September in Minnie Roseberry's Kindergarten and lessened the terror of the appendicitis pain returning. Minnie's exuberant and sustained expectation for achievement provided me with the confidence and courage to experiment and explore once again. Unfortunately my first probe into the unknown was a disaster. Walking home five blocks from school while approaching the bridge abutment over the River de Flag I won-

---

STAGE FOUR—INDUSTRY OVER INFERIORITY TO ESTABLISH CONFIDENCE (6–11 YRS.)

Children are at the stage (aged 5 to 12 yrs.) where they will be learning to read and write, and to do things on their own. The peer group will gain greater significance and become a major source of the self-esteem.
There is now the need to win approval by demonstrating competencies that are valued by society, and to begin to develop pride in accomplishments. If encouraged and reinforced for their initiative, a feeling of industry and confidence in the ability to achieve accrues. If initiative is not encouraged, and restricted by parents or teacher, a child begins to feel inferior, doubting abilities and suppressed from reaching his or her potential. The inability to develop the specific skill demanded by society (e.g. being athletic, academic) may develop a sense of inferiority. Some failure is necessary to develop some modesty.
Success in this stage will lead to the virtue of competence.

dered if I could walk the remaining half block toward home with my eyes closed. Not a good idea. Smarting from a bloody lip and loose tooth I got another lessen of consequences in making bad choices.

FOOTBALL

My dad had taken me to see the local Arizona State College Lumberjacks play football and I immediately became obsessed with the excitement generated by action and the screaming fans; the actual payoff of ecstasy when a touchdown was scored and the hyperactive and classy uniforms of blue and yellow. I saw that one could earn identity and popularity – the subject of cheering crowds – by intense practice and emulation of being a Lumberjack. I acquired pads and uniform and would often play with neighbors on the lawn between houses often beyond sunset all the while singing in a high pitched tone, "When the Lumberjacks all fall in line, they're going to win a game another time, they are going to fight fight for every score –."

THE DOG

While living on Santa Fe Ave the most memorable, precious and treasured being I ever had as my friend came into my life— "Jippy" a splendid canine combination of border collie, spaniel and certain other breeds. Friends in the old stone house up on Santa Fe Avenue had rescued Jippy from the dog pound. At first interface Jippy and I forged an eternal bond of unconditional love. When the family moved up the hill to a huge malpais house circled by a low wall of the same material, I would spend Saturdays playing with Jippy. When the family decided to move to Phoenix, they asked my parents if they would take Jippy to live at our home on Birch Street. He came to Birch Street and lived with me for two years until my family moved to Denver. "Goodbye my Jippy," I said as the Buick pulled away from the curb at Birch Street in Flagstaff—off to Denver. The unfathomable mystery and unforgivable act was the fact that I never found out what happened to Jippy – a precious and faithful friend abandoned never to be seen again. Returning to Flagstaff several years later, I could only stare at the spot on the Birch house lawn where Jippy lay in the shade of hot summer days. "Biscuit Eater" was my favorite movie. Dogs, because of their unconditional love, became a life long and critical part of my life. The love a dog is that quintessential mystery of the universe, that unshakable purposefulness of being, which psychologists, philosophers and intellectuals can neither define nor explain. They have paraded through my life to always and faithfully be there to love and comfort me—Frosty, the water spaniel; Skippy, the feisty terrier; and much later Bo And Arrow the gold blue eyed Wolf-Malamute; and standard poodle, Zhin Zhin (Navajo for "Black Black"). Now in the sunset of life I have the Labradoodle, "Yanavia Che," ("Pretty Caramel Girl" in the Comanche language) and once again a standard poodle "Nishoni," (Beautiful in the Navajo language) as constant companions. I can not help that at times when Yanivia puts her head on my chest inches from my chin and gazes straight at me with those beautiful green eyes that for a fleeting moment I was once again seeing Jippy. The newly elected Pope Francis of the Roman Catholic Church stated that humans would be joined on the other side by their pets in life. Thinking back over the years I realized that the unconditional love of dogs and the support of some significant others like Minnie Roseberry actually affirmed to me that love, care and support did in fact exist somewhere in what had seemed to me at times to be an uncaring and threatening universe. Such insensitivities often brought to mind my bitter stint at St. Anthony's School in Flagstaff.

Competence Over Inferiority

St. Anthony's

Switching Schools

Mabel's motives for moving me from the Elementary Training School at the Arizona State Teacher's College to the Catholic school, St. Anthony's, could only be guessed at. Mabel had left the Catholic Church nearly ten years earlier in Jerome for what she claimed to be the sickness she experienced at the aroma caused by consumption of frijoles by Mexican-American residents which could partly be a prejudice or mind set attained

St. Anthony's

from her Texas linage. She wanted me to go to a Catholic school and that meant rejoining the fold. It could also be that she saw the support and counter-force of Roseberry's sane nurturing of me in the Lab School. It could have been Mabel's own belief in structured Catholic education as opposed to the progressive 'hands on' John Dewey approach of the lab school. Nevertheless I entered the coffee pungent aroma of the halls of St. Anthony's that September of 1939. More specifically, I crossed the threshold of Sister Mary Vincent's and the Sisters of Loretta's third grade lair to face another great challenge of life—"Can Do Versus Can't Do"??

Failure

My skills I got at the Training School were simple addition and printing letters to make words, doing beadwork and cooking Hopi piki bread were a sorry match for the scriptwriters and subtraction masters under the rule of Sister Vincent. The intense humiliation of appearing totally inept in front of thirty or more third grade classmates made life very painful and anxious for me. Leaving school in early September to gather autumn gold and red leaves was the only relief I got from the dogging regimen that plagued me. Jippy was like a warm soothing balm to my tortured soul. The awareness of my peers about my weakness and their humorous and sarcastic looks at me made me want to disappear. But, where could I go?? Amid the trauma of my exposed ineptitude I took a gut wrenching hit from Sister Vincent, who all of a sudden glaringly accosted me loudly in front of the whole class and asked what I was doing with my hand in my pocket! "Are you fondling yourself Gerald??!!" The next day Vincent announced in front of the whole class that I would be moving across the hall to Second Grade because I could not do the work in third grade. My mother and father acquiesced to the St. Anthony nuns and promised me a bicycle if would move back to second grade. The Second Grade teacher, Sister Anne, became the bodily prototype of what I thought angels must look like — short and stout with brown mottled teeth, but blessed with a sweet voice and smile. Her infinite sense of patience, assurance and encouragement in her endless after school tutoring sessions snatched me from the depths of hopelessness.

Mary Ann

A great and saving benefit for my stint at St Anthony's was that I could walk Mary Anne W to school each day. Mary Anne lived up the street and walked by each morning on her way to school. I would wait on the front steps on Birch Street for her to come from her mansion house up the street. I thought she was the most beautiful girl in the world in her blue and white trimmed school uniform. I was required to wear a tie, which I once wore around my neck with a shirt without a collar. Mary Anne was the second female with whom I had had an "intimate" relationship. Both Mary Anne and I had stuffed our bodies in Jippy's doghouse. I had never been that close to a female ever. I had always believed in the "scent of a woman" to be something like sweet onions and something else I couldn't quite figure out that summer of 1940. In later years I would walk up near the old sled run on Mars Hill to a place I calculated that Mary Anne and I had cook outs of hot dogs and Van Camp's pork n beans cooked over a small stack of pine branches. Mary Anne's mother Beulah was always the organizer of these events packing pans, water, beans, bread and hot dogs from the W's house up into the pine forest. Years later I wondered about Beulah's motive and came up with the idea that it was done to introduce Mary Ann "to safe partnerships." I guess I take "safe" as a compliment for an eight year old. Mary Anne and I were "skiing buddies" operating at different levels of competence, Mary Anne progressing toward Olympic style capabilities while I was avoiding losing my hand stuffed in a glove on its way up to a grinding pulley perched atop the ski tow. The theme song from "Sun Valley Serenade" featuring Sonja Henie, a movie star of the same movie would loop over and over again on the ski shack speakers. "Why do roses bloom in December, I know why and so do you," lilted through the aspen grove from the ski cabin at old Sisabel Park. That song and memories of the pungent smell of ski wax reappeared again and again in my mind, totally engulfing my being one day while visiting Mary Anne's grave. She had passed away tragically in her 30's. During those St. Anthony days I delivered handbills advertising Saturday sales. I worked from three am until I completed my route on Milton Road. I received 80 cents, which I could use for red hots and tickets for Mary Anne and I to attend the Orpheum's Saturday matinee. Such a mission was never consummated. To my distress I did see Mary Anne accompanied by an older boy one Saturday attending a Nelson Eddy and Marie McDonald film, "Desert Song" about the Riffs in Arabia. I hoped Mary Anne was in the stands to see me play starting end for the Winslow Bulldogs. Returning to Flagstaff six years later in 1948 I found Mary Anne betrothed to an older gentleman and ski partner.

LIFE ON BIRCH

SURPRISE

One bitter November on my ninth birthday I played football on the frozen lawn way after the sun went down and darkness engulfed my Birch Street home nestled below Mars Hill. Every five minutes after dark my mother would open the door and insist that I stop playing and come inside. I operated under the assumption that practice would result in perfection and the day would come when the cheers would rise out of the stands for me and I would know that I was OK and valued like everyone else my age. Even more important I would be admired and treasured by such girls as Connie and Mary Anne W. "Gerald, come in here this instant or I am going to whip you to an inch of your life," my mother's voice rang out across the dark and empty Birch Street. Knowing that I was running out of any birthday good will she might have left in reserve I picked up the football and my coat and went up the steps through the front door of the old malpais volcanic stone house.

"Happy Birthday to you," rang out from the crowd of four fellow friends gathered around the dinning room table— Kenny and Dickey from old Grand Canyon Avenue and neighbors Bruce and Jack from across the street. A dinner of fried mock chicken legs (alternate one inch squares of veal and pork) was served with hot cocoa followed by the presentation of a lovely chocolate cake covered with the candy flowers and lighted candles.

What a surprise! And of more importance the realization that my mother really did care about me within her continuing war to dominate, control and make me that perfect child that would make up for her unruly and misbehaving brothers. Those wild orphaned brothers she could never seem to chorale but always had to play the understanding and supportive surrogate mother that they had lost at such a young age.

Years later I suspected that I acted as a lightning rod for allot of my mother's pent up anger over forms of physical, sexual and other abuses she had suffered by being the only female among those five brothers and growing up in the early years with a unfaithful and alcoholic father who had been killed by his own fire engine. The accidental and tragic death of her mother, Maggie, who had fallen out the second story door of the hotel in Cisco, Texas, caused her to be sent to the Convent in Fort Worth to eat hated cod fish balls. At fifteen her Aunt Mabel and Uncle Kenneth who lived in Arizona in the Mexican border town of Douglas took her in. Her high school classmates immediately dubbed her as "Tex."

STIMULATION

Life in the small hamlet of Flagstaff was broadly varied and intensely stimulating which acted as a buffer and educational tool for me. Flagstaff lay at the center of a number of National Parks, monuments and historical sites. Nearby was the Grand Canyon; Anasazi Ruins of Wapatki, Montezuma Castle and Walnut Canyon sites of the Sinagua People; the Hopi and Navajo Reservations; and only a short drive from Oak Creek Canyon and Sedona, the most beautiful areas of red rocks on the planet and the backdrop for many a Hollywood movie. I sat in the back seat of the old Buick in 1940 and could have touched Cornel Wild and Gene Tierney walking back from a scene up in the red rocks while filming "Leave Her to Heaven." Director Michael Curtiz of "Casa Blanca" fame chose Flagstaff as the location for the filming of Virginia City featuring Errol Flynn and Humphrey Bogart. I was fortunate to be in the audience the day Errol Flynn appeared at the Orpheum stage during the filming of Virginia City.

Excursions

It was only years later that I figured out why there was a constant trail of my mother's brothers appearing at the family doorstep – Uncles Bill, Ben, Ray, Holland and Tommy. Such interfaces always included trips to the Grand Canyon and the swimming pool in Oak Creek Canyon. Sunset Crater, the thousand-year-old quiescent volcano, was always mounted to the summit followed by rolling down its slope through the fine black cinders, which activity at the time was still legal.

SLEDDING

Winter in Flagstaff meant skiing on the San Francisco Peaks at Sisabel Park. But greatest thrills came with the sledding down the steep run on Observatory Hill. At some sections the sled run was as steep as a 45-degree angle. The sled run ran a quarter of a mile through the pine forest and could catapult a sledder one block down into residential Birch Street. Luckily, the traffic in those days was minimal. Sledding required a very tedious and exhaustive climb up the run, rewarded, of course, by the thrill of speeding down hill with extreme abandonment. One snowy January day one Eddie T hit a tree head first requiring a silver plate to mend a fractured skull. The site of Eddie gurgling and his eyes rolling back in his head punctuated one of the many lessons for me about how unforgiving Mother Nature was. My sense of confidence and freedom allowed me to immediately reject the accusations that Jippy was one of the barking dogs that had distracted Eddie's steering into the tree. I announced the fact to everyone that Jippy wasn't even on the hill that day.

An Abyss Of Terror

Trust emerges after birth governed by the degree to which the infantile psyche senses caring and comfort in the face of a changing and sometimes painful environment. The challenge is to retain trust through the trials and tribulations faced in each evolving phase of development. My trust of adults was sorely tested one dark night.

I stood frozen in front of the door peering into a black abyss. "Don't be silly. Go into the house," my mother hollered as she crossed the lawn into the street in front of 810 West Birch. Just as my mother had unlocked the door to our house, a car honked out in the street with a lady's head peering out its window requesting directions. I had quickly and quietly replied to my mother "there is someone in there."

My memory of having been frightened in a darkened house by my Uncle Gene Reedy when I was three had forever traumatized me of being inside of a dark room. Even as a teenager I slept with a 22-caliber rifle when my parents were absent attending a pharmacy convention. Sleeping out in the wilds of northern Arizona, however, under the sky held no threat for me. But staying inside a dark house was an issue, one that only subsided later in life.

That moonless night of June 1939, I sensed a living presence somewhere within the pitch-blackness of the small malpais dwelling. As I stood paralyzed staring into the abyss of the open door "a loud bang, crash and thump" emitted from the right side of the house. I saw a dark figure plunge out the window and run off into the back yard and beyond disappearing into the night. The split second activity was an accompanied by a jingling sound, which turned out to be my piggy bank containing 15 dollars and change accumulated by my handbill delivery pay. My mother ran to the street just as the car took off with great speed. In ten minutes the police arrived and took my mother and me on a cruise through the neighborhood. Four blocks away a Hispanic figure stood under a streetlight, quickly disappearing as the police care approached. I later picked a Hispanic gentleman out of a lineup; he looked like the man seen under the streetlights. No one was ever arrested for the burglary, and I often saw a figure in my dreams chasing me down the street. For many years afterward, I projected guilt and fear toward Hispanics under the onus that I had mistakenly fingered the wrong man.

SNATCHED FROM PLUNGING INTO THE FALLS

Uncle Bill had come to Flagstaff late the spring of 1939 to begin the tours that Jack loved to share with those who visited that northern Arizona city. Grand Falls of the Little Colorado River lay north of Flagstaff on a very bumpy black cinder road; they were a favorite destination for my father, Jack, as both a photographic subject and geographical phenomenon. The ancient volcanic flow from the south blocked the little Colorado stream and created a dam with water higher than Niagara. No water flowed during the dry season of northern Arizona; at other times a heavy stream poured over the Falls. When rains or snow melt flowed from the White Mountains in central Arizona, the little Colorado flowed with a brown soupy stream and spilled over the falls below, fine spray from crashing water wafting upward, rising higher and higher until it finally turned into dust.

At a most exuberant seven, I had devised the habit (acquired most likely from comedic great grandfather Phillip Lynch) of creating clever pranks to entertain and get attention. Thus it was that on a fine spring day my mother, father and uncle Bill's family had made the expected trek out to the Little Colorado River famous site of Grand Falls where the Little Colorado cascades down further than Niagara Falls. I conceived and executed a great performance better than a barrel over the falls. I darted from the back seat of the Buick and ran hell-bent toward the dangerous precipice of Grand Falls to fake an accidental plunge into the Canyon.

Uncle Bill Mason's comment rings as clear as though it were yesterday – "Mable, you-all got to do something about that boy before he kills himself." My mother Mabel had her back to the Buick but my screeching caused her to reach out and grab my arm as I dashed toward the edge of the gorge above the Falls. I'd exited the car in full sprint toward the swirling chocolate waters that lay two hundred feet below. Years later I shivered to think of the day I almost accidently went over the Falls, still with no idea what crazy chicanery had possessed my seven year old mind that July of 1939.

NIGHT TRAIN TO THE COAST

The monstrous metal machines rolled through downtown Flagstaff in a steady stream each day. Standing on the tarmac at the Flagstaff Depot when the trains came roaring down the track and thundering through, shaking the ground, never ceased to give me a high. Seeing the strange faces peering inside the windows and racing through the night puzzled and mystified me—who and where were they going? Now as I boarded the train to LA and on to San Diego my excitement was intensified.

The night in the sleeper room was punctuated by stops at Kingman, Barstow and Needles, and San Bernardino.

The morning breakfast corn flakes impregnated with rich cream never tasted so good. The poise and friendly air of the diner filled with the syncopated chatter of the cooks stationed below near a floor level kitchen accompanied mother and I into the final run into Los Angeles.

The train trip ended in the La Grande Santa Fe Station in Los Angeles. The day was spent in LA visiting the Farmer's Market wherein I consumed strawberries capped in a shell of sugar and listened to Ozzie and Harriet Nelson's band.

My Grand Aunt Mabel and friend Dorothy had met the train and would drive me and my mother down past San Diego south on to Chula Vista.

The War

The radio crackled in the living room of Birch and a sudden voice proclaimed that the Japanese had bombed Pearl Harbor in Hawaii. I had already experienced the dead seriousness of somber reaction that war brought to Birch Street. I was with my father hiking in September on the side of the San Francisco Peaks when the radio announced the German invasion of Czechoslovakia. I had the strongest desire to go up to Grand Canyon to see Kenny because his presence always seem to signal resolve and hope. That day brought a sense of panic and frantic thoughts about what to do and what could come next. I sensed a sea change in my life and knew that life would never be the same again.

My Dad Jack had the option of buying the Flagstaff Pharmacy across from the Depot, which he had managed for 5 years. Old Mr. Grager, the scarred and crippled World War One owner of the store depended on the store for his sole income, Jack knew that his purchase of the store would drastically reduce Grager's income. He could not in good conscience take the store away. I learned at an early time a critical lesson of morality— there exists values above and beyond the strict application of rules and rights.

Jack also wanted to join the Navy to do his duty in the War effort. However, punctured eardrums disqualified him. Ashamed of his inability to fight for his country and his unwillingness to take the pharmacy away from Grager made him decide to move the family to Denver to work as a pharmaceutical salesman.

DENVER

The first week of September 1942 the Buick left the curb on Birch Street and headed for Denver through Gallup, Farmington over Wolf Creek Pass and on to a motel on Colorado Blvd in Denver. My best friend, Jippy, was left laying in the yard looking expectantly at my face in the car window. I would never see him again and I somehow knew it in my heart. The theme from a recent movie about a deer named Bambi, whose mother is shot and killed by a deer hunter while trying to help her son find food, leaving the little fawn mournful and alone replayed over and over again in my mind.

The thought of Bambi wrenched in my soul during the whole trip as I felt like an abandoned fawn that ninth year of my life.

ADAPTATION AND REVELATION

Death off Table Top Mountain—

One had to adapt in life and I completed my first and only fisticuffs in back of a motel—one punch and the perpetrator ran. Physical violence seemed to work to provide protective boundaries and respect when life threatened. Denver also provided diversion and excitement to ease my depression, loneliness and homesickness. The circus was held on a stage in a steep amphitheater. That same year my presence with my Dad at the Lime House Blues musical was confusing in terms as to why I was exposed to the rather risqué dressed women. But I did enjoy the melodies. It was not the first time I found out that men, including my dad, were interested in naked women. I had found the picture in the Birch Street closet of the shirtless lady taken at the Phoenix Pharmacy Convention. I never confronted dad about the photo, which meant that I could not proffer total trust or respect for my father on sexual matters nor to any adult for that matter.

THE B CLASS

I was placed in the "dumb section B" of the fourth grade in a Denver public school. Although it only lasted by several weeks, it again reinforced my failure to perform in a crucial phase of my entry into society. But fortunate for me the family found a home near Annunciation Catholic School. It was here that I, absent the bias of the St. Anthony's nuns, began to slowly achieve and progress in the three R's aside from any feelings of inadequacy. My love for dogs was manifested in every part of my life. At Annunciation I copied a favorite reading story, "Jacques, A Red Cross Dog" as part of a reading lesson. The story was written from the dog's perspective. Jacques was turned loose with other Red Cross dogs into the World War I battlefield in search of the wounded.

From Jacques' thoughts – "Running over the field we began to search for wounded soldiers. I was the first to reach a big ditch. I heard a low cry and looking down I saw a man lying on his back with a pile of earth over his legs. Sliding over I soon reached his side and what a surprise to look into the face of my own good master! I dared not back off. I licked his face and his hands and wagged my tail really hard. Soon he opened his eyes and saw me. Oh, Jacques! He knew my lick at once for a good master always knows his own dog. 'Good old Jacques,' he said, 'how did you ever get here?' How happy I was to hear him speak those words."

Denver Days

In Denver I fortunately once again found the needed comfort of the extended family in the form of my mother's distant cousin Lela B and cousin Beverly who provided guidance and mentorship for my country boy's maneuvering among the city streets and canyons of downtown Denver. Explorations and expeditions riding the trolley to the end of the line, solo trips downtown to the Paramount theatre on Saturdays and frequent journeys south of the duplex on Josephine street to the Zoo expanded my self confidence. However this carefree wandering suddenly changed when the Denver Post featured the South Table Mesa's Castle Rock at Golden as the site of a teenager's murder of a ten year old by throwing him off the top of what was later the mountain featured on Coors Beer cans. Unfortunately Beverly's early death prevented me from making amends to her for my bullying her in 1942— an anomaly in my history of interface with females.

One of the favorite Sunday pastimes was to visit the graves of the family's Irish relatives. It was my first introduction to Thomas O'Mara. Excursions into the cemetery were followed by visits to the ice cream shops. The idea of death was not only unpleasant but an idea that I had difficulty processing at all, even though it played a key role in directing my life in the those early teen age years.

Independence and freedom was also enhanced by my weekly trip to the dentist in downtown Denver to correct the position of one of my front teeth. The trip down town also enabled me to attend the matinee at the Paramount Theater. The toxic fear I had attained earlier in life was fleshed out in spades when I watched the then famous "Mummy" movies featuring the quintessential monster-man, Boris Karloff. So intense were the feelings that I would not go downstairs into the men's room alone. I would wait until another movie attendee went and I would follow him. At night I was frozen with terror believing the "Mummy" was under my bed in the downstairs duplex.

A continuation and extension of the carefreeness experienced within the streets and hills of Flagstaff found many opportunities in Denver. The favorite ploy of my friend and I was to travel on the trolley to the end of the line and return home on the same.

When the Denver Post published a half page spread announcing and picturing the butte in Golden from which a teen-ager threw off a seven year old the forays on the trolley abruptly were abandoned.

III. QUEST

Earner—Albuquerque—

My father was reassigned by Sharp and Dome Pharmaceuticals to Albuquerque. The high desert and Sandia Mountain of Albuquerque seemed as a warm and sunny place in contrast to what had seemed to be a dark, dank and dreary Denver. It was like going from gray to gold.

Freedom preface

Central Ave. Bowling Alley

Albuquerque restored the opportunity of extensive freedom that was lost in Denver. I could ride my Schwinn almost anywhere in the Nob Hill and the University areas up on Central Avenue near my home on Stanford.

Having arrived in Albuquerque in the last week of June, I armed myself with hundreds of ladyfinger firecrackers, which gave me some sort of personal power. Attendance at the Lobo Theatre and even at the State and Kimo theaters in Downtown Albuquerque were done unaccompanied by parents signifying my growing independence. The thrill of autonomy was heightened by the sense of threat from the urban myth about horse mounted "Zoot Suitors" raiding people at night. "Zoot Suitors" were supposedly teen age Hispanics with baggy pants and greased hair that wandered around at night. In spite of these imaginary beings I would still go to the Kimo both day and night be taking the city bus to downtown. I used that same bus each day to go to school in downtown St. Mary's. Seeing Casa Blanca at the Kimo, eating poppy seed rolls with ham, lettuce and mayonnaise at Newberry's dime store, attending University of New Mexico Lobo football games and eating the hot Mexican food in old town Albuquerque among the fumes of old raw cowhide chairs always spelled enchantment for me. The strains of the popular WW II song, "They're Either to Young or Too Old," (Lyrics: Frank Loesser, Music: Arthur Schwartz) (1943) based upon the score of "Lullaby for Strings" by George Gershwin: "They're either too young, or too old, They're either too gray or too grassy green, The pickings are poor and the crop is lean. What's good is in the army, What's left will never harm me." The strains could bring me back immediately to my days in New Mexico and especially the enchantment of Santa Fe.

POWER PLAYS

The clandestine exercise of control and influence were acted out in many ways. It was a way to manifest independence of sorts. A major prank carried out with me and the neighborhood chums was the act stringing kite string across Coal Avenue and draping newspaper over it and then lighting it on fire when a car appeared to be approaching off in the west. Capers with Buzzie, a same age boy and family associate from Flagstaff days, began to educate me about the dire consequences of dangerous pranks and delinquency. Of a Saturday matinee Buzzie executed plans to slam a bag of sand off the balcony onto the candy counter at the Kimo Theater. To my surprise he did it. As an accessory to the crime I took off into the dark depths of the balcony and escaped being caught. I had never suspected a crime of that weightiness. However, later that week while walking down an alley in my neighborhood and parallel to Harvard Avenue Buzzie without word or warning picked up a half brick and threw it through a bay window in back of a large home. I sprinted fast and far. It would be the last time I would ever see or hear about Buzzie.

DANGEROUS EMPLOYMENT

Friends and accomplices living on Coal Street cattycorner to my Stanford house were more "normal" than Buzzie and represented a group that did enjoyable and profitable things minus the extreme threat and danger. My friend and I got a job "setting pins" at the bowling alley up on Central Avenue. The work was not exactly safe by any standards as we had to duck flying pins every few minutes. It seemed that a bowling pro hurled his ball with such enormous force that pins scattered in all directions in what seemed to be a personal assault aimed at me. The great solace though came from the late night after-work raid in his brother's next-door bakery job, being rewarded with newly iced and hot donuts. I received my first Social Security Card that July of 1943 at the age of eleven, giving me a fresh sense of achievement, confidence and freedom.

ST. MARY'S AND THE "INCIDENT ON STANFORD"

SUCCESS AND HOODLUMISM

"Sure a little bit of heaven fell from out the sky one day" rang out from children's voices in the fourth grade basement classroom at old St. Mary's in downtown Albuquerque. Those Irish nuns injected an expectation of joy as the result of accomplishment which ignited my belief for the first time that I could achieve, be a part of and be accepted by my peers, not only as an equal, but even as one with exceptional skills and contributions. "Yes, I can!" My newly found confidence and freedom unfortunately stirred up the budding of arrogance, which began to appear in me as a player in the St. Mary's "gang." The "Gang" were a bunch of fellows who reveled in such mischief as eating lunch in the nearby Franciscan Hotel elevator by pushing the stop button until we exited at the pounding of the door. We later secluded ourselves inside the incinerator a site we abandoned when principal Sister Margaret whatshername grabbed and shook our cheeks with dire warnings of retribution of many years in Purgatory if we ever went in the incinerator again. I finally learned reading, writing, arithmetic and "Sure a little bit of heaven fell from out the sky" at St. Mary's.

RIGHT OF PASSAGE

St. Mary's playground tackle football with my friend Placido M honed my primal gridiron skills brought from Flagstaff. My football and fascination in general with athletics found deeper meaning by my attendance at the Knights of St. Mary's high football games against Albuquerque High. Attendance at basketball games even accelerated my interest and devotion to sports as a source of accomplishment to compensate the damaged esteem suffered from those early Flagstaff days. I accepted the idea that one could become perfect, prevail and become dominant in an athletic field by faithful and tireless practice.

STAGE FIVE— Identity over Role Confusion to establish FIDELITY (12—18 yrs.)
During adolescence (age 12 to 18 yrs.), the transition from childhood to adulthood occurs. The individual becomes more independent, and begins to look at the future, wanting to belong to a society and fit in.

This attitude and focus of controlling one's destiny by self discipline and tireless practice became an obsession with me after being jeered at by a group of a older fellows in basketball court play down the street one day. "This will never happen to me again," I pledged to myself.

"Mary Is a Grand Old Name"
"...But it was Mary; Mary
Long before the fashions came
And there is something there
That sounds so square
It's a grand old name."
(MARY'S A GRAND OLD NAME From the Broadway Show
"Forty-Five Minutes from Broadway"
1906, George M. Cohen, Featured in Forty-Five Minutes
From Broadway is a three-act musical by Cohan.)

It would be years later that I would understand the origin, need and passion for female associations (and i.e., 'girl friends'). I often dreamt of Mary D next door and our treks on bikes around the Nob Hill and University areas. These episodes were the closest thing to dating or having a relationship. Attendance with Mary and her mother at the movie "Oklahoma" at the State Theater embedded in my psyche a deep-rooted association of my relationship with Mary that was often triggered by the tune, "People With Say We Are In Love," (from Rodgers and Hammerstein musical Oklahoma! (1943).

My movie going days at the nearby Lobo Theater and the "B Class" movie house in downtown Albuquerque allowed the acquisition in my memory of a large repertoire of romantic songs—*Shining Hour, Stormy Weather, A Lovely Way To Spend An Evening*, etc. which provided me with a form of self entertainment. I sang, hummed and whistled such tunes all my life to relive those romantic moments with my past girls friends. Looking back I quipped the joke that "I hoped I would fall in love with someone I liked that year."

Attending the Jefferson Junior High football games with Mary and observing the intense emotion and caring focused upon the red and silver uniforms convinced me that the ultimate recognition and retribution I craved would be through sports. At the same time it would provide the hero and warrior guise that movie plots had demonstrated would appeal to females. There was very little to nourish my romantic fantasies except for those movies at the State Theatre; a wonderful day with Mary on Sandia Mountain's Cedar Crest in a roaring arroyo filled with gushing water spurned by a cloud burst; birthday dinners; cheering at football games; sitting together of a summer afternoon in the cool recesses of the Lobo Theatre with Mary; and riding bikes all over the Nob Hill streets.

Mary and I were "traditional, no nonsense bikers." We peddled $35 Schwinns, with no helmets, no shoes, no spandex, no gloves and whizzed down to Safeway and over to the bakery on Central for those hot iced donuts.

THE BOMB

I have firmly believed at the end of that summer in Albuquerque that the bright sky to the south beyond the mountains one July morning had been the first atomic blast. My love affair with New Mexico never ended and it was with deep sadness that I passed over the Rio Puerco River Bridge west of Albuquerque, as I knew I would never see Mary again, or enjoy all the wonderful things about New Mexico. "So long, Mary / don't forget to come back home."

I was now Winslow, Arizona bound and yet unaware that I would pass through a teenager's rite of passage.

TRIUMPH—WINSLOW

The individual wants to learn the roles he will occupy as an adult and re-examining his identity (the sexual and the occupational), trying to find out exactly who he or she is. The result is a reintegrated sense of self, of what one wants to do or be, and of one's appropriate "sex role" merged with a changing body image and the discomfort about their body until they can adapt and "grow into" the changes. Success in this stage will lead to the virtue of fidelity which consists of being able to commit one's self to others on the basis of accepting others, even when there may be ideological differences.

Fidelity

The individual explores possibilities and forms identity based upon the outcome of their explorations. Failure to establish a sense of identity within society can lead to role confusion. Role confusion involves the individual not being sure about themselves or their place in society. Role confusion or identity crisis may cause experimentation with different lifestyles (e.g. work, education or political activities). Pressuring into an identity can result in rebellion, a negative identity, and feeling of unhappiness

Good Samaritans

Returning to Arizona, especially close to my long time home, Flagstaff was not such a tough change for me. But, as is always the case, the move to a new place it did require the discovery of novel places, acquiring new friends and adjusting to fresh school classes. I entered fifth grade in Lincoln School in the April of 1944. Playground games at Lincoln were not like the tackle football of St. Mary's. The preferred game was a bully-like diversion of snatching a chap's hat and teasing him to "get it back if you can!" One Marcus B seemed to project the same sense of loss and being on the outside looking in that I often felt which had started that day at St. Anthony's. A mob had grabbed Marcus's hat and he was desperately chasing one after another fellow exhibiting increasing humiliation and desperation. I immediately saw myself again in that torturous day at St. Anthony's and sprinted after the fellow with the hat, pushed him against the fence, yelled at him and ripped the hat out of his hand. It was just like days at St. Mary's except instead of football it was a cruel and unfair sport. It was a rare act for me to challenge a group of peers, as I had no training skills for fighting with family siblings like most kids. Yet a warm sense of satisfaction and joy overcame me to see the shame and frustration leave Barrett's face and his return to his normal boisterousness. The first light and gift of empathy had dawned in my soul. By showing caring for another, in some strange way I had created "caring" and therefore came to believe that it really could exist in spite of those traumas and insensitivities I had experienced.

Lincoln School, Round Ball, and Buddies

Mrs. Leahy's, (Related to WW II Fleet Admiral William D. Leahy whose son visited the classroom in 1945), 6th grade Room in the northwest corner Lincoln School contained four characters that became a set of life long friends and members of the Tucker Flat Gang who probed the high desert around Winslow for hidden springs, special camping sites and secluded lairs. Terry N, a-look-a-like me fellow became my partner in basketball, remaining with him 2 and 3 hours sometimes on the basketball court in back of Lincoln. As eighth graders Terry and I traveled to Flagstaff by ourselves, stayed in a motel and attended the Northern Arizona Basketball tournament. Then there was Fredde C who was the spitting image of his great grandfather, J.D. Lee, who was executed in the 1800's as a central figure in the Mormon Mountain Meadow Massacre in southern Utah. Roger T was the crazy joker of the gang who was used to test out dangerous operations, obtain illegal sources of wood and to test dive off the cliffs of Clear Creek, a favorite haunt of the Gang. Roger was the "food tester" of potential escapades and fanatics concocted by the Tucker Flat Gang. One of the finest characters I ever have known was John P whose Greek father was the local maker of unparalleled delicious vanilla creams. John was a mark of patience, stability and wisdom that was sorely required by our unruly gang and disastrously prone team. He later starred as an all-state quarterback for US Hall of Fame Coach Emil Nasser of Winslow High School. The Tucker Flat Gang was a "Stand by Me" type group in whose members forged tight and lifelong bonds by surviving the woes of the wild southwestern high desert as well as the glory of Winslow Bulldog football. I so needed a group of loyal and trusted peers to aide in my socialization and teen-age quest for identity. That loyalty would be sorely tested several years later.

THE TUCKER FLAT GANG EMERGES

The First Expedition to the Little Colorado River resulted in yelping coyotes, a burnt leg and drinking alkali water.

It was my first but tediously long hike east of Winslow out to the cottonwood bosque along the Little Colorado River. I carried a cotton-padded blanket containing cans of fruit cocktail and pork and beans as well as biscuits, bacon and maple syrup over my back. At each step of the way the cans would slam into my back. The Gang set up camp on a sand dune in the middle of the dry part of the riverbed. The package of lessons I received during this camp out were invaluable. The pack of Coyotes yelling all night actually gave great comfort along with the existence of a campfire which being nourished all night with driftwood. That same expedition resulted in the disastrous cooking episode of dumping hot bacon grease on my leg causing two orange blisters and life long scars. The lessons of those initial treks out into the high desert of Arizona taught me how to camp cook with the right equipment; not to camp in the middle of a river bed when there are thunderstorms in the mountains to the south; and not to depend on drinking river water full of sand, salt and alkali. Future tours into the desert would take me along the yellow limestone cliffs overlooking the pristine and deep waters of Clear Creek, and the labyrinth of canyons to the west of town which hid the gushing spring at the old Tucker Cabin site which always provided challenges and adventures. The Gang tried coyote trapping in the snow and literally only ended up with cold feet. Our kind gesture to allow Eddie H to accompany us deep into the forest almost ended up in a disastrous forest fire ignited by Eddie's giant sparkler escapade running through the extremely bed of dry pine needles. Responsibility, adaptive ability and endurance were the virtuous gifts given the Gang's character those several years on their own out in the wilds. The camaraderie and spirit of independent survival on their many sojourns made them a fierce and undefeatable junior varsity football team. John P and Fredde C totally challenged Mother Nature one Christmas Eve by surviving a blizzard by secreting inside a lean-to within the local cemetery.

OWL'S WORST NIGHTMARE

OWL (O.W. Letts) was my 8th grade shop teacher. Next to being our junior high basketball coach he manned our shop class full of reckless adolescents scattered among electric band saws and motorized planes. We were certainly his worst nightmare.

It is impossible to remember OWL with a smiling face. His sullen and angry demeanor was something that one had to put out of one's mind or you could be overridden by fear and guilt. He governed our shop class with total eye contact and body language. His modus operandi was successful for I learned a tremendous amount about woodworking that I have carried all my life.

Mr. Letts apparently had been a race driver in younger days. He tells the story of speeding down a city street ally ready to mall over a cardboard box in the road when two children crawled out the side. Unfortunately, OWL had so little acumen as a basketball coach as we lost every game.

THE POLITICALLY CORRECT BASKETBALL TEAM

Quick side-glances from the waitresses and noon diners at McGee's Cafe at Keams Canyon in the Hopi reservation translated into "What's that white guy doing talking to that old Hopi for so long?" Four hours later, the waitresses were totally absorbed in trying to find out what my Hopi friend Jack C and my heavy extended discussion was all about. I overheard one of the waitresses whisper, "He must be a Bureau of Indian Affairs cop."

I had come to Keams many times asking about Jack and found out that he lived west of town where he tended his corn field and occasionally managed construction projects or went on the road to help build houses with Jimmy Carter's Habitat for Humanity group. One day the gas attendant pointed out the window and said, "That's his red tractor parked along the fence." When Jack had taken his cap off earlier that day, a shock of gray hair sculpted as a neat crew cut revealed itself and there was Jack, a little older and a little more guarded but the same jovial fellow who had so entertained the Gang fifty years ago on the long bus trips of the Winslow Junior High Basketball team.

My eyes had begun to water when the waitress had pointed to the corner table and said, "That's him sitting over there." Jack invented a code language wherein one communicated with great emphasis by saying opposites. When one had a bad cold the comment would be, "I'm well." The coded language became so sophisticated that the teachers and coaches did not know what we were talking about.

When I set out to locate each of the members of the old Winslow Junior High School Basketball team I dreaded what I might find out. We were truly a multi racial and ethnic novelty as functioning and closely nit basketball and football teams. What if the unique qualities I had attributed to each one of the team members would turn out to be only my projected wishes? And what if the potent bond I'd imagined to have been forged among the group was only wishful thinking fashioned by the liberal onslaught of the Kennedy years, the War on Poverty and the Age of Aquarius mentality impregnating society during the late 1960's and early 1970's. I was beginning to question my own commitment, my professional sacrifices in those days driven perhaps by a naïve, impractical idealism. The early bonds of lasting care and friendship, the sharing of victory and defeat, of being "us" against the rest of the world, of times of tricks, and fun and chicken fried steaks, of long days and nights riding and singing on the old yellow bus seemed to be the social glue that should hold people together in mutual care and commitment transcending time, space and the harsher episodes of life experience that characterized the fate of key members of the team who were all members of the minority mélange that made up the small railroad town in the 1940's. In addition to Jack, a member of the Hopi Tribe there was Pete, an Afro-American whose family had come to Arizona from the sawmills of Mississippi; there was Virgil "Sugar Bear", a member of the Navajo Nation from Red Lake north of Winslow, and finally 'Turo (short for Arturo), an Hispanic whose father had run a trading post at Na Ha Tee on the Navajo Reservation north of Holbrook. John P was Greek-American and Terry was just plain German-American. My mother's side of the family came from Ireland by way of Trinidad, Colorado. They were Irish immigrants to the U.S. in the late 1800's.

It has been said that genes, experience and a third factor, the expression of these elements' within recurrent problems, forge one's persona.

Jack, a member of the Hopi Tribe of Indians was born near Keams Canyon and spent part of his early life off Hopi Reservation at a private school near Sedona, Arizona. A wealthy family who owned the small community south of the ski resort of Sun Valley, Idaho had adopted his mother.

Seeing the slight tremors in Jack's left arm and having been conditioned to the suspicious and guarded response given me during my twenty five years working for the Navajo and Apache tribes, I expected that life experience and the accumulated insults flung at Jack's copper skinned persona would produce only a slight, brief and polite response from him.

"It's Jerry Knowles, Jack," I said as he sat down and looked into the gray-cast eyes. Jack averted his eyes slightly and blinked. Maybe he had Alzheimer's, I thought suddenly, feeling a slight burning feeling as the pores on my face began to dilate. "I really feel stupid," I thought. "My corny nostalgia has always gotten me into embarrassing situations. All this baloney I preach in graduate classes about the need for early bonding among youth to assure communities committed to equality, etc. has gone to my head and I am really beginning to believe my own B.S."

I began to stiffen my body to get up and make an excuse to get out of the awkward situation. I could feel the waitress and the Navajo people at the next table staring at me. Just when I was about to make my move, the gray eyes looked straight at me, twinkled and Jack's thick voice said, "Bean,(a special name given to me by Jack), you crazy guy, where the hell you been." I could smell the sweat of the little locker room under the Winslow High School Gym and it was as if no time had passed since 1946. "You still like chicken fried steak?" asked Jack, laughing. I felt comfortable and at home again. Jack, the master of mirth, the team joker, said "You ate two chicken fried stakes at the Elk Restaurant in Seligman, and O.W. Letts told you that you had to pay for the extra one."

DAN'S DEATH- FIRST DANCE, THE MOVIES AND THE POOL

The early days in Winslow introduced me to Death, Dancing and Drama at the Rialto and the Swimming Pool. The routine on hot summer days was the swimming pool in the afternoon and Rialto at night with frequent visits to the soda fountain for coke floats. Evenings were also spent trying to beat the odds of the local pinball machines in cafes along 2nd Avenue. I was exposed to my first dead body, that of Uncle Dan in his casket at the Scott Mortuary. It brought to mind once again the precariousness of life. Years ago in Flagstaff I was confronted by the incident about one Jackie Pylon's electrocution and broken neck caused by his fall during tree climbing. It was something I had never really dealt with completely. Now, here was the body of uncle Dan. The appearance of cousin Jackie in Naval uniform after the funeral provided me with a sense of comfort and reassurance.

ROMANCES

Females had always been significant in my life and my fantasies and, of course, the onset of puberty and adolescence only fired latent passions and created intense infatuations – there was Diane, Wemo, Oxley, Nancy, Barbara and sweet Lorraine. Dietrich had it right in her sexy lyrics:

> *"Falling in Love Again, Never wanted to*
> *What am I to do? I can't help it*
> *Love's always been my game, Play it as I may*
> *I was born that way, I can't help it."*
> (Reg Connelly,Marlene Dietrich, "THE BLUE ANGEL")

Bulldog pep rallies under the October Harvest moon began with the burning of the

"W" and ended up at the Walgreen Drug Store and the Rialto Theatre. Someone once said "he hoped he would fall in love with someone he liked this spring,"(Clancy I.).

Fantasies of nirvana and Shangri-La which invariably and suddenly appeared after the that first touch of a currently preferred female always fell short for me and sooner or later the infatuation would fade away. It would be years later and many intimate relationships, including four committed ones through marriage, before I realized why the chosen female always fell out of grace completely disappointing my expectations. Lorraine's mother Ruth had chastised me for calling and asking for her to "pick me up" for the movie date. Even though my house was much closer to the Rialto than Lorraine's, which was located way over on the west side of town, her mother Ruth had cut me off and quipped, "Nice girls do not pick up boys."

FRANK MERRIWELL AND SERIOUS SANDLOT FOOTBALL

The ultimate status achievement for a young fellow in Winslow was to become like the football, basketball or track stars that embodied that cherished glory and power— the stripes on the maroon (or white captain version) letter sweater were equivalent to local medals of honor.

In sixth, seventh and eight grade my friends and I fielded our own football and basketball teams to play against opposing groups. Each Saturday morning we would meet at a vacant lot and play tackle football without the protective pads. The radio series featuring a mythical Yale football hero, one FRANK MERRIWELL was listened to faithfully every Saturday morning. "*Frank Merriwell, the All American,*" was a radio series about that Yale football player who always left at the game's half time to solve mysteries and crimes, only to return late in the game to make the critical wining play. That large dose of football was usually topped off with the attendance in the afternoon at a Winslow Bulldog game at the local stadium, later named after Congressional Medal Honor winner Captain Jay Vargas.

SEVENTH GRADE BINGE
Kirk Clark, a violent fellow who later on identified himself as an alcoholic, strangely enough was one of my close friends. His bitter life of abuse by his alcoholic father, a prize fighter and persona of perpetual pugilist confrontation forced Kirk into golden glove boxing, preparing him genetically and by experience to be a classic alcoholic. The inevitability of the two of us thirteens getting drunk together was acted out one June day in Winslow. I believe that the moment I saw the Seagram's 7 fifth way up on the top shelf my subconscious had made a decision to consume it. All it took was an accomplice like Kirk to synergize the expectation of relief from any bad thoughts or circumstances with a shot of booze. Kirk threw up and went home. I went downtown to the drugstore to procure the pint of green-colored, mint-flavored vodka that had also lived in my subconscious for many months. Unfortunately, sitting at the fountain drinking a coke float my beyond-jubilant speech and body language was noticed by my father who immediately accosted me. I can't recall any details of what my father said but as always he had a way of signaling by demeanor, especially with eye contact, his deep displeasure at my behavior. This 1940's episode with alcohol left me with feelings of shame and uncertainty that added even more weight to a struggle for a self worth already careening from the burdens of early abuse. The effect of my first admonishment for alcoholic behavior quieted my obsession for alcohol until a sophomore in high school. The shame of that day operated to put me on the wagon for three years until the consumption of a beer in Freddie C's Chevey.

Season after season at old Lincoln Elementary, my friends and I formed teams and faced off on both courts and vacant lots. The Saturday routine was to meet at the lot next to the Church of Christ and square off against Pete Van's team in tackle football – tackle football without any pads for protection. The local belles were conned into coming to the game – for what was a warrior, a knight, without a lady Guinevere on the sidelines to revere, comfort and soothe? Lorraine, Barbara, and Wemo – they were in attendance there, in triumph and in tragedy. The only medical supports available were the stretchy Ace Bandages that I got from my Dad's Winslow Drug. One Saturday, Fredde was gang tackled and bounced out of bounds and had his breath knocked out. The Tucker Flat members of the team dutifully wrapped Fredde's chest with Ace Bandages and dragged him back onto the dirt field.

Bathed, glowing and adorned in a Winslow Tuxedos (white tee shirt, Levi's pants and jacket), we all went to the soda fountain for a Coke float and then on to Vargas field for the Winslow Bulldog/Prescott Badger game. The warm October sun and the beauty of the Winslow Belles magnified the primitive stirrings of puberty, and the glory of the game amid the red dust of Vargas seemed like paradise on earth to my friends and me. Surely, it was absolutely believed that passage into Shangri- La could be consummated by becoming a Winslow Bulldog.

I created my own basketball team which, and being of serious Irish origins, I dutifully out fitted with Kelly green "T" shirts. In addition to my solo sessions of round ball I also often practiced various track events amid the red dusty expanses behind the high school. I wound up winning the A Class 100, 200-yard dashes, the shot put and high jump events in the local Junior Chamber of Commerce Track and Field Day. Athleticism was a controllable skill to be perfected with intense and continuous practice.

A CRUCIBLE OF DEMOCRACY

Winslow High School Hall of fame football coach Emil Nasser's achievement in forging the unfailing loyalty and unity among youth from disparate social class, race, and ethnic groups was amazing. Nasser could create the support for one's fellow teammate that nearly equaled a soldier's passion for his foxhole partner. The heart, energy and principles gained from exposure to Nasser would be carried the rest of one's life. One of the highest examples of the many testimonials came from Congressional Medal of Honor Recipient Jay R. Vargas, "You came into our lives at the right time, for early in life, you taught us what leadership, never give up, integrity, compassion, teamwork, morals, and loyalty were all about." The championship team of 1955 proclaimed, "Your words echo into eternity-You did it all for us— we will never forget you."

SODA FOUNTAIN

The summer of 1946 I worked the soda fountain at my father's Walgreen Drug Store on the corner in Winslow. Today a bronze statue of Jackson Brown stands at that spot in honor of the corner's role in creating the song, Standing on the Corner in Winslow Arizona. The insanity and exhaustive work of soda jerking facing three deep screaming tourists pouring off of Route 66 doomed any interest I might have had in entering my father's business in the future.

NIGHT ALONE ON WILLIAMSON

My fear of being alone in the dark had still persisted from the time I was three years old. One weekend while I was in eighth grade my parents had gone to Phoenix for two nights. I slept in bed with my father's 22-caliber rifle. I became petrified at one point when I thought I saw a shadowy being pass by the back window.

CAMP GERONIMO

The Tucker Flat Gang went to Camp Geronimo, a Boy Scout Facility under Zane Grey's famed Mogollon Rim of Arizona. Imbedded within my tightly united peer group I learned to question authority that summer of 1946. The regime that controlled the scout camp routine required what the Gang thought were rather silly rules in contrast to their practical, carefree and boundless life on the high desert. Scout technique for lighting fires with flint seemed ridiculous and already had been rejected on the high dessert where fuel was scarce, the weather frigid and a little gasoline made a quick campfire. Sleeping in a teepee seemed weird to us and washing mess and dipping such into boiling water seemed unnecessary to us. We celebrated with great joy when we were relieved of the teepee and slept on our piles of pine needles we had built. We rejected the highly controlled routine that we were subjected to. The concept of questioning any authority was given birth in our psyches.

POIGNANT REVERIE

In the 1970's while having coffee with another alcoholic at a pancake house booth in Winslow I was introduced to a woman whom, when she heard my name, screamed "Jerry!!" in her thick Texan accent. She was Kirk's mother. She revealed that Kirk had been sober for 7 years prior to his tragic death in a 1963 plane crash.

While living in Winslow and running for County Supervisor I visited Daniel Kirk Clark's grave and said a silent prayer to and for him that I regretted that we could not spend old times together armed with the joyous spiritual gifts of those of us who found a higher power to relieve our alcoholism. That night at sunset on the way to

Flagstaff my silent radio barked alive after hitting a bump and Jo Stafford's "*No Other Love*" came lilting out of the Showlow FM. It was Kirk's favorite tune.

BULLDOG PLAYER

My persistence and passion in the quest for basketball and football fame was fleshed out and tested that sweltering hot August day in the red dust of the Winslow Bulldog practice field. The practice field seemed to consist of Baked Adobe. As the season progressed the Tucker Flat Gang made up the majority of the Junior Varsity team. I was fortunate to score a touchdown for the first time in one of the games that garnered the support and attention of my coach, one Jim Lovett. Lovett lobbied varsity coach Nasser's attention to promote me to a varsity position as right end. Fredde's brother Johnnie had injured his back in the

Starter as Frosh

Prescott game and the varsity needed a replacement at right end. Nasser had stated that no freshman would ever play on his varsity, much less be a starter. Yet I began my Bulldog career as a freshman starter for Emil Nasser. At first I made some critical mistakes on defense, but ultimately I was lucky to score a touchdown with a notable catch. I later stated in a book about Nasser, "You gave me a chance and changed my life forever." The touchdown was a breathtaking moment in my life. A rite of passage had been consummated that October day at Vargas Field. I played my last game as a Winslow Bulldogs on the cold frozen gridiron on my fifteenth birthday at Flagstaff. I was totally unaware of the tragedy that would follow. ("COACH, THE LIFE AND TIMES OF US HALL OF FAME COACH EMIL NASSER.")

THE COLLAPSE

Coach Lovett was also the varsity basketball coach and assumed I would be a talented addition to the Bulldog Varsity Basketball team. I was chosen as a member of the 1947-48 Bulldog Varsity basketball team. On a November evening just before Thanksgiving vacation I was running down the court in practice when my legs seem to turn to rubber and I fell prone on the court. At home that night I slept in the freezing cold garage so that Grand Aunt Mabel could have my bed. When I arose in the morning and looked at the coffee can that I had been urinating in it was colored a dark cherry brown. American Airlines flew me to Phoenix and the urologists at the St. Lutheran's Hospital diagnosed me as suffering from *glomerulonephritis*, an often-deadly kidney disease.

LEAVES AND FLAKES FELL—MONTHS CAME AND PASSED

I did not know that the somber attitude exhibited by my parents and my forced exile to a bedroom and bed 7/24 was being done because the doctors made a prognosis that I had a good chance of dying. I finished my freshman year in bed that was carried out because of the kindness of one selfless friend Billy W. He acted as a carrier of my assignments and homework. I gave up on Barbara H, tearing up her letters from South Bend and assuming with bitterness my status as a boyfriend could no longer be sustained. I was an invalid and imperfect. Kenny C. from Flagstaff came to visit me, which really cheered me up. Father Driscoll from St. Joe's brought me communion, confession and consultation once a week. The teenage fancy of the unending security of an earthly life was destroyed in my mind. Contemplation of the hereafter due to my desperate health plight was probably the genesis of my desire to become a Catholic Priest. From Thanksgiving through Christmas and on past Easter leaves fell and snow flakes wafted outside my bedroom window. Summer came and in early June of 1948 the family moved back to Flagstaff. My father partnered with one Fred Moore in ownership of the Moore Drug Company. I would become a Flagstaff Eagle and bitter rival of the Winslow Bulldogs.

LEADERSHIP—FLAGSTAFF

While I was rewarded by my old haunts and friends and by being back in Flagstaff I nevertheless felt left out, lonely and isolated without status as a sports figure. Achievement in sports had been a key part of my teenage identity and it had been left in Winslow. I faithfully acted as baseball manager my sophomore year at a sport I actually despised. I worked hard at basketball and football games selling mementos and refreshments. I never dated my sopho-

Spectacular run from fake punt-Phoenix 1950

more or junior year except when I escorted girls who chose me partners in some regal event or placed my name on a dance card. Sharing my identity with a girl was "verboten" to me without the veneer of esteem of sports to arm my ego.

Yet my sensitivity and empathy for the feelings of other people was still latent deep down in my character and even more poignant considering my own alienation at the time. Sadie Hawkins Day when I was a junior provided me a chance to get out of my own isolation and think more of someone else for a change. One Gwendolyn M, a frail and acne faced classmate, pinned her name on my back in study hall. The pinning required me to chaperon and stand as her date at the Sadie Hawkins Dance the following night. The teenage and love quest dimension of my personality balked at being seen in a relationship with someone less than an ideal queen. The sensitive and caring part of me could see what pain rejection would mean to Gwendolyn. I did accompany her the next night and somehow actually got with the flow of fun and enjoyment and accepted my role with class and caring. We became friendly partners.

CHEVY FORAY

That deep fear of the pain of shame was very powerful as it was associated with the 1945 episode, which exposed my alcoholism to my father for whom I had the greatest awe and respect. It dented my soul in such a way to have intensely killed an option of drinking until 1949.

Although now living in Flagstaff and attending Flag High my social group and buddies were still from Winslow. Fredde C had a four door Chevy and had come up to Flag with John P, Terry N. and a couple of other fellows. It was peer pressure that broke through my fear of drinking. The group consumed cans of Arizona's A-I Beer. It was a bad event. This was my first boozing party with my friends and it introduced and reinforced a feeling of being part of something that I had not known as an only child. The effects of the alcohol were like a Pavlovian association by bringing the feeling of joy in "belonging" and being a part of and having membership in a group of like minded friends and buddies.

The search for that belonging and communal joy experienced in Fredde's Chevy cruising the dirt road south of the Toonerville Bar between Winslow and Flagstaff became an obsession spanning nearly forty years. I intensely sought those feelings with my stature in football teams, in a society of seminarians in a monastery, within a college fraternity, as the leader of a Newman Club, as a member of a cadre of fellow students and educators, as an astute and synergetic pod of Illinois graduate professors and fellows, and as the committed activists at Purdue University and my associates in Gary Indiana during the civil rights movement.

THE LAST GAME—FRIENDS NO MORE

My life and self-concept at Flagstaff High School seems a strange anomaly now. I was welcomed with open arms by old friends and supported to the extent that they elected me high school student body Vice President for two years in a row—(I did not run for President because of the persisting fear of failure). My participation in Boys State opened a very painful wound of low esteem and was acerbated by my failure to "run" for any state office while my nemeses, classmate and class VP, Don C, was elected as Secretary of State of Boys State.

But the 'Sun Also Rises', (to quip the title of a famous Hemingway novel), as several key family friends (Principal W Killup) talked my father into letting me "punt and kick points after touchdowns." But, my lack of skill and performance as a kicker moved me over to defensive corner back – and also a ball carrier from fake punt position. The latter role played out in a sweltering Phoenix Indian game that earned me a front-page picture in the Phoenix Republic on Sunday morning. I had run once more from punt formation sprinting from left and right dodging the oncoming onslaught of those "Indians." In my plight to escape humiliation I had actually moved backward 20 yards behind the line of scrimmage. I began to think in a nana second mind's eye that my football career was over. Suddenly out of nowhere shot co-captain Walter B. who threw a body block that opened a hole in the Phoenix Indian Posse allowing me to break in the open and scamper all the way down to the 5 yard line wherein I was slugged by an angry Phoenix Indian player. Getting off the bus in Flagstaff the next day, I was accosted by one of my best friends who yelled, "Your picture is on the front of the Republic sports page!" If there is such a thing as "karma" I got it in spades that day as in later years I worked for the Navajos, Apaches and Zunis for over thirty years of my professional life. I ended up marrying a member of the Kiowa Tribe of Oklahoma. These were some of the best years of my life.

I came in fourth academically missing a chance as valedictorian, which I attributed to unfair grading by an English teacher on the one hand and a typing teacher on the other. It never had been my goal to excel in that way, but only to avoid bad grades and not suffer the shameful pain of failure.

TERRY AND I ~TUCKER FLAT HS VP'S

A poignant anecdote for integrity and mending wrongs was acted out my senior year. I was Vice President and my dear friend Terry N of Winslow was VP there. Terry, in a total out of character moment, gripped by disappointment and overwhelmed with rage had kicked the Flagstaff baseball coach "Frog" in the pants after losing a the Northern Arizona championship game. Flag High administrators implored me to encourage Terry to come to Flag and apologize. John P, the Tucker chum, urged Terry from the Winslow High School side. Terry came and apologized to a packed audience of students in the Flagstaff gym. John P and I introduced him.

BITTER SHOWDOWN

The Flagstaff Eagles would have been state champs that year except for one loss to my birth town Jerome. The Eagles had defeated a sound Bulldog eleven 39-7. There were always two games with Winslow as during a previous season a game was cancelled due to weather. The last game I ever played in was a bitter showdown between the revengeful Bulldogs and the Eagles. My friends gave no sign of recognition or welcome as they stared across the dressing room lawn— they could only glare at me. All concern about my kidneys was abandoned at mid season when I started receiving punts one of the most vulnerable acts on the gridiron. To say they "creamed" me at each punt reception puts it mildly. In spite of an inspired play by the Bulldogs, our all-state fullback, Garland Neal, and halfback, Walter Burton, were too much for my old buddies.

I limped onto the school bus to transport the Eagles back to Flagstaff. I attended the team dinner at the Monte Vista Banquet Room where I had to tell Patty M that I would not accompany her to the dance that night. After intense interface with Patty I admitted that I had a Greyhound bus ticket to go back to Winslow to stay with friend Billy W – the one who had given me a charlie horse that same day. "I can't get up there." I told Billy. "Why not?," Billy said looking surprised. "Because you hit me with your helmet in the thigh this afternoon," I said

I existed in a Jekyll and Hyde existence of good and evil. I was considered a fierce runner and defensive force but out of uniform I was a cheerful, kind and supportive friend. During that season I had identified Father Damien of Molokai as a hero worthy of emulation. (Winfrid. Herbst. 1924. BOYHOOD'S HIGHEST IDEAL: HELPFUL CHAPTERS TO CATHOLIC BOYS, AT THE PARTING OF THE WAYS. The Society of the Divine Savior).
Yet I had mistakenly made a necktie tackle flipping a Coolage High School opponent in the air in such a way that had the football stadium booing me. Not even beginning to own my own reality about who I was I was awarded the Babe Ruth Good Sportsmanship Award medal in tandem with one of my secret angels— one Barbara R.

VOCATION!?

I was chosen to read the benediction prayer at baccalaureate ceremony. Father Lindenmeyr, a mentor and facilitator for my entry into a vocation as a priest, had dictated the speech. Most of the speech was the usual sanctimonious pap except for the phrase, "And at the end of our lives may we be able to say,I have fought the good fight- as for the rest there is laid up for me a crown of unfading glory." That phrase sunk deep in my psyche and glowed like a neon sign many a time in my darkest hours. Yet I must admit that ego and arrogance played a large part of my persona not only during those graduation days but often times throughout life's challenges.

NEAR DISASTER

There were no drinking bouts during my high school years in Flagstaff except for the night of graduation. The opportunity to locate a group for all those reasons that break conventionalism under the onus of "graduation night" passed me by and I rode around with two friends, one of whom ran over a handle for a railroad switch. Fortunately there was no tragedy because of our failure to report the accident.

I was especially obsessed about Damien of Molokai, the Belgian priest who took his brother's place to go to the leper colony at Molokai in the Hawaiian Islands. Each Sunday Damien would address his flock from the pulpit with the salutation, "You lepers." One Sunday he announced, "We Lepers." Damien contracted leprosy and died on Molokai. He spent his life caring for the lepers battling the church and government for support. I think now that I was impressed that such caring

Friends Forever

could exist and be expressed by a human being. That gave me hope and encouragement and a worthy vision and destination to emulate.

I informed Father Lindenmeyer of the Southside Guadalupe Parish about my desire to become a priest and that I preferred the Franciscans. But, upon a session with the Bishop at Gallup, I was notified that he sent all his seminarians to the Benedictines at Immaculate Conception Abbey in Missouri, favoring their emphasis on the liturgy and the church cycle.

I would leave with classmate Alfred Tachias on a greyhound bus bound through Kansas City to northwest Missouri to begin study as a secular parish priest.

Certain events are burned into one's consciousness and associated with those watershed turning points in one's life. The theme song from "*Moulin Rouge*" about Henri de Toulouse-Lautrec's life poignantly flashes me back to the trip and my arrival at the seminary campus in Missouri. I had doused myself with Old Spice cologne on the bus— the scent of which would forever bring me back over and over again to that day of arrival at Immaculate Conception Monastery.

MASSIVE BUILDING COMPLEX

Immaculate Conception Abbey was a huge complex including a minor basilica layered inside with oak, marble and 50 monk stalls and 16 remote altars to accommodate the very large number of morning masses celebrated by the many Benedictine monks who dwell in the Abbey. The Abbey was established in the 1800's by a group of Benedictines who came from Switzerland. A number of the residents held the role as "fraters" (brothers) who were not priests.

Basilica

The designation of Basilica imposes on a church "the obligation to celebrate the liturgy with special care, and requiring that a church for which a grant of the title is requested should have been liturgically dedicated to God and be outstanding as a center of active and pastoral liturgy, setting an example for others. It should be sufficiently large and with an ample sanctuary. It should be renowned for history, relics or sacred images, and should be served by a sufficient number of priests and other ministers and by an adequate choir," (Wikipedia).

In 1951 there was a four-year high school, a two-year college, a two-year philosophy program and a four-year theology program to top off the whole programs of study. The motherhouse of the Swiss Benedictine monastery had come to and claimed a section of Missouri extending as far as the eye could see. Bishops from Arizona, Nebraska and Midwestern states sent novitiates aspiring to be priests to Immaculate Conception Seminary in deference to the Order of St. Benedict's emphasis on the yearly cycle of Catholic Church liturgy.

College Building

I both lived and went to class in the four-story College Building, sleeping on its top floor among some 50 beds, mine being atop a double bunk lining the east wall.

The were a huge number of buildings including a printing shop and a four storied building of single rooms for the major seminary theology students on their way to ordination. The College building included canteen with a pool table in the basement, a lounge and classrooms on the second floor.

The Conception grounds included a regulation football field and lake beyond which housed an island grotto dedicated to Mary.

Coming To A New Home

The bus trip to Missouri was tedious and exhausting. The magic carpet motif the trip and the destination I had projected to be was suddenly killed in the middle of the night somewhere near Salina, Kansas, which turned out to be a hated trail stop for me for the two years to come.

The huge red brick complex of buildings appeared through the haze and heat of that August afternoon. Fate had arranged for my first encounter at Conception to be with a seminarian named Elmer Joseph Mudd who eventually lived up to his namesake. I never really found out from whence he came and was afraid to find out.

I had left a house in Flagstaff with a view of the twelve thousand foot San Francisco Peaks out my window and a private room and shower framed from floor to ceiling with pink and maroon tile. These few days on the road were my first time away from home and outside of the West. I had gotten food poisoning from the dinner in Kansas city bus depot and spent my first night away from home in the second floor of the infirmary attended by a Swiss brother who doctored me with a white pill and mysterious brown liquid which turned out to be the standard dose given for any and all ails.

I was awakened in the infirmary at 5 in the morning and ushered over into the Basilica wherein I saw fifty monks in their stalls with heads bowed singing Gregorian chant. One monk stood out who had a poorly fitting red wig. "What the hell am I doing here!"

College students were given a steel locker 7 foot high and 2 and a half feet square for in which to store all their belongings. I stuffed my total wardrobe into this small space. My Samsonite went into storage awaiting Christmas vacation.

GREGORIAN CHANT, LATIN AND GREEK

Daily mass was accompanied by seminarians chanting Gregorian, reflective of the season and the particular spot in the church calendar. I could sing 6 Kyries Eliasons by heart into my late years.

I attended Latin classes twice a day for two years to the point where I could read the Latin version of the New Testament and even use it as a pony (a literal translation of text) to interpret the Greek version of the same. To add to the mayhem an Italian Benedictine attempted to discuss the complex 24 Philosophical Thesis of Thomas Aquinas in a broken English accent. He called ice cream "*itchee creaham*" The very thought of the Theses, in addition to figuring out what the teacher was talking about, gave me head aches.

On the other hand our Greek master was a disgruntled monk who had returned from the "good life" outside the abbey to wreck havoc on and scapegoat my young friends and me. After requiring the class to repeat the Greek alphabet after a 5-minute examination of it on one page in the book, our class revolted and had the master removed as the teacher. One Father Placid, an Ed Win like bubbling wit, took over and we translated the Greek version of the New Testament using the Latin version as a pony.

ENGLISH GRAMMAR AND MONK PERSONAS

Gay Father Lawrence Giddly taught English grammar and half the class were so totally confused that I volunteered to tutor some of them on Sunday during a cheese and cracker snack. One St. Patrick's Day morning Fr. Giddly was faced with extreme sanction for his derogatory comments made citing the non-contribution of Irish to western culture. The sudden deep purple appearance in Dick McNeal's earlobes prompted me to tap his shoulder and warn "Don't Hit Him." In April Giddly standing as point man aside the Missouri River bank helping contain a spring flood slipped and fell into the river. Heaven could wait apparently for Fr. Lawrence Giddly.

Father James Jones was the epitome of action and joy of living. He often joined us sems in softball games. He subbed for the pastor at Our Lady of Guadalupe in Flagstaff and had a spaghetti dinner with my family in the later 1950's. He later became the Abbot of Conception Abbey

Then there was the zoo teacher Father David who used embalmed cats – red for arteries, blue for veins – for dissection. James Daily from Great Bend Kansas partnered with me in the dissection enterprise but refused to touch the cat. Father David was never forgiven for the awful act of cutting the phrenic nerve to the heart of Bennie, a revered terrier and mascot around Conception. Yuk!

Father Ignatius Potts had the bad habit of creating an early morning trauma by rapping his flashlight of the corrugated door to the dorm. One January mourn Chuck Chester, a Sioux from South Dakota, upon hearing "rise and praise the lord," from Potts' mouth, yelled, "Get me an ice pick first!" The reverence of silence was completely destroyed that morning by 50 odd sems roaring with laughter.

The major player and immediate supervisor for the college sem (seminary) fellows was father Joachim Schreiber, a Burt Lancaster persona and look-a-like.

He epitomized an excellent merging of honesty, practicality and spiritualism— a welcome refuge from the exposure to the wide-ranging characters wearing the black robes of St. Benedict down the halls of Conception. He often took groups of sem students to Nebraska football games and other special excursions which manifested his compassion and care for young men in such a constrained environment.

Father Edmund was the music master of Conception and taught the sems chant, current liturgical music. He composed many hymns we sung at mass—*From rosy dawn's far eastern door to golden sunset western bound, around the world His song resounds –*" stands as an example of his poetic talent. Of a Saturday music session a sleepy inattentive group of us sems jerked to startled attention when he declared that we should *Do Everything with full malice.*" No one has ever figured out what the hell he meant, but I have used it as an excuse for a myriad of different behaviors.

My smoking and adversity to the chow hall had caused me to lose about 30 pounds causing Jackie to remark that I had better "get out of Conception" which encouraged an alternative for me in juxtaposition to the stance of the rosary ladies who thought it was so great that I was studying to be a priest.

JOKES

As I found out with an upcoming paint episode/fight with the bowling alley, young men can be cruel and concoct many serious pranks. Humor existed as continuous cacophony of quips and pranks. A favorite time for jokes was at the dinner table wherein ten sems were seated. Positions at the table were rotated so as to create a mix of fellows getting to know each other over time. So it was during a several weeks of dinning at the table I was at that one Jim R., a graduate of Boys Town Nebraska and past enlistee in the Navy, sat at my table. One of the fellows created a phony "Joke Club." To be accepted or voted into to the club one had to tell three jokes that received considerable laughter. One of the leaders at our table set Jim R. up by coaching our table to laugh at Jim's two jokes, but to turn our backs on him when he went for the third joke. There is nothing like good old Christian charity! When everyone turned their backs on Jim, he lost it, picked up a pitcher of hot tea, and began sloshing tea up and down the table. The head perpetrator of the joke started a fistfight with Jim. The monk in charge broke the fight up. Jim and the table leader challenged each other to a fight behind the Basilica. Two other episodes seemed really funny in retrospect although not so humorous at the time. The Benedictines of Wisconsin sent applesauce and apple "juice" down to our Abbey in Missouri. Eating applesauce got real old quick-like. However, the slightly fermented apple juice made a huge hit causing the break out of fisticuffs over who got his hands on the most. It was fermented and a gallon of it would give one a slight buzz.

Humor played a critical role in reducing stress among a mass of young men. Homesickness and depression weighed heavy on me as the first autumn began to shift and all the leaves had come down. Although not so apparent in 1951 the extreme quietus about no talk after 8 o'clock especially in the dorm sleeping quarters, was a defense against any acting out of homosexuality. So, the excitement arose with the expectation of Thanksgiving break, a wet toilet paper fight erupted in the sleeping quarters and I, being one of the participants, was "caught." Unfortunately, Father Ignatius Potts caught me and the other perpetrators. A close friend from LA said he was in on the "pot" which was a toilet in a small enclosure in the sleeping quarters. However, prefect Joachim thought he said that he was in on the "plot." It took several minutes to get my friend off the hook. I did not escape. I was 'campused' for the Wednesday before Thanksgiving. The punishment was devastating for I had existed in a different universe in my first experience "away from home." I was scheduled to have Thanksgiving with cousin Jackie in Kansas City who was like a brother to me. Homesickness and depression weighed heavy on me as the first autumn began to shift and all the leaves had come down. The planned trip down to Kansas City to have Thanksgiving with brother-like cousin Jackie Bean was extremely critical to my mental health and spirits.

THANKSGIVING CAPER WITH COUSIN JACKIE

As a consequence of the wet toliet fight and being campused and I would have to take a milk train Thanksgiving at four in the morning from Conception Junction. Cousin Jackie met me at the KC station and we cruised away to his apartment in downtown, me being petrified at the roller coaster speed of 50 mph, which I had not experienced in months. Even more bizarre was Jackie's mother in law who poured hot coffee down my back at breakfast – I felt she must be possessed and a candidate for exorcism.

A family thanksgiving dinner had been set up. Awaiting being served out of the corner of my right eye I saw a flame and I grabbed the water glass to put it out and almost succeeded when Jackie yelled "no don't." It was turkey flambé at a fancy German restaurant in the Plaza, supposedly the first shopping center in the US.

The other item that brought out some violent interfaces was, of all things, Franco American spaghetti out of can.

"FOOD"!!

The refectory as the chow hall was called – refractory would have been a more appropriate name – was the source of severe penance for me in the form of liver, brains, head cheese (pig snout hairs and all) topped with Saturday's 'mystery stew' a concoction of all the meats served during the week thrown together.

Roast beef was served each Saturday noon, a treasured feast day when we got cream for our coffee. "Oh! Oh!" Dick M screeched. Everyone at the table looked to see the large cockroach in the bottom slide out of the gravy bowl.

Again, Apples from the monks in Wisconsin guaranteed applesauce, sometimes with rhubarb, for dessert each night.

All meals were preceded by blessings in Latin with final punctuation by a major seminarian, who, frequently was late and would come busting through the door adjusting his roman collar, breathlessly quoting the final phases of the blessing.

MARTINI INCAPACITATION

An experiment with alcohol –one to ward off the gloom of returning to Conception – was the train stop of the Grand Canyon Limited for one hour in Gallup, New Mexico. Bill M and I had planned to get off and eat hamburgers at the White Café immediately across from the Santa Fe Station. As we left Holbrook Arizona we decided to go to the lounge car. We discovered that we could purchase high balls there. Martinis had always fascinated me so I ordered one. The buzz felt too good, especially as it wiped away the gloom, that I had a second drink.

It was mid afternoon and my stomach was empty from the early morning breakfast in Flagstaff.

Bill and exited the train with some difficulty and when I stood next to the passenger car I knew I could not walk across the street to the White Cafe. I had the taste of shaving lotion in my mouth- my first hit of a martini.

FRIENDS AND FELLOWS

I fell in with the sems from Omaha and of all places, Mark Twain's Hannibal Missouri. Dick M and Don K were from Omaha and Jim K was from Hannibal. Sports, touch football and basketball had been a common experience and base of identity with these fellows. Don had been offered a major league baseball contract and turned it down, becoming a priest. Dick got a PhD in language and ended up as a top administrator at Cleveland State. Koch was chosen to be sent to Rome, but left the sem, got married and had five or more children and ended up teaching at St. Edwards in Austin. I hitch hiked across Missouri with Jim one Easter morn to Hannibal. A family on their way to church gave us a ride, inquiring whether or not we went to church on Easter and we informed them that we had just spent four hours in the Basilica the night before. Jim could have easily been taken as Tom Sawyer's twin because he manifested all the myths about Hannibal, Missouri.

My friends drove out to Arizona and spent a week there, including a visit to the Grand Canyon. Efforts made to reconnect to the three fellows were unsuccessful. I had disenchanted Dick by appearing drunk at his job interview with me. Jim said he would come to Taos if it had a good golf course and frequent inquiries for Fr. Don were never answered. The priest who left Arizona with me to Conception informed me that Don was living with a female. A dejected and disenchanted Don had contacted me in mid 70's to share his plight about being bypassed to become a bishop because of church politics. My situation was less than admirable and I never heard from Don again.

Conception forced me to adapt to the social requirements of a group of peers in a daily, intense and comprehensive way— a necessary socialization, but it did not move me to a level to overcome the tendency to isolate.

MAY DAY

Sometime in May a bell would go off early in the morning without warning to signal May Day, a full day of track and field events complemented by fun things like "piggy back races." I won first in high jump and the standing broad jump, records I have seemed to hold in perpetua. My high jump style was an unorthodox straight run. I would run headfirst and lift my whole body over the line.

These achievements gave my identity a special recognition among the community, which seemed to be a needed dimension of my personality in a milieu where status was achieved by behaviors that were uncomfortable and difficult for me— much like the sense of failure felt at Boys State.

THE HUBBA HUT

Being some forty miles from the nearest town the few times the sems were allowed to visit either St. Joe or Maryville were exciting and cherished times. Conception bused us to these towns two or maybe three times a school year, usually coinciding with a holy day. Both intensive and innumerable activities were jammed into those days— several diners, movies and girl watching at high school lunch times.

St. Benedict's day in St. Joe of 1951 was densed out by watching girls at lunch dismissal at the local high school— two major dinners and a movie at the Robidoux Theater.

On another occasion the sems loaded into four taxis and took off across the Missouri border into Kansas to a place called the Hubba Hut Bar— a railroad car in front with a dance hall attached on back. Since Kansas allowed beer consumption at 18, it was a common event to go to the Hut. However the little old lady attending bar was totally stressed out soon after our arrival in several cabs. She had no idea why all those fellows ordered so much beer before lunch and then, of all things, began dancing with each other.

One October Saturday the sems went to the Robidoux Theater to see ACROSS THE WIDE MISSOURI with Clark Gable and John Hodiak. The second floor of the theatre had a large TV that was broadcasting a Notre Dame game and I was trying to identify my high school buddy trumpet playing Bill McCullough marching in the band at half time.

Father Giddly's Shakespearian personality prompted him to use feast days to expose sems to cultural events. One bitter February day he piled us all in for a forty-mile ride into Maryville, Missouri to attend a Shakespeare Play. We all purchased cigars after the performance and lit up once the bus was down the road – creating a dense cloud of tobacco smoke in the bus and the screaming voice of Giddly to "put out those cigars fellows or you will have to get off the bus."

CLOISTER AT CLYDE

Only ten miles from Conception was a cloister containing a huge community of nuns, who as contemplators spent the majority of their time in prayer. The sems were brought over to empty the construction materials from an underground water storage cistern.

The event included a meditative and solemn prayer visit to a chapel of perpetual adoration, which exposed the consecrated bread thought to be the actual body of Christ. Some one was always in the chapel seven days a week for twenty-four hours a day. Midlevel around the wall of the chapel were small niches with glass fronts supposedly containing relics of a saint. Monks of Conception joked that one of them contained a feather of Archangel Michael.

Most of our sems meditative time was spent gazing at the young female novitiates popping their heads up and down like turkeys giving us the eye. We guessed that bob and weavers were obviously signaling us and exhibited vulnerability enough to later leave the convent to hit the "golden trail" out into the wicked world.

The mother superior could have been an angel or even the blessed mother for her body language and kindness. Breaded veal was served at the banquet she hosted to honor us sems for our volunteer efforts.

We were not so lucky helping those Belgium nuns one infernal August day. Wearing military combat boots those nuns were pitching hay up into the barn so fast that we could not keep up with them and feared we pass out with heat exposure.

RECREATION

Smoking in the lounge to the resonating ballet of Richard Rogers' *Slaughter On 10th Avenue* and eating Oreos, playing pool and listening to Joni James sing *"Why Don't' You Believe Me"* in the basement recreation room were the daily forms of leisure at Conception.

But there were also very special occasions. Movies were shown and the most memorable was the one about a group in London who declared a section of the city to be separate country. It was a comedy about their absurd resistance and survival.

The major seminary theology students produced "ARSENIC AND OLD LACE," a play that is a farcical black comedy revolving around the Brewster family who descended from the' Mayflower,' but are now composed of insane homicidal maniacs." (From Wikipedia) Major sem fellows with unbelievable skill, especially the Teddy Roosevelt characterization,

Coffee, Oreos & Joni James

played the parts. Football games were broadcast on TV in a large auditorium, which on one occasion resulted in a chair throwing fight between Notre Dame and Oklahoma football loyalties. Most Saturdays were spent among the furrows in a nearby field listening to Notre Dame football on a portable radio. One such Saturday I mistakenly tried to grab the tale of a large bull snake side winding across the landscape. It almost knocked me down. Autumn, football and Notre Dame always generated a sense of hope.

"Touch Football"

The college and philosophy sem fellows played "Touch" football games on Saturdays. I had spent the prior season in high school experiencing rough play catching punts etc., but nothing was as brutal as the touch football of those sensitive sems. After the short prayer breaking huddles, one south Omaha fellow would often say, "Someone block that son-of-bitch end."

"Wow," Jim K said when I snagged one of those impossible catches fashioned from the incessant basketball practice days. Again, a needed case of the recognition needed by an ego that was an esteem project in progress.

PAINT FIGHT

Certainly there was a strange conglomerate of personas congregating at Conception that autumn of 1951—from distant spots across Nebraska, Kansas, Missouri, Oklahoma, the Dakotas, Arizona and California.

Everyone maintained a false standoff of politeness and reserve, afraid to expose themselves. What was needed was a ground-braking event to chill the icy atmosphere of those first few weeks. An extraordinary experience for bonding and introductions occurred.

An event happened that was just what the doctor ordered. Father Joachim Schreiber, prefect of the minor sem, accepted the responsibility for painting a bowling alley. The major sem had a two-lane bowling in their basement building. The light green paint was peeling off the wall. Since there wasn't enough of the same color green the seminarians knew that had to mix and match to get one single batch, not knowing of course that a single shade would be impossible.

The whole college crew was sent over with the variety of green paint. There were many "characters" among that first year college roster and the one of the most striking fellows was one Nick O. from somewhere in Kansas. Nick was a sports nut who preached incessantly about softball exploits, particularly his own. His constant bragging grew in irritability to the point that unkind jokes were being leveled at him. Atop an eight-foot step ladder Nick was busily brushing the ceiling when one sem (Jim Koch) crossed that Rubicon of behavior and sent a thin swab of green paint that hit Nick across the left chin and neck. Nick was startled and jerked his around to preview the room looking for the guilty part and decided it was Jim Dunphy who suddenly got a full brush in the face. Many other sems got part of Nicks spray. Dunphy in turn dunked his brush and hit Nick on the back of the head. Sems who had been hit by Nick's second spray began retaliating and bedlam came necessitating the re-sanding of the alleys. I had to wash my hair in turpentine along with the rest of the crew—burning scalps.

TRAIN TRIPS HOLIDAYS

"Its beginning to look allot like Christmas" came across the airwaves in the canteen one afternoon and caused a ripple of excitement and joy. The expectations of the onset of the Christmas holidays, was exhilarating and very uplifting in a drab routine and the stark landscape emerging with the onset of winter in Missouri.

The day finally arrived when my Samsonite came out of storage, got packed and stowed on the waiting Greyhound bus to Kansas City. Nothing but joy looking out the windows as small hamlets and leafless forests passed by until we pulled into the Greyhound station in downtown Kansas City. Two hours before boarding the west bound Santa Fe Grand Canyon Limited through Kansas, Colorado, New Mexico and on to Arizona and California—plenty of time for a banquet at the Emporia Cafeteria. Nearly four months of lousy food had fused an obsessional appetite for roast beef, scalped potatoes, biscuits, corn on the cob and peach cobbler. I once filled my tray with double the number items I could possible consume.

As much as we tried we could never locate the chips from the gangland bullets that had hit the side of the Depot – a high-ceiled wonderful old building with at least ten tracks into a covered Ramada.

The ticket agent stared with deep doubt as to whether Bill C deserved the clergy pass like the rest of the sems. Bill had a tendency to get loaded when he hit town and was held up with a sem under each arm to obtain his pass. (Bill C became a Catholic Priest and disappeared in the bowls of Kansas somewhere.)

Morning broke through the window of the diner on my cream and cornflakes. Real coffee aroma filled the air. Soon it would be time to go to the window between the cars to search the horizon for the white peaks of the Colorado Front range. This always occurred at La Junta, Colorado. I often remained near the window to see Trinidad and get the thrill of the slow wind through Raton Pass.

The train stopped for a full hour at Albuquerque, which allowed a scrumptious lunch at the Fred Harvey's in the Alvarado Hotel. "*Silver Bells*" sounded out over the station intercom. A sense of the nearness of Arizona and home was evident from the silversmiths and Navajo weavers in the Alvarado Indian Room.

It would be deep in the night when the Grand Canyon stopped in Winslow. I would look out the window at the grey buildings of the depot and La Posada Inn and try to remember the Winslow Days, reminiscing with sadness and visions of banquets, pep rallies and lights at the corner of the Dad's Walgreen Drug store and the Rialto Theater down the street. I thought mistakenly that entry into the priesthood would forever bar me from Winslow days.

Finally, the train would roll through the winter storm and heavy snowfall up into Flagstaff. I had told mother and father that I was not getting out of sem until December 22 which was 12 days after the actual Conception dismissal date of December 10th. I walked up Aspen Avenue through the five inches of snow to the front door, rang the bell and got showered with surprise, joy and Christmas cheer.

Since Conception posed a somber existence, Christmas passed like a flash of fireworks, but enough to shroud the darkness left behind in Missouri.

There is nothing like a wedding reception. Friend Bill McCullough and I served both as greeters and qualifiers in our roles of filling cups with strawberry laced Champaign, which we generously sampled after each wedding guest lilted by. Needless to say the reception team could hardly stand up after the event.

A trip down the Sunset Boulevard slope at the Snowbowl on the Peaks resulted in a disaster for me as a came speeding down on my back to the amusement of the hot chocolate sipping people on the lodge deck. It was a case of the wrong ski boots and skis (Dad's) and no skills beyond the "snowplowing" days of the 1930's on Sisabel Park.

Boarding the train at 3 am was the depths of depression – going back to Conception- I always woke up in Salina, Kansas that caused an exponential accretion of depression. Yet the second year at Conception being at home in the Basilica brought a sense of joy and security not apparent or accessible in Arizona.

I refused to sit with my fellow Arizona sems on the trip back. We were quite different personalities. My care for Alfred and Lawrence never altered all through life, but my skill in interfacing with gay men at that time in life was undeveloped– they seem to bicker and argue all the way to Kansas City and I was depressed as it was and needed solace, quiet and isolation. In truth as I look back, the fellows I chose to get close to were themselves gay – Father Larry D., my best conception friend.

Of a trip home the first summer I routed from Omaha to Denver and met my cousin for a day, taking the Santa Fe to Albuquerque and on to Flagstaff. My reception in Denver was cool and formal. Beverly still incensed from my bullying episode.

During my last train trip to Conception I would get off at Kansas City and Bill M. would ride clear to Chicago and there on to South bend. We had a fifth of whisky, which was never opened on the train because of continued interruptions in the bathroom waiting area. The foyer to the bathroom was continually occupied, blocking any attempts for a cocktail hour. We finally stayed in the Independent Hotel in Kansas City and quaffed only a couple of shots. Walking Bill to the train station was just one of many sad goodbyes in life the accumulation of which began to signal my psyche about the futility of always moving to a different place.

LEAVING CONCEPTION AND THE "VOCATION"

My commitment and fervor for becoming a priest began to wan the spring of 1953—a multi regression brought about possibly by a combination of concerns for my health on the part of cousin Jackie and friends, Kenny C. and Dick L.; exposure to the body and beauty of the frequent retreaters parading on campus; the knowledge of the diverse personalities of monks and seminarians; and some disenchantment because a number of sems seemed unhappy, uncaring and downright contemptible in physical and behavioral attitudes. In fact I have concluded that many were there with clergy exemptions from the Korean War draft. I also learned that Justice Thomas of the US Supreme court left Conception Sem because of its racism. A Navajo friend informed me he also left for the same reason .

I left with my parents the last day of May 1953 never to return as a seminarian. I have had some regrets especially at the ordination of Father Alfred T. However, as years of have passed I have realized that the role of a priest is not the only way to do good, in fact in some cases it could be restrictive.

DARKER DAYS

As the days passed by at Conception Missouri, my skies looked darker by the minute and loneliness and depression set in. I was terrified of being trapped into becoming a priest for fear of "God" and the Flagstaff Catholic Society – but most of all, I was fearful of my own shame, of my inability to dedicate myself to something I had built up in my mind as a life's goal. As a senior knocking people down on the football field I had been reading about Father Damien, the priest who served lepers in Molokai. I found myself enthralled at the idea of being a priest, and fantasized about the joy of being one.

My best friend at Conception proved to be a salamander that lived in the wall of the common bathroom. I had always had a canine pal, and the salamander was the closest I could get to that. I used anthropomorphic projection in assuming that it knew me and was my friend. Not much maturity there. The pathetic condition of my life had reached a new level.

Returning home to Arizona was my only option short of suicide, unthinkable for a Catholic. My first legal imbibe occurred with my folks at the Congress Hotel Restaurant in Tucson. I had a martini and spilled gravy down my shirt.

Wedding Day - August 24, 1955—Libertyville. Ilinios

IV. COMMITMENT

NUPTIALS

COLLEGE CAMPUS

ARIZONA STATE COLLEGE AT FLAGSTAFF

In the autumn of 1953 I registered at Arizona State Teachers Flagstaff to continue my college education begun at the seminary. I was a lost soul without focus. The energy and activity toward becoming a priest had been intense for three years and now the goal and the process were gone. There was ease at being home in Arizona and living with my parents, but underneath there was a feeling of defeat, sadness and isolation — a fire had gone out in my heart and nothing but reveries of the past were there to replace it. The college reluctantly accepted enough transfer credit equivalent of one year's work-30 hours of Latin being the prime transfer.

FRIENDS AND ASSOCIATES.

BILL R.

During pre-seminary days I had been a close friend with a family of Catholic converts – the R's. Bill R. like me had just mustered out of an institution to be a priest, which had come to a crashing halt in a Utah Trappist Monastary. Bill climbed on the table one morning at breakfast and screamed that the Virgin Mary had spoke to him and it told him it "was too God Dam quiet" in that place. He threw the tray of bread down the table. They escorted him to a local psych ward. He was released without prejudice to come back to Arizona

Our similar backgrounds provided a bond between Bill and me. Bill and I in turn befriended a previous acquaintance from the Birch street days that was a fellow who suffered from frequent seizures. We took him under our wing and he eventually joined the Catholic Church, married and managed a newspaper distribution business.

INFATUATIONS

The fires and desires – the need and time– to fuse my identity to another human being was intense and became a substitute focus of my libido away from Christ to a human being. Dateless in high school, a virgin I had accepted a vow of celibacy and had abstained from all sex for two years. My status posited a guy vulnerable as hell to engage in any kind of relationship. At the same time I suffered from the continuation of an obsession with romance. Years later this character dysfunction was defined as "love addition"-which is not so much about sex per se, but more about the search to find a "mother" to recapture that warm and secure bliss imprinted long ago in my soul. I learned that it would never happen and is not in reality a possibility.

I wish I knew then and could have spared both my pain and that of the many females who looked to me to make life long commitments. Of course, none of them met the criteria I had in mind for the ideal mother.

Strict Catholic rules and their regimen encapsulated my conscience to the extent that all interfaces with females had to be limited, to what in those days was called "necking," which was allot of kissing and hugging but nothing else

STAGE SIX—INTIMACY OVER ISOLATION TO ESTABLISH LOVE (18—35 yrs.)
During ages 18 to 40 yrs.), sharing more intimately begins. Relationships are explored leading toward longer-term commitments with someone other than a family member. Successful completion of this stage can lead to comfortable relationships and a sense of commitment, safety, and care. Avoiding intimacy, fearing commitment and relationships can lead to isolation, loneliness, and sometimes depression. Success in this stage will lead to the virtue of love.

My episode with a beautiful Italian American student at the college one night ended in my refusal to not go beyond "necking." I later informed friend Bill R. about her "assault" and how I had resisted her advances. So much for buying into the 'loss of one's eternal soul.' Do regrets come from what we did or didn't do in life? I had denied a request to escort a prominent family's daughter to a Christmas dance a year earlier. I responded to their request by stating that, "don't you know that I am going to be a priest?" One Easter holiday away from Conception in Omaha I had to fight off Dick M's cousin with the same mantra "don't you know ——" while Dick acted out a most passionate and hot necking episode in the front seat at the drive inn theatre.

I now believe my parents had and still were quite concerned about me not having a close relationship with a female— they might even believe I had homosexual tendencies which was totally taboo in those days.

There was the time that a girl, Betty D, a senior high school classmate, asked to meet me at the Orpheum Theater at a Saturday matinee. I believe that this rendezvous was set up by my mother through a business acquaintance in hopes it would jump-start me away from asceticism and even my isolation and celibacy before graduation in high school. Betty never showed up which meant my shaky ego took another hit. My suspicion about my mother's role in setting me up was enhanced years later when Betty and she became close confidents without any apparent connection.

My romantic fantasies at that time and even and most of my life has envisioned idyllic females devoid of imagining any sexual episodes. It seems that allot of my energy had been played out as described in Neil Young's song which declares, *"I want to live, I want to give, I am a miner looking for a heart of gold, I am growing old."*

You don't allow in consciousness to imagine having sex with your mother. I have been looking for a combo of Minnie, Mabel and Irene. Neither both the impossibility of such a myth nor chance of engagement eluded me for an eternity.

Enter Sophie Bennett

Over aggressive and active females frightened me and as my choice of male friends exemplified, I was drawn to the kind and the sweet ones. Of one November afternoon in my senior high school year I was pinned by a junior to be her date on Sadie Hawkins Day— a plight that traditionally can't be refused. She was a member of a prominent Flagstaff family. I thought at the time she was welded in a tight relationship with our football guard – an immigrant from Tennessee whose southern accent and demeanor made me unjustly devaluate him. I had thought all year long, " Why is she hung up with him?" We had been classmates at St. Anthony's years earlier. I had ended my only "love affair" at Flag high with "Patty" who had been jilted by my decision to return to Winslow after the last football game. I had no self-confidence relating to females and the rapprochement of the junior from the top social class signaled some special value for me.

Sadie Hawkins was followed by a December trip to a clearing up on the San Francisco Peaks. We had decided to go ice-skating on a remote pond that was frozen solid.

We ate roasted sweet potatoes with large cubes if butter melted in the center. What a romantic setting that was and of course— right out of Sun Valley Serenade! The setting and Sophie's

Sadie Hawkins Day
FHS — 1950

charisma planted in my naïve and immature mind that some eternal bonding and commitment had been sealed and that I had found a soul mate. Even of today the strains of What Are You Doing News Year's Eve?, inevitably brings me back to the arrival of new year's1951 and dancing in the basement of the hall of St. Anthony's with that same junior Sophie B.

WHAT ARE YOU DOING NEWS YEAR'S EVE?,(Frank Loesser,1947)
"Maybe it's much too early in the game
Aah, but I thought I'd ask you just the same
What are you doing New Year's
New Year's Eve?"

I followed up with an anonymous delivery of flowers to her after the junior play and spent many an eve by the fire in her living room throughout the winter hours –

"LET IT SNOW!"
When we finally kiss good night
How I'll hate going out in the storm!
But if you'll really hold me tight
All the way home I'll be warm
(Lyricist Sammy Cahn and composer Jule Styne in July 1945)

However, the day after my high school graduation while lounging in Oak Creek Canyon at Bill M's house, I said to myself a goodbye not only to the relationship with the junior Sophie, which was Bill's cousin, but to the life in Arizona. But, the lovely junior never left and was living all the time enduring deep in my psyche to return again and again in dreams. Upon my reappearance back home in Flagstaff I immediately thought of the junior Sophie as I felt that I desperately needed a female relationship. I was able to spend that summer of 1954 movie going and swimming in Oak Creek at a deep pool down stream from Sophie's family ranch. Those summer days back home provided an emotional balm to ease my disappointment and doubts about ending my religious vocation.

Sophie registered at the University of Arizona at Tucson and joined a well-recognized sorority. I went to Tucson several times. Sophie and I attended an Arizona Wildcat football game. We also took a trip up a beautiful Sabino Canyon. Sinatra had introduced the song, *Ebb Tide*, and that became the epitome of my romance with Sophie. I wrote to her and included a translation of *Sonnets from Portuguese* into Latin.

Credit to Sophie she never committed in word or writing any promise or expectation about me. On my part it was all fantasy.

As our dates became more frequent and seemingly more serious a conversation was broached with her mother, Sophie the senior. The mother asked me if I was "interested in a business career" as Sophie's mother was part of a vast family business entity in Flagstaff and all of Northern Arizona. I told her I wished to become a teacher.

It was not apparent to me until late the autumn of 1954 that a romance had ended. I received no more letters from Tucson and the party at the Bennett ranch in Oak Creek made me feel as a misfit among elite students from Phoenix Union. I was driving an unclassy Willy's Jeep at the time and was dressed in less fashionable cloths. A sense of self-loathing engulfed me. It was a scene right out of Fitzgerald's Great Gatsby. Spring came and I found out that Sophie's mother had taken her to Paris and eventually back to California and the house on the beach in Santa Monica.

I am not sure how I surmised later but I concluded that Sophie's mother and the local priest Father L, who had ushered my religious career, had conspired to end the romance so I would return to Conception Seminary.

(SONNETS FROM PORTUGUESE ,How Do I Love Thee? (Sonnet 43)
"How do I love thee? Let me count the ways.
I love thee to the depth and breadth and height
My soul can reach, when feeling out of sight
For the ends of Being and ideal Grace."
(SONNETS FROM PORTUGUESE, Elizabeth Barrett Browning, 1806 – 1861)

In Latin— *"Quid ergo amo te? Fiat mihi computat in via.* —————.*"*

The height of my naiveté was manifested by a trip to LA coliseum to see Notre Dame play USC in hopes that I would get a chance to see Sophie. Months passed without any returns to my letters. I regretfully accepted the fact that the romance was over. The unresolved issue of this relationship, my quest for the consummation of a fusion of identity with the ideal I had created, haunted my dreams for decades to come. The theme always repeated itself – the rendezvous with Sophie that never materialized, liaison within the grasp that always disintegrated in thin air. Actual interfaces at school reunions seemed to suffer the same fate as our interface was always interrupted by some simple nonsensical event. Sophie appeared at a 1981 high school reunion, informed me of her marriage annulment, and invited me to visit in California. Delphia, my second wife had accompanied me to the reunion, signaling my unavailability to an imagined attempt at reunion seemingly suggested by Sophie. Again, my imagination probably projected an unreal scenario.

I planned and created a DVD for the 2012 reunion. Responding to my mail announcement Sophie claimed her delight at hearing from me. I sent her an audio clip of Michael Feinstein's *My Favorite Year* to which she never acknowledged or never opened as an attachment.

My Favorite Year
"You

"Reappearing in my mind
You were right & I was blind
But that was long ago
Now
Do I ever cross your mind
Are your memories like mine
OR have they let you go
After all the loves I've lived through
All these years
I had to go so far without you
Now it's clear
You were my favorite love.."
That was my favorite year." (Michael Feinstein)

A planned dinner in the mid 80's in California during my attendance to a conference and meeting with an old revolutionary from Purdue Days never materialized. I had left my phone and address book in the car at the Phoenix airport and had no way to get to Sophie's home and waiting dinner date on the shores of the Pacific. I called everyone I knew in Flagstaff to get her phone number without results. Her friends and relatives had a field day trying to figure out what was going on.

I am thoroughly convinced that Sophie was completely oblivious to my fantasies, plans and expectations and it would make me very ashamed and sad if she were to find out and be in any way harmed. I had let go of Sophie emotionally and said good-bye and God bless deep in my mind, realizing both the futility and foolishness of an 80 plus year old romantic. I made some amends to her without uncovering and the machinations. I had gone through for thirty years and she responded that she remembered that 'adorable boy,' which of course acted as a defaulter to once again get my heart beating for Sophie. Just because I had accepted my 'love obsession' status did not mean I was going to give up the quest to find a "mother."

Courtship

Sometimes the best cure for obsessions is an "out of sight, out of mind" status. Such was the case with my preoccupation and remorse over the shattered romance with Sophie. I was a full time student on the ASC (Arizona State College) campus and I began to notice a Gene Tierney look-a-like, (star of the Movies Laura and Leave Her to Heaven). She was gliding around, across campus and showing up at Newman Club meetings. Upon a short conversation with her in the student union one day I found out she came to ASC from Illinois State College at Dekalb, Illinois. She was succeeding her brother Bob who had been expelled from the ASC for setting off dynamite in the middle of the campus. My awareness of her presence and the excitement it generated could have been classified as minor stalking as I made it a point to be where I knew she would be. Charlene and I began to date, attending college dances and other affairs and I was chosen as the "Most Eligible Bachelor," an honor I neither coveted nor understood. I despised the macho locker room talk about females and still do because it totally is calculated to put them down—pervasive misogyny.

Charlene met all the criteria that my ego and libido could desire—Irish Catholic, smoker, beautiful, simple and "wholly" like the idyllic female of my imagination. An intense early relationship in the spring of 1954 ensued (absent sexual intimacy). The climax of this phase relationship prior to a marriage engagement was a meeting we had parked at the city pond. She had been dating a fellow and one night he slipped her a very strong drink and she became very drunk. He proceeded to have his way with her and once this had happened he continued to have intercourse with her over a long period of time. She was resigned to bear a child should there be a conception. Fortunately she shared, she left Dekalb and transferred to ASC Flagstaff in the autumn of 1953.

I could blame it on the Catholic Church's liturgical fetishes about virginity, purity and other BS dysfunctional expectations of celibacy for young passionate people, or I could acknowledge the core role that was being played by my shallow and shaky male identity. Regardless of the cause or causes Charlene's life experience she shared with me they set up a never ending feeling of inadequacy in me of not being "good enough" or as "good as the other guy" or being "first." I recall that Charlene had picked up my deep disappointment about her persona, but I feebly expressed to her in so many words that I was willing as a "saintly soul and champion guy" to accept her as a "soiled dove." How terrible that was. Dr. Shatala Mishra of University of Arizona years later quipped a poignant concept in telling me, "What do Americans make such a big deal about sex!!??" There was no turning back from my dilemma of a twenty-two year old's raging sea of passion, my total codependency of "taking care" of the "needy," filling the hole left in my soul by the loss of Sophie. At this stage in life there was a search for consummating that necessity to find a soul mate with which I could fuse my identity. I needed the closure as a young adult. In reality I was incapable of seeing the real Charlene— a simply beautiful, sweet, innocent, honest and talented female. She was a star of the ASC College drama club, a cheerleader and a queen. Why did I have to mature enough to see the truth until after Charlene was buried in the Flagstaff Catholic cemetery 56 years later? On the other hand I was an emotional cripple with no self-aware identity or perceived value that I could offer to fuse with a life's partner. I sat in the living room up on Aspen street and squeaked out a feeble sharing with my mother Mabel about the fears of a committed relationship. The lack of the knowledge and acceptance of an identity I learned later was the prime source of my fear. Isolation had protected this poor self-esteem for most of my life. I got a quick fix and a standard tenet by her simply saying, "Don't be silly, stop feeling that way."

IDENTITY CRISES

The early days upon my reconnection in Flagstaff, the attendance at NAU, the consequent pre-marriage relationship with Charlene, couched in the uncertainty and sadness at the belief in a seeming abandonment of a priesthood vocation created a dense black cloud of dejection and uncertainty. The idea of a fusion of identities in marriage terrorized and depressed me as my poor self worth and image could not contemplate matrimony. All of the failures to acquire adequate capability outcomes from previous stages of development – in terms of a strong combination of hope, willpower, keen purpose, self-competence, and faithfulness – crippled any robust consummation of identification with Charlene. The only glue left to combine our relationship was the passion of youth and intense infatuation.

Targeted—Most Eligible Bachelor

ENGAGEMENT

I cannot remember the actual engagement interface as to where and what was said that night. But it did set up enormous issues and conflicts inside of me. Although a member of a fraternity at the college, I basically operated from a standpoint of insecurity within a social milieu wherein I perceived myself in lacking of those attributes most attractive and favorable to the opposite sex— no sports identity, no significant leadership roles, and still without much of the outer props of car and reputation of fast and furious activities. Sledding down Observatory Hill and swimming at favorite holes down in Oak Creek comprised most of our activities. The popular Hit Parade featured current songs that provided the context of the relationship between Charlene and I were—*Three Coins In The Fountain, Once I Had A Secret Love, She Wore Blue Velvet*, and Nat King Coles' *Ruby*.

The social events that we attended – picnics, her holiday performances, dances, her major role in a college play, her selection as a top female in various contests – only served to heighten my sense and pain of inadequacy and always requiring severe drunkenness accompanied by bizarre behavior to make up for my perceived lack of attractiveness in competing with the field of other available males on the ASC campus.

My constricted experience from high school and through sem days left me with few roles and scripts to assume in the context of a life commitment I had made as a partner to another human being. Unable to see and independently care for another person, I assumed the 'courageous' and 'saintly' role of life sacrifice to 'take care of' Charlene that would be a minor role in a quest for grandiose accomplishments. It was a set up for disaster. The thin veneer of this 'courageousness' completely covered my deep need for dependence – dependence on the existence and return of a mother figure that I had known long ago and not the need for an equal interdependent partner for life. Not only Charlene, but also other females would fall to the same fate of not fulfilling the role and expectations of the 'mother' ideal. The dire incompatibility of my relationship with Charlene went totally unnoticed in my Christmas visit to her hometown of Libertyville, Illinois the site of the same high school Marlon Brando attended as a truant and incorrigible. There was a myth that Marlon had ridden down the high school hall on a motorcycle. During the year of this writing the high school was torn down.

Trip to Libertyville

I accompanied Charlene during her trip home for Christmas vacation of 1954. Charlene's family was to say the least seriously dysfunctional. Brother Bob was anger personified and had been kicked out of ASC because of his participation in setting off dynamite in the middle of the campus. Petey, the youngest was using baby talk because that is what he was modeled by significant others as an infant; brother Donny, a fine fellow and quiet member of the Coast Guard was at that time and ever sense then a kind and supportive gentleman. Sister Barbara Ann echoed the father's boisterous in your face jolly persona. The mother, Sally, was a telephone operator who did little or no cooking for the family— a handicap passed on that burdened Charlene. Father Barney, served in the Navy, built the family house and grew corn on the side while selling butcher supplies across the Chicago suburbs and Illinois. For me, he tended to be loud, overbearing and controlling which I felt his persona was the result of the "farm boy not letting city slickers get me" syndrome. He managed the local VFW Club that gave him cover for his cheating on Sally, even to the point of having his girlfriend at our wedding. An episode in Las Vegas was a poignant example of Barney's the need to outdo the city boys. Barney went around a line of twenty people to hand a maitre d' a hundred dollar bill to allow his group into the Las Vegas show. It shocked my whole egalitarian being to the bone.

The melee that Christmas in the house in Libertyville left me feeling so severe at a loss as to how to cope that I would get up and out of the house early and go down to Joe's Fireside Restaurant to drink coffee and eat cinnamon toast. The cacophony of high-pitched chatter in the house deeply unsettled me. Recognition of the potential and one-day divergence between Charlene and I, aside in my quest for a mother-like character, totally escaped me amid the throes of coping with a tough situation. It was years later that my father said, "That family was crazy." The Irish side of Charlene's family had a brace of problematic characters ranging from an acrophobic— financial destitution and to an aunt who experienced three husbands who committed suicide. In spite of the obvious problems from Charlene's side combined with my weak identity and maturity, the powerful glue of passion and my newly assumed role of saving an idyllic fallen angel cemented my commitment.

At this time there had been no sexual episodes between Charlene and I. The two-year mindset of celibacy foisted by Conception days had blocked the acting out of any sexual desires I might have had. I was without any form of self-analysis to determine what I needed and wanted in life. It was too bad Tina Turner's lyric "What does love have to do with it?" was popular and embraced by me at the time.

WHAT DOES LOVE HAVE TO DO WITH IT?
"What's love got to do, got to do with it?
What's love but a second hand emotion?"
(Tina Turner, Britten, Terry/Lyle, Graham Hamilton)

A mature attitude about sex could have made a difference in my life starting with a natural response to ASC coed Beverly D. Even of today it is mind boggling that the many Catholic Bishops are so obsessed with sex that their diatribes are often nothing but anti-abortion and anti-gay propaganda. In the meantime the poor, the homeless, the hungry and the sick do not get the attention that their Boss missioned them to carry out.

The powerful notion of interdependence necessary for a long term loving relationship was totally unknown and unavailable to me, much less my capacity to develop and implement it in my premarital relationship. It was the 1950's of Doris Day and Cary Grant. The cultural mores were impressed upon my age group through Saturday matinee movie plots. Infatuation blinded any true experience of love, which was defined by my wonderful spiritual advisor, Ed A., as "caring from the deepest part of you what happens to another person." The locker room culture of the day certainly didn't think of relations with females as caring about them. Again, George Clooney's quote from "UP IN THE AIR" — "The notion that couples are classic romance partners and forever paired and committed geese is not true. We are sharks." The ballads of the day, which persist in popularity into contemporary society, (Sinatra's 100th Birthday), suggest acquisition of Shangri-La when there is consummation with a chosen female. Significant divorce rates stand in opposition to the idea that couples naturally mitigate differences. A healthy existence of interdependence is the exception and codependency is often the norm. {CODEPENDENCY VS. INTERDEPENDENCY By Darlene Lancer, JD, MFT)

FIRST SEX

The night finally came when Charlene and I consummated our first sex act out by the old Flagstaff Golf course, quite sickened and conventionally in the back of my new two tone Ford Fairlane. What a horrifying way to be introduced to one of the most precious gifts given to a human being. Having had no knowledge of the structure of female organs or even having seen such genitalia the whole act, an awkward fumbling, was not what a romantic novelist would want to write about. Without going into great detail, the episode did satisfy my first experience and completed the necessary end to my celibacy and "virginity," delivering me across the contemporary Rubicon into "maturity." What I did not realize and would have been a great help at that time was the significance of being able to empathize with Charlene as a person and consider her as an equal partner. The culture had taught me that sex delivered me to some kind of nirvana and in fact that making love (sex) was synonymous with love. A friend one stated to me that "lovers come and go, but friends last forever."

The failure of Charlene and of future of either temporary or marital partners would always crash with my deducing that "You're not a Mom."

The abusive treatment and mental disabilities that had impacted me in my early childhood days caused me to disrespect the integrity and actions of women. Deep down inside I believed you just couldn't trust them. And because of that mistrust and their ultimate posture of an impotent mother, I concluded eventually as each relationship devolved that my partner didn't deserve commitment and I shouldn't stay and remain in the relationship. So it was Bye Bye quietly undercover out the back door armed with excuses and rationales why another partner had failed again. Large and frequent bouts of drinking of dark side Mr. Hyde were necessary to overcome that Dr. Jekyll "caring" conscience that I had for everyone. After all, Charlene burnt the spaghetti and announced that it didn't make a difference because food all went to the same place. Charlene's failure to entertain with parties during Purdue days I believed was a necessary role to ensure my rise to a full professorship, I figured such was totally unacceptable and reason for my excuse for a more "caring" and adequate partner. In addition it was the 1960's and I was up to eyeballs in Aquarius, revolution, professional summitry cultivating some serious arrogance and grandiosity.

There was no one more idyllic and caring persona on the roads I was traveling than the ex Sister Of Mercy Joyce D who had left the Order as a teacher in at Xavier in South Chicago to attend the University of Chicago. She was intensely involved in techniques to learn how to reduce stress. It doesn't get any better—a perfect metaphor and prescription for a practicing love sick alcoholic whose stress was off the charts at that time—the rest of the story later.

MISTRUST— MALIGNANCY— MASTITIZING

Knowledge of her being the victim of a date rape while at Illinois State in Dekalb unleashed a malignancy of distrust as to whether my meager identity credentials matched or even exceeded those of the mysterious persona lurking from the past. Fr. Piquet the Purdue Newman Club Chaplin appeared in the living room one morning after a nightly bout of my alcoholic rage. He suggested that I did not "trust" Charlene.

MARRIAGE

Plans were made and all arrangements were completed for an elaborate wedding at St. Joe's Catholic Church in Libertyville. It was father-in-law's Barney's show with a large set of wedding attendees. My best friend Bill M was my best man. Bill G from Flagstaff was also part of the wedding party as an honoree along with Charlene's brothers.

The wedding proceeded as a standard Catholic ritual without any notable difference. I felt extremely self-conscious, out of place and awkward at the wedding. The whole affair had been totally scripted by father-in-law to be— Barney A. However the tension was very great and showed itself when Barney slapped my brother-in-law Donny. The reason for that outburst is lost in time, but it fit Barney's personality and was probably motivated by the degree of uptightness and false sense of wellbeing covering the family conflict. I picked up on the lack of any sense of joy or happiness and got drunk, actually kicking someone in the pants while dancing. Charlene's mother, poor soul, sat immobile staring into space with a deadpan and depressed look. Charlene and I would spend the night in separate beds capping Barney's ultimate need and message of control. I looked foreword to exiting Libertyville just to be relieved of what seemed to be a very uncomfortable and captive-like place.

I never realized later that the medium is the message, i.e., Barney having his girl-friend at the wedding in front of Charlene, his wife and children was not a brilliant model for the commitment it takes to create and maintain a life-long relationship like marriage.

COTTAGE CITY

Charlene and I traveled back to Flagstaff and set up house keeping in a very small stone building which was one in a horseshoe arranged group of cottages for married students. Charlene finished her teaching degree and I continued as an English minor, social science major to finish a high school teaching degree.

Life that first year of marriage at Arizona State College (ASC) represented a fairly normal college tempo with B's and A's, involvement in clubs and societies, achievements such as "Student Of The Month" type recognitions and president of the Newman Club. I accepted the responsibility as chairman of the ASC Homecoming Parade, which entailed a mission to construct a number of floats requiring the use of numerous flat bed trailers. These trailers had to be hauled in

CUT WEDDING CAKE—Mr. and Mrs. Gerald (Jerry) Martin Knowle

from farms east of Flagstaff. Accepting and playing out this near impossible role showed a serious lack of judgment and maturity on my part. To complicate life even more a sense of sadness, resignation and depression set in during this period. I had discovered that marriage was not the nirvana that I had expected to medicate and resolve those many issues I had carried through various stages of my life up to that point. Charlene was pregnant with our first child. Life was fully enmeshed and dependent both emotionally and financially on my mother and father. Easter picnics down at Peck's Lake in the Verde Valley and Friday night family dinners at the local Mexican restaurants represented our family's social life with all holidays spent with celebrations and turkey dinners "at the folks."

CHILDREN

Robert Christopher Knowles was born on Father's Day of June 1956. He immediately became the "apple of his grandfather's eye." As a conservative Catholics, the only acceptable form of birth control available to Charlene and me was called the "rhythm method" which was based on the avoidance of Charlene's periodic fertility conditions. The discipline and commitment to this "method" was totally overwhelmed by young adult passions and another baby was on its way to be birthed 11 months after Robert. Timmy Knowles arrived on May of 1957 one day after his grandfather's birthday. Tim joined his grandparents as the apple in the other eye. Charlene taught second grade at Mt. Elden school while I finished my teaching degree and certification.

Dear Jacquelyn, named after her grandfather, was on the way and born in 1958. She was baptized by an old sem pal from Winslow, Father Lawrence Flores. The local college registrar at the time remarked the foolhardiness of having so many children one after another. He was not a Catholic and why he would assume such counsel and control was a mystery and resentment to me.

The strange red coloring in Jacquelyn's face, which we thought was a birthmark that would disappear, turned out to be the manifestation of a deformed heart that was missing the left chamber. "Don't let her cry," the doctor instructed. Such a regimen meant many sleepless night sessions. In her third month Jackie began to smile and it was decided to take her to Children's Hospital in Chicago. I drove Jackie and Charlene to Winslow to board a plane flight to Chicago. Two weeks later I was awakened by a knock on the door at 3:00 AM in the morning. It was my mother in her nightgown. My dysfunctional fear of darkness prompted me to answer the door with a 38-caliber revolver in my hand. "Jackie passed away late last night," she announced. She stayed at the house having coffee and I went back to bed only to be awakened by my mother who warned of a large black widow spider crawling up the bed spread towards me. Looking back at that night in Flagstaff I realize I had no grasp, ability nor recognition of my emotions and met most situations with falsetto optimism of a Catholic perspective attained during seminary days. I requested and got the Nativity Church Choir to sing the Gregorian Chant rendition of the *Mass of the Angels*. The massive antique pipe organ accompanied the choir.

There seems to be no reason why the next child, Maureen Anne, came after a four-year delay. She arrived and I was able to name her for St. Maur, the child raised by St. Benedict at the Monastery on Monte Casino, Italy.

HOUSE

With the help of my parents a house was purchased in a new subdivision north of Flagstaff. The fates (God, Higher Power or what ever) had other plans for me during that period. It is totally amazing that I did not cause an explosion and raging fire in the new house. I had painted a brown stain on the new cement with horrible results and spent a winter day removing most of it with paint thinner, which, if the furnace had been on, would have blown the house off its foundation.

During the five married years in Flagstaff with a large growing family and the increasingly serious professional roles the responsibilities of them began to weigh heavy on me. Every chance I got I went "duck" hunting down into the Verde Valley. Often at night I would go out and have a beer and pizza at the Stein Club on Santa Fe Avenue. I began to feel more and more alienated by the fact that breakfast was only a

STAGE SEVEN—GENERATIVITY OVER STAGNATION TO ESTABLISH CARING (35—65 yrs.)
During middle adulthood (ages 40 to 65 yrs.), careers are established and a quiet and steady life within a relationship. Families are begun and a sense of being a part of the bigger picture is developed. Giving back to society is done through raising children, being productive at work, and becoming involved in community activities and organizations. Failing to achieve these objectives, results in stagnation and feelings of unproductiveness. Success in this stage will lead to the virtue of care.

coffee and donut at the local long established downtown bakery.

Charlene and my mother did not get along. As my mother was always busy with garden and other projects, Charlene tended to dismiss her efforts to help the family as an intrusion. It is true that Charlene had what is termed a "stubborn Irish" constitution – the reality of which was not an excuse for me to avoid the support she needed as a mother. The same old embedded rationale, "Your not being a Mom," began to color my judgment which would eventually blossom in to a rationale and excuse for infidelity and divorce.

During those years in Flagstaff one old classmate, "Betty D," would show up visiting my mother in a tête-à-têtes meeting that I could never figure out. My best working hypothesis in retrospect was that she was being groomed by my mother as a sub to replace Charlene if I left the game.

PERFECTION PARALYSIS

In early years of marriage the responsibility of marriage and children pressed hard on my attitude. I felt trapped with all the pressures of home and profession. I worked very hard at teaching by getting up early hours and staying late hours to perfect my lessons. The family and especially the children suffered from neglect. There was so much in the Flagstaff area— skiing, fishing, hiking etc., — that the family never enjoyed because of my quest for perfection to meet the ego needs of success and recognition. The NAU lab school job ignited the fires of arrogance and grandiosity because of my higher status in the local education society. Both attitudes were projected to compensate for poor self-concept and esteem. Yet, my parents in many ways, especially in terms of financing, supplied most of the actual family recreation and support. Whenever alcohol was involved I went to the excessive level – one time getting deathly sick from crab meat combined with hot apple cider and vodka. Even that passing bout seemed as relief within the dark clouds of life.

TEACHING

I completed a degree in secondary teaching, but there was no job opening at the local high school, so I switched to elementary teaching by taking a few extra courses. I was hired as a sixth grade teacher.

THAT FIRST YEAR

So my first year of teaching was in the basement of the high school in a room with a sub pump covered with an orange crate – no bulletin boards and windows at ground level. I found out later that there was no roster to assign students. They just "walked in" from four different 5th grade classes to become my class members, creating a group of 20 of the sweetest and most intelligent girls and 12 of the worst trouble-maker boys.

THE PADDLE

While swats down the hall tended to cow and calm my class I had to use a paddle myself at times. While I accepted corporal punishment as an institutional "given" at that period in time I also felt shame and guilt deep inside for the actual administering such an act on twelve year olds. I often wonder if such treatment did not contribute to the dysfunction that allowed a fatal car accident to one of those fellows as a high school student-Kenny P. Even after 60 years I have not been able to make amends to his buddy whose arms he died in for the same abusive treatment administered to him. My first year of teaching I performed amid two quite different teachers. On one side was the Latino (Basque) fellow Tony G who was the high school player who had kicked me in the mouth and chipped a front tooth. On the other side was a very angry gentleman who seemed at times to actually hate his students. My uncertainties about my own persona and capabilities caused allot of conflict for I could not buy into either of their perspectives.

I continued teaching sixth grade and taught two years at Mt Eldon School, continuing to look for things to excite, motivate and engage children. One young Hopi child, who later became a professional educator himself, built a "foxhole radio." The specs for a foxhole radio were found in one of the old Boy Scout manuals. Its genius and novelty were that it required no power and could be constructed of everyday materials—a spool of copper wire wound around a used toilet paper roll, a blue razor blade, a safety pin with a pencil lead tied to the end, and set of ear phones which were the only out side equipment needed. Owen S. could pick up any of the Flagstaff radio stations by scratching the tip of the pencil lead across the blue razor blade—which essentially functioned as a station tuner. Owen had strung aerial wire three blocks through the trees in East Flagstaff.

DROWNED REMORSE

At the ordination of my Flagstaff seminary partner I felt deep sadness and regret as I had left the lofty ideals of the priesthood for a humdrum life. The disappointment reverberated in my self confidence for many year afterward only being extinguished when I stopped drinking and worked on those deep issues caused by the accumulation of defects of character because of the failure at each stage of life to acquire those capabilities for a happy joyous and free life- hope, will power, strong purpose, feeling of competence, unselfish love, and mature caring.

After three years of classroom teaching I was appointed as an assistant principal over the heads of other worthy candidates—a position I never sought. I was told I would never go back in the classroom. Mount Eden School which was under the principle ship of one Manuel de Miguel who had been chosen as an all state fullback while playing with a cast on one arm. Once again, my appointment as an administrator at Mt. Elden was a surprise to me as I never applied nor broadcast to anyone my desire for that role. I can only guess that my life-long mentor, Wilfred Killup an assistant superintendent of Flagstaff schools at the time, had lobbied for and requested my appointment. I was slightly concerned because the Latino contemporary sixth grade teacher was passed over for the position. Maybe Killup was 'making amends' for the scar he put on my forehead by a misstep years earlier. Tolerance of ambiguity and command and control of 1000 elementary children acted as a boot camp for meeting the challenges later with the White Mountain Apache Nation.

SEVENTH GRADE

Serious Education

I was told I would never return to the classroom again. The next fall a principle of another elementary school asked me to take over a self contained 7th grade, which was housed in an L shaped former basement kitchen. It was one of the most notable teaching years of my career. Each morning as I appeared around the corner into that room I never knew whether I would see kindergarten characters or graduate students. It depended upon a lot of factors – barometric pressure, seasonal and holiday times, snow rain or whatever. That year my students published an underground newspaper that bugged the principal to no end. We had a great interschool football team with an ambidextrous quarterback; we had folk dancing; and we had an exciting science program featuring the distillation of water from a jar spoiled by a dead clam. Nearly the whole class agreed the water had been purified by distillation. Only three students agreed to drink the water. One of my more foolish science projects was to keep black widow spiders in huge gallon jars, feeding them grasshoppers, which they hung in their webs like a meat house. Fortunately for me there were no accidents.

Haunted House

My seventh graders decided to create a haunted house for Halloween and entice high school students to tour. The project was located beyond the basement walls into and under the floor of the main building. The class created a number of horror scenes with shadowy lighting. The most spectacular and ambitious project was the creation of a paper mâché Black Widow spider. The specter ended up six foot in diameter with appropriate green eyes and the red hourglass mark on its abdomen. Two ropes in the furthest recesses of the basement suspended the spider. Senior high school students were

naturally making fun with sarcastic remarks about the class's exhibits. So it was
with great joy that when our students lowered the Black Widow onto the none expecting visitors they screamed in horror.
One senior high boy actually broke a door
off of its hinges running out of the cavern.

Haunted House Black Widow

STARE, GLARE AND LAUGH

If one waits long enough the sweat, pain
and frustration of trying to teach what
seems to be uncaring and unresponsive students will be rewarded in wonderful and
unique ways. At a meeting with a Justice
of the Peace I was earnestly trying to ex-
plain my failure of my driver license renewal due to unavailability of a motor vehicle
facility on the Navajo Reservation. Since the JP had a Latino last name I had brought
my Navajo business partner with me, hoping to play an ethnic card to my advantage.
The JP just sat and glared at every word I uttered to the point where I wondered what
the hell was wrong. Just when I was ready to make a nasty remark and march out of
his office, the JP burst out with hilarious giggles – "Don't you remember me, I am
Jimmy Sedillo your seventh grade student!!!!" JP Sedillo tore up my ticket and we
laughed and hugged and talked about the Black Widow spider caper. Representative
Sadillio became a member of the Arizona State Legislature, but sadly passed away in
2005. The last time I saw him was at a downtown Flagstaff celebration and he introduced me to a very beautiful lady.

LABORATORY-DEMONSTRATION SCHOOL

In 1960 the height of esteem, achievement and recognition as a teacher would be attained by the securing of a position at a university laboratory school— an ultimate
symbol of excellence and skill as a teacher.

When offered the job as the sixth grade teacher at the ASC Laboratory School (aka
'Training School') I was both thrilled and terrorized by what expectations I faced and
whether or not I could deliver. I not only would have two or three student teachers in
the room to nurture and mentor but I would be demonstrating my teaching in front of
groups that sometimes would number as many as 30 college students. In addition, I
was responsible for teaching my first college class, a beginning class about teaching.

The 'Training School,' the same institution I had attended from kindergarten through

'CHRISTMAS CAROLE'—Lab School

second grade, had moved into the basement of a new building called "Eastburn Education Center" honoring a previous president's namesake. And, down the hall of this lab school twenty three years after I had sat in her room as a child, was one Minnie Roseberry—my third "Mom." Over the years I have a strong hypothesis that it was Minnie who got me the job in the lab school because I had done none of the politicking necessary to prepare me as a candidate for the job, The only other factor would have been my father's close friendship with Virgil Gillenwater, the Chancellor of the University, and basically the major majordomo along with Roseberry who functioned as the ruling junta. Gillenwater would also play a key role in my choice and entrance into advanced graduate work and degree. President J. Lawrence W., the actual president of the university, (as commented by my son Timmy who interviewed him), rarely completed a sentence in his discourse.

The regimen of being on stage at the lab school acted a strong catalyst for my creative tendencies. First I was free of the public school administration and peer group monitoring and judging my work. Whether or not the Lab School staff or the College of Education staff paid much attention to my work or judged its efficacy was little known or was I ever given formal feed back. Some of the most talented teachers, especially fourth grade teacher Dr. Ivernia Tyson, were the best professionals I had ever observed. Tyson was the chief mentor and supporter with me of an individual who would become one of the most tragic and heartbreaking cases of a student to ever attend the Lab school and my classroom.

The Lab School setting provided a great stage for development, demonstration and experimentation of techniques that did not depend solely on textbooks and chalkboards. First of all the roster of students was representative of the broadest spectrum of society – college professor and administrator's children, business magnate offspring; Afro-Americans, Native American and Hispanic American representatives as well a special needs children who the public school either would not accept nor had programs to serve their needs. Whether it had been my exposure to people like Ed Walker or my own personal life experience I saw education as a process that addressed not only the cognitive needs of kids, but it also had to address their emotional, social and physical needs. Intensive analysis of achievement data was used to identify status and needs of students in subject areas. Sociograms were frequently given to assess where children were in the classroom and school social structure. A rudimentary form of prescriptive teaching arose which based classroom experience as much as possible on the needs of the student.

SCROOGE

While reading was carried out in "reading groups" many other activities were complemented to the process. In one case a student we will call Bob B was reading at 3rd grade level measured by an achievement test at the beginning of school. Bob had been exposed to myriad forms of "remedial" reading and hated the "subject." I wanted students to appreciate literature and with Bob's deficit in mind I conceived of a potent reading strategy in addition to a number of other objectives. I read the first phase of Dickens's CHRISTMAS CAROL to the class. "Do you want to act this out? Who wants to be Ebenezer, Marley, Tim ——?" There was no script nor would there be any— the students had to construct the whole play. Years later Bob B. —now a PhD and school principal—admitted I had framed the drawing of straws so he would get the part of "Marley." His father, who was a close friend of mine, informed me that Bob studied the 8th grade tale intensely and would stay up all night if he could to practice his role. Bob B, went from 3rd grade achievement level to 9th grade in reading that year in 6th grade. The class put on a two hour, three act performance without a script and directed by one of their own classmates. No one was more surprised than me, the teacher, at the capabilities of those 12 year olds. Bob was eventually offered a professional career in acting, but chose education instead. He earned a Ph.D. and became an elementary principal and recalled how I had set him up in the role as "Marley."

In the case of the special need student Bobby M, who exhibited both difficult physical and behavioral presence, a key inhibitor of his focus on reading was his lack acceptance by his fellow peers. Special practice and help for Bobby to attain football skills were executed. In the succeeding football games teammates shouted such cheers as "great Bobby," and patted him on his back! The greater acceptance by classmates resulted in Bobby's greater concentration on skill development and considerably enhanced his academic achievement. Bobby attained measured reading skill in prison and sent me letters in a cartoonesque format. He was in prinson for murder which is addressed to follow.

WHY EGYPT EMERGED

One of the things I learned about middle school students is that, although they are on the verge of abstract and logical reasoning, concept development still required manipulations and display of concrete materials. The sixth grade that year had studied primitive societies that had depended upon hunting and gathering for the most part. On a planned demonstration day session to be attended by twenty or more college education majors I covered the classroom walls with scenes from National Geographic files depicting all facets of the river valley civilizations with special emphasis on Egypt. Students had been exposed for several days to these pictures. The demonstration session was begun with a formal review of the picture display, citing the content and purpose of each of the pictures. The identification of each picture was followed by the questions, "What happened? Why did these vast cities, monuments *et cetera* arise? Where did they come from and what caused them?"

As hands were raised and suggestions offered I made separate lists on the board categorizing the suggested causes – religion, science, farming, water, organization etc. The class was more or less evenly divided among five categories. I suggested we debate each "category" (cause) to determine what the answer might be to explain the rise of river valley civilizations. Making a long story short after two weeks of "debate" with students using resources from the Laboratory School library and even the university library the final conclusion of the major cause undergirding the rise of Egypt was formalized. Except for a couple of holdouts there was a near consensus: "an excess production of crops (food) to feed the entire population by a minority of farmers allowed for people to direct their attention and concentration on other areas of the Egyptian society and culture — engineering, science, writing, religion etc."

INTERNATIONAL CONNECTIONS

After the presentation of the Christmas Carole during the Laboratory School days, the students sang *"Let There be Peace on Earth."* The war in Vietnam began with passion in the early part of 1960's. There were a number of people opposed to war and "… Peace on Earth" seemed appropriate at the school plays in 1961 and 1962. I had begun an international project that was a deeper and more involved pen pal operation. My students prepared sort of white-information papers to be sent to their various school counterparts in other countries. I had contacted the embassies in ten or more countries requesting the identification of schools and classes of comparable sixth graders that would agree to be involved in an exchange program based on mail, photographs and audiotapes.

A class from Bath England was contacted and a rich exchange occurred. My students commented on the "Queenship" concept being slightly undemocratic. The Bath children wrote/talked back that the United States was fickle in its policies by having the election of a president every four years. Our class received wonderful files of info and pictures about the history of Bath and the presence of the Roman Empire there.

SCIENCE

The science program of my sixth grade consisted of a "hands on" approach using simple materials and simplification of concepts. A barometer was constructed using a gallon jug with a balloon placed over the top on a day when the barometric pressure was "normal." A straw was glued in the center of the top. As the pressure outside the balloon changed the constant presure on the inside would move the straw up and down like the needle on a gauge. At low pressure the straw would move up and move down with high pressure.

The principle of transferring sound to electrical impulse and back again to sound was demonstrated by the use of a permanent magnet wrapped with copper wire. The contraption was hooked to the leads from a record player and placed under Pork in Bean can, exuding beautiful "Music from a Pork in Bean Can."

The generation of sound into electrical impulse was demonstrated by the use of a pencil sharpened at both ends placed between carbon rods from flashlight batteries glued on a cigar box and hooked to a 12-volt battery. As a voice resonated inside the cigar box the pencil resonated and modulated the electrical current between the two rods creating sound out the receiver.

Thus Science consisted of hands on construction of workable barometers, motors, foxhole radios, simple microphones and earphones.

STUDENT TEACHERS

Over my three years at the Laboratory School I mentored 15-20 student teachers in my sixth grade. Most notable was a Navajo gentleman, Phillip B. who later served on school and university boards. Mr. Jim P, an Afro-American became a school superintendent. One lady, Diane C., was chosen as the "student teacher of the year" and became a very close friend of mine. It was at this time that I experienced but never objectively accepted the ease at which one could began to move too close to associates. My religious, personal and professional acumen prevented any acting out of such feelings. However alternative potential relationships to marriage begin to settle in my unconscious to the point that fantasies and intentions at a later time became real. A different environment and developing roles and alternative ethics can operate to open the door to changing behaviors. The sexual revolution has been partly blamed on Second Vatican Council of the Catholic Church. Entrance into graduate school and subsequent entry into a high powered field also enhanced a change in my behavior.

Bobby Moorman came into my sixth grade room my second year at the Lab School. His reputation was well known to me because of this presence in the 5th grade below. I didn't have much respect for the 5th grade teacher because of his general attitude and his statements about Bobby. He claimed Bobby had threatened a girl with a pair of scissors. A most respected and talented staff member, Dr. Tyson, who was a long time advocate and deeply cognizant of Bobby's background and condition, informed me that Bobby's blindness in one eye forced him to hold up shiny objects to see a glints of light.

Bobby was adopted and he was in an accident as a baby that had killed his mother. His adopted parents were long time residents of Flagstaff. His father had a taxi business and spent allot of time with Bobby in hunting trips and other outings. Bobby's mother was a chain smoker and appeared as a frazzled and confused person – very nervous in any conversations about Bobby. It was humored that she was an active alcoholic. Bobby also had meningitis, cerebral palsy and was blind in one eye. The good eye side of his glasses was painted black under the assumption that it would force the bad eye to correct itself. Bobby's tested IQ varied back and fourth above and below 70— certainly a level cited as mental retardedness.

Bobby obviously could become a serious behavioral problem but never once under my supervision did anything to threaten another student. Many times the look in his eyes appeared like a wild animal in a state of desperation. I always interpreted this facial expression to be the feelings of a human who knows there is something wrong with him, senses the rejection of his peers and desperately doesn't know what to do about it. His wild eyes, shaved head and gangly walk on his toes made him a specter amid the other students.

The ancillary activities of the classroom – like the production of Dickens' CHRISTMAS CAROLE – provided a context into which one could help Bobby find a niche of respect among the rest of the class. He played a key role in the CHRISTMAS CAROLE. I had a big stamp collection as a child, which I "loaned" to Bobby, as it was his favorite hobby. On one occasion I took a group of my "problem" students and Bobby target practicing near Sedona, Arizona. It is clear as yesterday that I can see myself setting up soda cans and looking back amid the troop 30 yards or so at Bobby holding my semiautomatic .22 caliber rifle. I had a sudden fleeting thought that this was not a good idea, but immediately dropped it. I never felt threatened by Bobby. When he became uncontrollable I would grab both of this arms and quietly tell him everything was OK and that always had a calming effect. He knew my heart went out to him.

Futile Clemency

Fifty-five years later I addressed a Clemency Hearing for Bobby and was asked how I felt about his execution. I said I thought it was "absurd." Bobby had spent 25 years on Death Row at the Arizona State Penitentiary in Florence, Arizona. According to his attorneys Bobby was exhilarated to find out that I would be there at the hearing.

Upon entering the Clemency Hearing chamber I found Bobby placed in a cage. I said "Hey Bobby, how you doing?" "Hi Mr. Knowles," he said and I looked into a set of eyes that seemed much calmer than they had been fifty years ago. As I had looked around the room prior to my testimony I actually thought the County Attorney looked much more sinister than Bobby. I watched him take copious notes except during my testimony. I actually believe the Clemency Board feared anyone who described Bobby as a human being in defference to his posture as a caged animal. I had spent nine months five days a week with Bobby and he knew I was aware of the real story behind his horrid public image. He had killed his mother in a local motel one week, dismembered her body and placed the parts in garbage cans all over Florence,

Years earlier I had exchanged letters with Bobby who used a comic book format for his letters. He said how much he enjoyed corresponding and had been tutored in prison by a sweet old couple I met at the hearing. Sadly, as months went by I quit answering his letters because I could not get up for the task. Every year living in Taos I planned to visit him in Florence, and went as far as getting his identification data and the procedures for visitation. The Florence Prison was described as an institution where death row inmates could only see sunlight only one hour a day.

Bobby left the Lab School in 1962 and was not accepted into the Flagstaff Public Schools. I moved to Illinois to go to graduate school and subsequent jobs at Arizona State University at Tempe, Purdue University and Temple University in Philadelphia kept me preoccupied and far from my past and Arizona days. Returning to Flagstaff from New Jersey in 1971 I became aware that Bobby, now was 21 years old and working as waiter in a little restaurant on the main street of Flagstaff down the street from my father's Moore Drug Store. I had no or little interface with Bobby and I was uneasy and aversive about reconnecting in any way with him. Again, I think "how sad" as I might have made a difference in his life.

Doing Only Naturally

Two months back in Arizona the Daily Sun Headline read that Bobby had been arrested after kidnapping a teenager, taking her to Nevada and driving her back to Flagstaff. Of course an innuendo of "molestation" had to be floated to whip up public outrage and prep them for the ultimate sentence Bobby would receive from the local

District Court. Inside information related that his "victim" had willingly gone with him, was untouched in "captivity" and when she asked him to go back he immediately drove back to Arizona-what I thought was quintessential Bobby. Dr. Tyson and I stood up in court testifying not to send Bobby to the Florence, but to a special facility that could address his special needs and development. He was sentenced to life in prison.

I retain a one foot thick Capital Punishment Defense file, including psychiatric reports that reveal the real story about Bobby— the narrative that I knew all along. The State Penitentiary had a policy of allowing inmates to spend weekends in Florence with relatives. Bobby and mother checked into the Blue Haven motel where she died and was cut up into pieces. I must complement the County Attorney and prosecutor for a very sophisticated scenario about what happened that weekend. What really happened was totally opposite of the truth.

The Victim

The hidden story of what happened to Bobby and what happened that weekend in Florence will be revealed in the book, "Justice Undone." But, it is important to briefly summarize Bobby's story for it stands as such a travesty of Justice and a black mark on my home state of Arizona.

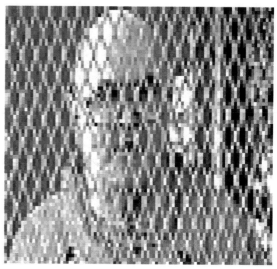

Bobby was first abused by his mother at 9 years old when she forced him to have sex with her. Such abuse was regular throughout his life. As a teenager Bobby's rage spilled out and he shot her the stomach with a .22 caliber rifle. When social workers, counselors and myself had sessions with the mother she always was very nervous and closed.

The weekend visit in the motel with his mother ended in her being smothered with a pillow. During a sexual episode the mother began screaming and Bobby placed a pillow over her head. When he removed the pillow she was not breathing. He wasn't sure what her status was so he put her body in the bathtub with cold water. Upon realizing that she really was dead he totally panicked. What to do!!!!

Bobby's dad took him hunting all the time and they often bagged a deer and even an elk. Remember, we are talking about a retarded person who learned and depended upon certain habits that automatically motivated his action in certain situations. Bobby most assuredly helped his dad dress and cut up many a game animal and some of this was done in the field. A panicky Bobby reacted impulsivity to do what he could to hide a terrible accident. He cut up his mother's body and hid it in garbage cans all over Florence.

The prosecutorial murder book included "facts" that tried to establish premeditation. But I knew what the truth was and the State of Arizona was going to execute a compromised retarded person (in violation of the US Supreme Court's Prohibition against executing the retarded.) Arizona claimed that Bobby's IQ testing scores jumped above 70 points on occasion.

HIGH FIVE ON BULLET PROOF GLASS

The prison administration bumped a number of people in line to talk to Bobby after the clemency hearing. Bobby had requested to talk to me first.

We spent an hour after lunch talking about his days as my student and actually laughing at some of the events of that time. No mention was made of the actions and events that would take his life. This "killer" who had morphed into a kind, simple and sweet old man after 25 years on Death Row told me, "Don't worry Mr. Knowles, I am OK. I am going home"

I said, "I love you Bobby." So much more to say but I couldn't talk as tears began to water my eyes. We did a high five on the bulletproof glass and I turned and walked away never to see Bobby ever again.

The other inmate on death row said they should never execute Bobby, as he was harmless gentle man.

Five days after the clemency hearing they executed Bobby by lethal injection. Reports indicated that he twitched a squirmed allot before he died. Subsequent reports of executions across the land indicate that many lethal injections are causing lengthy and excruciating pain. The State of Arizona in the execution of Bobby Moorman violated two Supreme Court tenants – the execution of retarded people, exercise of cruel and unusual punishment for the crime of what should have been manslaughter.

My decision to appear on the steps of the old United Verde Hospital (Jerome Grand Hotel) to burn documents – birth certificate, baptismal certificate, high school diploma, BS and Master Degree – are still on hold mainly because no one would show up and the event would never make the media. U-tube?

My six years of teaching laced with a half year as assistant principal and three years as a laboratory school demonstration teacher at ASC Training School provided no special impetus nor greater vision, except a creative and aggressive strain began to emerge and, without too much of a heady claim, I believe I was buying into Robert Kenney's favorite quote way before its appearance. "There are those that look at things the way they are, and ask why? I dream of things that never were, and ask why not?"— Robert F. Kennedy, *Robert F. Kennedy in his Own Words.* .

UNIVERSITY OF ILLINOIS

MASSIVE SEA CHANGE – OFF TO GRADUATE SCHOOL UNIVERSITY OF ILLINOIS

During my tenure at the Lab School I carried on with advanced graduate work, research and all manner of professional activities. Two statistics courses and exposure to mentor Dr. Ed Walker hastened a growing belief that I could in fact survive a big university and garner a doctor's degree, which degree I was

CHAMPAIGN-URBANA, ILLINOIS

told would be required for me to stay in the university arena. Walker said, "Go to the best; they'll work your butt off no matter where you go." My father's friend and NAU chancellor Dr. Virgil Gillenwater was a graduate of Illinois and a close friend of Dr. Frank Finch, the co-author of the Kulman-Finch Intelligence test – the gatekeeper for entrance into Illinois graduate school. One hot June afternoon I took the Miller's Analogies Test, the only screening device for entry into that school. I feared a diminished performance due to the summer heat, so my father gave me an amphetamine that kept me awake for two days. The Miller's was a one hour test with 100 analogies requiring closure. For example – *Henri de Toulouse is to Lautrec, as Rimsky is to <u>Korsakov.</u>* A tougher analogy required answers to the likes of – "*infinity is to the square root of the number 2 as <u>XXXXX</u> is to <u>XXXXX</u>.*" I never understood that one. The cutoff point for passage of the test was 40 out of a hundred, to be finished in one hour. My core shame base and lack of self-confidence had me believing that I had failed, and might only be allowed into grad school for political reasons.

However, a grad school letter of admission arrived – proof that I scored above the cutoff point.

There was a sea change coming up, and it would see our family vacating the nest in Flagstaff for one in Illinois to face a totally different life.

GREEN STREET

I moved into the Green Street dorm – a ten-story building adjacent to the main campus – instead of Newman Club Hall. My job with graduate assistance was that of supervisor and counselor to student teachers in Hinsdale, a posh suburb of Chicago. Once a week I would travel 100 miles north and stay the night in La Grange, spending the next day visiting classrooms and conferencing with student teachers. One late November day the weather was gloomy and overcast – and the date of my mother's birthday. A student stepped out of the main entrance of the elementary school I was visiting and said that someone had shot the president. I immediately left for Champaign and, arriving at the dorm television station in the lobby, heard the announcement of Kennedy's assassination. The next day I realized I was witnessing the murder of Oswald on live television. I immediately left for Libertyville. A deep gloom awaited me at the house, as Charlene's people were very serious Irish.

SAMMY K

While yet immersed in my small town naiveté, a gentleman whom I will call Sammy K befriended me. He was an enormous help in introducing me to the area in general and the College Of Education in particular. It was one of those unfortunate interfaces when I discovered that Sammy was gay and that I of course could not and would not be cooperative. My advisor asked me if I was married and I of course said, "Yes," not realizing at the time the significance of his interest. Instead of having frank conversation and arriving at a mutual understanding, Sammy ignored me and never spoke to me again. I had not reacted with disdain – only with surprise and unresponsiveness. I recently emailed him in Hawaii but he didn't respond. Sad – but as of this writing, the 'times are a changing.'

LIBERTYVILLE – BARNEY

My small town background and general lack of streetwise maturity forced me to adopt a plan for the family to live in Libertyville. I wanted us to be secure in father-in-law Barney's home with his presence to aid our family.

My boys were just starting school, Maureen was only a year old and Gregory was scheduled for birth any day. Charlene's mother Sally had passed away in late 1950's. But, when the family arrived in Libertyville, father-in-law Barney moved posthaste around the corner to stay with his girlfriend and her two children. He rarely came to his house to see any of us. He was no help nor should I have expected him to be a surrogate man of the house. That first year was really tough on Bob and Tim who suffered abusive treatment in the Catholic school of St. Joe's and froze at night without any heat upstairs at home. Gregory was born on the way to the hospital while I made my first trip to Champaign. I rushed home. He was baptized at St. Joe's and was my only child not born in Arizona. Charlene was totally overwhelmed, a situation I realized with shock one weekend when I found feces in the diapers in the washing machine.

My parents came to Libertyville for Gregory John Knowles's baptism. I had foolishly driven through sun-lighted fog into O'Hare Airport to pick them up.

Christmas was spent alone in Libertyville without immediate family, the only saving dimension of which was that I had bought a remote controlled car racing set for Bob and Tim. Up until that time my parents had been the major source of presents.

FINANCING

At this writing I cringe contemplating what it would cost to earn a doctorate by current standards – whereas back then, I was granted a graduate assistant position with stipend and all tuition paid. In addition my parents supplemented the family's income with a substantial monthly amount. My graduate school peers were much more effective in planning for their family, one actually purchasing a home in Urbana. It was obvious that there was and still is a dimension of my persona that did not do an acceptable job of taking good care of myself and my own.

CHAMPAIGN-URBANA

Champaign-Urbana was actually two cities joined as one urban conglomerate with the University of Illinois spread out over the whole area. In addition to the formal century-old campus complex there were residential type dwellings, housing departments and special projects space. My first visit to the education bailiwick took place in a two-story edifice that was residential at one time.

Within my first year at Illinois, the College of Education moved into its new three-story building with the top floor perimeter lined with offices and second door opening onto a balcony. One set of grad students were located in a large room called the "Bull Pen"— all metaphors intended.

ARRIVAL – CONNECTION

My preview of the campus was almost overwhelming. Two bus routes ran on the grounds, and the danger of being run over was apparent due to the rule that traffic was not required to honor pedestrians. I had originally planned to stay in the Newman

Club Dorm. My first exploration of the place included a visit to the chapel where I lit a candle and prayed to survive. I was told that if one received three "C" grades I would be dropped from graduate school. I discovered during my first month that once accepted as a doctoral student, the college of education adopted you as a member of a cherished "pack" and one would have to deliberately cop out to fail the program.

THE BRACE OF PROFESSIONAL TALENT

Dr. Foster McMurray

For many years, in response to queries about my major college focus I would of course answer, "Education." I have never apologized for my education degree for Illinois was one of the premier if not the top Colleges of Education in the country, much of its faculty with national and international visibility. Standing-room only students from liberal arts, impressed with his keen intellect and observations, monitored Dr. Foster McMurray's course. A debate with Arthur Bestor of the History Department resulted in Bestor leaving the university. McMurray was unique in not being vociferous or competitive but graced with an infallible use of logic and discourse.

Dr. Harlan Shores

I chose Harlan Shores as my major advisor. He was a wonderful Gary Cooper type character and an international curriculum leader by virtue of his co-authorship of the top book in his field, along with his presidency of the Association for Supervision Curriculum Development (ASCD) – the most visible and most powerful organization in education at that time. I was told years later that he had selected me to take his place as president of ASCD. In my placement office resume/papers he described me as "the best graduate student he had ever had." Not embodying much in the way of emotional maturity, my unassuming nature would not allow acceptance of that sort of endorsement. Illinois Profs may have said that about all their doctoral candidates but still, the affirmation did boost my self-confidence somewhat. Unfortunately, I never understood the real significance or value of Shores' comment – and, still suffering from low esteem, I parlayed the compliment into professional arrogance and grandiosity. I simply did not realize that my scope of abilities might have been given me to serve others rather than inflate my ego.

Doctors Smith and Stanley

One of the most intense and ultimately most valuable courses I took was "Education and Social Integration," taught by Professors "Bunny" Smith and Bill Stanley – co-authors with Dr. Shores of "FUNDAMENTALS OF CURRICULUM DEVELOPMENT." The value of the course was its intense analysis of the major social theorists of the times thereafter applying their concepts to current issues. Most influential to my thinking were Karl Mannheim and Gunner Myrdal.

Mannheim described the required dynamics of a viable democratic society and Myrdal theorized that social change in the U.S. would occur if and when the culture moved toward the realization of those principles in its founding documents, the most significant of which is "*all men are created equal.*"

"*The big majority of Americans, who are comparatively well off, have developed an ability to have enclaves of people living in the greatest misery almost without noticing them.*" Gunnar Myrdal. 1944. AN AMERICAN DILEMMA: THE NEGRO PROBLEM AND MODERN DEMOCRACY: Harper & Bros.

DOCTORAL THESIS

I had to choose a research problem for my doctoral thesis. National events occurred signaling the onset of the civil rights movement. My closest graduate school buddy was an Afro-American, Frederick R. I read an article about Afro-American students who preferred "empathy" to "sympathy" from their teachers. At the same time my research revealed a study by THE COLEMAN REPORT – "*Equal Educational Opportunity and School Desegregation*" – which examined major factors impacting Afro-American student achievement. School curriculum, teachers and a broad array of variables were analyzed and a surprising discovery emerged amidst the mass of data. It was found that the most significant factor fostering the achievements of Afro-American students was simply their attitude – the belief that they could control their own destiny by their own actions, by their own internal control. This factor was termed the presence of a sense of 'internal locus of control.' Years later I heard President Obama and his wife Michelle state that the belief that they could "*do it*" was a major factor driving their success. It is no surprise that the "*can do – can't do*" conflict plays a major part in the process of human development. (Erikson's STAGE FOUR—Industry over Inferiority to establish CONFIDENCE   (6—11 yrs.)

 The question I asked was, "what can a teacher do to further the development of the belief on the part of students that they *can do it*." One report about Afro-American students identifying the relative importance of certain teacher attributes cited empathy – a sense of being understood by teachers— as the most important influence on them during their school days. People when identifying their most memorable teachers often report the concept of *understanding*. In addition to the feeling of "*can do*" (internal locus of control) two other variables were selected to assess the relationship of teacher empathy on academic progress – *achievement motivation* and *self-concept*. Needless to say my doctoral committee had to be convinced that all these factors existed, and that research and epistemic correlations (observation of projected behaviors attendant to the concept) were offered to support the reality of such thesis statements. Hence "TEACHER PSYCHOTHERAPEUTIC EMPATHY PERCEIVED BY STUDENTS IMPACT ON INTERNAL LOCUS OF CONTROL, ACHIEVEMENT MOTIVATION AND SELF CONCEPT" became a thesis topic. Details of the obtaining of relevant data were complex and time consuming. Arrangements to use a sample of Afro-American students from Racine, Wisconsin fell through at the last moment, and elements of varied social class levels were substituted for race – i.e., *Social Class* differences being substituted for Afro-Americanism.

THE ILLINOIS CENTRAL RAILROAD

That first year at Illinois eventually came down to my using the Illinois Central Railroad to travel back and forth from campus to Libertyville and then the Milwaukee Road Suburban to finish my trip home. Walking across Chicago in the early mornings and evenings from station to station allowed for inexpensive meals (Tad's Steak and Salad for $4 – breakfast for $2).

The family moved to Champaign to a student housing in a complex called Orchard Downs. Residents looked like representatives to the United Nations, giving my children broad exposure to a vast array of different friends and their cultures.

FOOTBALL

Illinois was my first experience with big time college football and it was exponentially enhanced by the presence of famed linebacker Dick Butkus. Illinois had a great team those three years at Champaign and played Washington at the Rose Bowl in 1964 wherein Illinois was behind at the half. I told my father on the phone "Don't worry, the defense will win it." That is exactly what happened. My oldest boys Bob and Tim were inculcated with football fever, which pleasant obsession passionately transferred to the University of Arizona Wildcats – "Bear Down, Arizona!!"

Bob and Tim spent the summers in Flagstaff with their grandparents traveling all over the southwest and cruising on Lake Powell in Dad's boat. We took the boys to O'Hare in Chicago for a Phoenix flight to their grandparents. The airlines required verification of the pickup in Phoenix by a personal phone call to the grandparents.

Summer life in Flagstaff was a paradise for Bob and Tim compared to the unpredictable havoc of Champaign-Urbana and the resonance my dark attitude had on their

Acceptable Inebriation
Graduate school attendance at the University of Illinois opened the gates for the supreme nurture of my budding arrogance, armed as I was with a doctor's degree from a big ten major university. It was the practice of grad students to attend conferences in Chicago and spend most of the time drinking and carousing. In later years such forays devolved into wretched, dangerous episodes.

small, nurturing souls. Trips to Mesa Verde Ruins, picnics in Oak Creek, the All Indian Pow Wows and the thundering showers of early July made for an exciting, entertaining life. I existed in those days under the illusion that time spent with their grandparents in Flagstaff compensated for the deprivations of Illinois. I know now that this was an erroneous interpretation.

Chief Illiniwek

Chief Illiniwek dressed in buckskin and full headdress would dance at half time – a lively, dramatic presentation. Unfortunately an oversimplified interpretation of the idea that any Native American symbols used for sports were disrespectful caused Chief Illiniwek to be dropped as an Illinois mascot. However, some schools – Florida State's "Seminoles" for example – are allowed to keep those names. A great number of high schools within the largest Native American nation in the U.S. – the Navajo Nation – have mascots that are Native American – Braves, Scouts, Redskins and so on. I am tempted to invite NCAA officials to address Navajo high school assemblies about changing their identities to some respectable animal.

Thunderbird

The best sandwich I ever enjoyed anywhere could be found at the Thunderbird Restaurant – a symbol attendant to my Arizona southwestern tribes. Of course, the restaurant was symbolic of the Fighting Illini. (The Illinois Confederation, sometimes referred to as the Chief Illiniwek, or Illini, was a group of 12–13 Native American tribes in the upper Mississippi River valley of North America).

The sandwich was called the Italian Beef Sandwich and it consisted of very thin beef cooked with pepperonis and stacked on a bun. There was no red sauce.

Campus

The Illinois campus and greater Champaign-Urbana area offered rich, diverse entertainment venues. That last year my mother and father came to visit and we all took in "The Sound of Music" – a cheerful musical capturing the joy that filled our lives at the prospect of my finishing a doctorate and moving back home to Arizona.

Advisor Harlan Shores counseled not to take a low paying job promising "the blue sky" of the Southwest. I was offered a position at the University of Illinois, but could not bear the thought of living any longer in the Midwest.

I was receiving offers from Emory in Atlanta, from Buffalo, Stony Brook and New Mexico as well as from NYU, Florida, New Hampshire and other state universities.

Rumor was that the Champaign staff were promoting me as a department chairman within the emerging Chicago Circle Illinois campus. But I still had no real understanding of who I was or of my capabilities. I had no knowledge about what possibilities existed, of the value of moving into positions of power and leadership or the significance of being part of any specific university or community. I was unaware of how faculty leadership – especially my advisor Harlan Shores – pushed graduates into key positions. I had no notion of my identity or options. I just wanted to return to Arizona. Still handicapped by failure to accrue maturity and a realistic identity, I was left to navigate higher education lanes with a thin veneer of the same old arrogance and grandiosity.

OVER THE RUBICON TO INFIDELITY

FIRST INFIDELITY EVENT

As a graduate student in my last year at Illinois I was invited to go to New York City to visit "inner city" schools as I had expressed a desire to focus my professional career on those underserved groups – Blacks, and Native Americans.

I created the opportunity to act out my latent 'love obsession' and the need to prove my independent charm and attraction as a male. A perfect stage was set with the famous *Blackout of New York City* in 1966.

Once out of the Warwick Hotel 24th floor and down the service stairs my partner Ted M., a professor from UI, and I hit the bars and the blackened streets. We hooked up with two young ladies from Canada and in my alcoholic delirium I planned an intimate liaison with one of them. The lights came on in Times Square near 5AM and the Cinderella scene reverted back to reality.

I learned a powerful lesson about cheating on one's wife when Dr. Ted M. said he could not do that sort of thing and honestly interface with his wife. In other words, cheating kills the veracity and intimacy that is essential to a loving and supportive relationship. Unfortunately, temptation, passion and future opportunities were opened up in those dark streets of New York City and would find ways to express themselves in the future.

As I flew toward Phoenix to be interviewed by the Education Department at Arizona State University in Tempe I could see my beloved snowcapped San Francisco Peaks off to the north and tears came to my eyes—I was finally coming home to indulge my deep feelings for the Phoenix area and southern Arizona. I took the job at ASU and rented a house in Scottsdale. It would be a Rubicon with my crossing into a totally different life.

Purdue-Gary Early Childhood Institute

GOIN' TO YPSI

PURDUE

TRINITY BAPTIST CHURCH

V. CHALLENGE

ARIZONA STATE UNIVERSITY

The ASU campus of 1967 was growing fast and only beginning to have any definition. As an institution it was a far cry from the University of Illinois; the university car I used to transport student teachers was one beat up old can. Greater Phoenix and Scottsdale were arresting locales rife with impressive choices. The Town and Country

Arizona State University

Shopping Center boasted a generous array of food outlets in one large location wherein one could get Mexican cuisine, BBQ, Chinese dishes, hamburgers, hot dogs and a whole lot else. Variety aside, I was not comfortable with the opulence and narcissism I observed in the greater Phoenix area. Trips back and fourth to Flagstaff for holidays and other events were frequent and something always to look forward to.

I was responsible for both graduate and undergraduate classes and recall that I either lectured for the total undergraduate class time or referenced various cherished topics in graduate class. One fellow thoroughly lost it when I challenged the whole idea of human learning and development as being a simple case of behavior reinforcement (vs. a vs. B.F. Skinner's "OPERANT CONDITIONING").

The elementary education Department Chairman, one Richard Bullington, was a prince of a fellow and supported me at every turn. He had me pegged to take his place as Department Chairman, a first step in climbing up the hierarchical stairs of higher education. Jean Piaget, the Swiss psychologist, had risen on the scene as the prominent authority of human cognitive development and I had become a protégé of his theory gained from my study under Cecelia Stendler Lavatelli at Illinois. In the process of writing a proposal to apply Piagetian theory in science curricula I was coordinating closely with two professors from the university science community. They started to make fun of the Piagetian theory, probably because their unfamiliarity with his work was threatening to them. It was the first turnoff at ASU and my proposed future there.

I was appointed Department Chairman for the summer session and found myself in Lloyd Wright's famous "*Birthday Cake*" Center counseling beginning education students. The president of the university was a Dr. Benson who later became the President of the Mormon Church in Utah; I was aware that an assistant to the Dean of Education was also a member of the LDS church. Without any attempt at condemnation, I knew from my days in Arizona that the LDS Church maintained a sophisticated system of extreme control in religious, social and economic realms aimed at protecting and perpetuating its institution and supporting membership ascendance in all realms. I have always been an expert at reading thoughts and feelings based on facial expressions and one day the assistant dean gave me the strangest look; I realized then that I had a powerful enemy with regard to any future positions with the university. An official informed me that the next time I taught the graduate course in curriculum I could not use the same class textbook again. I had chosen "FUNDAMENTALS OF CURRICULUM DEVELOPMENT" by Smith, Stanley and Shores. The authors of the book were considered *social reconstructionists* and that was unacceptable at ASU. However, the content of the book did not emphasize any social theory but only those elements necessary to consider for curriculum development. As I write Arizona seems to have gone even further south in irrational conservatism.

JACK D AND MARGARITA IN THE HEAT

I launched a professorial career at Arizona State University. I was back home, but there was no professional balance to my life due to the lack of internal self-awareness with respect to my motives. Now that I was outside of the support of the Illinois academic "pack" I had nothing to rely upon but the deep files of information I had garnered and a superior attitude adopted to make me feel okay.

However, it soon became not okay at ASU. I perceived an assemblage of less than dedicated professionals that fueled my disappointment, depression and rudderless existence. I began to consume half pints of Old Grand Dad with increasing frequency to fight the Scottsdale heat on the outside and my coldness on the inside. It was a miracle, "bombed out" as I was with that pint under my belt that I could drive up to Baskin Robbins to get a cup of Lime Margarita flavored ice cream. I cannot count the times I escaped vehicular homicide then and in later years.

ASCD ELEMENTARY ADVISORY COUNCIL

My advisor at the University of Illinois, Dr. Harlan Shores, was the President of the Association for Supervision and Curriculum Development. Upon graduation from Illinois I had neither definitive knowledge nor understanding of the professional association national power structure, much less any plans to ascend its hierarchy to attain a position. Again, my advisor had stated in my placement files in a letter of recommendation that I was his top graduate student for the past 20 years. The reality was that my identity was very thin and covered with a counterproductive veneer of arrogance and grandiosity. The ASCD Elementary School Advisory Council was a seven-member committee that published position papers and held national conferences on current issues and topics. The Council was the most powerful elementary school organization in the US. I never accepted Shores' evaluation of me or the significance of its professional value. I received a letter while at ASU inviting me to be appointed to the Council. I wavered about accepting the appointment or turning it down! I was also invited to publish articles in the ASCD Journal, Educational Leadership and presented several articles in the journal beginning with a piece about ACHIEVEMENT MOTIVATION. I accepted the appointment to ASCD and Without realizing the heavy professional value of being on the Council.

Attendance at National ASCD conventions along with the planning and conference sessions of the Advisory Council exposed me to the elite in the education profession, enabling me to exercise complete freedom in acting out with alcoholic escapades and liaisons with female colleagues. Unfortunately, my romantic mindset was faulted by the dysfunctional expectation that I was always in the process of finding and uniting with my ideal – that mystical and unreachable mother. My close friend at Purdue was a quintessential womanizer, facile and successful in his conquests. I did not possess the same skills, and had no *chutzpah* for his *shtick*. Actually, my friend and some associates from south Chicago enjoyed great mirth at my expense regarding my obsessions and failed attempts to make female friends. Of course, the few acquaintances I made suffered the same abandonment I relegated to partners who did not possess the expected motherly attributes.

Attendance at the ASCD National Conventions and Elementary Advisory Counsel Meetings introduced me to a brave new world of alcohol and potential love affairs. At my home in Scottsdale I began to drink a pint of whisky on weekends and toss the empty bottle high to see if I could catch it before it hit the ground and broke. The temperature that summer in the Phoenix area was as usual very hot. I could not get the house temp down below 80 because we only had an evaporative cooler. The heat of the sun storing up all day radiated into the bleachers at the ASU football games making attendance a tortuous time, even at night.

The time came when in Dallas at an ASCD Conference that a certain connection was established with a jet-black-haired barmaid at the Adolphus Hotel. I asked about open late clubs and she said she could take me to one. It was 1967, three years after the Kennedy assassination. The shadowy fog hovering over the city combined with a lot of beer clouded my mores enough that I located a motel for me and the barmaid, which hoped for tryst ended up instead as an intense therapy session in which my overflowing dam of unexpressed issues were poured out to a very confused yet enduring lady. This act completed my total isolation as an alcoholic – position and a superior attitude would hold me in stead for the next five years. Fear and guilt weighed heavy on my mind.

It seemed that being thrust into the powerful, prestigious subculture of higher education and national organizations, combined with expectations placed upon me by my jobs, my peers and my professional associates from Illinois created enormous stress and confusion. I was trying to operate, as they say, way beyond my pay grade. I not only didn't understand the nature of the forces impacting me, but also, I had neither capacity nor capability to capitalize on the opportunities. Hence, that same relief and ease that had anesthetized me during the appendix operation was once again employed to relieve the pain of stress, shame, fear and loneliness.

ASU did not exude the power and sophistication I had been used to at Illinois, and with that realization it seemed to me that a viable university environment was more important than being in Arizona.

At an ASCD National Convention I had dinner with a former Illinois graduate student who was now at Purdue. He asked me about coming to Purdue. One rainy February in the Pizza Hut in Tempe, Arizona I decided to run back to the "Big Ten" milieu where I felt most comfortable. I accepted an associate professorship at Purdue in West Lafayette, Indiana.

Wife Charlene had preceded the family to Indiana to search for and purchase a house. We decided to buy in a new subdivision named Bayberry Heights. The house was a three level, five bedroom, two and a half bathroom place with oak floors. A large kitchen, portioned off by a wrought iron rail, faced a spacious family room three steps below. It is still a mystery as to how I threw a large pressed wood dining table over the rail into the family room in a drunken rage.

Purdue University

Purdue University was renowned for its excellence in engineering education along with the team that always beat Notre Dame and which produced as well NFL quarterbacks like Bob Griese and astronauts. The university campus lay above the Wabash River in the community of West Lafayette, the larger portion of the area located on the east side of the river in the city of Lafayette itself – a very old town with marble-counter concession stores and aged brick buildings. One evening I looked in the rear view mirror and could not believe that I was being followed by a massive train engine. The train tracks in Lafayette went right down the middle of Main Street. There was a "town vs. gown" face off between the two towns – mostly dormant until student sit-ins began in the late 1960's.

SOVIET UNION

Newman club chaplain Fr. Piquet termed the Purdue campus student center the "Soviet Union," which pretty much characterized the complex of buildings making up the campus. Notable was the strong engineering influence of Purdue, which may have been the first educational institution to have a high rise parking garage for easy access to the campus. The cyclotron buried underneath the area in front of the Administration building was impressive. Purdue claimed the largest marching band in the Big Ten yet it had no music department. There were those who claimed the university was a "hotbed of content."

PURDUE FOOTBALL

If one dropped into the local cafeteria on the highway bordering Bayberry Heights, one could determine the latest status of football programs.

Purdue football games were thrilling. They beat Notre Dame all three years I was there and I attended two of those games in person. Purdue had a future NFL quarterback in Mike Phipps and a second runner-up in the Heisman award – halfback Leroy Keyes, an amazing runner who could and did turn certain losses into victory. He was a Black Red Grange galloping ghost. "Black Jack" Jack Mollenkopf was the coach and one of the most winning of all the Purdue greats.

EDUCATION DEPARTMENT

The Education Department had a cluster of leaders holding starring positions in their special fields. Most of the faculty had been there for a good number of years, and I was just one of several new staff. One of my closet friends and comrades in inner city projects was Ted Urich, a University of Iowa PhD in school administration.

I am not sure of the origin and creator of the "Gary Project." But, there was a need in the late 60's for universities to increase the enrollment of minorities and address the needs of the inner cities, especially in the field of education. I was appointed as the director of the "Gary Project" and began a liaison with Gary officials to set up the student teaching program. Two individuals who became very close friends and local leaders for the Gary Project – and later the Gary Early Childhood Education Program – were Dr. Carry Dawson, the first black female PhD from the University of Illinois College of Education and Bennie Mae Collins, a school social worker. These two ladies were handmaidens in the discovery and development of the famous Jackson Five, who were from Gary.

Gordon McAndrews, a very creative and foresighted individual had been chosen as a new Gary school superintendent. He had begun an alternative school method for dropouts like the Kangaroos. Learning sessions were held all over Gary in abandoned buildings. McAndrews was emulating a technique established in Philadelphia called the Parkway High School consisting of a system of cites scattered across the city, utilizing the city itself along with the institutions as the location and content of instruction.

STUDENT TEACHERS

The first group of individuals chosen to student teach in Gary represented both elementary and high school levels – all white, downstate Indiana Hoosiers. Both the departmental staff and myself were concerned that the students be adequately prepared and set up for success. I began a search for housing and ended up in Hammond in an old apartment building that smelled like years of sauerkraut cooking.

In order to prepare student teachers going to assignments in Gary, the Purdue Counseling Department hosted "therapy' type sessions – discussions that encouraged a delving into their personalities to determine who they were – thus to guarantee their authenticity to the Black students they would interface with in Gary.

I watched these sessions through a one-way mirror and found myself wanting to be part of what was going on – the first crack of light into the fortress of my mind where I hid my reality. I longed subconsciously to be part of some group work.

I worried about where the students would live. The students solved the problem on their own initiative by renting a house in the middle class section of Gary. The five-bedroom house allowed the segregation of the sexes with central facilities for cooking and relaxation. The picture I took of Gandhi the student teachers had hung on the wall has been lost somewhere along the way.

A serendipitous activity presented – a perfect way for students to be introduced to the subculture of the ghetto. The Kangaroos, local Gary gang members, came often to the house at night for beer parties.

GHETTO FIELD TRIP

One Jerry O. and I, (Jerry was a PhD.D. candidate in the Counseling Department), carried out a bizarre plan to introduce prospective student teachers to the 'Gary Ghetto.' We secured a forty-passenger school bus and covered the windows with newspaper. Fourty sophomores were jammed into the back half of the bus and roped off. Jerry O. and I had a large urn of coffee and boxes of Dunkin' Donuts up in the front seats of the bus. We had told the driver not to worry about what happened be-

Dire Consequences of Drunken Intrusions

The 'Sexual Revolution' was in high gear in the late 1960's. I had allowed myself to believe that my naïve concepts about how a fellow should or could "come on to a female – scoring techniques used by my buddy Teddy and other models of success.. – were in fact *acceptable.*

Every chance I got I began to carouse in bars around Lafayette and West Lafayette. I would like to blame my revolutionary friend Teddy for my attempts at modeling his womanizing, but blame is just an excuse for not accepting responsibility for my actions. Success in "scoring,, at these forays I feel were an attempt to prove my 'desirability,' which in turn provided balm for my poor self esteem. I had not yet 'sowed my oats' and seemed to be on mission to devour all the experiences I had imagined to be necessary to a male person. The damaged identity with regard to my marriage to Charlene seemed to demand attention by my scouring the terrain for un-biased females who would choose me not as 'the good boy next door' but as a charming, irresistible hunk. Forays late at night into bars in Washington, Chicago or Denver, aside from my woeful ineptness as a "scorer,, could at the same time be rather comical. My penchant for empathy and the need to get to know another human being, to care about a potential relationship was of no use in the wee hours in a tavern. Charm, manipulation, even outright bullshit was the most effective tools for success – and with none of them did I demonstrate any competency. The whole idea of "scoring,, I found repulsive as it conoted an attack on another person.

As years went by I saw my antics not as outcomes of the pressures of trying to do good, but resulting instead from my inability to accept myself and see my position as a blessing to be used for other people instead of hot air upon which to float my grandiose ego.

cause we would take care of any activity.

As we dug into our sugary, caffeinated treats some of our sophomore ladies in the back of the bus began to squeal about wanting some too. I went to the pack in the back and announced that the coffee and donuts were meant for them and we would begin distribution after they filled out a short questionnaire – a nonsensical survey about personal stuff. We collected the forms and feigned an examination. After a reasonable amount of time we returned with a new set of forms stating we required more information. "Whaaaa!" and similar whiny sounds were heard as we passed out the new forms. Suddenly several students began screaming "No more bullshit" in angry tones. They began tearing the newspaper off the windows and finally disengaged the rope boundary. Jerry O. and I saw no point in escalating the scene to angry confrontations. But, the discussion with the sophomores during the last segment of the journey confirmed that the scenario had created some understanding and empathy for Ghetto residents trapped and ignored by the bureaucracies that are supposed to help them.

Professionally, things seemed to be on the upswing—spiritually, not so much. I accepted the tenet and one Sunday eve Ted and I, soused with Golden Dawn Cocktails, (gin, apricot brandy, calvados and orange juice), left the gormet dinner gathering and went out the den ground floor window, into his Toyota and down across the Wabash River Bridge going the wrong way.

I would often come home late, once abandoning my car when a failing alternator dimmed the headlights. One night I met a lady in a German Biergarten. Expecting a sexual liaison, I instead wound up assisting her to raid her grandmother's antique cache which was located way out in the Indiana countryside.

Intense competitiveness at the university level burst the boundaries of civility during post-game celebrations. My arrogance often spilled out during these events with my admonishment of colleagues for their failures as educators and social change antagonists. Umpteen parties and absolute major drunken orgies took place after Purdue football games – win or lose. "Hail Hail to Old Purdue" was heard over and over again. Amid the reveling during a Notre Dame vs. Purdue party I was interrupted by my wife Charlene; I told her that the gang wasn't leaving until the game was over. She said it had been over "2 hours ago" - but the partiers were still cheering. Post football games at Purdue always meant a party at a faculty home. Unfortunately the inner tensions of a very competitive faculty were unleashed and resulted in unkind insults and put-downs.

A SERIOUS EFFORT TO STRUCTURE 'TEACHING'—THE DOSE MODEL

A group of staff representing all the sub disciplines had come together to design a model of teaching. The psychological paradigm of T-O-T-E: Test – Operate – Test – Exit had been used as a structure for many professional functions. The group used this pattern to postulate a D-O-S-E model of teacher behavior, one in which specific learning outcomes would be set up and upon which teacher competency would then be based. Diagnosis-Objectives-Strategy-Evaluation would complete an essential learning loop.

The group worked individually and came together two nights a week to discuss elements of the model. Each dimension of the model was designed with three legs. For instance the Objectives dimension of the model included objectives of the three behavioral domains – Cognitive, Effective and Psychomotor. In putting the model together new concepts were discovered and noted. The professors from the Purdue Educational Center (PERC) condemned the structure for not being a "model." I have subsequently decided that the DOSE team was a power problem as well as a political problem that threatened the Center and discouraged their support. Lamentably, PERC could have cooperated but did not offer any help. The DOSE team failed by not including a PERC member on their team. A detailed description of DOSE can be found in the archives of the EDUCATIONAL LEADERSHIP JOURNAL.

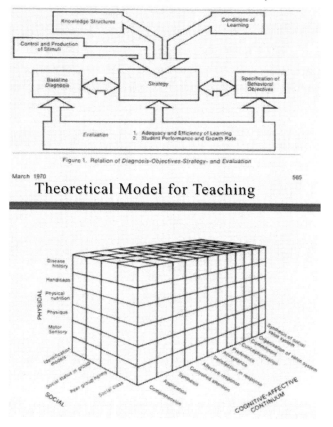

Figure 1. Relation of Diagnosis-Objectives-Strategy- and Evaluation

March 1970 585

Theoretical Model for Teaching

EARLY CHILDHOOD GRANT

From whence came the idea for a grant submission to train early childhood education personnel is lost in my memory. But, a group emerged that included Collins, Dawson and other early childhood staff of Gary with professors from the Lafayette campus of Purdue. The basement of the Trinity Baptist Church in south Gary was rented as the project site and the early learning center down the street was used as a complementary location for the Purdue-Gary Early Childhood Project. The church was located in a common city pattern of locales – church – bar – restaurant.

PURDUE – VORTEX OF FORCES AND OPPORTUNITIES

The position at Purdue University dropped me into a caldron and vortex of forces as well as into opportunities that levied intense pressure on all sides – personal and professional that acted as an accelerant to the existing fires raging in my soul. With no fire controls to quell unleashed resentment, arrogance, grandiosity, sense of power, righteousness and achievement my life spiraled downward from one chaotic episode to another. I was floating on clouds of delusion and denial unaware of the rapidly approaching crash landing.

THE GARY EARLY CHILDHOOD INSTITUTE

Theories of the Viennese biologist Paul Kammerer posits the belief that coincidences are really the tip of an unseen reality. So it was with the Gary Project. Several of the staff and myself had developed a hypothesis for testing the effect of school environments on student teachers in contrast to the "education courses" taken on campus. I composed a research project description for grant funding and was told by the PERC that it would be funded internally. A month or so later my mail in-box contained a 40 thousand dollar grant to test the effects of school environments on student teachers – plagiarizing my exact words. I slammed the document on the secretary's desk and screamed "God Damn It!" "Dr. Knowles!" she exclaimed as she handed me an envelope, "You have this letter from the U.S. Office of Education." The letter was an announcement of a 170 thousand dollar grant for the Gary Early Childhood Institute.

Again, serendipity reared its unpredictable head. I drove several days later into Gary, Indiana to initiate the Gary Early Childhood Institute – facing a trail of cars with their lights on and Black fist salutes coming out the windows. Tragic destiny and coincidence would have it that Martin Luther King had just been assassinated the day before. I felt so down. But, Gary Mayor Richard Hatcher championed interracial harmony and it was exhibited that day in Gary.

Thirty women were chosen for the project and sessions were scheduled on Thursdays and Fridays with practicum work to be done at the Early Learning Center during the first part of the week. Video tape recorders, cameras and other equipment were housed in the church basement.

The staff of the project might have been one of the most unusual within the entire Chicago area: a clinical psychologist, Mark S; Irene S., his wife, a developmental psycholinguist; social worker Bennie Mae; Dr. Carry Dawson, school principal; Bill M, a militant from South Chicago, my graduate student assistant – and a Director of the Gary Early Childhood Center.

Many a time my Gary Project students invited me to go across the street from Trinity Baptist Church to the corner lounge. I always refused because I peeked in one day and saw only figures in an area illuminated by "black light." I told one student, Helen King, "I can't go in there. Someone will kill me." Black women participants in the Gary program were such wonderful people – the more the years go by, the more my respect and admiration grows for them. They so patiently suffered abject discrimination, all the while manifesting not only hope but also significant progress and achievement.

My alcohol addiction resulted in me teaching in a drunken haze and I often didn't remember what I said. I actually flirted with a student (an ex-nun in a graduate counseling seminar) while following her down the halls of the Education building. (Many years and many Internet searches later were required to find her to make amends).

SUICIDE IN THE FIELD – MATH BOOK MILLIONAIRE

A significant event at Purdue provided me with a clue about the impact of alcoholism. One mathematics professor, who had co-authored a textbook series for elementary grades with one of my education colleagues, had a reputation for his inability to avoid alcohol. He was known for an attempt to break the addiction by drinking a German wine called Liebfraumilch.

I was told one afternoon that the gentleman had been found in a cornfield where he had killed himself with a .357 magnum to the temple. Fame, fortune and position in life were no buffer to the devastation that alcohol could wreak. The man was a millionaire based on the profits of the math book series. The lesson was clear to me – alcohol can capture you and it can take you away. Still, I wasn't ready to see myself going down that road.

One time I found myself traveling southward back to Indiana, awakening to what sounded like an alarm clock to discover I was off the road hitting the shoulder reflective markers. Another time I wondered who was screaming only to see smoke out of

INCIDENT IN BROWN COUNTY
At a conference in southern Indiana's Brown County, at a totally empty resort hotel, I embarrassingly quipped to all the Black staff that I "had their backs," which I doubt any of them believed given the shape I was in. The emptiness of that resort mirrored the way I was starting to feel about my life and my profession. I discovered later that the resort had been a stopping off point for pilgrims who once stopped there on their way to and fro from horse racing venues across the border in Kentucky.

the back window coming up from screeching tires of my spinning car. I would wake up in the second story bedroom in West Lafayette and look out the window to see if the Purdue car was in the driveway..

ATTEMPT TO ENTERTAIN

I did not like sucking up at cocktail parties and dinners but when I went ahead to start the effort, Charlene said, *"But they will get the kitchen floor dirty."* Instead of trying to support her concern and suggest ways to mitigate the presence of a lot of people, I simply gave up on her being of any help in my career ascendance. This was terrible on my part, and if I had it to do over I would have done it differently, the better to support her in the awful melee in which she was mired.

A Repose From The Angst And Bedlam Of Life Were The Christmas And Summer Trips To Flagstaff

The only break from the hectic, nearly desperate dynamic going on in Indiana were the few instances when the family boarded the Santa Fe Super Chief from Chicago to Flagstaff for Christmas. The thought of "Going home for Christmas" allowed bright rays of light to come through the dark and somber overcast of life on the Wabash. A strange event occurred on the train that has forever puzzled me. A professor, Ernie M, from the Purdue Educational Research Center was there and began to shed tears when he saw me!?

One of the largest snows in history hit northern Arizona that December – the Super Chief was rerouted north while my family and other passengers were transferred to a milk train in Albuquerque. As we drew into Flagstaff semi trucks were parked off the highway appearing as humps in the snow. My father met us at the Santa Fe Station in his Willy's Jeep and we road up the hill to the folk's home. Snow in Flagstaff at Christmas was white and wonderful with decorations, music and cuisine to match. We entered the front room of the house to fine a blazing piñon fire in the hearth with a beautiful Christmas tree sparkling in the corner by the picture window overlooking the neon-speckled skyline of the city below.

That Christmas of 1969 the family came into a Flagtstaff covered with five feet of snow. Christmas Eve My father offered me a drink of Kailua. I responded by getting a large water glass with crushed ice and filling it with Kailua. That was all I needed to super start my alcoholic addiction, and in a short time I was in the jeep and off into

GIN, BUNS AND COLD TIN
"Streaking,,,(running naked) was the 'thing' in the late '60,s and early '70,s. Of a drunken night in Bayberry Heights neighborhood I streaked out two blocks, dashed back rear-ending the cold garage door—a wake up call for me and the slippery edge of my life.

the night in search of a cozy lounge and imbibing groupies for a tiny drink or two. My father arrived near midnight that Christmas Eve at the Safari Bar where I had joined a group of holiday revelers. The family had been waiting at the house to open their presents, and Greg and Maureen had gone to sleep on the living room floor. Any shame I had at that time could not penetrate the grandiose veneer of my persona kept alive by my over-avowed belief in my importance and my role in the "major forces of social change," (no pun intended). I lived under the delusion that my career was a both a calling and a mission.

The boarding of the train bound back to Chicago was always a sad affair. The elevator music in the chair cars echoed depression and finality. It seemed that the goodbyes were going to be forever. Arriving at Union Station in downtown Chicago, we took a cab to the Berghoff Restaurant, famous for Wiener Schnitzel and Oxtail soup. The waiter that evening seemed offended by having to deal with a large family with four children. We waited for over an hour for our meals, and we did not tip that waiter.

We hailed cab after cab before one stopped to pick up my large, imposing family and after that boarded the Milwaukee Road suburban train to Libertyville. We decamped from the train baggage and all in the middle of the four-lane main street. Snow was coming down in heavy, wet flakes as we packed the Ford station wagon for our return to West Lafayette. Cruising on Interstate 55 south we experienced a problem with the window defogger and the windshield wipers due to a slack belt on the generator. Heavy splashes of sleet covering the windshield dangerously obstructed my vision to the point hat I had to pull off and get a motel, which decision incited rage on the part of Charlene.

Winnowing our way down ice-packed roads we finally arrived late afternoon in West Lafayette only to find our pipes frozen by the arctic temperatures. Small wonder further thoughts of going home for Christmas were fraught with uncertainty.

YPSILANTI

Ypsilanti Michigan was a site for one of the top early childhood projects in the country. Follow Through was a curriculum establishing experimentally designed programs that could take over where Head Start ended and was based on distinct theories of learning and child development. Ypsilanti housed a Follow Through, ('Follow Through' after kindergarten), based on Jean Piaget's theory of cognitive development. It was directed by Dr. Constance Kami, a Japanese American who had studied under Piaget for years and had designed a follow through program based on his conceptions of the geneses of cognitive development.

The Gary Project took a field trip to visit the Piagetian project with regard to assessing its possible application to the Gary Early Childhood Program. A limousine and station wagon were signed out to ferry the participants around. I had to change a flat tire on the limo. There was only a bumper jack and each time a truck swooped by at 85 mph the limo would sway back and fourth causing enormous anxiety on my part. When the spare was secured I remarked, "I really need a drink." Albertine Folks pulled a pint of brandy out of her purse and we passed the bottle around.

My drinking that night and the next morning negated any chance of attending the field trip in Ypsi. One of my graduate assistants took the wheel. Someone gave me a bottle of potent rum and I passed out while dressing with my pants around my ankles. Little did I know that my ideal, most sought after girl in Winslow High School, a resident of Ypsi, came into the hotel where we frequently stayed. The irony was that over 33 years later I would meet Lorraine once again in Winslow.

INTO THE DARK ABYSS OF "PATHETIC AND INCREDIBLE DEMORALIZATION"

THE DESPICABLE AT CHICAGO'S "DANCE ON THE BAR"

The third member of the "revolutionary" cabal, Tom P., had attended a Polish Catholic Seminary and was acquainted with a number of former classmates who were now priests in Hammond. I marveled at the fact that get-togethers with these priests, went in and out confessionals, as they swigged down sizable gulps from a glass of bourbon. "Wow! My kind of people," I thought.!

Then off our car pool went into downtown Chicago to a restaurant renowned for waiters dancing on the stage. I was sailing on the edge of consciousness when I ordered spaghetti.

To my right was an early 60's lady who caught my eye, and across the gap between the tables I began my usual ritual of verbal brilliance and obvious body English enticements. Just when I was beginning to warm to it, a wad of spaghetti involuntary spewed up my esophagus, out of my mouth and onto my plate in front of me. I thought this should not be part of the repertoire of charm and quickly covered the mess with my napkin.Fortunately no one in my group seemed to notice as they watched the waiters dance and sing on stage. However, the horrified look of disgust from the object of my advances signaled a necessary retreat from that night's sortie.

AN ABOMINATION

Perceived slights and putdowns along with my generally hostile feelings about people, institutions and events were planted deep in my psyche, waiting for the appropriate season to creep out. Alcohol always guaranteed that those monsters would raise up to haunt me.

Most days, my Chairman, John, and I operated in a civil, give and take manner. But once I had something to drink any miscommunications were stored as simmering resentment. Of a day when I was moving across greater Lafayette for lunch – too slowly for the Chairman – he quipped, "How do you think you like driving?" I made no comment, no visible reaction to the quip, but returning from Gary later that week at one in the morning and under the influence of alcohol my recollection of the comment enraged me so much that I went into the office complex and into the Chairman's office. I urinated on pile of computer output on his desk. The next morning, thinking my act was only a nightmare, I went to John's office and found the computer output laid "out to dry." The irony of the whole scenario was that the computer output was the data of a study being carried out jointly by John and I.

The next day, filled with anxiety and even hoping that my behavior was part of a nightmare, I mentioned to John that we should "lock the complex at night of avoid any intrusion or vandalism." No response from John. He did not make the connection that the damage had come from me. Years later on a trip to Anaheim I broached the subject of my drunken behavior at Purdue to make amends to John. John said, "Oh you were not so bad, Jer."

LAGUNA BEACH JAIL

The funding of the Gary project enabled me to attend an evaluation conference in Laguna Beach. The helicopter trip from LAX to Laguna was a bellwether as to what would occur while I was there. The copter cruised over a thick cloud of pinkish smog before descending down to the port side of a beach being lashed by huge waves.

Since I thought I was familiar with most of the material in the U.S. Office of Education workshop, I joined a Black gentleman at an outdoor bar protected by plastic walls from the wind off the Pacific. It was my first taste of Pernod, Absinthe and vodka.

That eve I partnered for dinner with a lady who directed an Upward Bound Program in Philadelphia. After dinner, my usual drunken riotous self came on to the lady but I was quickly rejected. She later handed me a pint of gin out the door of her room, which alcohol unleashed a hellish monster focusing on the evilness of President

PURDUE – BURGOMASTER ROBBERY
A favorite site for carousing was the Burgomaster tavern where they featured polka music and one could dance around stamping with a German staff. I established a relationship with a lady who asked me to take her to her grandmother's storage. In the wee hours of the morning I found myself filling the back end of my Ford Country Sedan with antique objects the lady friend was stealing from her grandmother's cache. I was harshly told that no intimacy would occur, at that point realizing that I was simply an accomplice in felony- robbery.

Richard Nixon. My screaming epithets caused the motel manager to call the police. Awakening within a Laguna Beach jail cell, I was summarily escorted to the judge's court and fined $25.

ENTER CRIMINAL BEHAVIOR

My penchant for driving drunk, laboring under the belief that I could maneuver regardless of my condition would sooner or later get me in trouble, likely into a long term sentence in the penitentiary even by the standard of the late 60's and early 70's. My first time for jail was therefore for public disturbance in Laguna Beach while at that U.S. Office of Education Workshop.

The second incarceration happened as the result of a DWI in Lafayette. I had busted up a bathroom at the Pig and Whistle Bar and then made an exit, got in the car and took off. The police had been contacted and were waiting for me. The night in jail this time was unpleasant, especially without cigarettes. The admission officer I interfaced with stood and glared at me for an eternity, giving me a taste of the kind of people who ran the jails – not good. My friend Ted bailed me out whereupon I immediately procured cigarettes and M & M candy, taking the haul back to the jail for the folks I left behind.

The judge released me on probation with the onus that if he saw me again he would put me in jail every weekend for the rest of the year. I was so relived about my escape, and still wearing the imagined cloak of a pseudo activist and revolutionary, that I looked at my incarceration as a mark of distinction and a plus on my resume' and reputation for the inner city people. I needed to celebrate so I joined up with Poem L at the motel lounge, got drunk and took off in my car. Flashing red and blue lights made me pull over. "You okay to drive home?" the cop said. I said, "yes" and he let me go. I have been convinced over the years that he had prviously been a Flagstaff cop known to my father who had in turn contacted him while in West Lafayette and asked him to "watch over me." There was no reason I would not have been in jail again that night. But, there would be more to come.

A PERFECT MOM??

At an Indianapolis Conference I encountered one of the most dynamic individuals I have ever known. And of course my fatuous persona immediately "fell in love" with her. She (Joyce D) had a personality that literally radiated unending joy and optimism. But, what clinched my obsession about her was the fact that she was an ex-Sister of Mercy from Xavier in south Chicago. She was a look-a-like for Kate of the character in the television show, Charlie's Angels. My "revolutionary partner," Ted U and I hung out with Joyce D at the Columbus Conference a year later. When asked by

Ted for the meaning and nationality of her last name, she said "I am Dutch-Hungarian, warm and clean." I have never accepted nor understood the reason why she said what she did. And I was not naïve. I became obsessed with the need to get close to Joyce, not in a physical way, but a spiritual-social sense. The theme song from Romeo and Juliet, "… *a time for us … someday there'll be, a time for us, for you and me*," was the backdrop for my passion.

100 MPH TO HYDE PARK, CHICAGO

It took only one martini to ignite my obsession about Joyce, and so it found me one summer night storming at more than 100 miles per hour northbound on a country road out of West Lafayette. I saw those red and blue blinking lights in the rearview mirror. The policeman handing me the ticket quipped that he had reduced the clocked speed to 85mph. And he also said as I pulled away onto the road, "You should not drink and drive a car, sir." The Purdue sedan and my position at the University had saved, or should I say had enabled me to continue my insane existence

My courtship repertoire with Joyce consisted of phone call after phone call, mad rushing trips at high speed up from Purdue to Blackstone Avenue in south Chicago, Japanese dinners complemented with plum wine, and finally a night spent sleeping with Joyce on her apartment floor.

"Man is the aggressor," I had always been told. I found such behavior awkward and a turnoff. However, the few moves I mustered the courage to make that night were not intrusive but more like a signal or message awaiting an encouraging response. But, there was never a response to this climatic interface with Joyce. In retrospect I realized that the history of my behavior resembled a mild form of stalking. For any real or imagined offense that had impacted Joyce I made amends years later and offered to do anything that would mitigate any negative impact that my behavior might have had on her. Her magnetism prevailed; in later years she earned a reputation as a prominent force in the development of social-consciousness in communities around the world.

A CHARLIE'S ANGEL
I had established an intimate relationship with an educational administrator from Memphis during a national conference in St. Louis, which continued on a trip to Temple University the following year. We were housed in a Buck's County Temple campsite in separate dorms but of course we remedied that easily, retiring as we did to the Delphi hotel in Philly. Serendipitously, a year later as I was in the Delphi Bar staring at the bottles on the shelves, the first thought of the peace offered by my alcoholic friends was negated and a sense of sadness begin to set in about my drinking.
While in deep remorse in New Jersey the following year I called Maxine's house in Memphis collect and was met with an angry retort – "Why are you calling here?!" The scene from the movie, "Up in the Air" with George Clooney was an exact depiction of my experience, minus the face-to-face interaction. Actress Vera Farmiga had convinced Clooney to end the swinger bachelor life and marry her. At her door in Chicago he was met with voices of children and her husband and her angry confrontation, "What are you doing here?"

Two tragic events ended my relationship with Joyce. The most poignant, the most heartbreaking occurred that one night when I was invited to spend that night at her Blackstone Avenue apartment. It always took a modicum of courage for me to initiate such direct affectionate behavior toward a female. Since there was no bed we slept on blankets on the floor. I felt that my position in the situation was an invitation to 'come onto' Joyce, which I did in a very gentle, loving way. Of course I was gently rebuffed, a rejection, which acted as, an enormous wound to my already weak ego. I have been confused for years about what occurred that night. I do know from accessing my own history, issues and persona that my behavior was not an exclusively selfish driven initiative. I remember having neither angst nor intention to press on in any way physically or even aggressive psychologically. In fact I believe the context of the situation made me in some way the unwitting player of some conscious or unconscious issue of some kind being unconsciously acted out by Joyce. (Yes, blame the female!)

INCIDENT AT HOWARD JOHNSON'S

Cocktail hours attendance by my associates accelerated, expanding into diverse and interesting locations – the bar at the best western, upstairs in downtown Lafayette – hot dogs cooked in beer, and honky-tonk bars down by the Wabash.

An incident at the Howard Johnson restaurant one afternoon during the dinner hour makes me tremble even as I write when I recall the scenario.

We fellows left the Purdue campus about 4 pm and traveled across the Wabash into far eastern Lafayette to Howard Johnson's bar for "happy hour." That happy hour ended but not our presence in the restaurant as we squatted there like slugs, continually consuming alcohol. I have no recall of any conversations until the setting turned into a candlelit scattering of tables with parents and children dining together.

I sat like a time bomb waiting to be set off by sound. Across the room and in the far

NON DEBATABLE
Of a Night in Indiana I found myself intimate with a graduate student and Big Ten University Campion debater. As irony and serendipity would have it I lost my original social security card that night. The event also acted to eat away at the innocuous shield I held up about my altruistic missions.

LIASON WITH POEM
I met a bar maid at the local Best Western and we became "lovers." She was from Australia of Dutch-Jewish background, daughter of parents that had fled Nazi Germany. She was the epitome of the girl in Carpenter's "—why do birds suddenly appear—." She was blond and blue eyes with an English accent. My gift of a high school sportsmanship medal engendered hilarity on her part. Sportsman had a unique meaning in Australia.

THE BENDER
One episode with my "friend Poem" involved her apartment several blocks from my residence in Blueberry Heights. I had begun drinking there and remained for three days in a stupor. Earlier that month I had taken her to Chicago for a stay on the South Shore while Charlene was at her parent's home in Libertyville. I walked around in a state of paralyzed terror that Charlene would discover my affair.

Although an absence for long segments of time, being drunk as one was, are not essential to an alcoholic's repertoire of disaster, I did go for a three day bender once, "waking or coming to" only to drink again. Such an experience rips away all the hope an ego loves to generate about one's life, and for that I am grateful.

corner of the restaurant the "n**" word rang in my ears, punctuated in the narrative of some "Hoosier sounding" characters. I turned purple and stood up shrieking, "you racist SOB!!" at the top of my lungs. Next thing I knew the police were at my side. "Do you have a car?" I said, "yes." "Then would you please leave," the two officers demanded.

The highway westward across the Wabash and up the hill to bayberry heights was a complicated construction zone where drivers were forced into a narrow pavement confined by sharp drop offs on both sides. Seeing two roads in front of me I stuck my head out the window with only one eye open, semi trucks zooming by on my left. I actually prayed for survival.

War zone at the Wabash café

It became a habit of Teddy and I to frequent a bar down on the Wabash with Black fellows working on the Upward Bound Program.

My friend Ted U. and I were instrumental in developing and supporting the Upward Bound Program at Purdue, and in our roles we worked closely with Gary staff. We often socialized by meeting at a Black-white bar down on the shore of the Wabash River. There was a mentally ill Black named Willy who one night threw Tom P. on the floor and stomped on his face. (Tom P. was the third, but "minor" member of the Ted and Jerry "revolutionary junta.") Fortunately Willy was wearing tennis shoes. We had warned tom that Willy's posturing was an urban signal that he was coming after Tom.

Any time we saw Willy we knew there was trouble. And there was trouble one night with Willy standing and holding a broken bottle, menacing a woman and facing Ted, me, and two other Black fellows from Gary. We were all sitting in both sides of a booth. The lady pulled out a .38 revolver from her brassiere and aimed at Willy. Our Black friends told Ted and me to "move right," but we went over the back of the booth and crawled out the door just as red and blue flashing lights appeared and the police pulled up.

ENTITLEMENT??

It is hard for me to believe that I actually 'came onto' someone down one of the halls at Purdue. She was an ex-nun, and a member of a counseling workshop for which I was teaching curriculum theory. I must say that in addition to my alcoholic-induced charisma I was driven by a sense of entitlement, one assumed when in prominent roles in institutions. It took extensive research to locate and send a letter of apology and offer to do anything to make up for any wrongs.

HIT AND RUN

Of a late night stop at a tavern I left just before closing. I heard a loud thump while backing up in the parking lot and in the rear view mirror appeared a long, four-door sedan. The doors swung open and longhaired bohemian types poured out, yelling and moving rapidly toward my Ford Country Sedan Station Wagon. A split second scan of the sedan revealed an old car covered with a latex type surface. "Just a bunch of hippies," I thought as I took off fast onto the highway.

Bennie Mea Collins

Bennie Mea Collins was the quintessential Black mama. Her husband, Slim, headed up the Gary Model City Project, a key program of the "war on poverty." Slim's quote about something being "stone heavy" was my first exposure to that sobriquet. The small sign on Bennie Mae's door read, *"poverty is not a moral issue, it is just awfully inconvenient."* If only this precept could be accepted to depict the human condition and not simply phony rationales that poverty is the result of laziness, stupidity and immorality.

Bennie Mea directed a Purdue program based from its Hammond campus. The goal of the project was the production of bachelor degrees in a broad number of areas to increase the educational levels of the Gary community and to arm its residents with credentials of empowerment.

Bennie was a Methodist, and one Sunday my family came up from Lafayette to attend services and be at a picnic in Bennie's back yard. I have never been proud of the fact that I turned down the opportunity to enjoy chitterlings and greens. Anyone who claims that they are not racist doesn't understand what that means, nor are they willing or capable of self-inventory. Fred R.,my graduate school friend, identified the quintessential symptom of racism when he stated that he,as an Afro-American, was "s*o tired of entering a room and feeling he had to apologize for being there."* I have never broached the subject with Blacks that I have gotten close to – but it seemed that many of "them" would place their hand on your arm or shoulder to see if you blushed. The department chair John B at Purdue often said about contact with Blacks, "Does it come off?"— A most contemptible thing to say, particularly for an educational leader committed to expanding knowledge and good will.

Bennie Mae's program during its course graduated 100 students. But as the emphasis on minority enrollment at universities waned and weakened and the grant money was not renewed, the program shut down. Many of the staff were let go, most notably a math professor who held distinction in his field.

Bennie mea and I co-authored an article in EDUCATIONAL LEADERSHIP about the need to extend and supplement the content of Head Start—*"BEYOND SESAME STREET,"* EDUCATIONAL LEADERSHIP, Association For Supervision And Curriculum Development.

Bennie Mae And Slim—Cabaret Fiasco

The Collins' were invited to West Lafayette for a football game and a Broadway version of CABARET. I was not prepared for the Nazi theme woven into the production depicting Blacks as gorillas. there was simply no way to tell the Collins that I had not planned to challenge or embarrass them. Once again, I lacked the inability to be honest and open without fear of failure.

The East Illinois State University CENTER FOR SCHOOL DESEGREGATION AND EQUAL EDUCATIONAL OPPORTUNITY.

THE CENTER FOR SCHOOL DESEGREGATION AND EQUAL EDUCATIONAL OPPORTUNITY located south of Chicago at east Illinois state (aka now as "CaruthersUniversity") organized a conference for all individuals who were responsible for grants and programs in urban black communities across the Midwest. The first one was held in Indianapolis. The black caucus separated and met by themselves. They told white members of the conference that they already knew the parameters of segregation and that they should conference among their own to both identify and plan to modify the dynamics of same. I learned the essence of emerging black power and how, if in any way, I could relate and co-partner in civil rights efforts at the institutional level. I met Bill M who was to become my graduate student assistant for the Gary project. In addition I was introduced to Jacob Caruthers who I soon learned was very knowledgeable and committed to civil rights.

THE FBI AND INTENSE PARANOIA

FACULTY ACTION COMMITTEE

"The system" was the choice cry of current "revolutionaries" – the Black Panthers, the SDS, (Students For A Democratic Society), and members of the civil rights movement. Robert Kennedy and Martin Luther King had both been assassinated. The bitter taste of JFK's death was still in my mind. Add to those events fear, disappointment and cynicism and you had emotional bombs waiting for a fuse to be lit.

PATHETIC AND INCREDIBLE DEMORALIZATION

Alcoholics had warned that my drinking would lead me in time to "Pathetic And Incredible Demoralization." Under the influence of alcohol the deepest and most primitive motives and behaviors come pouring out to exhibit themselves in outlandish ways.

One night while at Purdue I decided to cruise a restaurant instead of a bar. There was a small eatery located on the main drag located just before crossing the Wabash River into Lafayette. I was going from booth to booth coming on to undergraduates out for a Saturday night fling. I remember displaying a bon vivant demeanor and was slightly annoyed at the fierce looks and overall rejection I was getting at each stop.

Suddenly, I was overcome with a searing shame. I was wearing a Palm Beach suit – the only suit I had – one I had worn on bitterly cold days on Michigan Avenue in Chicago. It was made of a very light material that thirstily absorbed any liquid spilled upon it.

Rebuffs accumulated as I trolled down the row of booths and it finally got through to me that something awful was wrong, something way beyond my ridiculous flirtations. I noticed a cold feeling around the crotch of my Palm Beach trousers. I looked down and saw a dark, wet basketball size stain on my highly absorbent pants. I can't remember what happened later except that I retired from my spree.

Midnight meetings with comedian Dick Gregory and SDA counselor Jonathan Kozol intensified the power and meaning of my membership and commitment to a group. The belief that the FBI had tapped my phone and my establishment of a federal grant in Gary put the icing on the cake with regard to my belief in the significance of my work and the value and weight of my "comrades." it also created an additional vice of pressure and loaded an even fiercer desire for alcohol-intense paranoia.

Students at Purdue like many other universities were protesting and sitting in as activists in support of any number of issues, especially the war in Vietnam. Fifty Purdue faculty members from a broad array of different colleges and departments gathered to form a "Faculty Action Committee" to address concerns within the university involving student rights but primarily addressing civil rights questions implicating black students.

At the first meeting held, the FBI took pictures of the group and later I sensed from my phone's strange sounds that the phone was tapped. an FBI agent even came by my office to check me out under the guise of inquiring about one of my former students.

THE MIDNIGHT MEETING

A midnight meeting of the Faculty Action Committee was called to convene at a three-story home close to the Purdue campus. I walked though the door into a room and saw amid the usual committee membership one rather robust black women in the center of two nationally prominent men, comedian Dick Gregory and Jonathon Kozo, chief advisor to the Students For A Democratic Society – the notorious SDS. Kozol was well known for his book about the ghetto children of Boston and their "DEATH AT AN EARLY AGE, THE DESTRUCTION OF HEARTS AND MINDS IN THE BOSTON PUBLIC SCHOOL."— deaths due to the lack of effective education. I learned that the Black lady was Helen Bass Williams, a civil rights leader from Alabama.

DOESN'T ANYBODY CARE?

Shared, common peril is one element in the cement that today unites my sober alcoholic friends, that unity akin to the desperate gratitude of survivors of a Titanic-like shipwreck superseding the selfishness of the outside world.
This was unknown to me the night I was dragged across an Indiana lawn screaming, "Doesn't anybody care?" I screamed my abysmal terror at facing the eternal loneliness and abandonment awaiting me and everyone else some day. Consider King Albert's take on life as he observed a bluebird flying out of an icy blizzard into a huge hall with a blazing fireplace and feast-decked tables: "*fiat lux—let there be light.*"
My partner in the "Gary ghetto" trip, Jerry O, thought I needed to dump my anger and

anxiety and suggested opening the psychic gate with alcohol could do this. One night at the local motel restaurant and bar we consumed enough liquor to loosen me up, thereby allowing paranoia and mistrust to prevail with me screaming, "Doesn't anybody care,?" as Jerry O dragged me across my front lawn on Essex street in West Lafayette! He never spoke nor gave me eye contact again, even of a Sunday during mass. While the event worked to unleash my real issues of toxic fear and sadness, it did nothing to relieve them. The episode reflected my deep cynicism and distrust of what was coined in those days as the "system." It seemed as though all the supports of life— Catholicism, western values, institutional trust and the good will and intelligence of people were dashed on the rocks.

On another occasion I was present at a New York Times party in Chicago attended by some of the top people in my field. I took it upon myself to openly make derogatory remarks about their belief and support regarding what I thought was outmoded and ineffective methods of instruction. I began to act out the anger and bitterness I felt about the educational system. I went over to the window, opened it and put one leg out the window. Someone yelled, "Let the SOB jump" which prompted me to immediately retrieve my leg.

Abandonment Of Sons

After a trip to a professional conference held at the brown palace hotel in Denver, my entanglement with yet another "dance of the night" caused an ultimate abuse to my two sons, Bob and Tim, who, returning from Arizona, had been waiting for hours alone at the airport for their me to join them to fly back to Indiana.

RAGING

During binge at home I threw dishes off the kitchen rail in the family room and pushed the kitchen table over. All four of the children – Bob, Tim, Greg and Maureen were hiding in the attic quivering with fear. Not stopping there, I put my fist through the wall and gave wife Charlene a black eye whereupon son Bob challenged me with my 12-gauge shotgun. I did not remember either event but evidence of my alcoholic rage was revealed the next day bringing about great shame and disappointment at my

CONRAD HILTON – CLIMBING OUT THE WINDOW
Under the influence of alcohol I would criticize the educational society elites with coarse commentaries. One night at an Educational Conference at the Conrad Hilton in Chicago, something set me off. The raucous reaction of the crowd moved me to threaten jumping out of the window of the 14th story building. With one leg out of the window, I heard someone shout, "Let the son of a bitch jump!,, Since no one seem to care or would express remorse at my demise, I realized that suicide would be pointless and came back inside. Unfortunately I had sealed the casket of my professional death by attacking two powerful educators – Phillip Jackson of the University of Chicago and the Chair of the ASCD Elementary Advisory Committee of which I was a member. I also attacked a professor emeritus from New York University.(See details to follow).
MUGGED IN CHIGAGO
One night the unresponsiveness of professionals about my ravings forced me into the dark streets of downtown Chicago. A group of teenagers but without any physical violence mugged me.
That was then. Now, considering the current conditions in urban culture, I would have been killed.

persona, one allegedly devoted to caring for others except for those near and dear and those deserving of care and support.

During the last term at Purdue the Gary project was focused on what was called a *Career Ladder* designed to allow educational staff to move both laterally and vertically in pursuit of degrees and certifications in various educational roles. Bennie Mea Collins was admitted and worked on a Master's Degree In Administration at Purdue, which she completed in record time

Within several years after the end of the career ladder program all the supportive staff of the program were not retained. in the following narrative it is evident that the resistance to inclusion of Afro-American students and staff at Purdue has persisted to the present day.

The Gary project proved successful – half of the participating students eventually took positions in the all-black gary school system, at both the elementary and high schools levels.

FUTURE AT PURDUE

In spite of an atrocious reputation that had to be accruing among the Purdue staff and administration, my apparent success in getting grant money and operating effective inner city programs gave me a pass and an offer to limit my work load to one graduate class one night a week.

The family did not escape the impact of my complex life and my alcoholism. One night while dumping enormous rage and anger out into the universe, I managed to move the kitchen table over a wrought iron rail and chuck it down into the family room. And then, when I started throwing and breaking dishes into the family room, my four children hid in the attic upstairs. After giving my wife a black eye (which I sadly don't remember) my oldest son Bob threatened me with the 12 gauge shotgun.

The next morning I found the Chaplain from the Purdue Newman Club, Fr. Piquet, sitting in the living room in front of me. It weighed on my mind that someone I so respected for his courage – he stepped between cops with guns drawn and students with broken bottles – would show up prompted by my misbehavior. After all, given the turmoil and conflict that was going on in the world, I wanted to appear to be just like any other guy, not a goodie two shoes. Uneasy fear began to seep through my bravado when Bill M, the Black graduate student in the Gary Program, asked me why I was "destroying my career"? His confrontation pierced the macho illusion, the fragile protective shell, and all the mindless grasping rationalizations for my downward spiral. I had identified my behavior as that of a "caring activist." I even dismissed my father – he had journeyed all the way from Arizona to confront me. I concluded his visit by telling him that things were "Okay, Dad." The fires of rage that flamed during my drinking bouts begin to dampen more and more as my escapades became more and more bizarre and outrageous.

I received a letter from Purdue Vice President Freihofer about the incident in the Pizza Hut lot. I wrote back and covered the event by claiming it was a consequence of the university's obligation "to operate in the inner city." I had no memory of the accident, as I was probably drunk.

Another time I tried to get to Bill M's home in south Chicago and came to a house with bars on the window and three guys drinking out of a sack. I asked where Bill M lived and they just stared at me, unbelieving. Bill later said I had gone into a part of South Chicago that he always avoided.

MYSTERIOUS NUDGE ON THE SHOULDER

Drinking episodes became more frequent and more consequential as time went on. One night in Gary I left the Holiday Inn tavern avoiding certain fisticuffs with the bartender and headed in a Purdue car west on the skyway leading to the south part of Chicago. It was my purpose to hang out in those bars that stayed open to the early morning hours. My last memory before my escape with death was feeling dizzy and tired and turning around to return Gary and my room at the Holiday Inn.

I felt something like a hand nudge my shoulder, and as I opened my eyes expecting to see the ceiling of the motel room, I was stunned to behold the bright orange pumps of a gas station moving towards me at 60 miles per hour. The road split on the east side of Gary, the left lane moving westbound and the right lane moving eastbound. Right in the middle of the split was the gas station. I grabbed the wheel and pulled into the right lane, by a nanosecond missing a fiery collision and certain death. As I peered out the window of my second floor room around four in the morning, I noticed a car down in the parking area and could see half of a face revealed by the area lights The shadowy visage in the car window terrified me. My theory has always been that either the school or the mayor's office put a tail on me to save me from disaster. I think I was seen in some ways as an asset to the struggles of Gary. My bravado was severely compromised, and I sat in an elementary classroom the next day repeating the word "Responsibility, Responsibility, Responsibility," over and over again. I was beginning to question my behavior and moving toward the "bottoming out" of my alcoholic addition.

"Has anybody seen my old friend Abe, Jack, Bobby and Martin – where or where have they gone?" That old melody flowed out of the Pizza Hut Wurlitzer on the corner in West Lafayette as I downed glass after glass of Stores beer. Alcohol was becoming my common friend and response to every crisis, real or perceived.

I sensed, after contacting a group of known sober alcoholics across the Wabash River in Lafayette, that I was talking to some old geezer in an empty room. It seemed fruitless to even be there. The severity of my drunken behavior made me want to find out the origin of my rage, to determine why alcohol was my choice to kill pain. I made an appointment with a psychiatrist. He opened me up and helped me to realize that I had a mother who said," Don't feel" and a father who signaled "Don't Listen." My father actually left the room in the middle of my heavy, intimate conversations.

The psychiatrist prescribed antabuse and told me of the dire consequences if I drank while taking the drug. I palmed my potion in front of Charlene. Two days after that dose I drank a beer and turned cherry red.

"Do not drink alcohol while taking disulfiram. Flushing, fast heartbeats, nausea, thirst, chest pain, vertigo, and low blood pressure may occur when alcohol is ingested during disulfiram therapy."(Wikipedia).

I believe I survived the dose of Antabuse because it reduced my extreme high blood pressure rate, a condition unknown to me at the time.

My out was that the psychiatrist was hard of hearing and my group were all drug addicts. I was convinced that I needed alcohol to carry out my quest for revolutionary change on all fronts. Unfortunately there was no way to communicate this to the blue-eyed, glaring cop who was fingerprinting me after I busted up that rest room at the peanut-shelled floor of the Pig and Whistle. Nor was the judge the next day sympathetic to my professorial status. He said I would spend weekends in jail for six months if he ever saw me again.

The pileup of negative consequences could not be brushed off as the expected affects of a socially conscious person. I started having sessions with a West Lafayette psychiatrist. I was individually interviewed and identified several issues I had with my parents. I joined a therapy group but was turned off by being the only alcoholic amidst a bunch of drug addicts. I still believed alcohol was necessary to function in the "special" work I was doing. The psychiatrist prescribed Antabuse. At one point after a daily dose of Antabuse I drank two beers and immediately turned purple. Charlene would watch me take the Antabuse each morning but I only palmed it. I still was not convinced that I could live a joyous life without alcohol and still believed I could drink if I were careful about the amount of consumption and what I did.

I have made concerted efforts to offer amends to any one of my romantic partners with a willingness to do whatever necessary to make things right. As I write one of my prime relationships, an internationally known business-social psychologist, passed away with complications from Alzheimer's disease.

The decision to take a position at Temple in Philadelphia – I thought my mission would be found in the inner city – was symptomatic of my arrogance and grandiosity, of the cover I had used for so long to compensate for my lack of esteem, my uncertainty and my consequent inability to plan and perform realistically.

NEVER EVER CHANGING PURDUE

As of this writing and with regret I review news on the Purdue University website: "PURDUE ELIMINATES CHIEF DIVERSITY POSITION"– 8:14PM EDT JULY 13, 2015 –

Purdue's chief diversity officer, G. Christine Taylor, no longer works for the university. Her position was eliminated July 1 after two months of talks with Provost Debasish Dutta, who has assumed Taylor's former role.

"We have made progress but a lot more needs to be done," he said.

Dr. Taylor was pushing very hard to analyze the Ferguson and other events involving Black people in her discussions and was promoting action for change. She made too many people nervous at Purdue.

When the program was in its preparatory phase the Hammond campus director, a native of Tennessee, was throwing roadblocks every chance he got to sabotage the Career Ladder Program. In retrospect it was probably not a good strategy, but I invited Jacob Carruthers and Barbara Sizemore, a serious Black rapper team, to come to a meeting for the purpose of "sensitivity training." After that meeting the resistance of the Hammond Campus Director ceased.

Because so much of my energy was directed by clandestine liaisons with ladies in order to get closure on my need to have a "sympathetic" partner (e.g., a Mom) in my life travels, I wasn't aware how much I respected and loved Bennie Mae. Over the years I would periodically call her and she would exclaim, "Jerry Knowles. What you say?" I attended her birthday party at the Genesis Center in Gary on my way to Montréal in 1985 and ten years later I traveled to Charlotte to celebrate her birthday on a Lake Norman steamboat. She came to Taos while I was working at Navajo (Dine) Community College and we toured the Navajo Reservation. She adored Indian turquoise and I got her some each time I had the chance. Diabetes claimed one of her legs in the mid nineties. Last time I called her voice was distant and weak. We never wish for nor do we accept the passing of old times and acquaintances. I would rather think of the day she recounted her nightmare about the "Chicago police attack on the

Black Panthers and saw herself chasing me with a hatchet."

"What you say, Bennie Mae, you know I could never be part of that," I told her. As my classmate and close Mexican friend from Winslow, one Fred Rubi once proclaimed, excluding entire categories of people and demeaning their value weakens the viability of the culture in general.

Descriptions, efforts and activities of the Gary days are in no way an attempt to claim neither gallantry nor special distinction. They are but an opportunity for me to creatively practice of my deep need to believe what I had learned about the Christian ethic— "he ain't heavy, he's my brother."

TEMPLE UNIVERSITY

My move to teach at Temple was driven by elaborate fantasies of a city life style, a small MG with the wind in my hair and of course the making of what I thought was a contribution to inner city education *vis-à-vis* an attack on the condition identified by Jonathan Kozol's "Death At An Early Age" – stories of black youth in the ghettos. While I accomplished things of which I am professionally proud, my personal life had spiraled downward. Brief experiences in south Chicago and Gary in no way prepared me for city life in Philadelphia. Lost was the energy that kept the light on in my soul – I had been surrounded by bright, dedicated, quality people in Gary and the Purdue Camp.

Life in Jersey within the Temple Camp community and my drinking bouts in Philadelphia and New Jersey – not to mention the alienation of my family at home – created a terrible sense of isolation, loneliness and fear driving away the joy, leaving me with only a sense of resignation. It didn't take much time for me to realize the folly of my justifications for being on the East Coast in Philly.

New Jersey House

The trip to Pennsylvania and Philly with two sons Bob and Tim I can hardly remember, but it was a journey aimed at procuring a home for the expected arrival of Charlene, Greg and Maureen.

I had walked away from the Education Building at Purdue holding back doubt about my decision and uneasiness about my competence to perform at a city university.

Bob, Tim and I breezed into Philly, got a motel and immediately went to supper at a swell-looking restaurant named Bookbinders which we later found out was one of the top seafood places on the east coast. The waiter looked at us with some disdain as we all ordered hamburgers.

House rental ads in the newspapers listed very expensive options in the greater Philly area, but the town of Willingboro across the river in New Jersey offered reasonably priced housing. Although compared to my salary at Purdue Temple representing a 30% increase, the relocation from Indiana to Greater Philly actually meant a 20% drop in my standard of living for many reasons, chiefly due to the daily commute from Jersey to Philly.

Willingboro was named after Benjamin Franklin's son William, "Willy," and was in fact a Levittown of over 50 thousand residents occupying three different house models varying only in landscaping and paint color. At the writing of this book the town has devolved into a very dangerous area. Even in the early 70's there were serious incidents of crime; if one knocked on a door, chances of a German Sheppard dog peering through a crack in the door were good. The papers reported the bludgeoning death by a night intruder of a couple two blocks away from our home.

Bob and Tim registered at Kennedy High School where Bob found his first love, Beth. Maureen and Gregory suffered a very bullied and hectic life at the local elementary school. Though I operated with some effectiveness professionally, I could barely manage to keep my personal life from drowning. All the props that smoke-screened the very real plight of my alcoholism — Gary associates, friends and "co-revolutionary" Ted, the DOSE Model fellows and the prestige of Purdue — were jerked away leaving me naked in front of a hostile and unfamiliar university scene.

LEFT ALONE

One night a poignant reminder of the dysfunction wrought by alcoholic addiction occurred when I left the house unlocked with Bob and Tim asleep. I went out for a "few minutes" at 10 pm to the nearest bar for a "quick drink." I ended up in a three-story house in the company of a strange lady and an old sea captain on the couch who I was told produced pornography. The only memory of the lady was her bitter put down of her husband being a low paid teacher. I left the house at 3am and returned home to an unlocked house, Tim and Bob never aware of any danger. Doubts about my glorious activist persona began to eat through my denial and delusions, and the paranoia became so great that I slept in the back bedroom with a baseball bat. I was only a door away from Charlene whom I was using as a burglar alarm should an intruder enter the house and come up the stairs.

I continued being a victim of my addiction by going out in the New Jersey nights, once finding myself lost in a jack pine forest and another time leaving a bar parking lot.

CALL TO MEMPHIS

I made a pay phone collect call to a current romantic liaison in Memphis. To emphize once again, my interface with 'Norma' was reminiscent of the scene in the film "UP IN THE AIR" whereupon George Clooney appeared at the doorstep of his lover actress Vera Farmiga. After numerous liaisons with that character, Clooney finally imploded, decided he loved someone and was ready to commit long term. He appeared at her front door in Chicago to tell her he loved her and wanted to marry. Farmiga answered the bell – the sound of children's voices in the background – and quite irritably opened the door exclaiming, "What are you doing here at my house?" In the background the voice of a male is heard, "Who is it honey?" I got a similar response on the phone – "Why are you calling my home? Never do that again. I never want to see you again." Years later I contacted the offices of that individual in Memphis to make amends to her only to be told that Norma had passed away ten years earlier.

Plans to find Shangri-La and enter nirvana into a realm of never ending bliss were left on the barroom table along with a chunk of my naiveté. It was unfortunate that a deep need to find that heart of gold, i.e., that reunion with the perfect Mom was still buried deep inside and was very active. Some animals are meant to marry each other and live symbiotically over a lifetime – star struck lovers and monogamous swans. However – "We are not star struck lovers nor monogamous swans, we are sharks." (Quote by Bryan Bingham (George Clooney) in "UP IN THE AIR." Unfortunately due to the constellation of attitudes my personality comprised in those early years, each relationship ended like the old cowboy song, "You are everything I never wanted." It seemed that I lacked an operational definition of what "love" was, and until I could grasp it and nurture it, I would continue to flounder in the dark. It was a pretty precarious plight for someone who had a personality akin to a film featuring a character combining the personas of Rodney Dangerfield and Mr. McGoo.

The challenge of young adult hood, which had eluded me for such long time, and the crises of intimacy vs. isolation were not successfully met because the failure to form a solid and positive identity interfered with any ability to bond with another human being. The function of shame as a prime emotion always ended in me thinking I was not good enough for someone else.

The true meaning and definition of love would have to wait until my spiritual father and counselor, Ed Aston, reviewed my alcoholic addiction that gave me some answers.

GONE IN AN URBAN JUNGLE

MIDNIGHT ON BROAD STREET

Nightlife around Temple University reflected some bizarre but lucky consequences. Temple had a locked parking lot with a security guard. One evening in Philadelphia I decided to leave my car in the gated Temple lot and take the train down to Penn Center where there were a number of bars. I took the subway to the Pen Station area to hang out in the bars. Returning in the early hours I had to tap on the door and awaken a drowsy security guard to get my car out of the lot. Having just turned on Broad Street said car suddenly coughed to a stop. A small hose from radiator to motor had split. As the bitter wind whipped through my jacket I dialed at a pay phone for help, but to no avail. I could barely see a Shell sign way down on Broad Street so I got in the car and ribbed the misfiring engine up, not stopping for a red light. The only cops in east Philly had to be there at that very moment. Barely able to stand or even lean against the car under the influence of the booze, I explained my plight and they let me go. I believe now that cops in Philly would not bother you unless you shot someone right in front of them. I got to the Shell Station and had the water hose repaired. The misfiring had blown a hole in the muffler, which sounded awful. Yet in due course I arrived home in Jersey and went to bed only to rise after two hours to head back to Temple and face 30 Black teacher aides who were part of a program to equip them as certified early childhood teachers. Not being castigated for alcohol consumption was one of the few advantages of teaching in the "inner city."

My position was in the early childhood department at Temple, sandwiched between two prominent professionals in the field. Evangeline Ward was president of the most powerful early childhood organization in the world and Lois Macomber was president of the Jean Piaget Society. I taught early childhood classes, but my main responsibility was directing, teaching and matriculating 60 Black teacher aides from Philly early childhood and Head Start Centers toward qualifying for their degrees and certification. My commitment was not without a socio-theoretical basis to serve civil rights – I thought. At this time, early in the civil rights movement it was believed that if the "community," through its members, could be moved into the schools, their power would serve to transform education and two, they would be very effective in teaching their "own People."

COLD BOX AT MALCOLM X

I also taught an early childhood class in Malcolm X High School. I carried a cooler full of resource files in and out of the building under the questioning eyes of high school students, one asking what I had in there. "Booze," I said.

The Main Line in the area west of Philly contained a number of Ivy League Universities with whom Temple wished to identify in their quest to become an urban Ivy League school. Because of this dynamic, the administration, particularly the assistant dean, felt uncomfortably split in their devotion to the inner city and the main line shtick. The assistant dean did not want to deal with "those ladies" matriculating and transferring their credits into Temple – see no evil and hear no evil. A 'militant activist' like me had the opportunity to hit a home run for justice when the assistant dean gave me the power to transfer courses toward the degrees of my 30 "ladies." That responsibility almost ended in disaster and possibly my murder. Attendance at a soiree of parties across town caused me to lose my leather brief case chocked so full of "the ladies" transcripts that when opened, papers would fly out of the top of the case. Frantic trips all over town backtracking my trail found me with great relief grabbing the case from the hand of a drinking compadre.

Bessie M had two years of course work completed in a South Carolina "normal school," the latest course completion in 1932. I was able to transfer the entire set of courses into Temple.

BUCKS COUNTY JAIL

At a party in Bucks County north of Philadelphia, I decided amid the frivolities that I was not having fun nor being successful at whatever flirtation I was involved in and so, I opted to leave the party, raining regret on the group for my departure. Unfortunately, someone anticipating my exit (which I guess I had been threatening) let the air out of the failing station wagon tires. When I took off down the cobblestone streets hearing the tires bonking and flapping it was not enough to stop me before a county gendarme arrested me and put me in jail. It seemed that I was becoming a seasoned inmate; I knew things were not so bad when the jailer did not take my belt and I was right, for someone came within an hour to bail me out.

HIGH BLOOD PRESSURE

The stress of my lifestyle, both professional and personal, was unbeknownst to me starting to take a dangerous toll. Of a day after swimming in the Atlantic at Long Beach, New Jersey I was sitting in a chair in the back yard when I sensed what I thought was salt water pouring out my nose on to the lawn. Looking down at the ground I saw a red pool forming. The doctor in the emergency ward, upon clocking my blood pressure at 120 over 200 immediately put me on a gurney and gave me a shot. It was a close brush with expiration; once again the veneer of bravado and minimization was pierced by reality. I was taking firmer steps toward an odyssey that could lead to incarceration, insanity and even death. The hot air under my wings, that false idealistic virtue was beginning to grow cold. I was literally writing letters with crayons while publishing articles professionally in major journals. My boss at Temple, Dr. Hilsinger, was a true hero and had disarmed a hand grenade-wielding militant in a flight from Europe. He was a practical and unassuming individual who had a message for me – do not take yourself too seriously, but just quietly do your best for your students and the institution.

OK TO GO HOME

It was beginning to grow on me that there was no nirvana of professional existence, especially in an urban environment where I had few skills and little of the knowledge needed for survival. It was time, and it would be okay to go home to Arizona. A letter from the Northern Arizona University home in Flagstaff came in the mail with an offer to run an early childhood project on the Navajo Reservation. It was like a life preserver in a stormy sea. As I write I surmise that a combination of my father's friendship with Chancellor Gillenwater as well as other political connections – even including a program director at the Office of Education who had overseen the Gary project – worked to give me chance to escape disaster, in reality creating the project with me in mind. Though the work that I was doing was certainly valuable, it could have been much more productive and would have had long-range impact if I had been more mature, more wise and more careful. Bennie Mae had advised me should I want to leave Purdue that I consider teaching at a Black college like Howard instead of rushing to save city people. But, an ego fed by arrogance and grandiosity could not accept a position that had no apparent glory nor visibility.

My term on the ASCD Elementary Advisory Committee had run out and I was no longer getting the all-expense paid trips to Washington and other major cities where I could run up hotel bills with large bar tabs and spend all night going from club to club. I took a dive into the depths of despair upon learning that a member of the counsel had maneuvered to be appointed for another term by sleeping with a senior member from a Big 10 University. That same person, who was a young but senior member of a church-run university in Hawaii, gypped that poor people at the Washington monument "should just get a job – that they were ignorant, immoral, lazy and dirty."

DARKER, MORE ISOLATED AND LONELY

Nights became darker, more isolated and very lonely. I was once rolled in Chicago by a bunch of teenagers who by contemporary standards would have simply shot me without compunction. As the theme from "Valley of the Dolls" played in my mind I found myself one early morning entering the Catholic Church in Atlantic City to light candles, to try and get some light to shine down my darkening alleys. I didn't realize until forty years later that I had gotten help that day.

EXIT FROM TEMPLE

Like any upstanding professional I exited from the Temple position with my usual flair, i.e. bring in the clowns. I taught one class during the summer and was scheduled to teach several classes in the fall. I left a handwritten note on the Dean's desk that I was leaving, and never had a face-to-face goodbye with him or my two faculty members, McComber and Ward. Fifteen years later I called Ward at Temple to apologize. She told me it was okay.

What wire did I have loose that would explain such passive behavior? All my life I found it difficult, indeed almost impossible to face people in situations that revealed some fault or failure on my part. Why did it take so much turmoil and trouble to get to the bottom of this lack of interpersonal skill? What had I missed somewhere in life's journey? Unlike many I found the loose wire and have been re-soldering it to my psyche and soul.

Culturally, the Temple experience offered trips to Atlantic City and clam chowder, pretzels at stoplights, a birthday cake looking City Hall, Philly's baseball and the strange New Year's parade of men in satin gowns and big hats – the Mummers – along with trips to Cape May. A café across from Temple had a horseshoe-looped conveyer belt to deliver food and return dirty dishes. It was a very long and narrow room without any space for tables.

Accessing the George Washington Bridge through an underpass always echoed the strains from Karen Carpenter's *"We've only just begun to live... ."* Apparently in spite of the dire straits of my existence I could yet find hope deep inside.

PIAGET CONFERENCE – RETURN AND SURRENDER IN PHILLY

I would return to Philly and Temple one year later in May to attend a conference establishing the Jean Piaget Society initiated by Dr. Macomber, a recent co-partner in the Temple Early childhood department. The trip and the accompanying personal change for me were astounding.

Sons Tim and Bob went to Kennedy High School in Willingboro, the same school that Olympic Champion Carl Lewis attended. He won nine Olympic gold medals.

Bob sang in the school choir and suffered through his first love affair with 'Beth.' He was almost killed in a wintery car accident a year later on his way to visit Beth, who, to his sad discovery, had joined the drug scene at the University of Colorado.

Visit to Ted

My pseudo revolutionary partner, Ted U, had taken a job at the University of Hartford, an act I later recognized was probably the impetus for my move to Temple. Ted bragged about the heavenly hot dogs of Nathan's in New York. My family and he toured Manhattan and ate at Nathan's while standing on a street corner.

A visit to Manhattan and New Jersey to long time friend Kenny from Grand Canyon Avenue days reestablished the fact that there were good people and good times, that they had not been a dream. Kenny had ascended to the Vice Presidency of Hess Oil Company— a very prestigious and well paid position.

Three Hundred Navajo Teacheer Aides Graduate and Become Teachers

VI. GENERATE, TRANSFORM, AND ACHIEVE—FLAGSTAFF

THE NAVAJO NATION

The offer to come back to Arizona to do an early childhood project on the Navajo was a heaven sent for my failing ability to cope.

BEAUTY OF THE NAVAJO RESERVATION

Coming back to Arizona from the east coast, from stark loneliness and a personal crash like the scene from the classic movie, "Lost Horizon" (the cold, hungry and hopeless plane crash group stuck in a blizzard) entering the Navajo Nation was like the movie scene of Ronald Coleman's coming over the pass into Shangri La. The beauty and diversity of Northern Arizona, particularly the mystical, magical Monument Valley was a spiritual triage to my soul. It was a gift.

However, during the early days, start up and operation of the Early Childhood Program my alcoholic personality and carousing were in full force. The need to confront universities and institutions in general were still with me.

The props that shielded me, that justified my use of alcohol – civil rights and desegregation; educational reform; the misery of war; did not follow me back home to Arizona. But my alcoholism and dysfunctional persona came back with me.

The beauty of the Navajo lands and the thrill of a new creative project continued to temp my use of "feel good" from the bottle creating the pathetic, preposterous and the passionate.

I had no premonition that the end was coming, that I was about to face a transformation from despair to an embarkation on the road to Shangri La.

The continued and obsessive need to attract and acquire affection was considered as a healing, as a soothing balm to my uncertain, damaged ego. Of course the expectation of such relationships to fill the empty hole generated by the absence of a caring mother never bore fruition. With dedicated insensitivity those notions were abandoned in a continual search for the perfect female. My lack of empathy for such acquaintances astounds me to this day. Empathy was the core of my coherency, yet relationships with females were totally blocked from empathy.

ALCOHOL – JAIL AGAIN

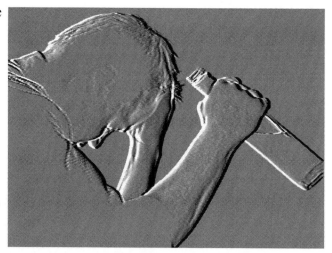

Since I had anointed myself as the chief arbitrator of both the education and the training of future teachers, and that, combined with my ever present arrogance and grandiosity fueled by a scorching alcoholic mentality caused me to take an angry but quiet exception at the deliberations of a faculty meeting. The dean seemed totally compromising and patronizing regarding the ideas of the conservative wing of the faculty. As always the resolution in my conflicted mind was to go to the new bar in town called "Friar Tuck's" (with a monastic motif) to drown my wrath in one martini after another.

At approximately 9 in the evening, after consuming at least five martinis I put my shades on and got into the Country Sedan for what would be my last ride in the old station wagon. Cruising north on Santa Fe Ave (Route 66) I miraculously drove under the underpass, turned, and headed east through downtown Flagstaff. Suddenly I both heard and felt a crunching sound as the Ford began to lurch and I could not steer. I pulled off the highway and turned left into a fast food concession, got out of the car and headed east down the street on my way to a bar with an African safari motif. It wasn't long until my eyes were squinting at the flashing red and blue lights of several cop cars surrounding me. I awoke to the cold reality of a jail cell. My father arrived within a short time and bailed me out for a rather small amount at that time —$500.

As the early sun hit my face next morning on Mead Lane in north Flagstaff it melted the delusion that had been locked out of my mind for such a long time. I murmured to myself that, "I cannot drink alcohol and predict what is going to happen." I had lucked out that one night in Gary and didn't get killed. I had lucked out again last night and didn't kill anybody, which, if it happened, could have doomed me to spend my life behind bars. The arresting officer informed me that I had run through a red light and sideswiped two cars. Fortunately, due to fate or unseen forces, I did not injure or kill anyone. I claimed to my lawyer, old friend Joe Bennett that I was "heading back to the scene of the accident." He indicated that at the site where I was arrested I was observed walking eastward, leaving the scene. The next day I appeared in the office of one Judge Brady. Years later I went to the grave of Judge Brady to thank him for that day in his office (the following day) when he told me that if he saw me again I would "end up in Florence in the Arizona State Penitentiary."

THE NAVAJO EARLY CHILDHOOD PROJECT

Science— Vince Randal, Apache

Navajo Children came to school not speaking English. This required the BIA (The Bureau of Indian Affairs) to provide a pre-kindergarten program for beginners to learn that language. National programs such as Head Start and Follow Through were placing heavy emphasis on a hands-on mode of instruction. It was this mode that the BIA from Washington wanted to include in their program and they funded, along with the Department of Education, a project establishing pilot program sites at five schools spread across the 200-mile length of the Navajo Nation from Flagstaff, Arizona to Albuquerque, New Mexico.

I was given the task to co-manage the project with Navajo lady Mrs. Marjorie T who had been an activist in developing effective, hands on, culturally relative materials for Navajo children. A third individual made up the staff and we teamed in two routes, one traveling south one week from near Winslow to Cañoncito near Albuquerque, and the other north from Kayenta to Teec Nos Pos (Round Trees) at the Four Corners of New Mexico, Arizona, Utah and Colorado.

EARLY CHILDHOOD PROJECT

The Early Childhood Project I had agreed to direct contained all the professional and personal dimensions of what I desperately needed at that time of life. My efforts at making a contribution had run aground, had lost its potency in Philadelphia to the degree that the crash was inevitable. Blood pressure of 120 over 200, bleeding nose, abject demoralization and rampant alcoholism eroded my enthusiasm and my ability to be productive came to a halt.

The early childhood project provided opportunity to ascertain immediate classroom impact. These were Bureau of Indian Affairs classrooms – notoriously rigid, and situated in prison-like boarding schools across the Navajo Reservation. I had come out of an inner city world where injustice, poverty and poor education were a combined challenge to overcome. The Navajo people were (and still are) suffering from a very high unemployment rate and an average annual income, at that time, far below the poverty level. Educational achievement was beneath the national average and continuation of education beyond 8th grade was low, with high school graduation a dubious probability. Navajos had basically no management over their education; Rough Rock Demonstration School was the first Indian controlled school in the U.S.

One of my major contributions was the demonstration of Piagetian concepts in the acquisition of scientific and mathematical theories through the manipulation of concrete components. Mrs. T emphasized the creation of culturally relevant materials and Dee C, the other staff member, worked on principles of child learning and development. The project served the five BIA schools and a group made up of administrators, teachers and dormitory overseers as well as educational aides at each school. Thus relevant education and lifting of community members in the form of teacher and dorm aides into Navajo education were the two main factors driving the program.

Sessions were held once a week for nine months; one week it would be Mrs. T and myself with Dee C doing a solo, and the next week it would be a revised combination of staff. The major capstones of the project were the field trips to Old Town Albuquerque to the Marie Hughes Follow Through Program. Marie Hughes and her program represented the crème de la crème in early childhood and elementary education, and I had always felt that "seeing it done" was the most effective means of educational change. The culminating activity to the program was a summer session held literally in my former lab school classroom and other rooms utilizing two classes of Navajo children wherein curriculum materials could be both tested and developed. The project team made site visits to all five BIA Schools to organize and prepare for the program. Each site was located in a distinctive subculture and topological part of the Navajo Reservation. The sites had been chosen for their representation to defend variables that covered the whole panoply of the Navajo reservation. Although like most federal grants the it was only funded for one year, the impact on classrooms was observed but proved over the years to be sustained, in some cases permanently.

Dances with Wolves Days

"I Don't Think She is a Navajo!"

As I sat one October day of 1971 at an initial meeting facing a group of participants in a small room in the Kayenta Boarding School – expecting to encounter familiar Navajo faces – I noted a face across from me and in my mind I thought, "I Don't Think She is a Navajo." The statement is not meant to be derogatory as there is wonderful, disparate beauty in the many faces of Native Americans across the U.S. The faces captured by the famous photographer Edward S. Curtis are mystical, and majestic. In my days to come with the Navajo, the Hopi, the Kiowa, the Taos and the Zuni I would come to distinguish striking differences. So it was that I learned that the stunning lady (Delphia) sitting across from me was a member of the

Delphia

Kiowa Tribe of Oklahoma, one of the most respected and, earlier in history, the fiercest tribe in America. Professionally, Delphia was one of the most effective teachers I had ever seen in working with Navajo children. Her grandmother and her grandfather, a Four Square minister, raised her traditionally. She won awards for cut beadwork and created exquisite buckskin dresses and moccasins with ease. She was crowned as the Kiowa Princees early in life and her family currently were sought after as head dancers at local Pow Wows. She attained a Masters Degree in Education and held many administrative positions, including principalships across the Navajo Reservation. She possessed a skilled empathy in working with her students, often involving them in Pow Wows. Two of her children attended the Navajo Academy in Farmington, were recognized as All State in sports and excelled in academics.

That soft part of the soul still searching for the "heart of gold" began having visions of an Indian maiden by a misty lake – Pocahontas, perhaps, or Saint Kateri Tekakwitha.

With Freudian thunderbolt transference I immediately abandoned the obsession about the ex-Sister Of Mercy from Chicago and switched it to Delphia H. She had four children; the youngest was Carly, the oldest Mattie. At the time Delphia was a much more sophisticated practicing alcoholic than I. She came to town each weekend with BIA staff friend, Martha F to drink on south San Francisco Street at Griegos, a tavern frequented by the local Latino population. The inevitable liaisons began at a motel in Kayenta and continued on in Flagstaff and on field trips to Albuquerque.

MEXICAN HAT

Driving up and back from Kayenta to Mexican Hat, Utah, was a dangerous affair even when sober. Alcohol was not legal on the Navajo Rez so one had to go forty miles north into Utah to "the Hat" bars to drink. I miraculously maneuvered the road from the "Hat" with Delphia and her BIA friend Martha one night.

DELIVERANCE

EL VADO MOTEL IN ALBUQUERQUE

Even though I had begun to recognize and accept my alcoholism, I still reached out for booze as an emotional crutch to snuff out feelings of inadequacy and poor esteem. I had established an intimate relationship with Delphia, a member of the early childhood project participants. The group from Kayenta had come to visit Marie Hugh's stellar Early Child Hood Project in old town Albuquerque. Inflamed by the fact that someone in the group was hitting on Delphia drove me to new heights of drunkenness after which we holed up together in a cabin at the El Vado Motel.

On another fieldtrip to Albuquerque I had to consume three cans of beer and a half glass of vodka just to get out the motel door.

ROMANCE IN THE RAIN

I had been banned from the BIA compound by the BIA principal because of a drunken collision with a car within that housing compound. In order to be secretly with Delphia, we found ourselves northeast of Kayenta out in the middle of the red sand dunes under a blanket as the rain poured on us.

A FINAL STRAW—NAIL IN THE COFFIN

Some of my most humiliating and macabre events occurred while I ran the Navajo Early Childhood Program. My co-director was an astute and very committed Navajo lady who I will call Shama'. At one of the five field trips to Albuquerque I had "come on" to her while drunk. The look she gave me in subsequent weeks acted to drain a lot of hot air from my grandiose, arrogant ego. It was Shama' who later as a key member of the Navajo Teacher Education Development Program (NTEDP) Board, cognizant of my fight for sobriety, overlooked my indiscretion and supported me as the director of the program – a program that eventually degreed and certified over 300 Navajo teachers. More humorously, she provided me with the Navajo term for "margarita"— *Toe Dethlil Ashee.*

Long Lonely Summer

The summer program of the Early Childhood Program was a significant success involving two classrooms of Navajo children and a curriculum center for creating culturally relevant Navajo materials. Three significant consultants were engaged to address the group and may have been the cause for the second year obtaining no funding. First, I had my old friend Ted U from Purdue days come to Arizona to discuss the importance of involving the community in the schools. In addition, I had two controversial figures who may have doomed the ultimate support of the program at the University, the BIA and the Office of Education in Washington – Dr. Robert R., an Anglo married to a Navajo, whom I considered the "John Brown" radical supporter of the Navajo people, had been an extreme anti-BIA activist. Dr. Robert R had bitterly confronted the BIA, other federal authorities and even private businesses and foundations about the plight of the Navajo people in order to establish two Navajo educational institutions – Rough Rock Elementary School, the first community controlled school in an Indian Nation and Navajo Community College, the first Indian controlled college. While his advocacy was strong and successful, his rhetoric and tactics tended to turn off bureaucrats. Several accomplishments of Dr. Robert R represented great progress for both the Navajo and native communities across the land that began establishing control of their educational institutions. A crucial understanding gleaned from early successes was that it was necessary to build into any new model the ability to acquire sustained funding to keep afloat in the long run. Dr. Robert and his wife had published significant works about the history of the Navajo people.

The second individual I asked to address the project was Vincent Randall, a member of the Yavapai Apache Nation near Clarkdale, a hamlet below my birthplace of Jerome. Vince, as if it weren't challenging enough just being an Apache and the representative of a people who held off five thousand troopers in a multi-year chase of Geronimo, was also a bitter antagonist to reform services being provided by the government to Indian people. Vince wore a huge ten gallon hat topped with an eagle feather, and when asked for a name to be called when his lunch was ready, he replied "George C. Custer." Ambling up to a lunch counter when his name was called brought the house down in hilarious laughter. Vince was a member of the Tonto Apache who were known being related to the Cibecue Apaches who were located at the spot igniting Army conflict with Geronimo. Vincent's sister-in-law was my secretary at NAU for two years.

Oblivious to the politics of inter-institutional affairs, I had attended an ASCD conference in Minneapolis to present a talk to a scheduled session on the needs of Native Americans. Two individuals from the NAU Teacher Corps also were invited to address the session. One was a Hopi and the other a Navajo. As had been my experience at Purdue and Gary, I assumed my job at the session was to give a heavy rap and to confront the need to change what was being done in education with Native children. Hence I prepared and delivered a very critical talk, based on the book "My Brother's Keeper," a decisive treatise about the BIA. My sense of politics was way off and though it fed my arrogance and grandiose ego, it probably did more harm than good. My two partners from the Teacher Corps made sure they sat far away from me to show their disassociation with my views.

My speech probably got back to the authorities at both NAU and the BIA in Washington. In addition, my liaisons with Delphia, plus my rule-breaking habit of taking NAU cars to Albuquerque was casting a shadow on my reputation as perceived by NAU officials, especially by Chancellor, Dr. Gillenwater and the University President, J. Lawrence Walkup, whom I had loudly accused in every bar in town of being a "G*d D*m Corn Farmer from Missouri." Walkup had fired a Native American staff member who dared to attend the trial of several Navajos who had committed offenses unrelated to NAU. My alcoholic friends reminded me that I had to make amends to him for my behavior, which I did in due time. I can't fault my heart for those days in Gary and NAU, but my sophistication, with which I had seemingly been successful in those earlier days, had suddenly turned to zilch.

BECAUSE THE EAGLE FLEW

His daughter, ("Why did you leave?") confronted Tom Lee Jones in the movie "MISSING." Jones replied, "Because the eagle flew." I find this to be as good of an "excuse" as any as to why, in the dark of night in 1974, I left Charlene and my family to return to Window Rock. It was a lonely and anxiety-ridden ride ending at 3:00 in the morning. Sad – yet as I write I have made progress at mitigating and resolving differences with contemporary significant others without suddenly going out the back door. This behavior had become a problem-solving mechanism, which I began using all too frequently.

Charlene and I separated in 1974 and were divorced in 1976. I shifted to become a partner to Delphia and stepfather to her four children. We were married traditionally by Medicine Man James Silverhorn and were blessed with cedar smoke and eagle feathers at a site way out in the country west of Anadarko, Oklahoma. I thought I had truly passed into the Valley of Shangri-La and the realization of all my dreams, both professional and personal. I had a perfect combination of elements that seemed to match life long dreams – the exquisite beauty of the Navajo Reservation at Canyon de Chelly and Monument Valley, partner to a mystical Lady of the Lake who was active in high impact projects and immersion in roles of power and prominence wherein I could twist the Tiger's Tail, act out resentments and settle the score for what I saw as institutional incompetence and lack of creativity within universities.

THE KIOWA GOURD DANCE

The Gourd Dance is a type of Native American celebration ceremony and it is believed that the dance originated with the Kiowa tribe. Gourd dances are often held to coincide with a pow wow, although the gourd dance embodies its own unique history. Gourd dancing may precede the pow wow or it can be a separate event not directly connected with a pow wow.

I had even been anointed as a Kiowa Gourd Dancer – but accepted the role with reluctance. I did not wish to be a "wannabe" since Native communities had enough trouble already with outsiders entering to assume aspects of their culture and their rituals. I give myself credit that although designated as a head gourd dancer, I followed the rituals and régime, as would traditional Kiowas. However, one afternoon in the Kiowa capital of Carnegie, at the bequest of Delphia's medicine man Uncle James Haungooah (Silverhorn), I was told to go out in the arena and dance. As fate would have it the aluminum top of my gourd came off and flew through the sky. Although James was revered enough to receive a horse when he showed up at a gourd dance, he could not get me a pass to be the only white guy to dance at a Kiowa Ceremony in Carnegie. But this narrative is getting too far ahead of itself. Both Delphia and I had to go through a critical and personal metamorphosis before our ceremonial marriage.

A Kiowa story recounts the tale of a young man who had been separated from the rest of his tribe. Hungry and dehydrated after many days of travel, he approached a hill and heard unusual sounds coming from the other side. Upon investigation he saw a red wolf singing and dancing on its hind legs. The man listened to the songs all afternoon and through the night and when morning came, the wolf spoke to him and told him to take the dance and the songs back to the Kiowa people. The "howl" at the end of each gourd dance song is a tribute to the red wolf. The Kiowa Gourd Dance was once part of the Kiowa Sun Dance ceremony.

The dance in the Kiowa Language is called "Ti-ah pi-ah" which means "ready to go, ready to die."

The Kiowa consider this dance as their dance since "Red Wolf" gave it to them. It has spread to many other tribes and societies, most of which do not have the blessing of the Kiowa Elders. Some gourd societies do not distinguish race as a criteria, and even non-Indians can and are inducted into their gourd societies. The Kiowa gourd dance society however only inducts Indians of half blood or more. Many participants may be older men, and the dance is less energetic and less physically demanding than most pow wow dances. Some of the Gourd Dances that are held go on all afternoon and into the evening when it finally cools off enough so that more energetic dances can begin. Some Tribal dances feature only Gourd Dancing.

The gourd or rattle is traditionally made from aluminum can. The gourd rattle can have beadwork on the handle. The gourd sash is tied around the waist. Either a gourd blanket or a vest may be worn over the shoulders. The vest or blanket has two colors: with the blue being worn over the right shoulder and the red being worn over the left to symbolize the heart.

JAMES SILVERHORN

"That white man may tell the federal government on us," James Silverhorn (Haun-gooah) said quietly that day out in the middle of nowhere in western Oklahoma. Delphia and the family were visiting with Uncle James Silverhorn once again during the many forays to his house out in the wilds. There is no other explanation I have for the great fortune to be introduced and then come to know such an awesome man.

The significance in which James was held not only by the Kiowa people but also by southern Tribal groups across America cannot be overstated. He was revered as the mentor for Native American Church members who flocked from across the land to his doorstep. He was the keeper of five of the ten sacred Kiowa bundles.

Arrival at his "ranch" down the rutty and bumpy dirt road was always fraught with some anxiety. It wasn't James. It was his dog that liked to bite tires and could actually puncture one.

Delphia and I were married in the back bedroom of James's home where he kept the sacred bundles. The Kiowa bundles, the "Ten Grandmothers" as they were known, were the spiritual manifestation of the existence of the Kiowa people. If and when the bundles were gone, the Kiowa would cease to exist. Traditionally a bundle would re-side with and be taken care of by a designated Kiowa family. Four families had be-queathed him with five of their bundles.

Five large medicine sized bundles hung from the bedroom ceiling covered with fresh buckskin. The bundles contained artifacts of great significance to the spiritual and his-torical record of the Kiowa. Sometime after James' death the H. family and I were visiting Uncle Bill Hunting Horse when he discussed the bundle he kept and even opened it up. I was startled and surprised. He had earlier shown Delphia and his wife some of the contents of the bundle, which he said could not be revealed. To me he revealed two objects. The first was an extinct bird known as a sea hawk. The second was one of the most amazing things I had ever seen – a small white buffalo body with hair, horns and all. It was not a made up like a doll. It looked just like what a normal sized buffalo would look like if it were shrunk to the size of a chipmunk.

The day of my marriage to Delphia, James put a large frying pan on the back burner in the kitchen and once it had reached maximum temperature he placed cedar branches from the sacred Rainy Mountain in it. As the dense smoke poured out and rose through the air, he took an eagle feather fan and began brushing the smoke from head to toe on Delphia and sang in a deep baritone some sweet Kiowa blessings. The Kiowa language is beautiful. It has a nasal twang that seems to emit right out of the nose of the speaker. James's surname, Haungooah (Hahn Goo' Ah), is a classic example of that sound. On the other hand, the Navajo language has more of a guttural sound with glottal stops ending the vowels, chopping off sound with constriction at the back of the throat.

Cemeteries generally give me the creeps and bring up some confusion as to what death really means. But, the Kiowa-Comanche Cemetery where my son Jerrell is buried is a quiet and serene plot of cottonwood trees towering over the red soil of western Oklahoma. James, his two sons and many other Kiowa elders, including Uncle Max, have been laid to rest out there. On son Jerrell's gravestone I left a mug from the University of Illinois. Inside is a little plastic bag with a note on it addressed to him. "Behave yourself – listen and pay attention." A psychic from Denver told me that Jerrell did not want to stay on earth too long and that is why he left so early in life.

James's comment to me that hot and humid summer day in the Oklahoma wilds was in response to the thirteen eagle feathers Delphia had given him for his creation of a fan. Being in James's presence gave me a feeling of reverence that superseded anything I had experienced from the monastic Benedictines on the day I asked permission to become a priest. James's stoicism and sense of universal awareness and power in the face of the alcoholic death of two sons, Bo and Billy Joe, the horrible persecution of the Kiowa people and the abuse and murder of his cousins in Oklahoma jails had not dampened his spirit.

While I believe the poem I wrote in honor of son Jerrell was a construct of my literal brain, James offered the musical strain that emerged to give life to that poem. Kiowa oral traditions note their migration from the north in Montana southward, following the sun into Oklahoma where they reside today.
There is a reason why one of the most potent weapons of the United States is a Kiowa

helicopter. The Kiowa are renowned for the fierceness and bravery as partners with the Comanches. There is a reason why the National Congress of American Indians initiates their annual conference with the appearance of the Kiowa Black Leggings Society.

DOHOSAN, KIOWA WARRIOR
From the southern plains My Grandfather
By sash belt anchored You dodged Osage lance and arrow
Like an eagle soaring through the sun,
You brought my heart your fire and destiny
Dohason, my Grandfather from the Southern Plains,
Kiowa Warrior
Aho Aho Aho, (lyrics and melody by G. Knowles for son Jerrell)

INSANELY SOBER

Attempting to relate to Delphia in a sane and sober way got more and more difficult. One day at Griego's Tavern the bartender asked me if I wanted to have a drink with him. He was a strange looking dude; the end of his nose had been bitten off during a bar fight. When I told him I wanted a Coke he gave me such an angry look that I felt I was back at the bar on the Wabash in West Lafayette. That was the last time I was in Griego's.

One Sunday while heading back to my Title I project site at Kayenta I arrived at the BIA living quarters and walked into Delphia's house to find her embarrassingly compromised. Later that week I told her I could not see her again because I needed to avoid situations that tempted me to drink. We talked briefly in Flagstaff and agreed to stop. I was in Flag with three busloads of 100 Navajo teacher aides on the way to a conference in Anaheim.

After a two-hour drive from Kayenta, of a rainy Friday I arrived in Flagstaff at the back room of a steak house for a meeting with my alcoholic friends. They had a birthday cake with one candle atop it in the center of the table. I was totally surprised that they remembered I had gone a whole year without alcohol.

DELPHIA IN SAN DIEGO

Life in San Diego that summer of 1973 was a magnificent time for me to heal the past five years of turmoil. Each afternoon I swam and sunbathed off the shores at La Jolla. I saw change occur in my personal life as I attended a meeting of alcoholic friends at which a lady revealed the deep problems and issues that were the bases of her addiction to alcohol. My God, I thought, a person could in fact lift the hood of his spirit and psyche and find where the wires were loose. I went to my apartment and began a 12-hour writing marathon, producing 15 legal sized pages identifying the anxious, egotistical, angry roots of my soul. It seemed like the first time I allowed myself to take an honest look at myself without the filter of arrogance, grandiosity, shame or unworthiness.

I had arranged for Delphia to spend two weeks with me in San Diego. It was the first time she had seen any ocean, and at the beach she turned her back to the incoming Pacific rollers and was literally knocked off her feet by one big wave. She started cursing me as though it was my fault. Amid our laughter at the local fish market I suggested the sea bass. She ordered a hamburger, disdaining the fish. Finally, she grudgingly took a bite of sea bass and ended up eating my entire portion.

On our way back to Arizona the last weekend together a tune came over the radio. Expecting that my relationship with Delphia would soon end, Dion Warwick's song, *"Touch me in the morning, then just walk away, we don't have tomorrow, but we have yesterday,"* brought about a deep sadness in me. As we rolled into Flagstaff little did I know that it was not the end, but "the end of the beginning."

Delphia called me three weeks after I had told her that we could no longer continue the relationship and asked to attend a meeting of my alcoholic friends. As I write she has not had a drink in over 40 years.

Kiowa Princess

RICK HYDE—A MARK TWAIN APPEARS

The deep terror, loneliness, remorse and shame gnawing inside me seemed to melt away each time I talked to Rick and his friends who insisted that I deserved to be happy, joyous and free. For the first time in my life, and in the presence of other alcoholics, every cell in my body seemed to relax. I learned quickly that I could contact a group of recovering alcoholics almost anytime and anywhere. This fact was confirmed by me many times – one noon in Manhattan, one midnight in Washington and down a dark street in Kino Bay, Mexico, where I always found a group of alcoholics gathered who never failed to excitedly welcome me as though I were a long lost friend. I also found that being with a group of recovering alcoholics was a safe place where I could tell the truth about what was going on with me without fear of judgment or criticism. I didn't need to worry whether or not my acceptance was dependent on whom or what I was outside the group. I had seen a very powerful Senator as well as Navy admirals at a Georgetown Episcopal church interfacing within the local community of fellow alcoholics with no acknowledgment or deference toward status, power or prestige. One left resumes at the door of these meetings, absent of any need to identify worldly achievements to gain respect. Those fellows treated me like a survivor of a shipwreck— glad I made it into the lifeboat.

Rick Hyde and other alcoholics shared with me how they had overcome the domination of demons that had driven them to silence the cacophony of voices, the lapses of sanity and morality with alcohol.

Asking question of everyone, I learned why folks with such horrid stories could laugh and rise above all the "arrows and slings of outrageous fortune" and I began to practice their regimen. They said I had "to open up the hood and find what wires were loose" in my soul and psyche. I had to find the loose wires and reconnect. They said I was not an inherently rotten person, but that I was born a wholly valuable and lovable being who had acquired some very bad behavior causing me harm to people and even institutions but more often than not to myself. I learned that I had to make direct amends to people and entities for the harm that I had done, and that I could be relieved of the weight and consequences of my bad habits. I was promised that over the years I would be given gifts of body, mind and soul that would provide that lasting joy and freedom I had fruitlessly pursued through the use of alcohol. One group of these alcoholics retained a room in Gallup, New Mexico with a mural covering an entire wall depicting an enormous black thunderstorm with an eagle flying above it. I was told that if I did my best to do all the things suggested I would realize joy, which is "the happiness of the soul lifted above all circumstances" – the exact motive, always, for my drinking.

My certainty about the regimen my friends had given me to help in avoiding the black abyss of alcoholism never really left me. But my naiveté and belief that I was not naturally attractive nor charming prompted me to use alcohol to rid myself of the fears, inhibitions and low self esteem repressing any conviction that I was a caring and charming being. Also oppressive were the impediments of my Catholic conscience and the awareness of my marriage commitments. Again, and luckily, the repeated drunken escapades did not end in tragedy. However, I was told prior to my second year at Kayenta Boarding School never to enter the teacher subdivision of the BIA again. In one of my local drunks I had backed out of a driveway into a car parked across the street from Delphia.

OBSESSION

The continued and obsessive need to attract and acquire affection was considered as a healing, as a soothing balm to my uncertain, damaged ego. Of course the expectation of such relationships to fill the empty hole generated by the absence of a caring mother never bore fruition. With dedicated insensitivity those notions were abandoned in a continual search for the perfect female. My lack of empathy for such acquaintances astounds me to this day. Empathy was the core of my coherency, yet relationships with females were totally blocked from empathy.

It is reasonable but not justifiable that this disdain, this empty consideration for the feelings of those with whom I had serious relationships could have been caused by the abusive experiences with my mother. This is an explanation – not an excuse, nor a defense. The recipients of my insensitivity and pain were hardly assuaged by the probable dysfunctions of my personality. Again, I must note that I do not 'blame' my mother, but hold her behavior responsible for its impact on me. She was a victim of abuse and did the best she could all of her life. (Yes, I love you MOM).

Kiowa Black Leggings Society

DEEP INTO THE SOUL

I still remember the night in the old Flagstaff Hospital malpais building when they poured ether alcohol through the gauze over my nose, giving me that first hit of false joy and ease. Along with the intense pain of an infected appendix those demons of shame, fear, loneliness and anger suddenly vanished. From that night foreword alcohol became my solution to all trials and tribulations both in life and in my head.

THE DAWN BREAKS

I received notification of a special conference to be held at Temple featuring Jean Piaget, a famous zoologist who had revealed significant theories about early childhood cognition. I had not had a drink for several months and was committed to stay away from alcohol.

However, cocktails at the conference reception for Piaget overpowered my resolve and my old hunting habits kicked in. Complete failure to locate any excitement brought me to the Delphi Hotel Bar. Something clicked deep in my mind that alcohol would not bring me the sense of peace, the escape from disaster that I had gained by being supported by other alcoholics who had shown that they were having a 'happy, joyous and free' existence without alcohol. Out on the streets of Philly I located a restaurant and begin using sugar in place of my customary medication, consuming a large amount of strawberry shortcake.

I had no premonition that the end was coming, that I was about to face a transformation from despair to an embarkation on the road to Shangri La.

I landed in Farmington, New Mexico and was met by Delphia at the plane. After a quick supper at a root beer restaurant we went to the "Office" – the Office Tavern, that is. I began drinking beer and at closing time I held a half-quart of Budweiser in my hand on the way to a motel in west Farmington.

A brilliant light exposed the folly of my illusionary romantic mind when at the hotel I saw signs indicating that the bed had already been used. Any sanctimony had been wiped out long ago by my carousing and drinking, and I did not react with any defference to Delphia. I had seen the Navajo gentleman at the "Office" and noticed his keen attention toward the two of us. That was my last drink of alcohol. It was the early morning of May 28th, 1972 – over 45 years ago as I write.

I had been made aware of the existence of support groups for alcoholics and I was given a local Flagstaff phone number. I called the number late that Thursday afternoon. One Rick Hyde answered with a deep resonating velvet voice and told me he was with a bunch of alcoholics and that I was welcome to join them. The first person I saw in the halfway house that night was a Mark Twain look-a-like who identified himself as the person I had talked to—Rick Hyde. Our brief interface that night initiated a 25-year friendship. Rick had taken a tough withdrawal and separation route away from alcohol and heroin addictions. He had done Cold Turkey at separate times, getting off of both. He had survived a very tumultuous life – he was wounded in the Korean War and had been bayoneted in the stomach when the Chinese overran a field hospital. He claimed he was supported by a universal 'higher power.' His life of recovery brought me back to the belief that there might be some power outside of myself that I could lean on to make it through those tough challenges that seem to bring me so close to self destruction and death. Any faith in the Catholic God of my youth had long been obliterated by cynicism and mischievous behavior.

Near the end of summer a grants administrator for programs at NAU informed me of the funding of a Title I program (for 'at-risk students') at Kayenta Boarding School, which I could direct. But, I was told that I could not "see *that* woman ever again" and of course, I had been thrown out of the BIA compound where she lived. It was 1973 and I was sober for one year, but still seeing Delphia in Kayenta and at Griegos' Tavern on south San Francisco Street in Flagstaff. During the Title I program year I, of course, spent most of my time frustratingly trying to morph the school's program to 'better meet the needs of the Navajo children.' I was also in a running battle with a new principle armed with a personality attendant to the culture of a prominent church group and the quintessential superior and dominant white overseer of the Navajo-(i.e., whom I annointed with a Navajo epithet, a *Chindee Beligana*— 'ghost of a coyote').

THE YEAR OF THE TITLE I PROJECT

Word came that the Early Childhood Program was not going to be continued with a grant renewal. It had only been set up for one year. I arranged for two Navajo Teachers to travel to the Offices of Education and the Office of Senator Ted Kennedy to lobby for funds to continue to educate Navajos to become teachers. The agent handling the grant from the Office of Education had switched to a women's issues desk and we did not meet with the BIA. However, we were able to meet with Senator Kennedy's staff that alerted me to the fact that a significant program with funding (called Title IV of the Indian Education Act) was imminent. The two teachers from the Early Childhood program were scheduled to go on to New York from Washington before returning back to Arizona and the Four Corners area at *Teec Nos Pos*, (Navajo for "Round Trees"). Fretting about the fact that these two natives could be extremely vulnerable to the wilds of the great city, I followed them to New York and found that they could handle the inner city much better than I had, and had toured all the key sites in Manhattan. The three of us spent an evening at the Cellar Door nightspot where we were treated to comedian Gabe Kaplan who would soon initiate the first of 97 episodes of "WELCOME HOME CARTER," also the debut of John Travolta.

ESCAPE FROM DROWNING – BUT LATE

Knowing I was struggling with difficult times including the quest to establish a new life sans alcohol, my mentor in sobriety, Rick Hyde, and another sober alcoholic, Rudy, traveled over 400 miles round trip to Kayenta to see me. We had a meeting scheduled and I waited and waited, feeling disappointed that they hadn't shown up when they came barging through the door soaking wet and covered with sand. They had hit a flooded spot in the road at full throttle

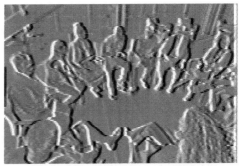
Alcoholic Brothers & Sisters

and turned their car upside down, barely escaping drowning. This poignantly reaffirmed my faith in the caring of alcoholics for one another, that they would go to any length to offer loving support. I would test their metal many times all over the U.S. and Canada and never found them wanting. I found them at midnight in DC, at noon in Manhattan, down a dark road in Mexico – and seventy thousand of them in the

Olympic Stadium in Montreal.

I had found other sober alcoholics in the Kayenta area and we would meet at the local city hall called the "Chapter House," a familiar community center in every sector of the Navajo reservation. That meeting was advertized at an international level. I would make twenty cups of coffee and wait and wait. Few people ever showed up. One night however four gentlemen from Mexican Hat Utah arrived but none of them spoke English. Not surprisingly, we as alcoholics understood each other without language.

SUMMER OF '73

At the end of my project at Kayenta I was frantically looking for a job. There was a strange situation at NAU wherein a regular position in early childhood education was being offered. I was highly encouraged to apply. It was offered with the support of Dean Faucet and most likely Chancellor Virgil Gillenwater. On the other hand and because of the always present Machiavellian politics of universities, Assistant Dean Dynoska was supporting a third member of the Early Childhood Project, one Dee C. The deep drama of being set up to compete for a position incorporating under the table dealings fired my hostility and, still suffering from arrogance and grandiosity, I obstinately refused to apply for the position. The Dean and others asked me, "Aren't you going to apply for that position?"

However, I did get my hopes up that I would have a job at International University in San Diego as I had gotten a summer teaching appointment there through the efforts of one of the evaluators of the Gary-Purdue Early Childhood Project. He was an Afro-American professor from the International University in San Diego. International University had campuses not only in San Diego but in London, Steamboat Springs, Kenya and Hawaii – a dream job. I wished to share my recovery from alcoholism with my classes at International University. Bad choice, as the President's wife was known to be a practicing alcoholic and he was not about to add one to his faculty.

I reached the last house on the block at International and didn't know where to go from that point on. I had turned down the application for the NAU job and had cashed in most of my chips from contacts. My file and my reputation at Illinois were suspect and things at home were in a state of estrangement. Son Bob and I reveled in the artist Steely Dan, especially his rendition of "*Reeling In The Years, Stowing Away The Time.*" I had reached a point like so many other professionals in the early '70's wherein a pedestrian, normal life was no longer possible for me.

Still being overwhelmed with self-centeredness, I did not consider the impact that another move would have on my family. They had just adjusted and settled in to the Flagstaff community and now they would be faced with a new place and peer group.

The Navajo Division Of Education
The Navajo Teacher Education Development Program

I can't remember what prompted me to write a letter to Ralph Davis at the Navajo Division of Education in Window Rock, Arizona, but I do know that within me there existed a great love for those Northern Arizona lands and for the Navajo people. At the time it seemed I had no control over the planning of my professional life. I felt that I was shamelessly inconsiderate of the lives of my wife and children who had been moving around from Illinois to Arizona to Indiana and New Jersey and back to Arizona. I felt ready to head out yet again through the back door of life and its problems.

Ralph Davis and other members of the fledgling Navajo Division of Education presented a perfect set of potential conditions that could benefit from creative planning and might well produce immediate, concrete change in educating dispossessed Navajo children. In some cases those children lagged eight years behind in achievement levels. The notion of providing linguistic and culturally relevant teachers capable of infusing community presence into the Bureau of Indian Affairs' ineffective schools was seen at the time as a tremendous opportunity just waiting for the Navajo to make it happen.

Ralph Davis

It was around three in the afternoon San Diego time and I was just about to head for the beach in La Jolla when the phone rang. Ralph was one of these quiet, intense Navajo gentlemen who spoke slowly, with great deliberation. I had been humbled by the support he gave me the first year of the Early Childhood Project. "Can you come to a meeting tomorrow in Window Rock, at 9AM?" Brushing aside the fact that this meant a 12-hour drive over the mountains and through a torrid desert, then through Phoenix and on to Gallup and into Window Rock, I said, "yes." The speed limit in those days was 85mph on the major highways. I arrived in Gallup, New Mexico at 4AM and went to bed in the motel for a 3-hour sleep.

Senator Kennedy had come through with extensive grant money under Title IV of the Indian Education act to create teacher education programs for Indian Tribes. The Division of Education (NDOE) received $500,000 every year over a three-year period to "train" Navajo teacher aides with regard to their certification and their teaching degrees. The Division of Education, with whom I had formed a robust working relationship were looking for someone to direct their program. I led the pack of potential directors but had to run the gamut before a very dynamic board of Navajo leaders. Too, I needed the blessing of the most influential Indian education leader in the U.S., Dillon Platero, the creator of the first Indian controlled school, Rough Rock, in the Bureau of Indian Affairs and the U.S. in general.

Dillon Platero

Dillon Platero vied to become Chairman of the Navajo Tribal Counsel, but his image suffered due to his being from Cañoncito, near Albuquerque – a separate group of Navajos known for siding with the U.S. Army in their war against the Navajo. Platero had a running mate from Kinlichee (red houses) area west of Window Rock. But the latent mistrust of Navajos from Cañoncito negated a successful bid for the Chairmanship, one that could have anchored in one of the most progressive epics in Navajo Tribal history. Platero had created a Navajo Education Association called DINE' BI-OLTA – Navajo for "People's Education." He also founded and was then elected as the first president of the National Indian Education Association. Platero was tightly connected to the U.S. Office of Education and to a complex of private foundations in New York, particularly that of the Phelps Stokes Foundation.

Dillon's partner had been Doctor Sam Billison, the president of the Navajo Code Talker Association. The Code Talkers, whose Navajo language befuddled Japanese access to secret communications, were reputed to have turned the tide of the war in the Pacific.

Platero's vision and energy knew no bounds and as I found out, it would be a thrilling but exhausting task to keep up with him. On the other hand, Billison would be a constant stumbling block to overcome.

The NTEDP Board

Though Dillon's office was located in a red stone BIA building, most of the Division offices were down the road in a complex of doublewides. I walked into one of the conference rooms at 9AM that August 15, 1973 and sat amidst the eagle eyes of eight of the most powerful Navajos in the Tribe. The grievous experiences of the dispossessed had been drilled into me in Gary, South Chicago and Philadelphia to the degree that I, even as a white male, was able to sustain the close scrutiny of the newly formed Board of the Navajo Teacher Education Development Program (NTEDP).

Board Members

Samuel Billison was the Board Chairman. Board member Mrs. Marjorie Thomas, Co-Director of the NAU Early Childhood Project, was a strong ally of mine. I guess I had convinced her of my commitment during that one-year cruise around the Navajo Reservation (Rez). She had apparently excused my drunken pass at her during an Albuquerque field trip to Old Town.

Board members represented various sectors of the Navajo Nation. A woman from Shiprock, one Stella Lee, was an in-your-face type whom you could never get past with a line of B.S. Another lady, a member of the powerful Arviso family of Crownpoint, made up the female threesome part of the Board. Another gentleman, a Council Delegate from Crownpoint, later became a Navajo judge. He was a gentle supporter all my days on the Navajo. My experience was that once you made through the right of passage with a Navajo and their families it was almost impossible to sever their acceptance of you. What a difference from individuals in our greater society, so often present only as fair weather friends.

Guy Gorman was co-founder of the Navajo Community College, a tribal councilman and a well-known and respected member of a prominent Navajo family. Finally, Tribal Councilman Don Noble from Steamboat rounded out the NTEDP Board. While certainly an imposing group to address, the process was nothing like those intense interfaces with my Black friends in Gary and South Chicago.

THE PROGRAM

The basic structure of the program outlined in the grant, and envisioned by Platero, was to establish five teacher training sites strategically placed at growth centers in each sector of the Navajo Nation – on the New Mexico side at Crownpoint in the Southeast, at Shiprock in the northeast and on the Arizona side at Tuba City, Ganado and Chinle.

Each site would contain a group of approximately 30 students for a potential roster of 150 students.

After passing their third degree, the Board voted to appoint me as the program director. I found that special dispensation had to be granted to me as a non-Navajo placed in such a position.

An upcoming issue involved selecting the institutions that would deliver the program at the five sites across the Navajo Nation. The next day the Board interviewed representatives from the Universities of New Mexico, Arizona and Brigham Young University. NAU was not interviewed. BYU was included to serve the Utah sector of the reservation but was ultimately rejected due to its insistence that students take mandatory courses in the Mormon Religion. As I write the urban myth persists that I had personally rejected NAU'S participation in the program when in fact I had no say in the choice of institutions.

STAFF

Dr. Allyn Spence

My associates in Window Rock and at the Universities of Arizona and New Mexico were quite different in their backgrounds, and quite exceptional. Allyn S at the University of Arizona had two PhD's in Anthropology and specialized in motives and personalities. His grandfather was the real lawyer character in the book, "To Kill a Mocking Bird." His expertise in analyzing and maneuvering institutional dynamics and organizational skills encouraged the college of education and university administration to make accommodations essential to the success of a field based program at sites 500 miles away from Tucson. It was almost impossible to determine Allyn's motives, but I knew they were always benevolent though not what the doctor ordered.

Dr. Don K

Don K on the other hand who directed the University of New Mexico program was an anomaly, and I only got what he was staging at any given time. He often wore black leather pantalones (black wide leg pants) and showcased the finest art quality Navajo jewelry. He was a jaunty individual with a perpetual mischievous smile. He did get things done. To my amazement he set up small plane landings for him and his staff by blockading a road at Teec Nos Pos; students with their pickups created a temporary runway. Unfortunately, Don's motives were often irregular, designed to further his professional advancement at other's expense. Appearing on the balcony of a motel during a program meeting it was apparent he had spent the night with one of the program students. In spite of these negatives Don did effectively manage a broad number of field-based programs all over New Mexico, including those at many Pueblo nations.

Lucille S.

Don's university assistant was a Navajo, one Lucille S from a Navajo Rez community northeast of Gallup. She was very bright, and a highly experienced educator. In the early stages of the program she worked in the field supervising practicum experiences of students from the Crownpoint site. Lucille later and for many years directed the "Native American Program" on the UNM Albuquerque campus. She struggled with fear of flying and was told by a medicine man to wear a scarf around her neck that cured her weekly anxieties on the plane flights to Tee Nos Pos.

Dr. Robert N.

Allyn S's associate in Tucson, Dr. Robert Norris, a Navajo from the Western part of the Reservation was of a totally different ilk than his New Mexico counterpart. He had a PhD from UNM (University of New Mexico) and a rather rude personality — a belligerent sort of fellow who would fire off confrontational comments at the drop of a hat. Appearing from out of a rainstorm in a trench coat and foggy glasses into a program board meeting one day he was accosted by boardmember Stella Lee, who asked, "Who are you?" Bob N retorted sarcastically, "Well, who are you?!" The battle lines were drawn and persisted for years.

Bob N appeared at student gatherings in Tucson in a standard Navajo ten-gallon hat and made outlandish statements. He was once responsible for a puzzling travel event: in addition to the use of a variety of forms of travel – plane, bus, hitchhiking, taxi – he had this time parked a Hertz rent-a-car that had been sideswiped on the right side in a rental return lot. University officials never learned the source of the damage. One afternoon in Manhattan a taxi driver kept putting an index finger at Bob's chest, calling him "Chief" until Bob finally grabbed that finger and disjointed it. Bob had a regrettable condition attendant to many Navajos, which made him look 90 degrees out of his eyes toward the left. I found this totally upsetting one afternoon dashing up a highway north of Tucson with an inebriated Bob N at the wheel. The overarching point is that Norris's brashness created conditions encouraging hundreds of Navajo women to become teachers.

Dr. Lawrence I.

Laurence I. was a graduate student at Arizona working on a PhD and became part of the Arizona staff during the program's second half. Lawrence had been a Navajo Ranger who intervened in an attack by Navajo Police on a helpless victim. Later caught alone he was badly beaten by the same Police, losing his sight in one eye. Lawrence came from an influential family near Cow Springs in western Navajo. His grandmother was a medicine woman and like many Navajos who travel far and wide, his grandfather had played in a jazz band in Greenwich Village in Manhattan. Lawrence later became the focus and center point for an "insurgency" at Navajo Community College.

Planes from Albuquerque and Tucson flew out each Friday morning with staff scheduled to teach all day at one of the program sites. The on-site teaching staff were not
graduate assistants, but many were full professors, excited and happy about coming to
the Reservation to instruct Navajo students. Later when I was teaching Ed Psych and
Child Development to the Ganado site students, the author of the textbook, David
Berliner, actually flew up and coached the class. I had this same professor honored at
a powwow during that same period. Face to face student exposure to leaders in education, I felt, countered the subservient position that the BIA and society in general imposed on minorities by holding their power and prestige over their heads.

The staff for the Navajo Division of Education included one lawyer, Rosalyn Silver,
who is, as I write, a federal judge in Phoenix. Platero's chief assistant was Tom F, an
extremely creative get-it-done fellow married to a renowned anthropologist's daughter.

NTEDP Staff

I had a series of excellent secretaries, or should I say administrative assistants. My
first was a member of a powerful Navajo family, the Bluehouses, and I believe
Platero picked her to ensure a good start to the program. Maggie A was the second
secretary who was a genius at reading my script, which scrawl deteriorated in quality
as the demands to produce proposals increased. An additional staff associate, Joan P,
was especially helpful, as she had worked in the U.S. Education Department in D.C.
for the director of Indian Programs. She was a member of the Crow tribe of Montana,
a tribe closely connected to the Kiowa tribe. The Kiowa tribe had resided long ago in
Montana close to the Crow people, eventually migrating south into western Oklahoma. The interface among the Navajo Nation committees and its departments such
as finance, along with the participating universities of Arizona and New Mexico, the
Bureau of Indian Affairs and the reservation-wide students in the program was a
quantitative enterprise fraught with complexity. The people I worked with were
bright, capable and copacetic with the cultural norms.

However near the end of my tenure I was faced with Joan P coming to work with
black eyes, injuries perpetrated by a husband who was from the Sioux Tribe and employed by the Indian Health Service.

One of my employees, Ray E, devolved into a "my man Friday" because of my inability to set either boundaries or expectations for him. He did not come to his job
with the experience and skill of my other staff. He was a kind fellow who lived in the
small shack without running water and took care of his grandmother and younger sis-

ter. He baked bread in large coffee cans and cooked breakfast in an electric skillet on his desk in our office. Staying with him at a large hotel in Tucson I suffered some distress due to the stench of unwashed stockings. I sprayed the room with hair spray but it barely killed the smell. Acceptance of the broad conditions existing among our human brothers and sisters looms as a superior goal of brotherly love.

My successor in the role as director of NTEDP, a Navajo, immediately replaced Ray who moved to Tucson to join another Navajo student in a private business venture. Actually Ray had been the needed emotional support from a male persona that completed the female part of my staff.

Rosalyn Moore (now Federal Judge Rosalyn Silver) was a lawyer exclusively for the Navajo Division of Education. She fit in a unique box of her own. She was a beautiful blonde without any of the mythical attributes attendant to that persona. She was very professional, easy going and stable. During a staff meeting one day Platero kept bending down behind his desk until someone finally asked what the hell he was doing. He replied that he was eating a hamburger and he didn't want to hurt Ros's feelings because he knew she was a vegetarian – quintessential Navajo humor. Rosalyn, Platero and I attended a meeting in Washington; I left the bar to meet with my sober alcoholic friends and she and Platero remained. Later I was called into Platero's assistant Tom F's office and was asked if I smoked pot. Apparently, Platero had mistaken the combined smells of my cigarette and Baron Cologne for the scent of marihuana.

PROGRAM INITIATION

After the appointment and my the decision to go with the universities of New Mexico and Arizona, I set about initiating the timing parameters inherent within programs and classes set at the field sites. I commented that we would probably begin the program in the spring semester, allowing enough time for all the startup tasks to be completed. It was around mid-August at the time of the board meeting. Platero said, "I want to start this fall." The faith in community leadership icons I had endorsed in my Gary and Temple

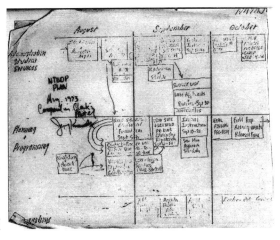

days caused me to immediately accept the fall launching of the program without question or argument. We had really bought the wild wind. There were students to identify and recruit, transcript acquisitions to institute, university contracts to be formulated and agreed upon and classrooms to be established at each of the five sites.

I developed a timeline/task chart vertically by weeks and horizontally by the functions of program. Peering at the chart one morning I realized it looked like the terrazzo tile in the floor of traditional bathrooms. Strangely enough, its existence provided me with a sense of control and do-ability.

A pool of potential students existed from the previous Early Childhood Program participants and they in turn acted as recruiters for the NTEDP. Only applicants with two years of college credit could participate. The Board members also had their list of potential students in their areas and made the appropriate contacts. My staff made the connections and set a deadline for delivery of transcripts to Window Rock. Transcripts came by fax, by mail, were hand carried and in one case delivered by horseback. We had only ten working days to recruit, record and analyze transcripts, establish university contracts, procure classroom space, forge a liaison with the BIA, with Head Start, with public school employers of the students plus send out notices for the first day of class.

I found myself signing one page working agreements stipulating the parameters of the program with both Universities. Still, I had no ultimate authority to commit the Navajo Tribe to anything. There was no hesitancy from the University of Arizona because a field based program serving many Arizona tribes had already been done. But, in the case of New Mexico, (UNM), it was not as simple. At the meeting in Albuquerque with the administrators and staff of the Education department the university was requesting financing for 40% of teaching staff salaries and a 20% overhead on the total grant, plus tuition costs per class per student. When I announced that we could only cover the actual operational costs and staff-prorated salary costs, the UNM reps balked. I then told them that the Tribe was also talking to Antioch College who had launched a number of successful field-based programs. I believe now that the strong presence of the Navajo in New Mexico, one member being in the state senate, and the need at the time for universities to show greater minorities in their student populations tipped the scales in favor of UNM accepting the Tribal terms of the contract. In ten working days we had identified and admitted 150 student participants with a set of unofficial transcripts for each one, a classroom at each of the five sites, notification and explanation of the program imparted to school principals, the BIA and Public school administrators, had signed working agreements with both universities and had set up a schedule for the first class meeting when the fall term began.

I now believe that at the outset of the second year of the program, Allyn S kept shifting the recruiting/admission sites as a means of screening students based upon their ability to find the correct site.

On Site Program Operations

The all day Friday classes onsite focused on the discussion of educational method and theory complemented by observation, analysis, evaluation and practicum in the student's respective classroom. Students were expected to develop relevant and supplementary materials focused on the language and culture of the Navajo. This model copied exactly what was done in many professional training programs, e.g., medical internships.

Abe Tucker of the BIA

The whole idea of allowing personnel to be released from their jobs for a day to receive "training" to upgrade their competencies as educators seemed a simple rationale justifying a key part of the program. But, for anyone in power opposed to seeing a flood of Navajo teachers come into educational operations, "released time" could be and was used as a weapon against the program. I got a call from one Abe T, head of BIA education, who yelled over the phone to me, "You cannot grant leave to teacher aides, you don't even work for the BIA!" I had told students to request leave or use any other guise to make the Friday classes, for I realized that if any entity forced our students to stop going to class the whole program would come to a crashing halt.

One winter evening I remained in a public school board meeting until very late without resolving the issue of released time. The superintendent claimed that it was illegal to pay individuals for "services not rendered." The position was ridiculous as there was a precedent for individuals to attend and receive workshops and upgrades to job skills all across the nation. I had to be in Phoenix the next morning to attend a National Indian Education presentation. It was an eight-hour drive, which I was able to complete by sleeping in the car at the Cameron Trading Post – and by licking my hand, holding it out the window, and then placing it on my neck for the freezing cold to keep me alert.

I was exhilarated that night by the romantic fuel of my relationship with Delphia and breezed through Kayenta in the wee hours past her house with the song "Summer Breeze" by Seals and Crofts playing on my tape deck:

> "See the curtains hanging' in the window ...
> In the evening' on a Friday night ... Little light is shinin' through the window ... Lets me know everything's alright."
> (Seals and Crofts. 1972. Summer Breeze: Warner Bros.)
> I could see the light in the BIA house front window as I road through 160

Shadowy BIA Overcasts

One official for the BIA announced that it was illegal for teacher aides to take federal money for a whole day without providing services. Individual boarding schools across the Navajo did not immediately enforce his decree. I was at a school in Chinle wherein a local supervisor informed the students that they would be fired if they left the "job site" for the Friday NTEDP class. After conferencing with Platero he contacted the two major newspapers, The NAVAJO TIMES at Window Rock and the GALLUP INDEPENDENT, about publicizing this attack on Navajo Education. The then head of the BIA, one Rebecca M, who at one time had worked for Platero at Rough Rock, fired the BIA supervisor.

The slang for NTEDP was the "Honky Program;" many educational officials saw it as an attempt to get rid of white teachers and replace them with Navajos – a gross distortion of the program's intent.

PROGRAM CONTENT

In depth analysis of prior classes and credits were carried out to design a program meeting the requirements for degrees and certifications in either Arizona or New Mexico. Later attempts by the State of Arizona were made to develop teacher exams designed to bar the emerging population of Navajo teachers ready to enter Arizona public schools on the Navajo.

Individual plans were composed for each student prescribing the liberal arts and other non-educational courses to be taken during the summer sessions on campus at Tucson and Albuquerque. Any questions concerning the capability of our Navajo students to cope with liberal arts and other courses on campus were quickly answered when students started earning A's and B's in competition with university wide populations. One 65-year old Navajo teacher aide, Fay Knoki of Ganado, attained an A in symbolic logic at the University of Arizona.

SCHOLARSHIPS FOR SUMMER CLASSES

Platero finagled the Navajo Tribal Scholarship office to provide summer stipends for student tuition, board, and room costs. I estimated individual stipends based on existing factors and sent an official list and a request for an issuance of checks, which checks were duly executed and given to the students. The Scholarship Committee of Navajo council delegates led by an aggressive newly appointed director, one Lawrence G, raised holy hell about my role in the unauthorized dispersing of Tribal funds. In line with the book "CHAORDIC ORGANIZATION," (Hock, Dee. 2000. THE CHAORDIC ORGANIZATION. Berrett -Koehler: Oakland, Ca.), " it is noted that things "get done," basically, by finding ways to get around rules and procedures in organizations – noting the newly accepted concept of chaos over formal organization.

Cigar smoking Eldon H, the Navajo Comptroller, along with members of the Tribal

Council's Finance Committee had to be convinced that the infusion of Navajo teachers into institutions across the reservation would have "some benefit" – a very puzzling request to have to make to Navajo officials and council delegates. To make things worse, I miscalculated the budget, was embarrassed in front of the Tribal Budget and Finance Committee and had to quickly return to the office to make corrections.

Approximately 120 students went to their first summer school sessions – 60 to UNM Albuquerque and 60 to UA Tucson. Each campus had its own unique beauty – UNM with its colorful Pueblo motif buildings and Tucson in its setting amongst waving lines of palm trees.

Bob N and Allyn decided that setting up the students in a frat house with common cooking facilities would be a good thing. Unfortunately, they didn't take into consideration that the Navajo people don't operate like urban aggregations of Pueblo people; they functioned in accordance with their own nomadic history, each family taking care of itself and doing their own thing. Hence the cooking was done in separate rooms on hot plates, totally ignoring the equipment in the downstairs kitchen. The hot plates and air conditioners generated a huge electric bill. Allyn S, under the assumption that Tucson Electric Power Company already owned Navajos back pay for undercharging for their coal, felt justified in challenging the payment of the bill. A Tucson Electric Power Company lawyer finally called Allyn about the unpaid bill. The phone number Allyn gave the lawyer for the NTEDP Student Association was a payphone at a Trading Post in lower Greasewood. After several calls to the number with some old Navajo "hostein" answering, "Yat tah Hay," followed by a conversation in Navajo, the lawyer slammed the phone and finally gave up his efforts at collection.

One late afternoon Platero called me down to his office and told me a student representative had called from Tucson and informed him that they were "out of money." Having just personally handed out scholarship checks, I was shocked. I left Window Rock, slept awhile in Show Low, Arizona, got up in the dark of night and drove on through Globe and south past the mining town of Winkelman and on into north Tucson just as the sun was coming up. Apparently my students had spanned out all over Tucson on a shopping spree, depleting their funds. I can't remember how we mitigated the situation, but as usual, my allies in Tucson and I found a way to replenish the coffers.

My son-in-law, a graduate of the University of Arizona and a current Coconino County planner found a database with colored dots representing the institutions where college graduates resided. All of the Navajo Nation in northeastern Arizona was covered in blue/red dots representing the University of Arizona. It is not unusual to be out in the middle of the Navajo and see caps and shirts with the U of A Wildcat logo on them.

ROMANCE – TO BE CONTINUED

After a long stretch of not communicating with Delphia and more less avoiding going to Kayenta all together, I called one day from Flagstaff to see how she was doing. "I want to go to your alcoholic friends meeting in Flagstaff," she stated. I was amazed, but of course ecstatic. During our ten-year marriage she claimed that I had conned her in San Diego into going to a meeting with my alcoholic friends. It must have impacted her much more than I thought. Nevertheless, I wasn't surprised, as I knew Delphia to be a very bright, strong person. It sealed my fate with that relationship and we were traditionally married out in the red hills of western Oklahoma by James Silverhorn (Hauangooah) among Tribal medicine bags with Kiowa chants, cedar smoke and eagle feather blessings.

DENNEHOTSO HOME WITH THE KIOWAS

I moved to Dennehotso (Navajo for "Grassy Plain"), a BIA school compound on the Navajo twenty miles east of Kayenta. I commuted daily to Window Rock 100 miles to the south to operate the NTEDP. Delphia became pregnant with our son Jerrell and literally kicked me out of the BIA bungalow. I later found out that this was a common occurrence for Kiowa women, so I didn't take it personally. We left the powwow grounds in Flagstaff and went directly to the hospital where I stood and watched our son Jerrell enter the world on June 27, 1976. He was the final link in the powwow troop of Delphia, Hattie, Patty Jo, Denise, and Charlie. Members and sometimes the whole family were honored as head dancers at powwows and I finally accepted a role as a Southern Plains Gourd Dancer, even acting as the head Gourd Dancer on many occasions and as a judge of various Southern Plains dance contests. I became invisible to both Kiowa family convocations and could listen intently to the old folks shared tales of days gone by. One fascinating story was told about Kiowas in a Mexican jail who claimed they could take out a steer's kidney before it hit the ground. Actually, as superb horsemen, Kiowas might possibly have accomplished such a feat by jamming a steer between two horses. Before the horse was acquired, Kiowas bonded with their dogs and still maintain a "Crazy Dog" society of warriors.

WARRIOR SOCIETIES AMONG THE KIOWA

"There were six warrior societies in the Kiowa Tribe during the plains nomad years. Five were for grown warriors, the sixth for boys. The military societies were called 'Dog Soldiers' because of visions and dreams of dogs. The Koitsenko were known as the 'Real Dogs.' All young boys were enrolled in the Rabbit Warrior Society; the sixth recognized warrior society. The other five could be joined as the boys

grew up. The Tiah-pah Society, O-Ho-Mah Warrior Society, Kiowa Black Leggings Warrior Society and Kiowa Gourd Dance Clan are warrior societies. The most skilled members and elite of all the warriors out of all the societies of every branch of the Kiowa were the Koitsenko. The Koitsenko was an honorary group of ten of the greatest warriors who were elected from the five adult warrior societies. The soldier societies policed the campsite and went on hunts and into war." (Wikipedia)

UNCLE MAX'S TALES

The most amusing story I heard was from Max Silverhorn who related a story about Kiowa Chief Dohasan, (son Jerrell's great great grandfather). Dohasan and a group of Kiowa Warriors were eating a meal on a sunlit slope when they sensed a group of horse-mounted men approaching from their backs over the hill behind them. A member of the group nervously told Dohasan that they must leave immediately, at which comment the Chief simply stared into space and kept on eating. The Dohasan team's frustration morphed into intense anxiety and finally into terror, thinking that the approaching group could be their bitter enemies from the Osage Tribe who had stolen their sacred "*taipe*" fetish. The team left Dohasan, galloped though a draw and up onto the side of a distant bluff where they peered at Dohasan, waiting for what they expected would be his tragic end.

Four Osage warriors galloped to the crest of the hill. Dohasan slowly put aside his food, drew an arrow out, placed it in his bow and shot the head rider of the Osage. Three more times, he calmly carried out the same act – killing all three of the other Osages. He then picked up the rest of his food and began eating again without so much as looking at his team across the draw in the distance. It was Dohasan who led a group of Kiowa and Comanche in the attack of Buffalo hunters at Adobe Walls in the Texas panhandle, wining the battle but failing to get Kit Carson who was saved by his two mountain howitzers.

UNIQUE AIRPORTS

The logistics of the Navajo Teacher Education Development program were a real challenge. The runway created at Teec Nos Pos by blocking off the highway with pickups was unsettling to me. In the winter planes coming into the Ganado site had to land early enough in the morning for the muddy dirt runway to remain frozen. Takeoff after classes had to be delayed until it refroze.

The Tuba City runway was literally in the middle of town and had to be buzzed and cleared of livestock before landing any planes.

The runway at Chinle was of red clay but unlike Ganado, dry most of the time.

The University of New Mexico used a paved runway at Crownpoint. At one time UNM attempted to move operations into its Gallup Branch Campus, but Platero, who considered REZ locations as having political significance, nixed the move.

Hudgins Air Company had the contract for the Arizona sector of the program; they were owned and run by fellows who had trained World War II fighter pilots. Their skill was crucial as the perils of navigating from Tucson north to the Navajo Reservation required flying up over the Mogollon Rim and the mountains of northern Arizona. There were hazard times, such as when clouds and fog required a pilot to fly down Oak Creek canyon to avoid a dense overcast.

It is amazing what with the many trips in single engine planes from Albuquerque and Tucson that there were no major mishaps. Such an event would have shut the program down, or at least discouraged any travel by the top faculty.

Almost Midair Disaster

A member of the Navajo Division of Education was scheduled to go with me to Tucson for a meeting. One Christine Bates, who later directed the Navajo Academy, was petrified about flying. I relayed to her all the successes without incident that Hudgins had executed over a two-year period and she finally agreed to come along. Approaching the Tucson airport I looked out the left window and saw an F-16 coming down for a landing. Fortunately, I mentioned this to the pilot, who upon spotting the military aircraft, instantly pulled the single engine up. The fighter went right under us. Bates never trusted me about anything after that event.

Consumed by Coyote?!

The unpredictable nature of small plane travel throughout the Southwest was tragically evidenced in January of 1976. Earlier that year Platero, my son Gregory and I had taken a flight from Window Rock to Santa Fe in a twin engine craft – a plane owned by a company stationed in Window Rock intended to serve the needs of the BIA, Indian Health Service and the Navajo Tribe. Weeks later in the coffee shop of the Window Rock Inn I asked one Jimmy X, the owner, chief pilot and the gentleman who had flown us to Santa Fe, about the perils of flying in northern Arizona and New Mexico; he singled out weather as the major mitigating force—especially the presence of snow squalls. The Window Rock company with Jimmy X as the pilot had flown a group of Navajo Nation Councilmen and a BIA Interpreter from Window Rock to Albuquerque to board a plane bound for Washington D.C. They were scheduled to attend a Senate hearing regarding Indian water rights – a risky, controversial topic. Jimmy X had made one trip to retrieve a group of Councilmen and take them to Window Rock. He then returned to Albuquerque, picking up two councilmen and the

BIA interpreter. One of the councilmen from Shiprock was known to be controversial, a bitter critic of then Chairman Peter McDonald. Jimmy X had mentioned the threat of sudden, unpredictable snow squalls occurring during the winter. Apparently Jimmy X and the last group he was bringing back to Window Rock ran into a sudden squall somewhere east of Grants, New Mexico. Informed sources reported that the pilot, Jimmy, had attempted to find and land at the Grants airport but instead had flown into a canyon near a roadside concession, hitting a wall at 200 miles an hour. The FAA blocked any attempts to tamper with the wreckage until they completed an investigation. The intensity of Navajo politics and their serious opposition to some of Chairman McDonald's policies quickly generated conspiracy theories about sabotage. The untouched remains of the four passengers of the plane being exposed to coyotes caused fires of controversy to rage. One passenger, Councilman Don N from Steamboat, was on the NTEDP Board. This sinister environment continued as a backdrop for my next job at Navajo Community College.

GAO Audit!!

Navajo Tribe Chairman Peter McDonald had expanded his power by forming the oil producing Indian Tribes into a syndicate. This posturing combined with other challenges and conflicts with the federal government raised the ire of Senator Barry Goldwater. In retaliation Goldwater ordered the General Accounting Office (GAO) to scrutinize federal funding for evidence of Tribal misuse or non-performance. Someone protecting the Tribe managed to have Platero's NTEDP audited because they knew we were a "clean machine."

Kiowa Family at Dennehotso

Two auditors showed up unannounced one day at the comptroller's office and immediately requested financial records for NTEDP. A clerk said they were too busy and to come back at the end of the week. The main auditor requested use of the phone (before cell phone days), and when asked who he was calling replied, "The FBI – we have directed them to seize your records." When Platero was informed of this he called me and asked that I speak to the gentlemen. Before I even arrived to meet with them, I had an office arranged for the auditors and gave them a glowing account of the program, volunteering my complete support with whatever they needed. I knew they saw the cold sweat on my brow and I told them the truth that I had been suffering from stomach flu all night. Of course I got that look that said, "Yeah, right!"

The two GAO auditors spent a whole week going through financial and operational files and even made visits to each of the five teaching sites to confirm the existence of a random sample – fortunately finding a 100% match in the sample of participants. The financial records and operational documents – planning, contracts, transcripts and so forth were all found to be in order. The only question they had, which was not listed as an exception, was a $500 consultant fee to Dillon's relative, Dr. Leo Platero. We explained that the gentleman in question was a doctorate MIT graduate specializing in linguistics. NTEDP passed the audit with flying colors.

SERIOUS BANQUETS!

Celebratory banquets to honor the graduates and their successful completion of the program curriculum and imminent graduation were held each of my three years as director of the program. Since enrollment approached 200 students at one time, this required accommodation for nearly 500 possible banquet attendees. Three flexible section walls of the Window Rock Inn (now the Navajo Nation Inn) restaurant were rolled back to allow seating for the first banquet which was packed with students and their families. The second year arrangements were made for a repeat of the large crowd. Sadly, the dining hall was half empty. The third year the banquet was moved to the Shalimar Motel/Restaurant in Gallup, New Mexico. We encouraged our students to invite as many members of the family as they could, including uncles, grand relatives and distant cousins. Because of federal regulations, funds could not be applied to food costs alone, but might be used to support "workshops." Students could be paid travel and per diem to attend such workshops. The headline "workshop" speakers were a very potent resource for our students.

People poured into the vast Shalimar conference hall and once totally filled, we directed people to the restaurant and informed the attendees to be free to order from the minue and told the restaurant manager that we would pick up all the receipts. The bill for the restaurant was $3,000; Allyn S and I discussed the situation and found a way to cover that debt.

ANAHEIM TRIP—120 STUDENT TREK

One of my stratagems as an educator was designed to inspire my students to believe in their own abilities, to not feel dependent, controlled or under the thumb of some superior knowledgeable authority. Many of the administrative people running schools on Indian reservations, particularly the Navajo, tended to act as governing experts of their institutions, keeping both content and processes of instruction under intense supervision. The BIA, originally organized by the war department, considered their facility as a military instillation, wherein one that could be written up and reprimanded for being AWOL.

The Association for Supervision and Curriculum Development had planned a conference in Anaheim, California – the home of Disneyland. As a former member of the Elementary Advisory Council I felt secure in taking all of the students to the Conference, thoroughly debriefing them in the selection of sessions they would attend.

We booked housing at the Space Age Motel, and I obtained a purchase order covering 120 Navajo students for Conference registration. We arranged for three Greyhound buses to route themselves across the Navajo reservation, one from Shiprock going west across the northern sector of the reservation, another from Albuquerque going west along the southern sector of the reservation, and a final bus coming from Chinle to other middle sites on the way west. All three buses rendezvoused at the Crown Restaurant on the east side of Flagstaff one early October morning. Once all had arrived, the convoy proceeded west on Interstate 40 on to Anaheim.

Somewhere in the Mohave Desert a coyote crossed the road and Narsisa Patrick screamed, "Stop the bus!!" It was a custom for Navajos to sprinkle corn pollen over the tracks of a coyote to remove the evil left by that wily specter of the desert.

And then the worst possible thing happened, exacerbating Ms. Patrick's worst fears: the dead-heading bus driver who had come out of retirement to make the trip to the West coast expired of a heart attack during the first night in Anaheim. The scenario at the Space Age boasted other interesting dimensions as well. One attendee/student was Larry T, a World War II veteran. The desk clerk informed me that he was upstairs, drunk, yelling about the "Kraut soldiers in the Black Forest" and requesting my presence. Larry again called me for help at the University of Arizona campus; upon arriving at his room I found him passed out, surrounded by empty bottles of mouthwash. I took him to a recovery center in downtown Tucson. A month later, the Director, a member of the Yuma Tribe, called me to come down for Larry's release and to act as encouragement and counsel. In a one sentence *bon voyage* he told Larry, "If you ever drink again, Larry, you will die." Larry finished a Masters In Special Education and taught for several years in Kayenta. Sadly, first his wife and then he died of alcoholism. It was an especially sorrowful time for me. I was in my third year without the need for alcohol and knew the deaths had not been inevitable for Larry and his wife.

We returned back to the Navajo Rez from Anaheim minus only two fellows who got drunk and wandered the streets of L.A. until they found a way back home.

The students returned to their teaching sites and their jobs with confidence, enthusiasm and the desire to be innovative in adapting instruction to the cultural and linguistic needs of their children. Attempts to oppose their plans by administers who chirped that such ideas were – according to certain authoritative sources – contrary to educational methodology were countered by a number of students who stated they got their ideas in Anaheim through personal interfaces with the actual experts across a number of current educational practice.

NEITHER ONE OF US

It was during this time that I had to finally discontinue my relationship with Delphia. We met in Flagstaff while I awaited the arrival of the three buses and said goodbye. In a strange sort of serendipity, a Gladys Knight and the Pips tune soared over the FM station in Flagstaff:

> "NEITHER ONE OF US"
> "It's sad to think, we're not gonna make it ... And it's gotten to the point where we just can't fake it ... For some unGodly reason we just won't let it die ... I guess neither one of us ... wants to be the first to say goodbye."
> (Gladys Knight and the Pips.1973. Neither One of Us. Motown Records on the Soul Records label.)

NTEDP REPRESENTATIVE MEETINGS

To maintain student, staff and field based professorial staff identity as well as morale, sharing of problems and technique, student reps from each site along with teachers and field staff met at a central location each quarter of the program years. The first meeting was held in a resort in Sedona, Arizona that had been a residence for movie stars acting in films made in the Sedona/Oak Creek area. Albuquerque was also chosen one year for its central accessibility. A fly-in to the airport in Holbrook, Arizona was an unusual event because of the need to retrieve student reps by plane at their work sites and then fly them into Holbrook. The most memorable meeting was held at the University of Arizona College of Education conference hall. The Dean of the College was there with other significant university personnel. I realized much later in the year that the University of New Mexico staff under Dr. Don K had decided to dismiss the entire meeting agenda by employing a nonresponsive wall of silence. The word "co-op for cooptation" was a salient concept floating around action oriented groups in the 1970's and meant that leaders and reps of the action group might be "bought."

Cooptation was effected by proposing various rewards for those cooperating with the goals of organizations being accessed by action groups with their own secret agendas.

As was my experience with Purdue PERC full professors, the University of New Mexico officials had included me in their personal and private events. When asked to make decisions favorable to the universities I always deferred to Gary Officials and Mr. Platero, or officials of the Navajo Tribe respectively.

During the second year of the Division of Education Programs for teachers, special education personnel, school administrators and I had been encouraged to apply for the UNM Department Chairmanship of Elementary Education. I did so and was told informally the night before the Selection Committee was to make their decision that I was going to get the position. Mr. Platero came over to my residence in Ft. Defiance and announced that going to UNM would be leaving the "real action" being carried out on the Navajo Nation. I called UNM the next morning and asked to have my name dropped from consideration for the chairmanship. Some of my close friends, notably an Illinois grad school buddy and now member of the UNM staff, never confided in me again. The family in Flagstaff, particularly my wife Charlene, was very disappointed about not moving to Albuquerque. That was the third time I had turned down a chance for a position at UNM. Not only were there the factors of commitment and creative opportunities inherent in my staying with the NDE, but also, the role of an outside force trying to make changes seemed much safer than actually operating within set institutional parameters. Failure at exceptionally complex tasks was not as embarrassing as failure at those standard administrative roles. The real impediments to my consideration of leadership positions within existing structures were deep-set fears – the shame of failure, the specters of inadequate esteem and self-confidence. All these factors made me shy away from performing the expected roles of mature leadership. The same weakness caused my rejection of opportunities at ASU, Illinois, Emory, NYU, Florida and a number of other institutions including a chairmanship at the University of Illinois Chicago Circle Campus. I passed through the school age period of "can do vs. can't do" challenge without enough "can do" confidence to avoid stumbling in later stages of life.

When fear of failure trumps the operation of self-confidence, people like me at certain times of life posture arrogance and grandiosity and attempt the "impossible dream" because it's a win-win. No shame for trying the impossible and falling short. The danger to the ego occurs when one is executing prescribed tasks that have a good chance of success. Failure in this case might reveal a weakness or inadequacy.

PROPOSAL AND PROGRAM DESIGN

Looking at my handwritten proposal documents I note that as each year went by my script degenerated to the point where I couldn't read my own writing. Associates who did the transcribing and typing could actually decipher it better than I.

I got a call one afternoon from Dillon Platero who said he wanted a proposal focused on community participation in education and that he needed it for presentation to the National Institute of Education the very next day. Although I no longer credit the viability of the National Institute of Education, (NIE), at the time I believed any request made to them had to be "stone heavy" as Gary's City Director Slim Collins would say.

I produced a proposal containing abstractions that could apply to anything someone might want. Reading it later to an alcoholic friend in Flagstaff she and I could not contain ourselves with halarious laughter.

LIFESTYLE

Every Wednesday night meant traveling the 30-odd miles from Window Rock or Fort Defiance into Gallup to a place called the Friendship House, a halfway house for re-covering alcoholics. The group of alcoholics gathered there had a chance to dump all the anxieties, frustrations and angers accumulated during the week in Window Rock.

It was also customary to eat Mexican Food at Pedro's, whose large Mexican hat neon sign could be seen a mile away. It was a vortex for Gallup society and it was full of dense cigarette smoke. I found out much later that the cuisine got its special flavor from the lard used to cook everything.

Later, Earl's Restaurant presented delicious meals at a reasonable price. Sunday mornings I always went into Gallup for breakfast and to meet with a group of my al-coholic friends. In addition one Andrew T, a counselor in a western Navajo recovery center, met with me each Tuesday morning for coffee at the small café in Ganado.

I also taught advanced statistics at Ganado College as a field based class from the University of Arizona. I reveled in keeping it concrete, simple and understandable in hope of neutralizing of the trauma that the topic engendered in most people.

> "Dear God,
> I have no idea where I am going. I do not see the road ahead of
> me.................... I will not be afraid because I know you will never leave
> me to face my troubles all alone." (Thomas Merton.1948. The Seven Story
> Mountain. New York: Harcourt.)

My divorce was finalized in the spring of 1976 and I moved out to the reservation into the Dennehotso BIA Compound with Delphia and her four children. The com-mute to Window Rock and back each day became an impossibility and I thus slept at noon to make up for an early morning rise – I had to get up at 4AM to get to Window Rock in time for work. One wintery morning I traveled on an ice-packed road to Win-dow Rock knowing that if I slipped off, hours would pass before I would be found. I turned my fear over to whatever Higher Power in the universe had protected me so often in places like Gary.

My alcoholic friend Ed A's wife Betty had given me a prayer written by Thomas Merton, the renowned Trappist monk whose life kept morphing from the depths of degeneration into realms of joyous spirituality. There would be many a time when I found myself quietly repeating that prayer:

LIVING AT A MOTEL

My first home in Window Rock, a small bedroom, was at a motel in the adjoining city of Bonito. Later I moved into an actual apartment in the same motel complex. Someone asked to move in and join me and soon there were a bunch of people in the apartment.

One of the employees in the division asked to borrow my car; I assumed they would be gone for a couple of hours. She returned the car – overheated – three days later. I found out later that Pat M was an alcoholic, and within a year I saw her near skid row in a meeting of alcoholics. I gave her a hug wished her well and that was the last time I saw her. I was told she died the next year.

One night I awaited Delphia's arrival back from Oklahoma – she and the children came busting in at 3 in the morning. It was a joyful, easy feeling to be with that family in Window Rock. I now believe Delphia was a partner through the next pass.

SCHOOL ADMINISTRATION GRANT

The Carnegie Corporation had agreed to fund a project providing a field-based program for Navajo personnel to attain a masters and a certification in school administration. I was chosen to prepare the program proposal in cooperation with the UNM school administration department—my worst nightmare. Platero had more or less committed to UNM in lieu of the University of Arizona, which made it difficult to attain leverage over UNM professors. I ended up sitting out in the hall outside the School Admin Offices revising program elements over and over again before the ED Admin staff would approve them.

Sixty Navajo men and women ready for administrative positions were chosen and all but a few finished the program with a degree and certification. Many attained top positions in Navajo Nation schools and in institutions off the reservation.

GRADUATION AND LONG-RANGE IMPACT

Graduation days on the UNM and U of Az campuses were spectacular. Amid the pin-stripe-suited men and jersey-dress-decked women were Navajo children, mothers and grand people dressed in their traditional garb.

The huge "Pit" in Albuquerque and the McHale Center in Tucson were packed to the hilt, and after graduation nearby parks were filled with celebrants eating lamb ribs and cutting decorated cakes.

There were over 300 Navajo teacher aides who obtained their degrees and certification from the Navajo Teacher Education Development Program. Another large group received special education degrees. The NTEDP became a model for many tribes to bring tribal members into their children's classrooms.

Nearly 60 Navajo school administrators received masters and certification from the Carnegie program.

Powwows

In my gourd dancing days, several episodes occurred that are today poignant memories. One Christmas Eve at a place called Red Lake I was awed by being asked to give the blessing. From a Navajo perspective this was highly unusual.

Delphia 's Uncle James Haungooah (Silverhorn) was considered the pope of the Native American church, and out and across the reservation it would have been hard to find some community wherein a ceremonial teepee wasn't standing with smoke curling out its top.

I was invited to attend a peyote meeting in Kayenta one night. I originally balked, feeling that since I couldn't take any mood-changing chemicals my refusal would embarrass the grand relatives staying with the families. I was told that all I had to do was rub some peyote on me. I did however participate in the spiritual sense of what was going on.

At a powwow in Teec Nos Pos several of the family had been honored as head dancers. The custom was to give out gifts to head dancers, upon occasion gifts such as Pendleton Blankets. I was called up as Mr. E and given a Pendleton. Much later I was called up as Dr. K, which I was known as by the Teec Nos Students. The sitting "Shama's" (Grandmothers) gave me the strangest stares at my apparent double identity.

One autumn evening I found myself dancing at the Shiprock Fair under a single 40-watt bulb and a dim campfire light. I realized I could be the only Beliganii (white man) in the whole city. Things had gotten a little rough when several teenagers pushed over an outhouse with someone inside. I used to describe Shiprock as the city of businesses with plywood windows.

The Navajo Nation Fair in September at Window Rock would test anyone's metal. One year the bathrooms near the powwow arena were ankle deep in mud. Camped on the side of a hill in a tent, on another occasion I awoke to an immense blast above my head and I peaked out to see a hot air balloon 30 feet above me. My final episode at the Navajo Fair involved the waft of tear gas coming through our tent at 3 in the morning. The Navajo Police were attempting to disperse a large group of loud winos. Delphia and the family climbed into the Toyota Van, but the grand folks got the full brunt of the gas, which floated through the chain link fence.

Stepson Charlie E would have won 1,000 dollars as first place in the Southern Fancy Dance contest but lost a single feather and had to disqualify him. Powwow events are totally unforgettable and at times, unforgiving.

OKLAHOMA

If Delphia 's relatives were not powwowing at our house and sleeping on the living room floor like stacked cordwood, the family was packed in the pickup and camper hurrying through the night on icy roads back from the Polman's Thanksgiving Pow-wow in Apache, Oklahoma. The Kiowa people were always so kind and respectful to me that I was left feeling somewhat abashed. Being honored by uncle James Silver-horn was almost more than I could take. The Kiowa Tribe had been one of the fiercest tribes of the early west. The Kiowa Black Leggings Warrior Society often opens the National Congress of American Indians.

ANADARKO FAIR

Each August the Kiowa Tribe gathers at the Fair at Anadarko, which locale was cited as the Indian Capital of the U.S. and where relatives, grand folks and families annu-ally reunite. Southern plains powwow drums echoed very late followed by the "49"er singers caroling all night – a stage for flirtation and courting.

Powwows can feature very competitive contests amidst a myriad of men and women dance styles with hefty rewards for the winners. The Navajo nation once offered an automobile as a prize to the winning fancy dancer. The H family often won first place at many powwows. I had attained such a high profile by association with family ap-pearances and my gourd dancing that I was frequently chosen to judge both and women dancer categories in the southern plains style. I think I may have been chosen because of my reputation of fairness, and because I didn't let politics enter my deci-sion. I chose the best dancers based on costume, style and skill.

Jerrell was just a baby and I felt I should be at home with him, Delphia and family. What with commuting back and forth 200 miles round-trip from Dennehotso to Window Rock, napping at noon became impossible. I decided to take a position as Director of Special Grants and Programs at Navajo Community College, (NCC, now known as Dine' College). NCC was becoming the model for higher education for Indian Tribes and had high expectations as far as developing programs consummate to the cultural preservation of the Navajo as well as desiring to prepare its students to excel in higher education and pursuit of an array of professional roles.

Little did I know I was jumping out of the pressure cooker into a holocaust of pressure and controversy.

NAVAJO COMMUNITY COLLEGE NIGHTMARE

Jerrell's birth in June of 1976 required that I be closer to home. I had been commuting 100 miles one way from Dennehotso to Window Rock. It seemed that the major problems with NTEDP had leveled out. I took a chance and moved up the road to NCC which shortened my commute to 70 miles one way. I began a three-year stint at the college in September of 1976 as Director of Special Grants and Programs of which a contentious plethora existed, but if I had known what was coming I might have changed my mind.

Navajo Community College was established by a special act of the U.S. Congress in 1968, becoming the first Indian controlled institution of higher education in the United States. Since Rough Rock K-12 School had been chosen to be the first Public/BIA School controlled by an Indian Tribe, educational self-determination flowed naturally toward doing the same for higher education. Major figures Dr. Robert R. and Dillon Platero were the chief players in creating NCC.

VOLATILE EXISTENCE

Like all institutions brought into the Navajo culture from the outside, NCC has had and is still experiencing a volatile existence. The 'Navajo are an incorporative culture' (Ed Spicer, University of Arizona) and they can take physical, institutional and even philosophical concepts into their way of life without disrupting the central core of what it means to be a Navajo. Almost like developing human beings, each newly embraced cultural form in the realms of government and economics – the Navajo Agricultural Products Industry and Kayenta Township – began as fledglings and went through difficult stages, morphing to meet the unique needs of the Navajo.

NCC began in the bowels of an existing BIA building complex at Many Farms, Arizona. It commenced with Dr. Robert R. as its president , but he was soon replaced by a Navajo, Ned A. Hatathli. Pervasive rumors accompanied Mr. Hatathli's death by "accident" while cleaning his hunting rifle. Financial complications attendant to Rough Rock School were also the plight of early days at NCC. Chief of the Navajo Fire Dancers and medicine man, Alfred Yazzie, shared with me that a large amount of money had been taken illegally from Rough Rock and that the person responsible had been removed from the school by Business Manager Susan A. and legal representative Emanuel D. from Dolores, Colorado.

A newly constructed campus complex was established at Tsaile (Navajo for "Lake") east of Many Farms and located near Canyon de Chelly. Distinctive to the campus buildings were their octagonal shapes – one a towering 7-story Cultural Center (the Hatathli Center), a beautiful edifice covered with bronze colored glass panels. The center of this building had a Navajo fire pit similar to what could be found in a traditional Navajo Hogan. The opening of the fire pit went from the first floor up seven stories and out of the roof. In the beginning the college complex was like a body without a soul.

One whole floor was devoted to a museum containing jewelry, artifacts and significant antiques including Navajo Chief Blankets, splendid products of Navajo Weaving valued at over sixty thousand dollars each. It would be the misuse of museum contents that ignited the battle initiating its first test of viability.

GREAT RED HOPE

Enormous creativity defined the first few years at the college, which operated optimistically on the premise that modes of instruction and even the content of courses could be integrated with Navajo culture. Many of the grant proposals I wrote during my tenure at the college had that concept at its core. In those early years, deliberations, curriculum alternatives and applications of Navajo ideas were included in the instructional process. Dr. Fred Begay, a Navajo and nuclear physicist from Los Alamos Laboratories, claimed that traditional Navajo lore cites the existence and use of lasers. The ebb and flow of emphasis on the incorporation of Navajo concepts and beliefs characterized the program at the college, but not without some frustration. The NTEDP program emphasized and was successful in using Navajo culture where it was applicable, this accomplished by simple supplements, the application of cultural materials for illustration and of course by employing the Navajo language to explain concepts. The prominence and power of the Navajo language spoken in World War II by the Code Talkers was well known on the Navajo. Use of the language was uplifting and motivating in contrast to the times in BIA schools when Navajo children were chastised for speaking their own language. The major force thrusting education into Navajo prominence has been attributed to Dr. Roessel and his wife Ruth whose names appear on the major curriculum source volume about the Navajo people. Mr. Alfred Yazzie, Head Fire Dancer and Navajo Medicine Man became a close friend and confidant of mine. He confessed to me that all the books penned about Navajos may have Navajo names on them, but Beliganii (white guys) wrote them. He wanted to write from his perspective as a Navajo and informed medicine man. I have always felt that from a moral and psychological point a view that it seems more effective to lend one's skill in empowering indigenous people with the competence to do and control their own destiny rather than to do it for them. I wrote a grant for Mr. Yazzie that was funded (Title VII —$175,000) for him to record a Navajo perspective of their history. A series of seven volumes entitled NAVAJO ORAL TRADITIONS were written by Yazzie and his Title VII staff, (Yazzie, Alfred.1984. Mesas Verde Press, Cortez, Colorado). The narrative was characterized by paragraphs in English followed by a paragraph of the same content in Navajo. Exquisite illustrations were created under the close direction and supervision of Yazzie, many of the drawings being his own which assured the authenticity of the material.

Thinking back about some of what I wrote about I see that my emphasis may have been in error. One cannot fault the sincere quest to honor the language and life of the Navajo who had been demeaned for so long. Still, a realistic perspective would have been more helpful than the pursuit of idealistic vision.

TRIBALLY CONTROLLED COMMUNITY COLLEGES

The Navajo Community College Act of 1971 became a model for the federal Tribally Controlled Community College Assistance Act of 1978 and has since been used to build 36 tribal colleges across the country. The American Higher Education Consortia (AHEC), located in Denver, strongly supported the base of policy and intelligence for tribally controlled Community Colleges. During my time at the College the majority of the AHEC staff were members of the Kiowa Tribe and associated in some way with my wife Delphia. This helped me to stay on the inside track regarding federal funding opportunities and pertinent contacts in the federal, private foundation and corporate sources of funding. The institutional integration into ecominic and political stuctures cause a problem sustaining the functioning of *ad hoc* funded projects. Many years later after intense lobbying, NCC was finally included in a stream of state funding.

In the early days, NCC funding was a bona fide dilemma. Direct funding came from Congress since the college was established as a federally supported institution. There was an assumption that tuition and other related expenses would supplement the entitled funds, but it did not. First, the sustainability of the physical structure was a critical weakness, that same flaw occurring with many other institutions created by ad hoc financial donations from foundations and corporations.

Upkeep of the NCC campus was very expensive and due to its remoteness, when such as the elevator in the cultural center broke down, it might be a week or so before it was made operable again. In 2009 I visited the Hatathli Cultural Center and found the huge mahogany doors chained shut. As years passed, key maintenance and upkeep requirements were apparently not being fulfilled.

The keen interest and extensive support for an institution that embodied Indian self-determination, for one focused on alleviating the plight of Indian tribes, had great appeal across American society. NCC was born with people lined up to give it funds, apart from the State of Arizona who refused funding based on the federal and sovereign nature of the College.

When I arrived at NCC the College was like a Christmas tree loaded and bent over with discretionary financial "grant ornaments" designed to accomplish a broad array of goals that were not really integral to the basic concept of teaching and housing students. The monitoring of grants to assure the delivery of their stated commitments was thin to non-existent. The organization of the College was not designed to function with regard to the delivery of commitments in spite of the grant monies pouring in. The ornaments pulled down hard on the tree and bent it over. Still, the majority of grants were sound which made it all the more important to deliver them to patrons providing financing. I found in my experience with the Tribal Carnegie Administrator Program that the foundation was monitoring the status of their grant all the way from New York.

LACK OF DELIVERY

An extreme example impacting the college's reputation, credibility and future support was one that surrounded the Kennedy Grant in Special Education. A former Illinois professor now located at the University of Arizona was the developer of the psycholinguistic assessment technique and had arranged a $100,000 grant for special education at NCC. He made a site visit to NCC and Tsaile and was told by the President that he didn't "know anything about the grant." Investigations as to the location and staff for the program were discovered on the third floor of the Cultural Center. The door to the office was locked. The director had been AWOL for several weeks and there was no report of program activities available.

I had learned in my Gary/Purdue, Navajo Division, and BIA/U.S. Office of Education programs that each dollar available should be applied and maximized to cover grant commitments and to bring about the most effective impact – the biggest bang for the buck – for the intended clients. If the patron or manager who led the grant did not have positive results to show his or her top administrators and boards, they would not continue to fund the enterprise.

GRANT MANAGEMENT

I spent many an hour writing grants, and a good number of them were funded. What was known as the Title III Higher Education Grant was one of the most demanding in its requirements. It was funded, although at my intense objection a section of the grant was misapplied and used to renovate the science office instead of assessing the college's science curriculum viability with regard to matriculation into advanced university courses.

My first task at grant management was to construct and legitimize within the system grant management regulations and procedures. It was important to protect the credibility of the College and to deliver the services and/or materials promised to the grant clients. I had also learned in working with other projects and university structures that it was essential to develop functional and successful processes because they would be adopted, modeled and incorporated by participating institutions. It meant "wiring in" management as an integral part of the college operations.

SEEKING MANAGEMENT

I asked President Thomas Attcity to have the Board of Regents pass a resolution making the Special Programs Management Procedures a requirement for any outside funding provided to the college. He replied that it would only be done administratively, which meant it would rest on the decisions of administrative personnel who had caused the problems existent to outside management of funds in the first place.

I had a premonition that the failure to place management of special funds as a basic tenant in the college operations was a bell weather for something ominous on the horizon.

The College had experienced a number of traumas unrelated to its central operations, but nevertheless the impact of these events tended to dampen both enthusiasm and unspoiled potential. A long line of quality people wanted to join the cause of Navajo

Higher Education.

There is no airport at Tsaile. One hot summer afternoon, a plane with four prominent staff members bound for Santa Fe took off, struggled to gain altitude and faltered, crashing and burning. I happened to be on the phone with the receptionist when she burst into tears. She had just been informed of the sudden death of a close friend.

Unanswered questions still hung around the Ned Hatathili death. Bypassing Navajo athletes in formulating the basketball team roster had caused college supporters some serious concern. Requests were being made for substantial supplementary funding from the Navajo Nation Council signaling a perennial problem with institutions that had been established with upfront initial funding, but who were without mechanisms to insure sustained financial support over time. Platero's decision to bypass the college's inclusion in NTEDP and other Navajo Division of Education programs was unsettling and I sensed that problems lay below the surface. I was rather surprised at Platero's reaction to my departure from NDOE, and I wasn't overly impressed with my status in that organization. You never know what people think of you until you decide to leave – which exit unfortunately was not the product of solidly reasonable humility, but more the result of the naiveté and codependence characteristic of "do-gooders."

THE REVOLUTION

The fires of discontent and dissatisfaction that had been burning underground for so long finally broke out in the open. Expectations that were the legacy of the college's creation were not being realized and concerns in all three domains – the students, staff and faculty – had been ignored for a long time. The President, Thomas Attcity, and the upper administrative officers ignored the petitions and were observed doing their own thing outside of their role and authority. Vice President Lawrence I. had been fired for unacceptable personal behavior; prior to that dismissal he had become a champion of student life on campus and was well regarded by the college community.

Several leaders out of the three sections of the college community called an organizational meeting referred to as "The Committee." My concern about the proper management of grant money prompted me to attend the first meeting. "Jerry, would you take notes?" Of course I agreed to take notes, not realizing that I was creating a core document of complaints against the President and current administration that would transform over several weeks into an indictment of their regime and a case for demanding their reassignment.

Former Marine Navajo Code Talker Teddy Draper, now a resident medicine man, acted as the guiding force and spiritual leader of the "Faculty, Staff and Student Com-

NCC Group Asks President To Quit

mittee" who claimed "We do not think of him as our president any more, so why should he represent us in Washington?" (THE GALLUP INDEPENDENT – January1979). The President and six Board of Regents members had gone to Washington to attend meetings.

Deliberations in the "Committee" reached critical mass with the decision to call a general meeting of the college with invitations to key Navajo leaders. The purpose of the meeting was to present key evidence in support of the indictment of the President and his regime, and to request a resignation. The meeting would represent a tumultuous three weeks of tension between the President's regime on the one hand and the "Committee" on the other.

UNCOMFORTABLE PROSECUTION

As committee meetings and plans of action emerged, an unpleasant realization became apparent. I was looked upon as the prosecuting attorney supporting the toppling of the College President who was the cousin of Peter McDonald, one of the most powerful Indians in America.

The possibility of a violent breakout was on everyone's mind. One college official, a Vice President, was sleeping on top of the file cabinets in the administrative offices. One committee member had breached the offices and had repelled off the top of Hatathli Center.

Bullets had been fired through a hood into a car motor.

I was living in a pie-like wedge of an octagonal dormitory. I would walk each night through the piñon trees to the meeting center, just waiting to hear a shot in the dark. As a safety precaution, I was invited to stay with a resident faculty member.

I was not privy to the creative source of a special Navajo Nation council session – a hearing on the grievances of the Committee. But I found myself in the vast council chambers with Committee Members testifying about complaints and requested resignations. Heated arguments exploded into yelling topped off by the appearance of an Aim Leader, Leroy Keams, dressed like chief Manuelito with a rifle in his hand. He was accusing a councilman and a member of the board of regents of embezzling

$75,000. Chairman McDonald's aide kept appearing and reappearing to relay his monitoring to McDonald. I was paranoid that someone would ask me to get up and testify; I felt more comfortable letting things play out as a strictly Navajo issue.

By way of accelerating my paranoia, a pickup truck had followed me on an ice-covered road from Tsaile until I ditched it in the residential area of Navajo, New Mexico.

Reluctant Prosecutor

Saying Goodbye to My Son

Adding to the somber atmosphere, my son Bob visited me for a night and two days, bringing his slide projector so we could enjoy some family memories. Late in the afternoon, just as the sun was setting behind the western hills I watched his Camaro disappear down the highway over the hill that led to Chinle. It was the last time I would see him in long hair as several days later he would enter Navy boot camp near Coronado Island in San Diego.

Standoff

In the small NCC college community – across its campus and within its buildings – tension, fear and bitterness showed in everyone's face. A rather bizarre event occurred in the large Hogan-shaped cafeteria. A nursing staff member, one Mabel G, was an alcoholic friend; an organized meeting of alcoholics was held each Tuesday noon in a side room off the main cafeteria. On the Tuesday of the week prior to the "Revolutionary" climax meeting, two of the "enemy" opposition administrators – two Vice Presidents – showed up and announced that they were "alcoholics." Their demeanor suggested that they were sincere, that their presence was not a ploy, or a spy tactic. The college vice president asked me if I would personally counsel him in his struggle for recovery. I have never regretted my decision, as the Vice President has been sober now for over 37 years. My standing quip to him was and always has been, "Gerald, I love ya guy, but I don't know if I'll ever like ya."

Feral Dog Attack

The remoteness of the campus made it vulnerable to unpleasant intrusions and unwelcome assaults. Fire was always a danger. Bears could be heard growling outside windows. One late afternoon a pack of wild dogs attacked a gentleman but fortunately the attack was seen from a window and a group of men rushed out, chasing the feral dogs away.

R and R from Desperation

Having spent nearly three weeks in a tense environment I needed a respite and decided to go to Flagstaff for the weekend. I doubt I could have survived Saturday and Sunday in such a way as to be ready for the Monday confrontational meeting, one looming to be a raucous, trying ordeal with any successful outcome in serious doubt.

As I drove northbound at sunset into the Flagstaff area, the imposing San Francisco Peaks covered by a rosy set of clouds soothed me and every cell in my body began to relax. And as I beheld the neon lights lining Santa Fe Avenue, I felt a sense of comfort and confidence about the future. A steak dinner at Mrs. Zipps and my room at the Ramada were a perfect escape from the Tsaile chaos, and gathering with my alcoholic friends at the Episcopal Church brought me into a joyous, optimistic state of mind. My meeting with the group at breakfast the next morning extended my satisfaction about life. I remembered Merton's promise that *"though I might walk through the valley of death I would never be left alone with my troubles ..."* (Thomas Merton, Seven Story Mountain).

Yet as the afternoon sun's rays lengthened the shadows of trees lining Highway 89 south of Flagstaff, my bravado began to wane. Doubts about the value of the upcoming mêlée began to creep in. "Why am I going back to Tsaile and the College? Why me, and why am I responsible?" I came very close to pulling a U-turn to re-enter Flagstaff. I wish I could come up with some heroic thoughts about what drove me on, but I don't recall them. I was totally turned off by what I was about to do. As I rolled over the summit I saw the panoply of twinkling lights in the gloom of the NCC campus. The "Committee" meeting with Navajo officials would convene in one hour.

As the weekend prior to the Monday meeting approached, key evidence supporting the indictment of the administrative regime was accumulating into a fat package prefaced by a seven-page summary. Desperation filled my mind when at a Sunday night assembly I was questioned about "What I was going to present" – emphasis on the "I." It had always been my understanding that certain members of the group would present the case, especially Teddy Draper, who was the chairman of the committee. Sitting in front of them all I challenged the idea that this was not my affair alone, stating that everyone had to chip in with testimonials and documentation. I made this passionately clear. Every soul in the group instantly pledged to function as a team. We worked until the wee hours copying and generating the package for the next day's conference.

THE MEETING

I opened the meeting by reading the seven-page committee position paper, and summarized the documents that were attached. I stood at the podium with Teddy Draper below and to the left of me. The scene appeared as if I were an aficionado heading the Inquisition. Draper was my assistant, translating into Navajo what I was saying in English. The objectivity apparent in all the testimonials, lasting for several hours, clarified that the entire college community was dissatisfied, and I was taken off the hook as the major perpetrator of a mêlée that had been instigated by a meddling "outsider."

Most of the committee except for Teddy Draper and a few others felt that the police power backing the Administration was too great to defeat. McDonald's influence across the Rez and his position in the United States community of Native Americans was robust, and an unvoiced consensus sensed that the Board of Regents in one way or another could be influenced by him.

However, one of the most prominent and powerful Navajo leaders had been invited to the meeting, although with little hope that she would appear. Dr. Annie Waunika was the daughter of the first Navajo Chairman, Chee Dodge. She had personally enlisted the Indian Health Service and the U.S. Government to provide the necessary support to combat high incidences of tuberculosis not only among the Navajo but also in various tribes across America.

Indian people had nearly been wiped out by "the White Man's" maladies – smallpox for one. They had no natural immunity to such diseases as did the Europeans who took centuries to develop resistance to contamination brought across the ocean.

Veterans of the NCC Committee forced the resignation of President Atcitty and his associates, crediting the presence and the words of Councilwomen Dr. Annie Waurika for saving the day. Dr.I. claimed that it was his grandmother, a medicine women, who provided the source of power. She had told Larry that the committee would prevail.

SUCCESS

The "Committee" held a celebratory dinner meeting down at Chinle. They quite appropriately awarded me with a trophy boasting a bent Coor's beer can on a wooden block with a horse's rear end on the top.

SETTLING OF SCORES?

Within the next several weeks I came down with a high fever and severe chills. I was at a motel in Flagstaff showering with water as hot as I could stand it. The next day I contacted my family physician, Dr. Sitterly, and told him that I was sure it was either hepatitis or a reoccurrence of the infection I had contracted in 1963. The symptoms were identical and that puzzled me; I thought one was immune from infectious hepatitis after a first episode. I learned much later in life that there are two types, an A and B version of the disease.

Sitterly admitted me to the hospital the next day. My blood levels indicated telltale evidence of hepatitis. It was Christmas Eve and I ended up laughing about the whole affair that startled the nurse as by then my skin had turned yellow.

I had gained considerable trust in my spiritual program and believed I was safe from ultimate harm; I knew I would recover even if it meant being in bed for a couple of months.

PEYOTE MEETING

My family in Flagstaff – my ex-wife Charlene, Tim, Gregory and Maureen made an early evening visit bringing good wishes and a jar of hard candy. Later that night my current wife Delphia came by with the two older stepdaughters, Hattie and Patty Jo, and that was encouraging. They informed me they were on their way to Oklahoma for Christmas. This was startling news and caused me to feel a little sad, a little lonely and somewhat resentful. They were leaving me on Christmas while I was seriously ill. I think it is true that Indian people are reserved and mysterious about what they are doing as I found out later that year that my Kiowa family were going to Lawton, Oklahoma to stage a peyote meeting for me to get well.

I spent February and half of March in bed in Dennehotso, spinning hypotheses about where and how I got hepatitis. It is transmitted by exposure to an affected person and/or from bodily materials or things that have been touched.

My prominent theory was that I had been a victim, attacked by a medicine man delivering retribution for my role in the resignation of McDonald's cousin. Navajo witches and skin walkers were prevalent in the Tsaile sector of the Navajo Reservation. Clyde Kluchohn, a major anthropologist in Navajo culture had located a skin walker cave in the Lukachukai Mountains just east of the site of NCC.

Navajo witchcraft is known to attack the pancreas, liver or gall bladder. My office – with no windows and with rheostat lighting – was on the second floor of the cultural center and designed for Navajo chant sessions. I was always with a cup of coffee in my hand, and I left behind many cups in my office. It is my prime belief that a Navajo witch laced my coffee with the infectious hepatitis virus. It would not be my last interface with Navajo witchcraft; another incident would materialize five years later on a dark New Year's Eve at the Greasewood Boarding School.

I remained an employee of NCC during my recovery and drew pay, sick leave and health benefits. In March I got a clean bill of health and resigned from NCC.

THE EARLY 80's TRANSITION
TUCSON DAYS

The summer following my resignation from NCC I contracted to teach at the University of Arizona in Tucson. I moved there by myself, chose an apartment that had been a motel and found that the room temperature would not budge below 80 degrees. I began inviting my family to visit and when my daughter Maureen spent several nights she almost passed out from heat exhaustion. Fortunately one of my alcoholic friends managed the Waterbridge Apartments; I rented a place there and kept the temperature at 68 degrees. One entered the apartment complex by walking through a tunnel under the second story. Just inside and three feet from my doorway was a hot tub, and several feet further on the shallow edge of a lighted pool – Shangri-la!

Son Bob was still in the Navy in the Philippines, but Maureen, Tim and Greg all came down. I made it a point to share with them the latest freshly ground coffee craze, real maple syrup on pancakes and fresh pineapple juice. For my own fare I crock-potted chicken breasts with vegetables and froze them for the future.

APPLAUSE PASTRY

Special pastries were sold in venues along major thoroughfares and often after movies we patronized the Café Applause. Being single and alone was a refreshing respite from the chaos of life on the Navajo. It was the first time in my life that I was totally free to decide where, what and when to eat or what entertainment attracted me.

There was a special club for alcoholics on Pima Street where I would go each night. Being not committed in a relationship at that point in time, I attended the single's dance held on certain evenings at the Angus Beef restaurant. I was no ballroom dancer so I launched into fast disco dancing, which only required sensing the beat and rhythm of the music and letting your body do the rest. I actually took my powwow dancing up a couple of notches of speed and gyrations and really "moved it."

Seven months in Tucson dancing at singles events netted me dates with two women, one of which ended in a consummation of the intimate. Sadly, even that late in life, approaching 50 years old, I was still stuck with the search for a "Mom" and could not invest much in the way of deep caring. I was not able to turn off the distrustfulness that had conditioned me in early childhood. "Why would anyone want me? There must be some hidden motive here." The downside of this for the other person was experiencing my exit without any explanation. They were left with the idea that I was merely an insensitive one-nighters looking for a quick sexual fix. I later interfaced with that same women at the desk at the singles club and felt no compunction to respond to her deep blush except to say "hello."

When I told inquiring friends why I had been married, why I had been involved in so many relationships they rarely understood much less accepted my explanation, which was that I suffered from what is known as a 'love obsession' – that I was searching for a warm, loving person to take the place of a deep-seated memory about what a real mother was like. No one ever fit the perfect mother label; they were quickly dropped and put in a box called "just like Mabel."

I met a wonderful lady, Marsha M, who was an emergency room nurse and who revered me for my work on the Navajo. We dated, and once met for dinner in north Tucson at a wonderful place. Alas, I had to say goodbye one eve as I was going back to the Rez. I visited her once again several years later while attending a nearby pow-wow.

Someone who is obsessed with sex is quickly satisfied with an orgasm and that is often the end of the relationship. I used to believe as one obsessed with "love" that my quest for the perfect women was nobler than any other male-female interface, but now I realize that great harm can be done by either obsession. Though I can't blame my behavior on my alcoholism, I still work at making amends to anyone that I have "dumped" without an explanation. I believe the heterosexual male has a primitive computer chip deep inside that fire off at the sight of attractive females. As George Clooney's character in the movie "Up in the Air" quipped, "Man is not a starry eyed lover nor a monogamous swan, but a shark."

CLASS IN EDUCATION

I had arrived in Tucson after another one of countless breakups with Delphia. My purpose for being there in late May was to attend the graduation of the Navajo Teacher

Education students and to be on hand to assist the ceremonies in any way I could. I was scheduled in the Fall to teach a course about instruction in elementary social studies education. My own experience as a teacher and the theoretical work I had done at Purdue formed a focus for teacher training that used a diagnostic-prescriptive formula – the old Purdue DOSE model and the approach I had used at that institution. I used a exemplary model wherein a teacher assessed what a child (her class) knew about the body –"Where does food go when you swallow it," and so on. Once you get a picture of what each child knows or misconceives or doesn't know, you formulate a set of objectives as guides to your teaching. Then you select various arrangements, sequences of media and activities designed to attain the objectives; and finally you measure, i.e., evaluate, the degree to which you attained your objectives. The approach is quite different than the traditional modus operandi goals of memorizing and regurgitating information.

8/8/80

Dear Dr. Knowles,

I attended your Social Studies Methods class in the Fall of 1979. During the semester I disagreed with your philosophy and methods of teaching.

As I prepare for my first year of teaching I realise what an impact your class had on me. I have referred back to the teaching strategies we developed and am glad that I have them to draw from.

I was not accepting of your technique, perhaps others felt the same. When you left the following semester something made me feel guilty. I hope my reaction to your teaching and from others did not influence your decision. Now I see what an advantage my classmates and I have, even now.

Any way, thanks for the excellent, teaching and for making me think! You might remember me, I was Frankenstien.

Juanita Diggins

Teaching Has Impact

The end result of the class was that all students would exit the class with a large file of diagnostic-prescriptive learning strategies that would act as a resource for their future teaching. The first segment of the course was to lay out the dimensions of a learning strategy model using the basic concept developed at Purdue. The remainder of the course was focused on one dimension of the "strategy" component of the model – the media aspect of the strategy dimension. Students were required to produce media examples for their strategies beginning with two dimensional media (pictures, for example) and examining one category after another moving up the scale from the abstract to the concrete, resulting in the use of personal testimonials from flesh and blood human resources. One student interviewed and taped an old cowboy in north Tucson, creating a continuous source for her unit on Ranch Societies. I invited Delphia to address the group as a resource on traditional Native American societies. Another student brought in the Tucson City Manager as a personal resource.

I wanted to arm myself with some data about the relative effectiveness of the model of instruction and wished to use a control group. Another section of the same class was being taught using a textbook identified as the course requirement. The professor for the course was a close friend of Senator Barry Goldwater and held a powerful hand at University of Arizona. I am sure that he agreed to play some role in my research, but in the end he maneuvered away any attempts to measure his class on cognitive and attitudinal changes. I therefore had no base of comparison. In fact, the dean floated the idea that any creative attempts at instructional alternatives would label one as a troublemaker, a "diva, a prima donna." With respect to this label I must defer to President Teddy Roosevelt's famous treatise entitled, "Its not the critic who counts .."

There was one student who raged about the fact that we did not use the "textbook." Sometimes the rewards for teaching come later and in different ways. The note I got out of the blue nine months after that Social Studies class was one of the greatest accolades I have ever received as a teacher.

THE NAVAJO ACTRESS FROM "THE OUTLAW JOSEY WALES"

Larry Isaac was a close friend of Geraldine Keams, a Navajo lady who grew up at Red Lake north of Winslow, Arizona. She attended the University of Arizona and obtained a degree in theatre. She also spent a year at Momma's Café in New York where she honed her acting skills and found a launching pad for a movie career, playing the role of the asstaulted Indian maiden in "THE OUTLAW JOSÉ WALES" (1976). The director of José Wales insisted that Geraldine speak all her lines in her native Navajo – but apparently New York had impacted her to such a degree that she picked up a New Yorker/Brooklyn accent.

I had to go north to Kayenta for two weeks and Isaac asked me if Geraldine could stay in my apartment as she had extensive dental work to be done at the Indian Health Service in Tucson. Of course it was an exciting honor to have Geraldine grace my Waterbridge pad. My apartment looked like a pack rat's paradise. I had a penchant for carrying my office with me wherever I went and the place was filled with stacks of files. When I returned to Tucson everything was neatly sorted into appropriate categories.

It would be Geraldine who would give the graduation speech to the first class of eighth grade graduates at the first Apache controlled community school. She has had roles in a plethora of movies and television series.

I returned to the Navajo Reservation and continued teaching for the University of Arizona part of NTEDP which tutelage involved three separate and distinct experiences. The first class ended up being an almost insane enterprise – teaching an audiovisual course in the middle of an isolated spot on the Navajo Nation at Cameron. The insanity had two sources. I had to haul in all the audiovisual equipment and secondly, I had quit smoking – from two packs a day down to nothing.

SMOKING QUIT

I used the principles learned from my alcoholic friends, which precepts had trained me to let go of habits and damaging conditions. I had a deep down commitment that I would not smoke even if I faced a firing squad. What with continuous coffee drinking and wads of licorice in my mouth I plodded through the days, guzzling orange juice and standing in cold showers to ease the obsession to smoke. After two weeks the withdrawal symptoms began to ease. Something strange seemed to be occurring which I could not explain; I sensed that my former partner in the Early Childhood Program, a Board member on the NTEDP, had somehow soured on me and was telling the Navajo class members to drop out. My assessment of this situation was based on reading non-verbal behavioral posturing.

CORTEZ

Every Friday eve I traveled 100 miles from Dennehotso to Cortez, meeting with alcoholic friends by way of gaining the spiritual strength to continue my abstinence from cigarettes. As I write it has been over 38 years since I had my last cigarette and never once have I obsessed about having one – a true miracle. Ex-wife Charlene and cousin Carole Humphrey could not beat nicotine and both passed away from emphysema. God bless. My best friend and counselor in the fight against alcohol once cold turkeyed alcohol and heroin, but in the end could not give up nicotine. But he died of the Hepatitis C that he had acquired from a blood transfusion while wounded in the Korean War. He had suffered being bayoneted by the Chinese overrunning his army hospital.

ISAAC AND KNOWLES

My contacts and my high visibility within the Navajo Nation prompted me to form a partnership with Dr. Larry I. to create a consulting firm. I learned the hard way however that private enterprise on the Reservation was 100 % politics. We scrounged a few contracts but never really got up and running with a constant cash flow. We had an office in Flagstaff and Larry's wife at the time allowed us to do copying at her firm.

COW EPISODE.

Larry's dog, *Ma'iitsoh,* had killed his heifer on the lot of his home in Flagstaff and I helped him butcher the animal on the ground. Pulling out the entrails and the vile odor produced almost stopped me from consuming beef ever again. A drinking episode on the part of Larry and the flight of the company bank account ended these corporate operations.

ISAAC FOR CHAIRMAN

Isaac became a candidate for Chairman of the Navajo Nation but did not make the primary cut. Larry had amazing drive and organizational ability and would have been a good Navajo leader.

POWWOWS

Life back on the Reservation with Delphia, the children and son Jerrell was a true retreat for me. Weekends meant either going into Flagstaff or Farmington to shop and to eat at Furr's Cafeteria – or to spend all day Saturday around the powwow drums. The beat of the drums and the singing, the ready hand of dancers, the hugs and smiles were soothing to what I realized much later was a professional burnout for me.

The malaise that always seemed to pack every inch of the BIA house in Dennehotso with family or powwowers drove me into making a corner closet in the garage as an office, as a sanctuary away from the chaos. I used my old scout bedroll for a wall. I strung a landline phone extension in there and plugged in an electric heater. One night I wrote from dusk to dawn creating a science proposal. I seemed to have no discretion and would agree to take on the most complicated and difficult tasks. I couldn't say no. Unfortunately, my ego and my codependency combined to force me into near impossible tasks and time frames.

As I look back at my life at Purdue and Temple I realized that coming to the Kayenta and Monument Valley sector of the Navajo was like passing though a dark and desperate path. I rambled resolutely into a valley of Shangri-La full of 500 foot red stone buttes, distant pine covered mountains and the sounds of Seals and Crofts' "Summer Breeze" echoing in my mind. "*Summer breeze, makes me feel fine, blowing through the jasmine in my mind.*"

GREGORY JOHN

Son Gregory was accepted and adopted into the H family and was loved by all.

The H children and Greg were good for his half brother Jerrell. I would take all six of the kids up into the red rock ridges that spanned the road from Kayenta to Dennehotso, formations generated by the dome-like uplift of Monument Valley. We explored volcanic outcroppings created by the geological cracks in the valley, we gazed at the Laguna Creek pools and their water creatures and we shot off rockets at 200 mph between the trading post at Baby Rocks and Dennehotso.

LAWTON, OKLAHOMA

Holiday trips were made to Lawton, Oklahoma to visit Delphia's aunt. Of a Christmas morning I was told there was a delightful surprise awaiting me. It was a bowl of menudo; Delphia's Uncle Mayonnaise (a corruption of Muñoz) was Mexican American and always had menudo at the holidays. It took me over an hour and 10 cups of coffee to empty my bowl and avoid the embarrassment of violating a native custom of not accepting hospitality.

Though the joy of family along with being in one of the most sought after sites on the planet were the context of my existence, being with Delphia was beautiful from many standpoints. She was a very good looking women, very strong, a product of a matriarchal Tribe, and her persona as that of a Native women was quiet and stoic. Dressed in beaded buckskin and moccasins she projected the quintessential Indian maiden that was the central theme of the song, Indian Love Call. The actual song that ran through my mind in those happy days was:

Loving You – *"Lovin' you is easy 'cause you're beautiful......*
.....And everything that I do is out of lovin' you
La la la la la la la la la la la la la la la
Do do do do do," (Riperton, Minnie.1975. #1, US Billboard Hot 100. MetroLyrics).

DISNEYLAND

One of the happiest times with the H family was our trip to the coast, which began at Disneyland. In addition to Delphia, the five children and myself were grandchildren Yanivia and Tallee. (*Tallee* is the Kiowa word for "boy" and initiated a family custom of using Kiowa names for children). Son Gregory, who was always accepted in the H family, joined the group. Visiting Disneyland for the first time with children is an unforgettable experience. Bob and Tim had gone there with my parents but I missed that trip. Still, the delight, the excitement of the children is etched in one's mind forever. Outings like Disneyland can heal as well; they can chase away the dark clouds of previous life experiences and replace them with hope and acceptance in life's journey. Time spent at Elitch Gardens in Denver burned off some of the gloom of my sojourn in that city. While in the Los Angeles area we went to Universal Studios and Knott's Berry Farm, each venue providing its own unique array of enchanting experiences.

From Anaheim the family traveled south to San Diego to the Crystal Pier Motel which sits on pylons over the Pacific Ocean; the ocean waves roll in and under the motel creating continuous ebbing and flowing sounds of water. It was the first time the children had seen the sea, had splashed in the waves. Son Jerrell, running from a big incoming breaker, was swamped by water – he almost drowned and he couldn't stop laughing. The Pacific had been magical to me since my first trip to San Fran-

Honored as Head Gourd Dancer

cisco. I think it had the same effect on the H family.

The eventual breakup of my relationship with Delphia and the children a year later was charged with bitterness and anger. Years later several children commented that the family had a great time traveling to amazing places – and that had been the good thing about being together. Those days were something to remember.

TRIP TO NORTH DAKOTA

The family, including son Gregory, took off one summer to Fort Yates, North Dakota to attend a Standing Rock Sioux Tribe Powwow. Delphia's aunt was married to a member of the Dakota Sioux Tribe. The trip north was intriguing and included visiting a tower in Wyoming sacred to the Kiowa. The Devil's Tower as it is called, in northeastern Wyoming, is an ingenious edifice. The Kiowa tribes along with the Arapaho, Crow, Cheyenne, Lakota and Shoshone have had cultural and geographical ties to the monolith.

KIOWA LEGEND
"Before the Kiowa came south they were camped on a stream in the far north where resided a great many bears. One day, seven little girls were playing at a distance from the village and were chased by some bears. The girls ran toward the village and the bears were just about to catch them when the girls jumped on a low rock about three feet high. One of the girls prayed to the rock, 'Rock take pity on us, rock save us!'

The rock heard them and began to grow upwards, pushing the girls higher and higher. When the bears jumped to reach the girls, they scratched the rock, broke their claws, and fell to the ground. The rock rose higher and higher and the bears continued jumping at the girls until they were pushed up into the sky, where they now are – seven little stars in a group – the Pleiades. In the winter, in the middle of the night, the seven stars are right over this high rock. When people came to look, they found the bears' claws turned to stone, all around the base. No Kiowa living has ever seen this rock, but the old men have told of it – it is very far north where the Kiowa used to live. It is a single rock with scratched sides, the marks

Powwow and Gourd Dance Days

of the bears' claws there still, rising straight up, very high. There is no other rock like it in the whole country. No trees grow on it, only grass on the top. The Kiowa call this rock 'Tso-aa' – a tree rock – possibly because it grew tall like a tree. (Told by I-See-Many-Camp-Fire-Places, Kiowa soldier at Fort Sill, Oklahoma, 1897. Devil's Tower, The National Park Service.)

"Fort Yates was the home of Sitting Bull. Before the Battle of the Little Bighorn, Sitting Bull had a vision in which he saw the defeat of the 7th Cavalry under Lt. Col. George Armstrong Custer on June 25, 1876. Sitting Bull's leadership inspired his people to a major victory." (from Wikipedia – the free encyclopedia)

Sioux Powwow

One noteworthy aspect about the Powwow was that piles of *star blankets* were given away to honor the head dancers.

It seems that all tribes have "fried bread." The H family were used to Navajo fried bread, salt and wheat flour pizza-like shape cooked in hot grease that becomes thin and crunchy. On the other hand, the Sioux bread stays in a moist gooey ball.

Rather than sit during the whole Powwow, Gregory and I opted to visit the site of Fort Lincoln – the point of departure for Custer's westward campaign culminating in his death at Little Big Horn.

The H family had a pickup with a camper mounted in its bed. While one could see from the camper directly to the floor or through the bed overhanging the cab, one could not get in the cab of the truck except by navigating one of the cab doors. Three times during the trip I was literally paralyzed with anxiety. The first time is when Delphia pulled onto a long sector of muddy road going uphill. Far ahead we could see a semi truck swerving back and forth through the quagmire but we made it okay. The second episode occurred when Delphia decided to breeze by her grandparents' homestead. That road was also muddy and so slick that the pickup slid into the ditch alongside the road. It took a farmer with a huge tractor to get us out. The third episode occurred while traveling through northern Colorado. Peering from the small window in the bed overhanging the cab, we drove through herds of deer, some of which had already been struck by passing cars. Fortunately, we did not hit one.

The gods were taking care of us while cruising in that pickup. Many a time we left powwows in Oklahoma to travel across Texas and New Mexico on ice covered roads. More than once I had to lick my hand and put it out into the freezing air and back on my neck to keep awake.

APACHE OK— TURKEYS

The H family always attended the Polman Thanksgiving Day Powwow in Apache, Oklahoma, preparing ten or so turkeys in ovens at the Community Center. The powwows often lasted until after midnight when we would finally depart for Arizona. Marceline Polman would put on the face of a contentious old bag when in reality she was as sweet as an angel inside. One Thanksgiving she offered the H family several hundred dollars for travel and Delphia refused the money. Marceline was of the Wichita Tribe and was often the recipient of large sums of oil lease money.

Back in Arizona months later, eating at Furr's Cafeteria in Flagstaff I found three one hundred dollar bills under my chair. Thinking it might have been lost by a Navajo family that frequented Furr's I took it up to the cashier – a foolish decision in retrospect. Days later it dawned on me that the money came out of my jacket pocket after being secretly placed there by Marceline.

THOSE TRIPS

Here, a caveat concerning my days with the H family and travels to Oklahoma.

The living conditions of many of the families that hosted us during holidays and powwows were in marked contrast to what I knew growing up in the American middle class. Before one gets comfortable with the idea that Native Americans and other minorities are "unclean" it is paramount to remember it was the European intruders into their land that brought a myriad microbes to which they had no immunity, subsequently wiping out large numbers with smallpox and other diseases – killing more than died in all the military campaigns waged against them. The death tolls from the newly introduced European diseases often reached 80-90 percent. Entire tribes vanished before the tidal wave of disease.

Natives existed for centuries within their natural environments without the decimation caused by European diseases. Having established the possibly superior status of Native American cultures in the realm of their distinct health and hygienic constraints – there was no Black Plague in their populations – it is possible for me to report the uniquely different conditions we faced in our travels.

My partner in the Early Childhood Program at NAU related that a pet prairie dog would upon occasion come up into their Hogan. I can remember round steak being hung on lines during the Flagstaff Powwow days that were covered with flies. If disease resulted as a consequence of this exposure it probably was born from sources inherent in the dominant surroundings.

Native peoples did not always make successful transitions from a teepee to the environs of a modern house. It was not unusual to see houses on the Apache and in Oklahoma subdivisions with boarded up doors and windows.

One time visiting Anadarko, Oklahoma the family stayed at a grand person's house wherein the plumbing had failed months before. In one case out in the Oklahoma countryside, the home of a medicine person had an outdoor john attached right off the kitchen with a curtain separating the two.

The younger members of E's family, having been raised in standard subdivision housing, were learning upkeep skills in what passed for modern housing. Some problems faced by Natives in their residence transition were caused by the failure of promoters and builders to provide the knowledge and technical support necessary to help them maintain the housing areas.

Injustices and wholesale destruction of Native American lives has been justified by = bogus ideas that they are unclean, unintelligent, lazy and immoral, (unChristian-like).

PROPOSALS

Having been identified as a proposal writer, I had many opportunities and requests to write proposals. I rewrote the proposal for the Navajo Academy in Farmington. Mr. Platero took over what was a Methodist Mission School to remake it into a super prep school for bright Navajo kids from the Rez. He also recruited top athletes for football and basketball. The teams did exceptionally well, and the *esprit de corps* in both sports and academe were superior. Two of the H family played in sports and were honored as all-staters—Charlie for football and Denise for soccer. Charlie turned down a scholarship to play football at the University of Arizona but did go on to graduate from the University of Oklahoma. Denise finished at OU with a degree in nursing.

Teaching Psych and David Berliner

I continued as an instructor for the U of A component of the Navajo Teacher Education Program, teaching Child Development and Educational Psychology at the Ganado College site. Dr. David Berliner, the author of the text we used, actually came up to Ganado and conducted a session. His presence empowered the students in the roles as teacher aides, protecting them from the condescension of supervisory personnel who lorded over them an errant superiority.

Traditional Navajo culture retained a bias against the handicapped. I emphasized the need to counter this concept by taking students on field trips to visit facilities wherein the handicapped were excelling. There existed a blind Navajo gentleman who was a skydiver. He would jump out of the plane and wait for a signal to pull his ripcord when his partner radioed him through his earphones.

Flag reunion 81

Delphia accompanied me to the 1982 Flagstaff High School Reunion. She stood out amidst the group because like many Kiowa her skin was very dark, making her all the more beautiful. One of my classmates, a fellow who had always been an adversary, slurred that he was "still married to the same woman."

Sophie Bennet came to celebrate with the class of '52 and pointedly informed me that she had had an annulment and that, although he was living with her, her ex husband had a bad heart and his presence would not be a problem if I wanted to come visit her in California.

Sophie Bennet Re-enters

Sophie kept appearing again and again in my life, in bodily flesh and in dreams. In both cases the rendezvous never materialized. Thirty years later in 2012 I saw her move slowly into the main reunion get-together. I managed to isolate her in the living room for a tête-à-tête but was interrupted by one of the classmates who said she had not seen Sophie in a long while and needed to talk to her. Once again, any obsession with Sophie was thwarted by the gods of love. I sent her an email attachment with a song by Michael Feinstein, "My Favorite Year," a passionate message to memorialize the year of the courtship that ended a romance with the Gatsby-like finality.

MY FAVORITE YEAR
"After all the lives I've lived through
All these years.........
..........You were my favorite love
That was my favorite year"
(Michael Feinstein, My Favorite Year
From the Album Isn't It Romantic.
January 1, 1988.

TUBA FLIGHT

Teaching courses for the University of Arizona brought me up to the Reservation on many occasions; I generally took the flight from Tucson to Kayenta or from Tucson to Tuba City. On one visit to Tuba City my associate Allyn S and I quickly boarded the single engine plane as a massive thunderstorm was moving in from the west. Conditions were forming so suddenly that the pilot had to take off in an unusual direction. The plane was buffeted by winds so fierce that I had to place my hands on the ceiling of the plane to stay upright. We could not land in Flagstaff because of the weather and had to go to Winslow instead wherein I would take the bus to Flagstaff. Winslow had a very popular Mexican food restaurant at its airport. While dinning with Allyn and the pilot, restaurant staff and customers kept meandering past, giving me the eye. Finally, one of them came over and asked me if I were Waylon Jennings. I laughed and said no, remarking however that I should have said yes – and I mocked lip singing one of the artist's songs on the jukebox.

COUNTY SUPERVISOR CAMPAIGN

My old football buddy Arturo Rubi invited me to run for Congress from the at that time 5th Arizona District. Never short of naiveté and grandiosity I of course agreed. I moved in with the Rubi family in Winslow, later residing in one of their rental properties near the high school.

Election Cancelled

I traveled to Phoenix to spend a day in the law offices of a Winslow high graduate researching the dimensions of what constituted a Congressional race. I talked with then Senator Dennis De Concini's office and learned about the hurdles you had to jump to run, and to win.

I even stayed with my alcoholic counselor Ed Aston and his wife Betty who were living in Tempe. I went shopping with Ed and Betty and inexplicably bought a pair of shoes that were too small and pinched my feet!

I appeared at a District meeting to announce my candidacy and lay out a platform. Somebody agreed to be my "advance man" which was something I knew nothing about. Ultimately, that visit to Phoenix convinced me that a run for Congress was near to impossible. The financial requirements, in spite of Arturo's assurance that the "money would come," seemed insurmountable. So I decided to run for County Supervisor of Navajo County – a position that 'Turo said was ten times more difficult than running for Congress. Speeches at the VFW and door-to-door canvassing of almost every home in Winslow occupied July and August. I now feel flattered that at least five or more candidates joined in the contest. My platform – plethora of platitudes one amusing to me now – could be used for any political quest, even for nation building. We established a raffle program, which prizes included a valuable pot from Delphia's brother's collection; he was a well-respected artist in the Santa Fe milieu. We also held a powwow honoring Mitsy B, an All-American Winslow High School basketball player.

There were two key furniture items in the house I lived in. One was a recliner and the other a mattress on the floor. Arturo's son overcame me with paranoia with the suggestion that someone might come in the middle of the night and force me at gunpoint to "take a drink." I had already attended a party at the house of a police chief who was later indicted and convicted of lying about an accidental death. Someone had offered me a martini glass filled with vodka when I had asked for water. I promptly went in the bathroom and poured out the booze and rinsed the glass, amused at the hawkeyed looks I was getting, eyes waiting to see me lose it in a drunken rage.

I played the FM station from Showlow into the wee hours to provide a sense of calm. One July night a violent thunderstorm roared through the Little Colorado River Valley and the town of Winslow. The force of the wind blew open my bedroom door. I grabbed the pistol Rubi insisted I needed for protection and realized I could have killed anyone coming through that door. I gave the gun back to Rubi and have often stated that my Higher Power would protect me against violence and that a friend had suffered a bullet ricocheting off his head. Son Gregory stayed with me that summer and slept in the recliner.

WINSLOW— KIRK'S MOM

I had a good sober friend, a retired Santa Fe engineer and one noon I was lunching with him at the Pancake House. He was with a charming lady and introduced me by name. "Jerry Knowles!," she hollered in her Texas brogue. She was the mother of my close friend from the 40's, Kirk Clark. Kirk had been a Golden Gloves boxer and football player. He was tragic character who had been beaten by his father with a belt and who had challenged the famous football coach, Emil Nasser. In the end, Nasser was the one who turned Kirk's life around.

Kirk's mother told me Kirk was sober from alcohol for 7 years before his death in 1964 caused by his continued use of an old rickety single engine plane.

Late that afternoon I went to the Winslow Cemetery to Daniel Kirk Clark's grave. Teary eyed I told Kirk that I wished we could have spent time together as sober alcoholics. The last time I saw him was in 1955 and all I got was a bitter glare. I walked away to my red two-door Toyota just as the sun was setting and headed westbound toward Flagstaff on Interstate 40. My radio speakers had a short, and the FM Showlow stations would crack on once in awhile when I hit a bump. I clipped a small pothole and on came the FM station playing Kirk's favorite song.

The Justice Department rejected the Navajo County's petition to increase its districts from three to five. Hence my only serious run for public office and an entry into the political realm of northern Arizona was ended when my bid for office was cancelled by no election.

CAPTURED BY THE APACHES

Few were surprised when one of the U.S. Army's most lethal weapons was commissioned with "Apache" in its label. The powerful effectiveness of the Apache Helicopter was manifested in no better way than in the mass of twisted equipment and burned out tanks strewn across the Iraqi desert after Desert Storm. What had once been the Army's unconquerable foe in the early West would later be recognized as the quintessence of fighting skill, endurance and ferocity. The long struggle of the Apache people, led by Chiefs Geronimo and Cochise, to protect their land from intrusion and to preserve their Apache ways against a tide of European invasion stands out with distinction in the annals of American History. It required 5,000 U.S. Calvary and one million dollars to capture and subdue Geronimo and thirteen other Apaches.

Apache Mountain Spirit Dancer

The Apache people, although physically subdued by waves of U.S. Calvary in the 1800's have never given up their quest for cultural freedom, economic self-sufficiency and national sovereignty. During the Nixon administration of the 1970's, tribal self-determination was given a quantum boost with the passage of the Public Law 638 Act known at the Indian Self-determination Act. PL 638 enabled the Apache people to contract for and run their own schools. The people of the small community of Cibecue decided to take over and control the Bureau of Indian Affairs-run School in their community. A bitter relationship between the BIA and the White Mountain Apaches, particularly the community at Cibecue, had grown even more hellish over the years but once again it was the tenacity, skill and intellect of the Cibecue Apaches that overcame massive obstacles and established their own Cibecue Community School. Today, Cibecue School has elementary and high schools that operate year round. They have distinguished themselves with state championships in basketball and are renowned for their student Mountain Spirit Dancers. The story of the School Board, parents, teachers and students who created the first Apache controlled education institution is a monument to their wisdom, courage, patience and that fierce and unquenchable energy of the traditional Apache.

APACHE SCHOOL

The Isaac-Knowles consulting firm had provided a management workshop to the School Board of the BIA School in Cibecue in the western sector of the White Mountain Apache Nation. I had finalized a curriculum guide that integrated Apache Culture into the school curriculum and was therefore well known and accepted by the people there. The White Mountain Apaches were notable on several levels. Their reservation contained the famous (or infamous, if you like) "Fort Apache" of western fame, and Cibecue itself was symbolic in that the site ignited the long war between Geronimo and the U.S. Army.

The School Board planned, submitted and was awarded tribal control of the Cibecue School. It was mid-summer and there remained a significant amount of documentation to seal the takeover. Judy DeJose, school board president and Tribal councilwoman, asked me if I would initiate and then direct the institution of the school. I was flattered and exhilarated. I believed that my experience and philosophy in elementary education gave me the confidence and vision to put the school on the right path at its very inception.

MOUNTAIN SPIRIT DANCERS

The early morning sun glowed bright and promising off the west wall and you could hear a pin drop in the vast expanse of the gym. The faint chant of Apache Mountain Spirit Dancers could be heard coming from somewhere off to the southwest. It was American Indian Day, 1984 and the initial celebration of that event by a fledgling Cibecue Community School. The White Mountain Apache people had wanted to have their own school and the control of their education as far back as the days following their final subjugation by the U.S. Cavalry. It was down by the creek, just over the hill from the school wherein the Apache scouts turned on the Calvary in the late 1800's, killing quite a few of them. The scouts had begun to lose faith in the good intentions of the U.S. government and became enraged after the wanton slaying of their medicine man. The same scouts were later hung in front of the entire community.

The heart and soul of the Apache people is expressed in the dress, chants and dance of the Mountain Spirit Dancers. It would be a symbolic return to power and self-determination for the Mountain Spirit Dancers to enter what heretofore been an alien institution and a symbol of restriction over their lives, culture and children. It would be the first time ever that the Apache Crown Dancers would enter the gym of a school controlled by their own Apache people.

I had become the newly appointed Executive Director of Cibecue Community School and had shifted my anxiety about school beginnings into a state of utter awe. As a boy the Apache Mountain Spirit Dancers had always dazzled me when the black hooded chanters, decked out with their gold-colored buckskin, snaked down the hot July pavement during the annual powwow celebration in Flagstaff. Later, as an adult, I had over many years frequently participated in Kiowa gourd dances at powwows. But I had never seen such deep feeling and respect given to a cultural event in a community as I did that warm September morning in Cibecue. Nor had I in all my time as a teacher and administrator seen an entire student body and parent-packed gym go dead silent at one time. The only sounds were the abrupt cries of tiny voices and the low wailing of infants in the crowd.

The charming, classic Apache face of Board President and Councilwoman, Judy De-Jose beamed with joy and pride. A long tough road had been traveled to grasp the reins driving Apache education in Cibecue. Great possibilities loomed on the horizon. But the trail to gain control of Cibecue School had been fraught with ambushes, traps and pitfall after pitfall and what, at times appeared to be insurmountable obstacles. Once the authority to operate the school was finally approved by the BIA it was as though the BIA had snapped a rubber band back into the face of the community with seemly impenetrable barriers deliberately designed to assure the failure of their community school. Yet, Cibecue Community School stands today as a monument to the beauty, strength and perseverance of the Cibecue Apaches.

THEY KILLED MY RELATIVES

It seems that the sunny August morning of 1984 was only yesterday. I can still recall every detail, including my fixed gaze at the namesakes of my Irish relatives chiseled on the granite block at the Cibecue Community Center. In the battle of Cibecue in the late 1800's Apache scouts, enraged at the murder of their medicine man, turned on the U.S. Cavalry, slaughtering a number of them. I remembered feigning solemnity, remarking to Board President Judy DeJose that her people "had killed some of my Irish relatives down here and I better get through the 'Pass' before sunset."

ELECTION CANCELLED

I was still on the ballot as a candidate for the upcoming Navajo County Supervisor election and was still bivouacked in an empty house in Winslow belonging to high school chum 'Turo Rubi. I was commuting back and forth to Cibecue to help the Board prepare a Public Law 638 contract to assume control over the school. However, when a week later the U.S. Justice Department rejected a redistricting plan for the newly created five Navajo County Supervisory districts, and the Supervisor election was canceled, I mused that the cancellation was a quirk of fortune for both Navajo

County and myself. Moreover, I was out of a job. Ms. DeJose's offer for me to apply for the Executive Director of Cibecue Community School came as a great blessing.

TOUGH BEGINNING

By sheer bureaucratic bungling or Machiavellian design the cards seemed to be stacked against even getting the school off the ground. First, there had been a long period of negotiation spanning years for control of the school, in conflict with stubborn BIA officials. The decision to grant a contract school to the Cibecue Community School Board was finally made on the brink of the autumn opening of school. As the first day of school rapidly approached, no contract had been signed nor did the BIA yet obligate critical funds. Points of no return and a dark abyss of chaos were fast approaching – a perfect storm guaranteed to accelerate both my creativity and any fear of failure I held dear. The future of Cibecue Community School was in the institutional dire straits.

Ironically, and in stark contrast to the apocalyptic backdrop of its institutional birth, the actual corpus of Cibecue Day School – as it was still known – seemed like a ghostly tomb at night. Tapping away at the typewriter under the light of a single bulb was like being in an Egyptian tomb. I remembered looking down the dark and empty halls, gripped by chills of fear. Rumor was that someone had been murdered within the school walls. I sensed an ominous force that whispered out of the blackness, "the school is not going to make it." Premonitions of crises, disappointments, anxiety, and frustration pervaded the ether. Specters of troubled and pained Apache children, teachers and parents appeared and then faded in my mind, intensifying my frustration as I wrestled with the massive bureaucratic red tape in front of me. There may be darkness before dawn but in those somber halls I could not at the time foresee the pride and satisfaction that would appear there one day.

STAGE FOR DISASTER

September approached within the setting of a classic Greek tragedy. All the props for disaster and destruction were on stage. There would be a seven-week period through September when the BIA could have opened and controlled the school. The current staff of BIA teachers were informed that they would not be rehired in October when the school was under contract. Most of them did not want to come back. The two teachers that did return during the short period of BIA control were the worst of the worst and epitomized those horror stories about incompetent and abusive professionals working within Indian nations. One gentleman had punched a student; the other had allegedly fondled girls during Physical Education. Both had been "exonerated" through a series of "BIA hearings," and they both came back for a short seven-week stint to draw their pay. That meant trouble – and it was.

Since phone service in Cibecue was sporadic and unreliable I charged calls to the BIA phone number in Cibecue from a pay phone at Safeway in Showlow. I made marathon calls to former associates at points throughout the U.S. My alma mater, the University of Illinois, contained a brace of innovative graduates; the University of Indiana, boasting an extensive outreach teacher education program that had operated for years within Indian communities, represented a potential pool of quality staff. I also had an extensive repertoire of associates and friends at the universities of Arizona, New Mexico, Purdue and Northern Arizona University. In addition, the Native American Placement Center in Denver was tapped as a resource for identifying management staff.

THE ACTORS

Only after an extensive number of phone calls and hastily summoned Board meetings lasting into the wee hours of the night did a pool of individuals become christened to commence working with the Apache school. That September at Cibecue, the first platoon of staff stood as profoundly diverse and creative as they were caring about the Apache children they had committed to serve. There was an English Major University of Illinois grad from East St. Louis who was a vegetarian. A child development major graduate of the University of Colorado accepted a position as Kindergarten Teacher. She was two months pregnant and also the first Fire Chief of Cibecue Community School! Bill Thorpe from New York, most appropriately a namesake after famous Olympic Champion, Jim Thorpe, became coach and Athletic Director. A young lady and member of the Navajo Nation was to begin her career at Cibecue teaching her cousins, the Apaches. A young woman with long golden hair and driving a silver Fiero took up residence as second grade teacher. She was the daughter of a wealthy dairy magnate and had worked previously as a bartender on Catalina Island. A participant in the second Wounded Knee battle and member of the Sioux Tribe committed to position of Curriculum Supervisor. A precocious and intensely Lilliputian accountant became Cibecue's first financial officer – a position essential to the overseeing of the large sums of money granted to the community. A special education teacher of a frontier, adventurous mentality left Alamo Navajo Community School on the Navajo to set up a special education program. The Apache teacher aides with their ancient roots within the community provided a cultural and human bridge in the transformation of the BIA Cibecue Day School to a Cibecue Community School. Betty Duyrea, a member of the White Mountain Apache Tribe who had grown up in Cibecue acted as an administrative assistant. Ms. Duyrea's adeptness, keen intelligence and boundless energy, so typical of many native American women became the vortex and stabilizing force within the frantic hurricane of activity characterizing those first institutional baby steps.

TROUBLE IN RIVER CITY

The authoritative voice of the Board's lawyer, "Manny" (Emmanuel) Davis, reverberated through my eardrums with its usual lawyeress twang – "you can't hire people – you don't even have a contract yet!" I had committed a plethora of staff – but without money, institutional or contractual authority – and they were already on their way to Cibecue. Moreover, for seven weeks, the BIA would still have control and would still be the only authority qualified to hire staff replacements – even I had to be employed by the BIA as the school's principal – forever 'tainting' my resume.

The BIA had emphatically said, "No, you can't hire anyone not certified on the BIA's roster of job candidates." All applicants for positions in the BIA had to be officially "certified" and placed on a list before they could be retained.

NO MONEY, NO TEACHERS AND NO AUTHORITY

The debut of Cibecue Community School was rapidly approaching – with no money, no teachers and no authority. I informed Ms. DeJose and the School Board members that there were no teachers for the children at Cibecue. They sequestered the BIA supervisor – one Nephi Cody, a member of the Sioux Tribe – from Fort Apache into the Valley of Cibecue – like Cochise did with Jeb Stewart. The BIA, confronted by the School Board, conceded that there was a way to hire uncertified staff. The Board and I were informed that the cadre of staff requested by me who were already on their way to Cibecue could be hired after all the names on the BIA's "certified list" had refused a position. Once again at a pay phone in Showlow, I called all candidates on the BIA certified list. The only candidate that accepted a position was a gentleman who became the future sixth grader teacher – the owner of a Showlow motel – who turned out to be an excellent teacher. So a corps of characters from all over the U.S., enticed by beautiful brochures of the Sunrise Ski Resort, the majestic White Mountains, the enchantment of the Apache Nation and the allure of Arizona came to the Valley of the Cibecue River, where Geronimo was first held captive by the U.S. Cavalry.

BUREAUCRATIC BEHEMOTH OF THE BIA

The bureaucratic behemoth of the BIA was not the only enemy waiting to ambush the fledgling school. The community was split over whether or not the school should go "contract." The flames of opposition were fanned by the political interface between School Board President and Councilwoman DeJose on the one hand and Marjorie Grimes, the other Councilwoman from Cibecue. The White Mountain Apache Nation Department of Education also wished to have prime authority over the school and soon, the school became a vortex of opposing powers. I felt that if the fledgling Tribally controlled institution were to morph into its ultimate potential in serving the needs of Apache children it would have to remain relatively free of the traditional canons of elementary education.

SUPPORT FOR TEACHER AIDES

Rumors had been circulated that the teacher aides, all of whom had extended family and cultural roots in the community, would end up with lowered salaries if the school were to be summarily "contracted." Meetings were held throughout the summer with this paraprofessional staff to squelch that rumor. Actually, under a proposed Community School Salary Schedule, all their salaries would actually go up significantly – the increase based on a new salary schedule with bonuses for educational attainments and quality of performance. The aides' salary schedule was modified by integrating local school district salaries within in the current BIA schedule, and providing those additional rewards for performance as well as educational advancement. The icing on the cake for the paraprofessionals was the proposal for a Career Opportunity track – an on site, school financed system of counseling and college courses though Northern Pioneer College which would provide a way for these dedicated paraprofessionals to advance toward certification and become teachers.

Rumors, myths and facts about Cibecue Day School were epidemic and lay heavy on my mind all that summer of 1984. My experience as a teacher, as a parent and as a participant in Tribal communities had shown me how unfair such negative reputations were to schools and how damaging they were to communities. The underestimation of the value, worth and abilities of their children choked initiative and lowered expectations for school performance and life itself.

THEY WOULDN'T LIVE THERE

Most of the teacher housing was empty. There was a belief that the community was very dangerous. Former staff had chosen not to live there but to commute round trip as much as 100 miles a day. I analyzed various points of view and the actual facts about the school and concluded that there existed a standard lack of achievement – three to four years behind in academic areas – which was often characteristic of Native American schools. All students came to school as dominate Apache speakers with limited English. There were rumors about attendance problems and serious behavioral episodes. There were stories of upper grade teachers chasing down students with their cars during class breaks to capture them and bring them back to class. The uncle of Delphia, stationed at Whiteriver Hospital loved to sit and tell Cibecue horror stories. It seemed like everybody saw Cibecue School as a depressing proposition.

A religious person in the community shared his grief with me about several suicides – one in which a boy actually used a chain saw on himself.

SOME VIOLENT PASTS

Unconfirmed by me personally, but shared by some trusted authorities were several extremely upsetting episodes. One involved a violent interface between a Cibecue gang and an opposing gang up the road in the small community of Carrizo. I was told that one of the gangs had cut off the head of the opposing gang member and stuck it on a pole at the entrance to the community. I was told that in the 1960's the original BIA school had been burned to the ground as a consequence of upper grade students having an issue with the principal. Not only were Cibecue School teaching slots vacant, but I was told the Indian Health Service personnel were not allowed to live in the community but had to commute from near by towns off the Reservation.

The most disturbing report involved the emasculation of an outsider because of his inappropriate relationship with a local female. I emphasize again that I feel these were only rumors – unconfirmed by me, but shared by sources that had no particularly sinister motive in mind. Still, such rumors had a very negative impact. Cibecue notoriously maintained the highest crime rates for any community in Arizona—primarily the result of intra tribal conflicts.

BUILDING A SHIP HEADED FOR DARK WATERS

The day after Labor Day in 1984, Cibecue Community School would embark into the murky, uncharted waters of community-controlled education. The fledgling institution would journey into an environment wherein a large, politically motivated anti-school segment of the community were hoping for its failure. They were watching for one mistake. Local paraprofessional staff were treading water with wait-and-see attitudes. The BIA bureaucracy – either by omission or commission – had put the school in a position like a hand that had been severed from a body. Students abhorred the school, because of its past history, expected boredom, the humdrum and the anticipation of hatred to be projected from teachers whose system they had long challenged with all sorts of misbehavior. Many parents despaired of enrolling their child, feeling that the environment was dangerous, weak and ineffective.

THE BEST AND WORST OF TIMES

The startling peal of the school bell at 8:30AM on Tuesday, September 4th, 1984 subdued staccato voices in the Cibecue lounge. High hopes as well as considerable dread dwelt in the minds of the staff. Surely many of them wondered that morning whether the bells tolled for a wedding or a funeral. During the first few weeks of school, students had to be literally disarmed of their summer's accumulation of weapons. Episodes of vandalism began to occur with increasing frequency. The newly appointed Curriculum Supervisor, one Ruth Hunsinger who was a member of the Sioux

Tribe and a veteran of the second Wounded Knee incident, reported that the students were doing "unspeakable things" at the back of the stage. (They were smearing feces on the walls, and having carried out a similar act myself as an infant I could emphasize with the students' motives.) The second week of school one girl went to the hospital – a victim of the paper clip rubber band war. Early reports from the Indian Health Service were touch and go as to whether she would lose her eye. Her father was intensely angry and indicated he would hold me personally responsible if that happened. One day while attending a standard meeting at the BIA office in Whiteriver, the supposed nightmare occurred. I faced a distraught and depressed staff. It was alleged that an attempted rape had taken place in one of the classrooms. However, after questioning all the students present at the event, I found that the incident was only pre-puberty play acting by a very young small boy and not a violent attack. Nevertheless, rumors of the event steamrolled and wreaked havoc throughout the Cibecue Community, including the Indian Health Service clinic that checked for evidence of rape. A very young child was simply imitating physical actions he had seen in a movie. It was absolutely a case for correction and counseling – but it was not a criminal episode. News of the affair made for bad PR and was political cannon fodder for those opposing forces in their obsession to "do in" the newly emerging school.

They Rode Away on Horses

One morning the 4th grade teacher ran into the offices and reported that half of her students did not return after morning recess. Amazed, we all asked, "Where did they go?"

"On their horses," sputtered the teacher. As White Mountain Apaches were accomplished horsemen, the students had tied their horses out in the bushes south of the building and when things didn't go their way, they would simply take off.

"I'll Cut Off That Beard!"

The seventh, eighth and ninth graders glared at me, smarting from the lousy treatment given them by the BIA over past years. They were itching to find out what made me tick. I had asked an eighth grader named Limbert Q who was the heir apparent leader of the upper grades to go to the cafeteria and he fired back at me, "do you want that red beard cut off?" Battle lines were being drawn. One afternoon Supervisor Hunsinger excitedly grabbed my arm, stopping me from going out the door. "Titus is out there with a pellet gun that has a scope sight on it!" Apparently Titus M, a 9th grader, was seen out in the bushes with a rifle, scope sight and all. I knew that to show fear would mean loss of respect and no hope of reaching out to other students. I casually walked outside and went around, in and out of buildings. Titus and his parents had a conference the next day and I expressed that it would be sad to see Titus leave

Cibecue and go to school at Whiteriver, which I indicated would be the case if Titus didn't 'shape up.'

The upper grades posed the greatest challenge to the teachers and administrators. They brought with them habits they used to confront the BIA over the years, such as taking off at the change of classes. They would disappear out into the mesquite bushes to smoke, drink and plot. A most frustrating confrontation to the fledgling institution involved the case of an 8th grader who lived in the hills and traveled on horseback, eluding Tribal police, parents, and the school staff. He would come out of nowhere to mock the staff by casually talking to upper grade students from astride his horse at a safe distance over the fence, avoiding anyone who approached. It would have taken a horse-mounted posse to capture him.

CONFLAGRATION

One sunny, lazy afternoon when the school finally seemed to be calming down, tranquility was shattered when two teachers came into my office and yelled, "It's on fire!" I looked out the window to see all the bushes on the south side of the school in flames. That October was particularly dry – a bad time for a brush fire. I grabbed an extinguisher, ran out and put out the blaze in several bushes, got another extinguisher and finished off some more bushes. The fires had been edging toward huge propane tanks located on other side of school!
"Thank God," I muttered, trembling inside my office. By this time, I had begun to overlook my own humiliation and frustration. I realized what creativity, what potential and what talent these Apache kids had. After all, they were made of the same stuff as Geronimo, whose energy, ingenuity and intelligence both baffled and demoralized an entire division of the U.S. Army. I knew that the students were capable of doing anything, and they sensed that I was very fond of them. Although even I laughed at what was going on, I knew I couldn't accept misbehavior, nonattendance and poor performance. To allow the youth of Cibecue to continue in total defiance of the school and the educational process would destroy their chances of becoming all those things that their talent and creativity could someday manifest.

SALVO OF BUREAUCRATIC BOMBS

The bureaucrats almost did us in. We experienced a bombardment – a salvo – a litany of blows – that came all at once in early October. The BIA announced it was taking our buses due to there being no lease agreement; the power company said they would cut off the juice on Monday because there was no deposit agreement; staff salaries would be delayed indefinitely because the electronic transfer of funds couldn't be coaxed into the bank. The Arizona Department of Education sent a standard letter rejecting our lunch subsidies because we didn't have a civil rights certification guaranteeing equal opportunity. Most of the school's equipment and transportation vehicles had been allegedly ripped off during the summer by nearby BIA schools, leaving us with piles of junk. As a last straw, one morning I was told that if I didn't get a signed contract to Phoenix by 4:15PM, the school would loose a $40,000 carryover of funds. I left on a chartered flight (weirdest plane ever seen) at 3:30 from Showlow, arrived and caught a cab at 4:30. (They said they went ahead anyway and obligated the $40K.) As my account was compromised to the extent I could not withdraw from the ATM, I only had cash to take a bus to a motel and write a check for a room.

HAND WRITTEN CHECKS

For the first payroll, I wrote out checks by hand calculating 'withholding' amounts for each staff member while watching football on TV. I was given Mexican food by the Illinois grad teacher – I found out she was vegetarian and I was eating her dog's food. She cooked them excellent meals!

Periodically, the phones would fail in the early afternoon. The BIA had ripped out the CB radio "because we were no longer a federal agency" so we had no way to communicate with either our buses or outside agencies. That's the way it was in October, 1984. Cry, or laugh. I could only laugh. Some mornings I played Kiowa gourd dance music on my stereo at full volume. My double wide would actually resonate and shake. Once I actually danced with my gourd. I would shoot out the door and rush down to school. The head of facility management, Tony Z, looked at me like I was crazy. Obviously, I figured that both students and others weren't buying into the Cibecue Community School. If for no other reason, I wanted to prove those insensitive doubters wrong about the school, the students and the community. I felt a dark cloud of negativity from the BIA area administration hanging over everything.

COME, STAY, WORK AND BEHAVE

It was clear that a primary issue was to get the students to come to school, have them stay there and behave within certain limits to maintain a learning environment. Also, we had to find a way to get them to perform up to their abilities, to realize their enormous talents and potential. *Come, behave and perform* were key foci. We needed to guarantee a safe place and an open environment welcoming parents and the community as part owners. We needed a climate where students could become motivated, interested and excited about what the school could offer. The school had to be accepted by the community. It had to be the resource base and dispenser of those things that would 'turn on' the students to the real meaning of education. We needed a staff who could create this environment and who could project a deep caring for the students and a concern and respect for the community.

A number of concepts had to be in place for the construction of the kind of school that would capture the trust and interest of the students. We emphasized school pride and achievement in athletics and in cultural events. We encouraged the staff to employ unique ways of learning. We began an Indian Club, which introduced traditional Apache dance contests, standard powwow dancing and the formation of Cibecue's own Mountain Spirit Dance Group. Students went to powwows in Albuquerque and to the Tucson Annual (Tohono O'odham Nation) Wa:k Powwow celebration. They started their own Cibecue Annual Powwow. The Cibecue Mountain Spirit Dancers became a favorite at the Wa:k Powwow and were invited to dance at NAU, the renowned Herd Museum in Phoenix and they were macho proud. Their costumes, made by local artists, were exquisitely beautiful. Vans were used to take the Indian Club to a wide variety of events. When I left Cibecue, arrangements for a trip to Japan by the Crown Dancers were being seriously investigated. It was crucial that Apache children recapture and respect their identity and their rich traditions. At the writing of this work the White Mountain Apache are having conciliatory rapprochement with the Tohono O'odham people to mend a historically brutal interface.

SCHOOL PRIDE

I felt that school pride through athletics was extremely important. Some community people actually showed up with clubs at our first football game. So-so and losing seasons seemed to be what was happening. So we got a young aggressive coach/teacher from New York named Thorpe who really pushed, along with two local Apache staff, emphasizing winning, and pride. Plans were made to change colors to forest green and gold and their name from 'Mustangs' to 'Cibecue Apaches.' Traditional Apaches headbands would be worn as a distinguishing mark of pride. Title IV (Indian Education Act) enrichment funds were used to send students to Phoenix Sun games, Arizona State University football games, and to summer basketball (Larry Nance, Phoenix Suns Player) and football camps.

THE SCHOOL BECAME LIKE A SECOND FAMILY.

Many of the students because of home conditions were not receiving proper nutrition. Some came to school only to eat lunch. We had started a lunch program serving the food distributor Nobel Sysco's "dinner menu" – the likes of steak, pork chops, dessert and ice cream. Then we added breakfast (not juice and bananas) – scrambled or fried eggs, bacon, buttered toast and applesauce. What a difference breakfast made!

COMPUTERS

It was felt that basic skill development – reflecting upon the old reading workbooks – along with timetable practice and similar modalities could best be done with Apple computers. We combined Title I (At Risk Students) and regular funds and purchased computers to be used for reading, math and language. We also used computers for special video games times during and after school.

"HANDS-ON" AND ACTIVE LEARNING MODELS

A critical emphasis was placed on "hands-on" and active learning models. The school was to look at a student's total development, not just his mind. His spirit and his body, along with his mind were to be exposed to experiences as truly related to life as could be generated – to bring the world into the school and to transport the student out into the world. An amazing number of activities, programs, and projects were generated based on this concept. We leased two 15-passenger vans and teachers were exhorted to schedule and to use these vans to the max. Requests for field trips had to be justified by a plan showing the trips as an integral part of ongoing instruction.

A SKI CLUB

A ski club was formed with approximately 100 students a week going to the Apache Ski Resort at Sunrise. Appropriate attendance, good behavior and dedicated performance were the criteria for participation in a Friday ski trip. A trip to Chaco Canyon was made as a part of a history class. A school newspaper stimulated three years growth in English achievement by 8th graders whereas in the past, only one-third of a year had been gained. Trips were made to Disneyland, San Diego, the Sonoran Desert Museum, the Tucson Planetarium, and Lowell Observatory in Flagstaff and to innumerable other venues. Field trips were seen as a vital mechanism in providing interest, intellectual content, stimulation, and curiosity for learning – they were not just a joy ride. One teacher, Sherry Mc., accompanied a group of her students on their first plane trip to Los Angeles and by boat to Catalina Island. Another instructor, Cheryl, took a trip to San Diego with third graders, thereby initiating a deep and sustained interest in school.

GENERATING LONG TERM INTEREST

First-hand, experiences to help the youth explore and discover ideas – involvements generating long term interest in math, science, English and art were strongly emphasized. We had one of the most talented, special education teachers in Dona Craft that I'd ever seen. Her room was like a microcosm of the outside world. One day on the football field Thorpe's class shot off rockets, using trigonometry and stopwatches to

calculate their velocity. Once at a Southwestern Social Science Conference in Durango, I
reported an enormous positive shift in attitudes toward science by doing these sorts of
things with Navajo teacher aides. Vine Delo-
ria, author of "Custer Died for Your Sins"
and Kenneth Begishe, an authority in Navajo
development, were proponents of a hands-on
approach being the key way American Indian children learned.

White Mountain Apache Children

EMPHASIZE CAREERS

Cibecue began to emphasize careers. Without direct contact and understanding of
"what's out there" to do in the world – and without ways to meet interests and develop talents – school makes no sense. School should have connection with reality
and those things that our students might want to do and become. Career education
shouldn't just be a comic book exposure to jobs or a series of lectures on how to find
them. Careers meant gradual exposure, including group field trips to Phoenix and
Tucson. Plans were being made for small groups of students to do both short term and
extended internships. Through cooperative agreements with such entities as Arabian
horse farms, we felt we would begin to get students interested, involved and exposed
to any number of rewarding careers. My best friend's career selection as a veterinar-
ian was no coincidence – he was raised in Winslow on a dairy farm. Life experiences
are powerful factors in the choices of career and vocations.

CHESS, GUITAR LESSONS, A ROCK BAND

EXCITED ABOUT LEARNING AND LIFE

Additional activities were integrated as a regular part of the school day. Pursuits like
chess, guitar lessons, a rock band – things that provided a full menu of experiences –
were made available. The setting up of a livestock business and a printing business
were planned as a cooperative venture with parents, who found the idea intriguing.
Students made a trip to Phoenix to take in the ballet. Plans were made to set up a
restaurant project to teach special cooking skills, and a bookstore was developed to
serve local needs.

Being at school had to become an attractive, stimulating, and comfortable place that
offered a broad array of experiences to meet the full development of Cibecue's children. The school had to become a place that would attract them and keep them in
school, that would require conformance to certain behavioral parameters as a requirement for them to participate, and that would push them and get them excited about

learning and life.

A special staff had to be supported in order to set up and keep this type of school environment going. The rule was that the students are "Numero Uno." We announced that "You can expect all the material and organizational support we can possibly give to help you." There was Carmela F, a Harvard grad from New York, who acted as an enrichment specialist; one Diana C from Washington, an English teacher and coordinator of the enrichment program; Donna C, the special education teacher whose classroom was a microcosm of the world. Then, there was Sherry Mc. with the long blonde hair who had just returned from Catalina and who drove that silver Fiero. She was a creative and caring teacher who initiated the Ski Club and other programs. On hand was Lynn N, a special education teacher who came from the Alamo enclave of the Navajo Nation. All of these individuals moved into and filled the empty Cibecue housing area. Raided in early summer by other BIA entities there was little material or equipment on the shelves – most of it was broken and inoperable. Again, I had to announce to the staff that there would be no salary for two more weeks due to inaction by federal bureaucrats. Behavior and attendance problems continued to plague the staff, but two things that sustained their loyalty were the continuous support and encouragement they received and a willingness to provide any resource they requested. A cabinet of representatives from each sector of school operations met once a week to collaborate in solving problems. Travel and participation in conference and workshop themes enhancing school programs were strongly recommended. Staff traveled to a myriad of conferences highlighting bilingualism, computer instruction, regional seminars, summer science institutes and even attendance at the National Education Association Convention. The purpose was to heighten staff morale, to bring back state of the art and applicable current knowledge for integration and expansion of the curriculum and school operations. It was critical to infuse excitement and hope in the school's future, and the staff were made to feel that they were leaders in the creation of excellence.

REDUCING STRESS

Humor, as always, along with social events were primary elements in reducing stress. Cibecue was located in a river valley within cedar country just off the Mogollon Rim of Arizona. The rim was a geological demarcation line ascending as high as 7,000 feet. The Apache people favored settlements in canyons and streams below the Rim. It was a thirty minute drive up and out of the lower country to the Mogollon Rim cities of Showlow, Pinetop and Lakeside. Southern Arizona residents escaping the heat in summer and who welcomed skiing in the winter used these communities as resort retreats. There were many fine restaurants and other businesses there and I even found myself retreating in the evening to one of those centers to relax and meet with my alcoholic friends.

Doberman Or Spaniel For Dinner?!

Just before the Christmas break I invited instructional supervisor Helen H and the finance director Cameron C to a celebratory dinner at a gourmet restaurant in Lakeside. Humor was a key element of my modus operandi because it helped unwind and encourage focus. Still, it was a mistake for me to ask Sioux Helen C whether she "preferred Doberman or Spaniel for dinner." The look she gave me simulated what Custer must have seen in the eyes of warriors in his last moments at Little Big Horn.

Paraprofessional Staff Advancement

The paraprofessional staff was offered nine semester hours of free classes, which included counseling, and a potential degree and certification from Northern Pioneer College, Whiteriver. Community School staff was paid for additional education, which consequently resulted in salary raises. Courses included written Apache as a base for bilingual education.

Several staff lived and traveled to Whiteriver and Showlow. The BIA kitchen staff had long tenure and large salaries, but were not rehired to work in the community school. Local people were chosen and they became great cafeteria cooks, adept at meeting the State of Arizona School Lunch Program requirements.

The beginning day of Thanksgiving Recess I found my self on the roof of the school hosing off diesel oil gushing out an air vent in the roof. The maintenance director had failed to open an internal vent.

Not All Staff

Not all staff turned out to be assets. One had no faith in the ability of the students; another was motivated chiefly by internal politics. The holdover staff from the BIA control prior to the school being contracted sat in class telling students "this school is no good" (he was the individual who punched a student the previous year). I finally commissioned him to do research in a remote office out in the gym and requested that he not go near the students during their presence at school.

Dedication

I interviewed over thirty of the staff members. The majority of staff made statements indicating that they were dedicated to the students and that they cared very much for them. I identified this as a distinctive factor characterizing the staff that had overcome significant social-cultural barriers by becoming involved and participating in community affairs, family events, Sunrise Dances and rites of passage into womanhood for young Apache girls. I met weekly with my alcoholic friends at the Community Center and felt perfectly safe walking through pitch darkness to visit with them. One of the staff sponsored and initiated a Girl Scout troop and solicited parents and community members to join in. Many community agencies used the gym for weddings and other events. School sponsored affairs were held to reinforce the idea that the school was not like a military fort but was instead a resource that was now in and of the community. A community Christmas party including talks with Santa Claus was established. The Powwow received recognition by elders along with political and religious leaders who participated as announcers, judges and dancers. Delphia's family supplied the head dancers at the first Powwow and I even participated as a Southern Plains Gourd Dancer. An Apache Arts And Crafts Fair with competition and awards was created and continued annually. The celebration was complemented by a 10K run.

Teachers were excited and eager to come back the second year. We made sure we had fun and as much as possible used humor to reduce stress. One morning I demonstrated the burning of sweet grass to my secretary and other staff. Sweet grass is used by northern plains tribe as incense and for ceremonial "smoking" by way of offering blessings. The Business Manager and Supervisor came running out of their offices yelling "they're smoking pot right in the building!" I launched myself after several students carrying stereos to investigate. Realizing by their bland and undisturbed looks that nothing was wrong it hit me that Helen and Cameron were smelling the sweet grass. After that we were always burning sweet grass or cedar (a Kiowa Tribal tradition).

FETAL SYNDROME

An appreciable portion of the student population suffered from Fetal Alcohol Syndrome. Supervisor Helen H remarked that these kids "could not learn." I informed her that we could not think that way and that we must use all resources available to encourage and instruct all students.

PLANS FOR HALFWAY HOUSE

A large number of students were from families whose members were dysfunctional alcoholics. These students really had no place to go for neither meals nor supportive living

CONGRATULATIONS
First Apache Controlled School

conditions. There were a number of empty houses in the teacherage, and a plan was evolving to make one of these places a halfway house, dorm-like facility for students who needed to live more normally.

"You get that upbeat feeling in the building when you walk in," non-educators would say. Teachers stated that they didn't feel isolated but experienced mutual support and sharing, and there existed a personal caring for each other outside of school. Kindergarten teacher Deena S mentioned her baby shower, and everyone came. Staff treated their compatriots as valuable and worthy persons. One teacher, Beth R from Indiana whom I had interviewed in Chicago, told me that her highest desire was to teach on the White Mountain Apache Reservation. She had done her student teaching through an Indiana University Program and wanted to come back to Arizona. When I interviewed her in Chicago she seemed far too gentle – almost naive. I was also concerned for her as well because she had epileptic seizures. I was worried. But her love for the junior high students – her honesty and simplicity – won their hearts. She epitomized the kind of caring and dedication that pervaded the staff. Beth died from accidental carbon monoxide poisoning in her house at Cibecue in December of 1986.

Cibecue Community School began with a reputation of vandalism, violence and the torching of the school hanging over its head. The first couple of weeks were bedlam fired not only by the students but also by the conflict that laced the community and the paraprofessional staff who had great doubts about the success of the school. Satisfactory attendance, behavior and performance had to be the first priority. In the early days we used traditional detention, but so many kids qualified that it became ridiculous. At the rate we were going we would have to put the whole school in the gymnasium and in any case, punishment and negative reinforcement has never worked. We had to come up with positive reinforcement and a reward system. The convergence of factors we induced into the system brought about positive changes including a significant reduction of absenteeism, misbehavior and poor performance. We set about to create a rich and stimulating environment. We stated clearly (by myself in the gym many times, to the whole school) and continually emphasized that the school was for the students to learn and grow, but that they must be there on time and not leave, and that they must follow certain simple rules of behavior – no violence and no vandalism, and that they must try to do the best they could at what the teachers asked them to do.

I had the same Titus M who had harbored a gun out in the bushes come in with his parents. I told them how talented and creative he was and that we didn't want to lose him – that we wanted him to finish and go on to high school. Limbert Q and his gang finally stopped lightning fires and arrived to negotiate, man-to-man, with me. This followed closely after starting of the Rock Band. The message was that the purpose of the school was for the development of their talents – not for the staff.

C.D. was called in because he had made fun of a teacher who had suffered a seizure. I told him - (I thought he could have difficulty changing as he was hyperactive kid – by the same token, he was mischievous, but beautifully happy) "C.D., we're going to miss you around here. I really like you because of your smiles and love of life, but if you don't get your act together you'll end up taking the bus to Whiteriver." C.D., to my amazement, really did well the rest of the year.

I have a long litany of stories. Garrett G – who was absolutely out of it – re-entered reality and started doing school. I mentioned that achievement jumped the first year in some areas which ascent was directly attributed to active learning. The misbehavior, poor attendance and tardiness were drastically reduced to normal levels. At night I could walk through the building and the bad spirits were gone. It was a warm, comfortable place to be. I felt at home there, and at peace when I ran through the woods.

We commenced with Gold and Green Days at Cibecue. Students, grouped by age and weight levels competed for track and field events. Teachers and students formed teams and together enjoyed tug-o-war, sack races, and various other amusements. The faculty played the students – the Gold against the Green, the whole staff and student body divided into two teams – in basketball, football, and volleyball.

Slowly, the community began to accept the school and the teachers. People began to smile at me. They began to believe and trust that the teachers cared, and that the school was a safe place for their children. It was important that action on my part showed no favoritism based on local politics or family to convince the community that it was "fair place." I know my trailer was unlocked most of the time. The school's parents began to exchange and interact with the powwow circuit across Arizona and New Mexico. Families had give-a-ways for beginning dancers. My family helped by making feather bussels and costume parts.

I doubt whether those former staff now make jokes about Cibecue. Cibecue boys won the regional championship in both football and basketball. A good number of students have gone on to high school, are on the honor roll and are taking advanced algebra. One graduate now wants to go to medical school. Incidences of suicide are rare compared to the past. Achievement has followed an upward cycle and Cibecue has received national accreditation. The community of Whiteriver honored one teacher; she was invited to adopt a child born of a teen pregnancy, thus admitting her into the

Navajo Actress

Tribal social fabric. Many of the teachers I talked to said, "Cibecue was the most satisfying job I ever had …" and "Teaching there was the most interesting experience I will ever have in my life."

The Class of 1985 on graduation day best reflected the strong spirit of it all. We had been showing the movie "The Outlaw Josey Wales" on the VCR to the kids. They knew that Geri Keams, the actress who played 'Little Moonlight' in the movie, was coming to Cibecue to speak at graduation. Geri – in her Hungarian boots and Navajo blouse and Brooklyn accent explained how her grandmother, who lived north of Winslow, encouraged her to go as far as she could go. Geri began speaking in the Navajo language – her grandmother told her, "Geraldine, you can do it." She explained how this self confidence took her from Tolani Lake as a sheepherder to the University of Arizona – to Ma Ma's Cafe at a drama center in New York – and finally to her acting career.

Another poignant memory concerns an interface with ninth grader Leonard Q., who had threatened to cut my beard off and who then came into my office months later, trusting me enough to ask me to get him a JTPA job, (The Job Training Partnership Act). We could not contain the smiles we gave each other. We knew we had both made it at Cibecue, maybe he more than I.

The sudden change in attitude on the part of Leonard and the gang happened that day at confrontation in my office. I noted to the fellows that they had been playing a rock type song tape and mimicking the playing of it on cardboard guitars. I asked, "What if you could learn to play real guitars?" Apaches can look right through you so that you have no idea what is going on with them. However, Mr. Leonard rendered a faint smile. He became a member of a guitar group formed by the special aid from New York who taught the entire group how to play a guitar.

Several events signaled a new and ominous phase in the school's journey – a fairly predictable reaction to a new institution in an indigenous peoples' community.

In January of that year, the School Board Chairwomen hired a totally unqualified gentleman to "train" the school board. The gentleman had a business-industrial background, but no educational experience. It was clear that now that the school was up and running and beyond the jeopardy of the BIA, some leaders in the community wanted to go beyond the role of a school board and initiated a micromanagement of the school. It is important to realize that the role of boards is to suggest and monitor policy – and that one tenet essential to the operation of a school is that board members do not usurp professional roles or responsibilities. Recent attempts of the Jefferson County Colorado School Board to dictate the content of history content were way

Alcoholism to Shangri-La   225

out of line. Same goes for like events in Texas. Boards should monitor and require professional decisions to select legitimate, professionally sanctioned historical materials, but never to dictate historical content or show bias.

Apaches accept that young girls in their early teens who have completed the Sunrise Ceremony are then considered to be women and own a right of passage into the adult world. As such they may began intimate relationships with the opposite sex. Consequently, a teaching aide, a bus driver, moved in with one of the eighth graders. The teaching staff, as members of a dominant culture with different mores went ballistic and wanted to intervene to "rescue" their student. School lawyer Davis said that the staff would have to testify in order to end the aide-student relationship, but none of the staff wished to stand up against the teacher aide.

The ninth grade student in question had in fact completed the ceremony and was therefore considered an adult female. However, moral values and even the requirements of the American Indian Child Welfare statutes did not sanction their involvement in sexual or cohabitation relationships before the age of 18 years – regardless of Tribal mores. The non-Apache staff was furious, believing that the student had been taken advantage of by the teacher aide. Again, legal counsel "Manny" Davis insisted that any action would require witnesses to attest to the love tryst. No one, and certainly no Apaches, were willing to testify. So, the situation was at a standstill – until a fortunate, or unfortunate, event occurred.

The standoff over the dismissal of the aide was not the first but in fact the final straw in a chain of events that I perceived to be community encroachment of the school's authority and operations. I was operating under the need to implement those things I felt necessary to assure the long range existence, the viability and the ultimate quality of the school's function. I saw my role as one of putting the school on the right track in exhibiting the best of elementary and middle school education. My plan required full cooperation of the board and staff.

Fortunately or not, the teacher aide drove the school bus drunk one Tuesday morning and I fired him. He was the son of a school board member. That school board member came into my office with another board member to request that I reinstate his son. My answer was that "as long as I am in charge here, this school will be safe for kids. No, I will not hire him back." That school board member and father was the only policeman in town, and he owned a .357 magnum.

The School Board Chairwomen and Tribal councilwoman had been meeting behind closed doors with the school curriculum coordinator. School counsel Davis said it was "OK." My lawyer from Flagstaff called it "insubordination."

Having been hired along with a Navajo wife, great expectations for the duo turned sour when the curriculum coordinator began derailing my plans for school development. The extremely negative response to his anonymous evaluation by the staff prompted him and his wife to resign before Christmas vacation. As for me I had done my job. It was time to go. I placed a letter of resignation on the doorstep of the school board chairman and moved out of CBQ.

My habit of avoiding conflict and contention caused me to head once again for the back door and I resigned my position at CBQ in April of 1986. I am not sure as I write whether or not my act was justifiable or simply a sudden impulse. Several factors may have combined to foster that decision. The school had reached a relatively smooth level of operation free from the original traumas characterizing its birth pangs. I had accomplished the mission to establish the school with all necessary components not only functioning, but also operating effectively and productively. The school was accepted and supported by the community and the Apache Tribe to the point that everyone now wanted to run the school they had condemned earlier. For myself, I was ready to go on to other things. As a member of the Kayenta Planning Board I was courted and encouraged to develop the Kayenta Township Project. I actually had begun to work on certain dimensions of the project by taking leave time from CBQ.

Manuel Davis interviewed the entire staff of the school by way of assuring, assumedly, that I did not embezzle, nor leave with the family fortune. He found nothing because there was nothing to find.

KAYENTA TOWNSHIP

DECISION TIME

I was the Executive Director of Cibecue Community School and had put almost all of its operations on straight and functioning paths. But, I began to experience micromanagement-oriented intrusions by community members into school operations. The time had come for me to say adieu. A more exciting opportunity and challenge awaited me. The Kayenta Planning Board, of which I was a key member as author of the Township Concept Paper, was moving rapidly to implement a Township Government and Land Use Plan. Albert Bailey was lobbying me intensively to take over the direction of the Township Project. I sat above the Kayenta Valley near Churchrock, meditating deeply about whether or not I should accept the challenge.

The Kayenta Township Commission

Second Public Hearing on The Proposed Amendment to the Kayenta Township Commission Municipal Tax Code

AN INCREASE IN THE SALES TAX PERCENTAGE TO 5%

THE TOWN OF KAYENTA PROPOSED BUDGET FOR FY 2002-2003

Kayenta Chapter House
July 11, 2002

ESSENTIAL AND EFFECTIVE MUNICIPALITY

Self-determination and economic independence had been a driving force in my psyche all of my professional days. What came to mind that morning amid the massive Navajo red sandstone buttes and the towering volcanic monoliths was a certainty that Kayenta had viable potential to become a model of Navajo evolution. All elements contained in the Kayenta Township concept could be fused to advance Navajo culture. We needed to establish an effective municipal activity center that would act as an economic engine to create jobs, and we needed support for a diverse community reflecting the Navajo way of life that combined the effective aspects of their culture with the tools of a larger American culture.

The extensive components characteristic of the current Navajo Nation – a variety of religious, governmental, educational, business and social groups – were well represented in Kayenta. Massive coal mining operations and a myriad of local, Navajo, Arizona state and federal institutions were located there and it lay at a junction fostering interstate commerce and travel. Perhaps most amazing of all, Kayenta was the gateway to Monument Valley – a top international tourist destination and one of the most awe-inspiring settings on the planet. To my way of thinking our objective was smart, sensible and possible.

Concentrated efforts were being made to the north and across the border in Utah to create a center serving Monument Valley tourists and travelers to southern Utah's red rock country. The famous old trading post of the 1939 John Wayne movie "Stagecoach" had been expanded into a vast motel complex and center for Valley tours. A new high school had been built, and the Seventh Day Adventists operated a hospital, medical clinic and dental offices just west of the motel complex.

The Utah sector of the Navajo Nation (Navajo Reservation) had been organized as a separate and semi-independent unit and was dominated culturally and politically by the LDS church. I felt however that Kayenta would best serve the basic Navajo ethos as opposed to embracing developments occurring over the border in Utah. Hence, a 'voice' told me that I should accept the challenge and assist the Kayenta Planning Board in creating the Kayenta Township Government.

KAYENTA TOWNSHIP ESTABLISHED

At this writing the Kayenta Township has functioned as a governing authority and an effective unit of local government within the Navajo Nation for 22 years. It is the only "township" formally established under Navajo Nation law. It is unique in that it operates as a city-type government with "home rule" authorities.

By the early '80's I had been a long time resident of Kayenta and Dennehotso and was known for my work on Navajo projects. In 1982, Mr. Albert Bailey, member of a prominent local family, was elected to the Navajo Nation Tribal Council. He was appointed to the all-powerful Advisory Committee, a screening subcommittee that initiated and cleared all the propositions that went to the Council. Bailey's best friend was one Marshall Plummer from a well-known Navajo family in Coyote Canyon located in eastern Navajo. The two of them represented a very progressive and visionary segment of the Committee. Plumber was a Vietnam War Vet who courageously took over the Tribal Chairmanship when Peter McDonald was forced to step down after his involvement in a demonstration resulting in the death of two Navajo men.

Because of the relative poverty, unemployment and dependency on the Federal Government, both Councilmen saw community and economic development as an essential to lift the Navajo out of adverse conditions. Bailey had been in contact with a Japanese corporation who wanted to build an international airport and resort in Kayenta, which locale was at a transit crossroads across the Navajo Nation, accessing Utah to the North and Colorado and New Mexico to the east. More importantly it was the gateway to Monument Valley. It was also a key service center for tourists heading for Canyon de Chelly and Chaco Canyon as well as the Canyonlands and the National Parks of Utah.

The Japanese firm researched the steps necessary to acquire land for their project. Navajo land was held in trust by the federal government and the Bureau of Indian Affairs. Obtaining land and a business site lease meant jumping over some high hurdles. Upon discovering that it would literally take years to acquire the land and the permission for the project, they abandoned their quest. Bailey and Plummer were shocked, and they vowed to find a way to cut the red tape holding back economic development and Tribal progress.

Bailey believed that the emergence of the Navajo people from a stagnant abyss would be found in the minds and hearts of the people and his first significant move was to form a local committee called the Kayenta Planning Board, an entity authorized by the Navajo Nation Council by resolution as early as 1962. The Navajo Nation did not accept the option of creating a Constitution under the Indian Reorganization Act of the 1930's. It operated by approving resolutions which could and did include Tribal Codes requiring a two-thirds vote to pass and a three-quarters vote to amend or void. The resolution form of government seemed more solid and less vulnerable to modification because each action acted as a constitutional amendment. The status of Tribal action would offer Bailey, the Planning Board and eventually the Township Commission a broad umbrella of protection from local and national protagonists.

Bailey understood that throughout the history of the Navajo people, final decisions were made based on groups of people residing in local areas. The Council, although it functioned as an overall government of the people and stood as the institution for interface with outside entities, was still an artifact imposed on the Navajo. In the early days treaties were signed by one group and broken by another band of Navajos.

Bailey understood that community-empowered development would happen through a local group. The Navajo Tribal Council had authorized Land Use Planning in 1962. Bailey also knew that the maverick efforts outside of and in opposition to the Navajo government most often failed.

Thus, Bailey instituted the Kayenta Planning Board of the Kayenta Chapter. He chose for the Board individuals from the community, both Navajo leaders and non-Navajos who were prominent and who qualified either professionally or politically and in some cases, those who fit into both categories. Even a naturalized American citizen from Iran employed by the Kayenta Mine as a computer expert was appointed to the planning board. Jim Brown, an administrator from the Kayenta BIA School, was also selected along with Bill Crawley, a long time resident and owner of Monument Valley Tours. Lillian Smith, wife of prominent local leader Keith Smith, became a wise, abiding member of the board. My participation with the Division of Education and Navajo Community College and my marriage to Delphia, whose family were known as pow-wowers and Native American church members, as well as my reputation as a grant writer and crafter of words made me a logical choice for membership on the Board.

Richard Mike, the local son of a Navajo Code Talker and a highly successful entrepreneur in the Burger King and Hampton Inn venues, along with Jerry Gilmore, BYU graduate and head of the local Conservation Office, rounded out the committee which included as well the head of the local Navajo Tribal Utility Authority, the agency responsible for water and electricity in the Kayenta area as a subunit of the total Navajo Reservation.

Concepts of a Township Government

On March 13, 1985, arrangements began with a plan of operation, some ideas to be tested and five-year goals to be discussed. A concept paper for a township and a plan of operation for the Kayenta Planning Board were set to be developed.

Bailey immediately made it the Planning Board's agenda to withdraw a large segment of land for development that could attract and establish outside businesses within a time frame common to most American communities. Most business interests like the Japanese entrepreneurs wanted their money to go to work as soon as possible, and the idea of waiting for years was anathema. ("Land withdrawal" is a term whereby the Navajo Nation stipulates a specifically defined piece of land for explicit use and under the control of a authorized entity).

The concept of identifying such a large segment of land evolved into an idea encompassing a "township." Reiterating, it was a regional center of business and tourism, public and BIA education and included as well Navajo, Arizona State and federal institutions and the residences of many coal miners. It embraced a large number of non-Navajo residents along with Navajo residents who cross cut Christian, Native American Church and traditional Navajo spiritual philosophies. Located as it was in one of the most beautiful areas on earth, the underdeveloped Kayenta had enormous economic potential.

By 1984, my observation over the 12 years that I had worked within the Navajo Nation was that the Navajo People never lacked purpose nor imagination. After all, they had survived for millenniums by adapting to changing conditions as they migrated across the Bering Strait and down into the southwestern part of the U.S. Still, of their many hopeful visions, few ever materialized due to the absence of planning, money, viable authority and competent staff.

On March 13, 1985 preparation began on a Plan of Operation to establish Kayenta as a township entity. Five year goals were set up, and certain ideas required testing. Bailey and Plummer were preparing to present the land withdrawal proposal to the Advisory Committee (AC) under the concept of a township – "The Kayenta Township Pilot Project, (KTPP)." Approval by the AC would enable the project to access finances, technical support and recognition from the Navajo Tribe as a Tribal program.

I was assigned to develop a 'concept' paper describing the objectives of operation for the land withdrawal and establishment of a Kayenta Township.

Most of the factors preventing community and economic development were informally shared, over and over again. But, it was important to identify and formalize the parameters necessary to establish and sustain a town within the Navajo Nation. There were a large number of sources that could be researched to state these parameters and deduce ways in which the Kayenta project would create effective and lasting mechanisms to structure such parameters.

A primary resource at the heart of the prohibitions against economic development was a paper rendered by the Office of Arid Lands Studies at the University of Arizona. Arid Lands researched both legal and business representatives to find out why they avoided investment in Indian reservations. The conclusions of the research were simple: (1) Entities could not afford to spend time and money going through the long list of red tape impediments taking years for the acquisition of land and a business site lease. (2) Investments within the trust land of an Indian Tribe could be lost, both the material and operational equity, if for some reason there was a decision by the Tribe not to renew or terminate a lease. Entities needed to secure investments in such a manner that their business could be transferred (with equitable finances) or that they could terminate their operations and exit with the equity common to financial operations outside Tribal trust lands.

One Alex Thal composed a doctoral thesis on the legalities surrounding Navajo individual and family ownership, or control of a piece of land. The 3,606 acres identified for withdrawal as the Township included land controlled by a number of Navajo families under BIA rules and regulations covering what was known as a "grazing permit" on an un-surveyed piece of property identified by topical and geographic elements.

Many families depended on their land to graze sheep, which for some was a critical part of the family income and identity. How could one convince the release of grazing lands by their Navajo owners without causing an area uprising?

CRITICAL NEED FOR LAND

The catch here, and this was not a manipulative device but a serious issue, involved the transport of sick or injured Navajos to regional hospitals. Kayenta had a dirt runway, useless in snowy or rainy weather. A Navajo child once fell through a plate glass window at a local motel and literally bled to death for lack of transport to an adequate facility. The case for an asphalt runway and for all-weather airports became key. Thal's assessment of the control of permit land was analyzed to project how permit holders could be compensated for their transfer of land or, in extreme cases, the making of their land into one public domain. A policy covering various types of compensation for land transfer would be placed under a plan of operation.

Tribal codes for land use planning attendant to the Council's 1962 policy were analyzed, and an existing land use plan of the Dilcon Chapter/Town (an area just north of Winslow, Arizona) was presented as a manifested model of Tribal code. It was offered as a future production model. I gathered existing maps and data to create the Kayenta Land Use Plan, a document presented by Bailey and Plummer to the Advisory Committee for approval.

OFFICIAL AGENCY FOR LAND USE PLANNING & TOWNSHIP GOVERNMENT

On June 10, 1985, the Kayenta Chapter resolution designated the KPB, (Kayenta Planning Board), as the Official Agency for Land Use Planning & Township Government for the Kayenta Chapter.

In June, in the summer of 1986, the H family was living in BIA housing at the Kayenta Boarding School. The family had gone to Oklahoma to attend a powwow at a place called Red Rock. I was to join them later, in Oklahoma. It was very hot in Kayenta and our cooler's pump was laboring. I had to take a bucket of water every so often and pour it over the mats on the side of the cooler and then go back into the house and continue working the concept document for the Pilot Project. The emphasis was always on "Pilot" because the Planning Board had no authority to establish a township, nor was it politically wise to use terms like "township" because it sounded like a long-term entity was actually being created. Navajos are very wary of new plans and schemes ever since the BIA under Commissioner John Collier devastatingly reduced their sheep herds back in the 1930's.

On July 1985, I drafted the KTPP, (KAYENTA TOWNSHIP PILOT PROJECT), Concept paper. The concept paper written that summer of 1985 focused on authorizing a pilot project that would target a township structure empowered under the Navajo Nation Code to carry out four essential functions: (1) Local control in land use planning, zoning enactment and enforcement; (2) Power to withdraw land and execute leases; (3) Ability to obtain and sustain revenue primarily by imposition of taxes, fees, lease payments and acquisition of funds common to regular municipal governments; and (4) Attainment of Township Status by inclusion in the Navajo Nation Code to be governed by an elected Township Commission.

KAYENTA TOWNSHIP PILOT PROJECT

On September 30, 1985, the Kayenta Chapter resolution recommended approval by the Navajo Tribal Council for the Kayenta Township Pilot Project (KTPP) and KPB, (Kayenta Planning Board), *Plan Of Operation.*

Achieving the sanction of the Kayenta Chapter to create a powerful subgroup, (Kayenta Planning Board and later the Township Commission) and give up land under its control was a complex, tedious and sometimes contentious process. Relinquishing power and land that had been in families for generations did not come easy. The process of approval by the Kayenta Chapter began with the presentation of a resolution to approve the project and to designate 3,606 acres as a land base.

In my travels I spent time taking pictures of what a township would look like, and what the benefits to the local community and chapter would be. The concept of a township entity being *the grandchildren serving the needs of the grand folks* (Chapter) was the chosen mantra. Of a Sunday chapter meeting at which the resolution was presented, I provided a slide show of various dimensions featuring a functioning township – the parks, businesses, government buildings, zones, utilities and so forth. Halfway through the presentation, School Superintendent Tommy Yazzie took over and addressed chapter members in Navajo.

A map with aerial-view boundaries drawn on a large chart was then presented. Grazing-oriented committee members whose land forfeiture was in question took a fractious stance. The exact geographical and topical lines where the township boundaries would lie had to be concretely determined.

The location of the proposed airport was the starter and the prime focus of identifying land for it was a community wide critical need, not only for medical reasons but also to enhance tourism.

A large rectangular gap was held out of the land base on the basis of a claim that it was farmland. Ancient irrigation gates dotted this land, but there had been no farming there since the 1930's. I knew it was not worth bickering about, for the future evolvement of the township would cause land parcels adjacent to its borders to be annexed.

I joked with everyone that the final configuration of the proposed township boundaries looked like "Snoopy." The day after the chapter passed the enabling resolution, I asked each of the Chapter Officers to examine the map and sign off on the exact, agreed upon boundaries.

I immediately went out and put wooden stakes at each point of the boundary lines. I found out later that Al Bailey had gone out and changed these stakes to expand the land base – excluding his own home site lease area outside of the township. Both actions would be become heated bones of contention in the future.

The township was surveyed by the Navajo Nation and presented to be officially filed in the Navajo County archives in Holbrook, Arizona. Metal cadastral caps imbedded in cement were placed at each point on the boundary corners.

LOCAL RESISTANCE

While the Navajo People are uniquely adept at dealing with change (Edwin Spicer, University of Arizona, CHANGING SOUTHWESTERN INDIAN CULTURES), the Township project and the growing power of the Planning Board were resisted by certain sectors of the chapter community inspiring an effort to renege on the chapter's supportive resolution. It was therefore necessary on October 16, 1985, for the Kayenta Chapter to reaffirm by resolution its support of the Kayenta Township Pilot Project for presentation to the Navajo Tribal Council.

The staff and myself prepared the resolution package for delivery to the Navajo Council. THE KAYENTA LAND USE PLAN was included as an exhibit in that package to give the impression that the Chapter knew what it was doing and had a strategy for implementation of the project. A critical tactic was accomplished when on November 5, 1985, Navajo Tribal Council resolution CN-86-85 approved the withdrawal of 3,606.3 acres of the Navajo Trust Land for establishment of the Kayenta Township site and authorized the operation and funding of the project. The "Kayenta Township Pilot Project" was approved to include authorities for local land use planning and land withdrawals and contained as well mandates for processing business and home site leases. The plan of operation for the Kayenta Township Pilot Project and Kayenta Planning Board were also approved, and the Land Use Plan became law. The action by the Council considered the Township project as having moved one step forward to becoming a Tribal resolution, for inclusion in the Navajo Nation Code. The status of the Township was now strong enough to confront the hurricane-force winds of opposition to come later. It would take a vote of three quarters of the Navajo Tribal Council to dissolve the township's existence.

Any council members voting for such would stand as being opposed to local government and in turn acting contrary to the Navajo tradition of homegrown decision-making.

At this period in time I was living out of my Toyota and using travel money from the Project budget to stay in Gallup motels. Between round trips from the Ambassador Motel and my office, the Kayenta Chapter Land Use Plan was born. A Tribal planner made a presentation to the Planning Board, citing the parameters of a town's zones and how they functioned and related to one another. His ideas were used to sketch the structure of Kayenta Township inclusive of existing areas and with the addition of new areas (industrial parks, major thoroughfares, etc.) so as to create an "organic" plot, or plan of development. Appropriate technologies were emphasized in the Plan's goals. Key individuals, both Navajo and non-Navajo leaders were consulted about the layout of the community and what direction development should take. In other words, the Township plan arose, was approved and eventually officially confirmed at a grass roots level and not superimposed from an overall tribal authority.

WITHDRAWAL OF TOWNSHIP LAND BASE

On November 13, 1986, the Advisory Committee of the Navajo Nation Council, pursuant to Resolution No. ACN-181-86 approved the withdrawal of 3,606.43 acres, more or less, of Navajo trust lands for the establishment of Kayenta Township. The boundaries of the Township were identified by a formal survey.

Township Planners—Ms. Worker & Ms. Donald

Locals evidenced opposition and some Tribal departments directly resisted the implementation of the Township Project. What with my experience over the years I was not surprised that absolutely any issue could turn into a raging forest fire dividing the community, and in fact the Township would sail on rough seas for the next thirty years. When on February 11, 1987 Chairman Peterson McDonald committed "general support" to the KTPP, the tribal departments and Navajo Nation Committees were officially obligated to provide assistance in material and technical ways. We enlisted Tribal support to propose to the FAA the construction of an all-weather airport. They approved the proposal and Kayenta was chosen over former priorities given to Chinle and Tuba City. The FAA chose Kayenta because it had both a concrete policy and the land for an airport plot in the context of a land use zoning plan.

I was made aware of a certified land use planner who lived in Window Rock and hired her to design the infrastructure for the township. It was interesting to watch her presentation as she was from Thailand; the Navajo community strained to grasp meaning through her strong accent.

PROJECT GOALS IMPLEMENTATION MOVED SLOWLY

Project Goals implementation moved slowly for the next few years. We saw continuous lobbying with the Navajo Tribal Administration and Council Committees to sustain annual funding for KTPP. It seemed that I was forever outside the Budget and Finance Committee meetings with hat in hand and a fat package of budget justifications. The Tribal Budget and Finance Committee requested a performance audit of KTPP, which was done by an impeccably competent auditor, one Lillie Roanhorse. Of course I had to produce detailed rationales as to why we had not completed tasks according to a given time line.

I was commuting from Taos, New Mexico at the time, which was over three hundred miles away. I was living in a trailer at the local Laundromat/RV Park. As time went on the water pipes cracked, the furnace failed and soon I had sewer problems. At one time I had an electric line and a hose strung out across several empty stations. The romance of roughing it wore very thin at times. I often got up early to take a shower in the Laundromat and when I turned on the lights, roaches would scatter every which way. The lady managing the 24-hour Laundromat was always hitting on me, and once I had to gently escort her out of my trailer. My bed was situated so that I heard patrons' vehicles coming and going all night. It is uncomfortable at this point in time to realize that I could not take care of myself, that in truth I could not extricate myself from what seemed to be a Sargasso Sea of inaction.

The KTTP trudged along. Every time I turned around it seemed that the Tribe had deleted my associate Lynne and I from their health insurance rolls. I had to go to Window Rock and plead for the reinstatement of our insurance status. There were times when I left Taos in a blizzard and questioned my sanity for doing what I was doing. However, Al Bailey was so energetic and optimistic, and my associate, Lynne Donald, was such an exemplary partner that I felt I could not disappoint them. And in reality, I had nowhere to go.

I knew that at 59 if I did not make a move I would eventually dry up and blow away in a spring sandstorm. Navajo Community College had advertised the position of Director of Development and I applied, which effort required facility with a computer. I quickly learned some computer skills using the DOS operating system. My old comrade from Navajo Division days, Lawrence Gishey, was now President of NCC and he gave me the job. I requested a Macintosh computer. I moved into an eight-sided, three bedroom house in Tsaile as the NCC Director of Development.

My associate was the wife of a Chief Justice of the Navajo Supreme Court who had received an international award for bravery for standing against a sinister plot by the then Chairman McDonald. McDonald wished to hold fast to those slippery strings of power, and with that thought in mind he instigated a riot resulting in two homicides. Chief Justice Long held fast and refused to rule in favor of McDonald.

I was able to fund a Quest telephone grant a called "Bridge" which was designed to assist Navajos coming from NCC to major university campuses in making the adjustments they needed to survive. There were a number of cases wherein Navajo recipients of Manuelito Scholarships ($60k at the time) left the campus to go back home before Christmas vacation. Not only are city environs and institutional complexities challenging in comparison to reservation life, but also powerful family connections and obligations are potent magnets to pull them back to the sheep camps.

DÉJÀ VU— STYMIED AND CORNERED AT NCC

I was disappointed that the support I expected from Gishey didn't materialize, but in any event he resigned and took a position at NAU in Flagstaff. One Al G took over as interim president and immediately insisted I provide samples of all my files. He sexually harassed my associate Christina C, a fine, competent woman with the skills of a legal secretary. There was no concrete reason that Al G should audit my office. I could see the light at the end of the tunnel and it was on a train engine coming straight at me.

Furthermore, the Board of Regents, whose chairman had been my student teacher at NAU years earlier, had summarily put aside my position paper justifying college funding for a state/county community college. Progress was glacial; success at NCC seemed unlikely. I resigned and sent a letter to the Board of Regents accusing Al G of sexual harassment. I received two weeks of sick leave and annual leave, one month in all based on a letter from my cardiologist (and kindergarten/high school buddy) Dr. Richard L. justifying that leave. I attended a writing workshop in Albuquerque by Anne Rule, well-known author of crime stories.

I requested reinstatement, was given my old job back with KTPP and set out to pre-pare the required five-year report for the Navajo Nation Council. It should be noted that many of the elements of KTPP imparting appeal had been cultivated through decades of dealing with institutions – the good causes, the pilot projects, the countless reports. All worked for those in power willing to take a risk.

In January of 1991 I completed "Kayenta Township Pilot Project: Five Year Report" for the KPB. The report was not formally submitted to the Navajo Nation Council until 1996.

ATTEMPTED EXPULSION OF SON JERRELL AT NAVAJO PREP

Son Jerrell was enrolled in Navajo Preparatory School (formerly known as Navajo Academy), went out for football and became a stellar defensive player and prized team member. The first Navajo Prep game in his career was at Monument Valley High School, just inside the Utah border. I left Taos at 4:30 the morning of game day to make a nine hour drive and was caught up for an hour in a Northern Navajo Fair Parade in Shiprock. I arrived for the kickoff, just in time just to see Jerrell nail a re-ceiver on the ten yard line. It was an exciting day. There were those many trips to Farmington, the site of Navajo Prep to see Jerrell play football. He joined the JV team in basketball as well and I went to most of his games even though my home base was in Taos.

When I got word in the spring that he was being released as a student at Prep I imme-diately requested a meeting of administration and staff to discuss their action. I knew that my previous role with the four children of my first marriage had been inadequate and unsupportive of the needs of developing children and youth. Gains I had made through the council of my alcoholic friends and my personal recovery improvement through sessions at the Meadows in Wickenburg, Arizona had armed me with the knowledge and confidence to support and defend Jerrell against what I thought was professional misbehavior on the part of the Prep administration. The Prep counselor, an Hispanic, was on Jerrell's side.

The criterion being used to dismiss Jerrell and several other students was that their achievement levels were below the level stipulated for entry into Navajo Prep. It was now March and the administration, who had admitted Jerrell based on the analysis of his previous school records, were now retroactively rejecting his admission.

Delphia had come to the Prep meeting in Farmington. We sat and faced at least 15 staff members, including the Executive Director, who was an Ohio State doctorate (sarcasm intended).

I excoriated the Prep group for abusive behavior and professional malfeasance for wanting to dismiss Jerrell in the spring of this first year. He would lose a whole year of high school. I remarked, "The only way my son will leave here is over my dead body!" They retained Jerrell and the other students to the end of the year. I am ashamed to report that I called the executive director and said, "You are an OU graduate, right? That explains it all." I had done the right thing for the right reason and yet negated it by acting out my anger on the Director.

A REVENUE STREAM GUARANTEED

The next step in the establishment of Kayenta Township was the fostering of a continuous stream of revenue to sustain its operations and retain competent staff commensurate with what all municipalities require. I undertook the production of a position paper

**The Kayenta Planning Board at Tribal Council Approval
of the Township Commission *Sales Tax Project***

and resolution approving a Kayenta Retail Sales Tax Project.

While the Navajo Nation Tax Commission made up of tribal councilmen and others had verbally given their approval of the Kayenta Township levying taxes, particularly a sales tax, the staff of the tax commission, all of who were *Beliganii* (white) lawyers seemed hardened against giving up any power to a single community like Kayenta.

To make matters worse, after a contentious meeting with the Commission staff I had gone to lunch with a couple of Planning Board members to the then Window Rock Motor Inn Restaurant. There I sat dumping out my anger by telling "lawyer jokes." My favorite joke was the answer to the question as to why the Harvard University Psychology Laboratory was seeking lawyers to replace mice. The answer was that, "The experimenters won't fall in love with the lawyers, and then, there are so many of them, and finally, lawyers will do what rats won't."

As the luncheon ended and we got up to leave I looked at the table behind us into the glaring eyes of the legal staff of the Tax Commission. I calculated that my anger had set back the acquisition of Kayenta Township taxing power for at least one year.

The approval of the Kayenta Sales Tax Project was essential in making the Kayenta Township operational by assuring it a source of continuous revenue and an empowered and elected body to govern it. However, a major lawyer (Steve B), counsel for the Tribal Council had intervened and derailed the Tax Project by faulting the election method of the Township Commissioners. At a meeting he quipped that "a child could be elected to the Township Commission under the Tax Project stipulations." One stipulation was that the election would be held under the direction and election laws of the Navajo Nation.

Again, it would be a Navajo elder on the Judicial Committee, one Carl Trodachini, who would put the kibosh on Steve B by angrily saying, "Stop throwing sand in their gears and let them have the Township.

The Kayenta Retail Sales Tax Project

On January 19, 1996, ten years after the establishment of the Kayenta Township Project, Navajo Nation Council adopted CJA-3-96, a resolution that established the Kayenta Retail Sales Tax Project (including the RETAIL BUSINESS SALES TAX ORDINANCE). The Navajo Nation Council, pursuant to Resolution CJA-3-96 not only approved a plan of operation for the "Kayenta Tribal Pilot Sales Tax Project," but also designated a Kayenta Township Commission to carry out such a plan of operation and tax project. The intent of the tax project of course was to provide a constant source of revenue for operation of the Township government.

Election and Empowerment of the Kayenta Township Commission

In order to remedy conditions set out by tribal lawyer Steve B on November 1, 1996, the Navajo Nation Council, pursuant to Resolution CN-76-96 (Nov. 1, 1996), approved an amendment to the plan of operation of the Sales Tax Project by way of clarifying election procedures. The establishment of an empowered

Swearing in of First Township Commission

Kayenta Township Commission was essential to pass a tax ordinance and implement the Kayenta Retail Sales Tax Project.

In April of 1997, certified Navajo voters within the Kayenta Township boundaries held an election and Charles Young, Richard Mike, Jimmy Austin, Yazzie Leonard, and Jerry Gilmore were elected as the first Kayenta Township Commissioners. Mike was a son of Code Talker King Mike and very successful local and reservation wide businessman; Jimmy Austin was an employee of the Navajo Tribal Utility Authority, a member of the Native American church and a traditional powwow dancer; Charles Young, a former Tribal Legal Department official, was the son of a prominent family of the BIA and Public school educational officials who were also members of the Mormon Church; Jerry Gilmore was head of the area Soil Conservation Office and Yazzie Leonard was an official of the Navajo Nation Business Development office.

On April 30, 1997 Charles Young, Richard Mike, Jimmy Austin, Yazzie Leonard, and Jerry Gilmore took the oath of office and became the first Kayenta Township Commissioners

THE FIRST TOWNSHIP MANAGER

I immediately set about locating a city manager as the tasks involved in running a city-like government required someone with education and experience. The position was publicized but at that time there were only a few applicants. Friend and former partner Dr. Lawrence I. applied and so did Peter Deswood, Jr. While Dr. I. was very dynamic and had performed well in a number of positions, Deswood had a degree from the University of Arizona and twenty years of experience working with top Navajo Nation leaders and departments. He had also been the Director of the Division of Community Development for the Navajo Nation. Because of his vast experience in community development and planning, the newly elected Commission chose him as the first Kayenta Township Manager.

Deswood enforced the Township's power in controlling business site lease tax payments and even stopped a $40 million subdivision project for non-compliance. Township taxes collected the first year totaled $350,000 and $500,000 the second year. As Navajo journalist George Joe stated, *"this tough attitude earned him enemies and pressure was placed on the Commission to remove him."* Joe claimed that *"jealousy was the nature of the Navajo people,"* citing personal reasons for his dismissal. Deswood claimed that he had to *"do what I have to do to get something done. I am sure there are those who disagree."* Deswood moved the township out of its office out of the old chapter building and into a large, elaborate, newly-constructed city hall near the center of town. Deswood's progress was primarily responsible for the receipt of the Harvard's JFK School of Government's highest honor award for economic development by Native Americans and its model was cited in testimony in the Senate Subcommittee on Indian Affairs—the only tribal entity asked to give testimony. Certainly Deswood's contribution matched his words – "*If I don't do this now, nobody else will. What we do today will set precedence for what happens years from now. We are making history here.*"

STANDING DOWN AND REDIRECTING

Whether it was fear of failure, naiveté or just plain burnout I was glad to turn over the reigns of my ten year development of the Kayenta Township. I would like to claim an ethic that emerged from my work in Gary – that people who want to help developing communities should teach them "how to fish" and not become the major supplier of fish. I had seen individuals come to the Navajo Nation to "assist" in a realm of development only to morph into power brokers abusing chances for leadership by locals and natives. I reveled in the role of "sheepdog" instead of being the "shepherd," so to speak. If this sounds altruistic, so be it.

FARSIGHTED MANAGER GARY NELSON

I continued to work as a consultant to the township, producing its first newsletter and providing positions papers on various and sundry subjects. The Commission chose Gary Nelson for its second Township Manager. Nelson was a Navajo born and raised near Canyon Diablo, just west of Winslow. He had proven his business acumen by raising the Pima Tribe's Industrial Park from a losing proposition to a very profitable one. Nelson was more business oriented than bureaucratic, which perspective was what the next phase required.

Nelson moved to begin a development authority and held a reservation-wide Economic Summit with a broad array of attendees and presenters including the Harvard Honoring Nations Director. Knowing the contentious interface between the now richly endowed township and the poorly funded Chapter government, I presented a paper suggesting the designation of the Chapter Chapter land base as a Development District under State/Navajo County laws that would enable the chapter to collect property taxes on gas and electric lines as well as on mining operations. A vast increase in funding for the Chapter would enable it to address water, electrical and transportation development.

The Chairman of the Commission, Charles Young, while claiming residency in Kayenta actually lived on the Papago (Tohono O'odham) Reservation west of Tucson where he managed a paving company. Commissioners received a $200 dollar stipend for attendance at meetings and in the case of Young, he received mileage and per diem.

Nelson's desire to move foreword with Economic Development, especially with the establishment of an Economic Development Authority, began to create growing conflicts with Young. In one instance Young called me in Taos and asked me to testify at a Commission meeting about Nelson's poor performance. I told Young that Nelson was doing an excellent job and that the Township was lucky to have him. Never too adroit in my political decisions, my support of Nelson compromised any chance of my future consultancy as long as Young was the Commission Chairman. I had always observed Young – even while he was a member of the Navajo Legal Department – to be driven by self-serving motives.

All Weather Airport Built

While Nelson was carrying out the sessions of the Economic Summit, Young and his allies on the Commission were plotting to remove him. They finally convened a meeting when Nelson's Commission supporters were unavailable, and they fired him.

Interestingly enough, in the course of managers coming and going one Daniel P., a politico absent any city management credentials, took over at a salary of $200K. Even amidst the strong existence of Navajo nepotism and local politics, the Commission realized that Daniel P.'s presence wasn't working. They asked for and received a benign resignation, honoring and saluting Daniel P.'s departure. "Hozho," (making everything right) reined and the Navajo adopted Irish diplomacy meaning that you could "tell someone to go to hell in such a way as they look forward to the trip."

I felt that the selection of township managers, capable or incapable, qualified or not, honorable or Machiavellian had to happen without destroying the basic institutional structure of the township. There were bitter assaults from business owners, particularly those owing back sales tax or lease payments. They were able to connect with Chapter officials and area Navajo anti-township protagonists to engender assault after assault on the Commission and the existence of the Township. It came to mind that the Navajo people, though they would eventually incorporate artifacts, institutions and even ideology from the "dominant" culture into the Navajo way of life, had a mindset against any significant change – a holdover from the time they were forced to reduce their sheep herds, a serious wound to their welfare. BIA Commissioner had forced the reduction of the number of sheep a family could have.

AUTHORIZATION TO APPROVE BUSINESS SITE LEASES

On January 7, 1999, the Attorney General of the Navajo Nation issued an opinion

(AG-01-99) that the KTC had been delegated the authority to approve leases of Navajo trust lands located within the boundaries of the Kayenta Township. It should be noted that one Herb Yazzie, a lawyer, now Attorney General and soon to be Chief Justice of the Navajo Supreme Court, was a fierce advocate of local empowerment and the enabling rights of the Kayenta Township as granted by the Navajo Nation Counsel.

On February 1, 1999 the Chief Legislative Counsel reinforced the Attorney General's opinion. (Letter from Steven Boos to Hon. Ben Johnson, dated February 1, 1999).

Regional Hospital Finally Built

As I journal the growth of Kayenta Township (History of Kayenta Township) approaches a thirty year anniversary – from 1986 through 2016. The original Kayenta Planning Board members, led by Albert Bailey and partnered by Jerry Gilmore, Richard Mike, Lillian Smith and Beverly Pigman, never gave up on their dream. Several of them were elected for long terms as Township Commissioners and rode over the bumpy roads of acerbic local and tribal opposition. To the credit of the Navajo Tribal Government and the Navajo people both the law of the land and due process have always prevailed, assuring the remarkable status it enjoys today. A recent issue of the newspaper KAYENTA TODAY details all the facets inherent in a modern municipality.

THE DAWN OF LOCAL EMPOWERMENT

It should be noted that the establishment of the Township Government spawned a surging effort to establish policies of local empowerment. The Navajo Nation passed the Local Empowerment Act with detailed items as to how local chapters could receive that status. The chapters of Chinle and Shiprock considered following in Kayenta footsteps as regards becoming townships, but their political configuration and history of factions has resisted serious attempts to organize as a township. Again, in the case of Kayenta, the Navajo people demonstrated their amazing ability to recognize and incorporate change in their way of life without so much as weakening the Navajo ethos.

In approving the Home Rule status of the Kayenta Township, the Navajo Nation

Council granted the KTC *"jurisdiction over all those areas authorized and designated by the Navajo Nation Council in November, 1985 (Resolution CN-86-85)..."* and stated that *"the authority of KTC shall prevail over all other authority contingent upon its consistency and compliance with all generally applicable laws and regulations of the federal government and the Navajo Nation."* This broad grant of authority is consistent with the concept of Home Rule, which is limited only by the generally applicable laws, and regulations of the federal and Navajo Nation government.

UNINTENDED CONSEQUENCES

At the onset of the Kayenta Township Project but not so much during its 10 years of operations and definition did I, Albert Bailey or the Kayenta Planning Board – and certainly not the Kayenta Chapter – intend or promote any colossal push across the Navajo Nation for local empowerment. Notoriety along with Township accomplishments within the Council and regional media motivated the development and establishment of THE NAVAJO NATION LOCAL GOVERNMENT ACT.

The Act was designed and focused to enable the local chapter governments (110 entities representing geographical/population sectors of the Reservation) to set up a structure of self-government. Actually, these local chapters were like county seats wherein determinative land adjudication of family gazing areas along with water and electrical resources were the prime issues. ("THE NAVAJO NATION LOCAL GOVERNANCE ACT.")

The passage of the act initiated a flurry of activity on the part of the many chapters to be certified as local governance chapters. Certain criteria had to be met for accounting procedures, administrative procedures and other systems to be implemented in the Chapter superstructure. Needless to say, since relinquishing power is no picnic, very few chapters became certified.

The real consequence of the Kayenta Township Project and the Local Governance Act was to focus on local planning and development essential to economic growth – a critical step away from the culture and mentality of dependence foisted upon Native Americans by the federal government.

Most of my days working for the Kayenta Planning Board on the Township Project found me living in a trailer at an all night laundermat RV park. Of a winter eve the electricity went out and left my water system vunerable to freezing and ultimate bursting. At one time both water and electricity could only be accessed by long lines of cable and hose to funtioning RV outlets. The sewere would often freeze and my machinations to make it work are too awful to put into words. Early morning showers were taken in the laudermat facility. When I switched on the lights in the wee hours roaches sped in all directions. Customer pickups would come and go all night. The lady who ran the laudermat once entered my trailer and I had to gently and kindly escort her out as I was not interested in any intimacies.

During another period of time I actually had no place to live and was living out of my gold Toyota, using project *per diem* to stay at the Ambassador Motel in Gallup. It was there that I wrote the KAYENTA LAND USE PLAN which was a document used to initiate the Kayenta Township Project.

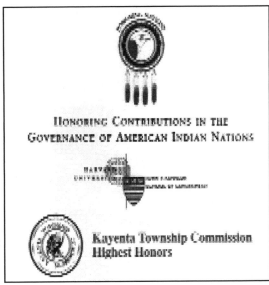

HONORING CONTRIBUTIONS IN THE GOVERNANCE OF AMERICAN INDIAN NATIONS

Kayenta Township Commission Highest Honors

What seemed so romatically "frontier" at the time seems totally rediculus now.

***YENAIDOOSHI!!*—**Skinwalker Intrustion at Midmight**

VII. REUNITE AND RELEASE—AFFIRMING LIFE

Love, Marriage, Death and Reunions , Death of Parents

In 1985 father Jack passed away at 77 years from a heart attack. Only a month earlier I had spent my birthday in Flagstaff feasting on a rump roast dinner and my favorite chocolate iced cake. My father had brought me a vest that I still have today, 33 years later. It would be the last gift I would receive from my father and mother. I had spent the day splitting wood with my dad.

About a month later and just before Pearl Harbor on December 7th I received a call at Cibecue informing me that my father had suffered a heart attack and that he was resting okay in the hospital in Flagstaff. I went to Flagstaff for the weekend to see him and was told he was experiencing a second heart attack. I actually met him as he was being taken in the elevator down to the emergency room. He looked at me and said "Jerry," with a pleading expression on his face as the elevator doors closed. It would be the last time I would see him alive.

Holding a vigil with my mother in the ER I looked at my father and realized there was no life in his eyes. He was gone. The cardiologist remarked to me and my mother that we "Might as well go home and watch pro football" – a crass, cruel thing to say. Thinking back to the context of that time my best guess is that one of the doctors took issue with my mother who could really assault professionals for supposed incompetence. He told the nurse to "unplug" my father from "that thing." Walking by the coffee room door earlier in the morning I had seen the same cardiologist laughing with another doctor. They both clammed up at seeing me.

My mother was a closet drinker consuming alcohol behind pulled shades. At one time she was diagnosed with water on the brain and was put in a strait jacket to avoid injury to herself and others. My Dad faithfully cared for her, taking on the cooking and housekeeping and the monitoring of medications. And my Dad fully expected to be there for her the rest of her life. But he died.

Christmas that year was depressing to say the least. Gregory was home from ASU and Bob had come from Levi's in San Francisco. We cooked Cajon blackened steak on the top of a stove grill shooting dense and greasy black fumes in a duct under the house to the north side of our property, driving the Golden Retriever in the neighbor's yard completely crazy.

Morphing out of the traditional role as a mother's only son into a new role of treating my mother as a "client" took several months. I spent weekends in Flagstaff away from Cibecue making sure she had food and all the things needed to support her solitary existence. It would have been delusory to assume that she could survive by herself with my father not there.

Throughout winter into spring and on into summer I became more and more frantic to find an assisted living place for my mother. She was alone in the house, functioning by herself but barely surviving. For any family, for any son or daughter it is painful to reach the point wherein a decision to execute direct intervention has to be made. I looked at private, public and Catholic social services and identified a number of alternatives. But, she rejected the options I offered and refused to consider even leaving the house on David Drive.

Her failing mental condition made it more and more difficult to deal with her and to assure that she was safe and healthy by herself. She took a shower standing in the bathtub in the bathroom she was accustomed to using when dad was alive. I bought her a rubber mat to stand on which infuriated her to no end.

I spent weekends in Flagstaff, sleeping in what had been my father's room with the adjoining bath. On weekends I bought TV dinners and did any cleaning that was required. Looking back I now realize it was a miracle that my mother did not succumb to an accident.

An event occurred one evening that changed my whole approach in caring for her. I was walking east down the hallway of the house when she came up behind me and hit me in the back with her fist. I could not get out of my mind the scene from the movie PSYCHO with Norman's mother wielding that large knife. I feared that my mother's mental condition might cause her to act out with violence some day. I quit sleeping at the house.

Son Bob had been executor of my parents' estate. Being an auditor and financier for Levi Strauss he wanted to do an inventory of all the assets and property of his grandparents. Son Gregory and I began one summer day to develop a written inventory of everything in the house, essentially everything in the estate.

Dad's half brother, my uncle Gene (who had terrorized me as an infant) came from Oregon and spent several days in Flagstaff while I was at Cibecue. I learned later that he shifted CD's around and apparently helped himself to a number of items belonging to my mother. His behavior may have fired the paranoia that governed my mother's call to the police to complain that Greg and I were trying to steal her things. The police arrived to investigate, followed by a social worker that insisted Greg and I leave the premises!!

I had borrowed my father's Jeep while my Toyota's transmission was being repaired. My mother had stopped driving long ago. But my use of the Jeep angered her to no end. In those days, in spite of my success at Cibecue and Kayenta Township I was not long on common sense, especially when it concerned my mother. I had lost respect for her and had not reached a mature level of determination to take care of her. I had a contentious phone conversation with her in early September. I had taken the position as Director of the Kayenta Township Project. I called my mother to check on her and was blasted with a blistering condemnation for not returning the Jeep pickup. I responded with counterpoints about my need and the fact that the Jeep was not being used at all. My mother slammed the phone down. It would be the last time I would ever hear her voice again. She was found the next morning on the floor beside her bed, dead from a massive heart attack. My son Tim had been called and was first on the scene. I rushed into town from Kayenta. Tim and I noticed that her heart and mood medications were scattered, with the tops off and pills loose on the shelf of the cupboard. No autopsy was requested nor executed.

An issue arose over my mother's death certificate. Her doctor was the same MD who had taken care of my father. There had been some question about his competency in that regard, for my father had suffered a second heart attack in the hospital and was in intense pain for over an hour before he received any help. One day upon meeting with that same MD with my mother and son Bob, we were told to see her psychiatrist to continue her care. Mother could say and do unsettling things and had probably attacked that same MD sometime in the past. The MD signed the death certificate with the cause of the death stated as "Probable Abuse." The mortician however was a long-term friend of the family and came to me with concern about the certificate. I registered strong objections to it and they went back to the MD who signed a new certificate indicating cause of death to be a heart attack.

Though I had weathered successfully the complicated and intense traumas of Cibecue Community School's establishment and sustenance, I was absent of the realization and movement to protect my mother and remove her to safer environment.

My mother was buried next to my father in Valley View Cemetery south of Clarkdale, Arizona. Mom and Dad had met, courted and were married in the Verde Valley and it was the place where many of the family were buried. The folks' full names are on the single gravestone with "Da" and "Nannie" inscribed underneath to signify the endearing terms given to them by their grandchildren.

While my history interacting with my folks was contentious at times, I in no way 'blame' them for my faults and defects of character. However, I was told by my alcoholic friends that I must identify the cause and conditions of my faults, identify the responsible events and remove the impact those events had on my character. Friends state that "I will not blame my parents … " but it is not about blaming. It's about going back in time to the incidents wherein one acquired deep shame, had unresolved anger and toxic levels of emotions. The pain of such feelings required medication with mood altering chemicals like drugs and alcohol.

My mother was the only girl in a family of six brothers. She was born sandwiched between the deaths of two sets of twins. She was sexually abused and deemed psychotic by my counselor Robert P. She was orphaned by my grandmother's tragic death at 15 and sent to a convent in Fort Worth and finally to live with her Aunt Mabel in Douglas, Arizona. I remember grand Aunt Mabel as an Irish drinker who killed my rabbit and threw it under the house. I know that all things considered, my mother did everything she knew how to do in caring for me. I know she was devastated by the misdiagnosis of glomerulonephritis portending my eventual death in Winslow.

My father was a quiet and gentle soul – kind and upright. Again, his refusal to take the option of owning the Flagstaff Pharmacy as it would end the income of Mr. Grager, the owner and an invalid from World War One wounds. Instead he moved us to Denver, to Albuquerque and then to Winslow and eventually back to Flagstaff. He joined the Catholic Church as a convert with the promise that if he did so, I would survive the diagnosis of terminal glomerulonephritis – a degenerative infection of the kidneys. When I was five years old and bent over with severe pain diagnosed by doctors as a non-serious appendicitis infection, he insisted on a white blood count and averted my appendix from rupturing which would have caused my death. I have strong reason to believe that my father had a close friend on the West Lafayette Police Department who interceded one night to prevent my spending six months of weekends in the Lafayette jail for DWI violation.

Skiing

As I indicated earlier in this discourse I had only rudimentary exposure to ski skills when I was eight years old, although the experience was exhilarating in its own right. The snow and the mountain gave one a magical sense of existence, even after my disastrous attempt to ski down Sunset Boulevard while home for Christmas from Conception Seminary. That was in 1952. It would be 34 years later when, coming alive about life and myself in general, I decided to ski from the beginner stage all the way up to the point where I could navigate the Black trails if I chose. The Purgatory Ski Area north of Durango, Colorado provided excellent slopes, wide and diverse, and I took lessons "A" through "F." Once I was comfortable on the Purgatory slopes I began taking my son Jerrell and stepdaughter, Yanivia Haungooah ("Pretty Girl of the Silverhorns") skiing. We would spend grueling but fulfilled days skiing all day followed by meals on top of the mountain at various venues. Within a year the Whole H family including Delphia came as a group. One morning Jerrell was standing backward on a mogul and a lady, fearing for his safety, cruised by and thrust him to the ground. Other times he would come off the lift with one ski caught in the snow and would go tumbling—true to his Kiowa genes.

On the other hand, Delphia in her earliest lessons on the beginner slope once slid backwards into a hole in the snow created by a tree trunk.

I did go back to ski in Flagstaff and successfully negotiated Sunset Slope with finesse. It made up for the humiliation I had suffered 34 years before.

Skin Walker- *Yenaidooshi*

New Year's Eve of 1985 I was "home" at the Greasewood Bureau of Indian Affairs School in the south-central sector of the Navajo Reservation. Delphia was the principal of the school, which for me meant a two-hour drive back to Cibecue.

The weirdest thing about the school was that there was a cemetery right in the middle of it – weird because the Navajo people have a very intense taboo about not having any contact with areas and objects associated with the dead. They had lived for centuries amidst the ruins of the ancient Anasazi inhabitants that preceded them with minimal disturbance of any of the archaeological sites.

The whole family was home for the holidays, including a visit by Delphia's uncle-Donnie A. New Year's Eve had come and gone with the last dregs in the bottles of fizzed apple cider. The girls – Hattie, Pattie and Denise – were gathered in the third bedroom in the north part of the house playing monopoly. Charlie, Delphia, Uncle Donnie and I were in the dinning room talking over a cup of tea. Suddenly there was a loud thumping sound on the north bedroom wall, bringing the three daughters out of the room with startled, wide-eyed fear in their eyes. What could be outside their bedroom at three in the morning?

Uncle Donnie was steeped in the Kiowa tradition of fearlessness and Charlie had just finished a season of football at Navajo Academy and had been cited for all state New Mexico honors. Both went outside to see what was going on.

Charlie burst through the door from outside and was screaming and crying. Donnie came in extremely agitated and said in a shaking voice, "Delphia, what the hell is that out there!!!"

Both Donnie and Charlie described a figure with black hair and bright red burning eyes peering out from the southern bosque of sage and cottonwood trees. It was what everyone on the Navajo described as a Navajo "Skinwalker."

The next morning the household went out to inspect the ground surrounding the house and found a very large coyote like paw print outside the north bedroom window – not a human, but an animal print.

A Kiowa medicine man not being available Delphia met with a Navajo medicine man. First, he told her to place traditional arrows on the seals of the windows in the house. Fortunately, I had purchased a set of traditional Apache arrows made in Cibecue for the craft fair during the powwow. Second, the medicine man told Delphia that the Skinwalker was probably curious about someone who had moved into what was considered the school principal's house and that it essentially meant no harm. The meeting occurred in the early evening of the first week of January in 1986. As both Delphia and Hostein Tso gazed at the sky at the rising of Venus, Tso remarked that man was not supposed to go up into the heavens. This was a strange statement considering the Navajo belief that medicine men could project and travel into space spiritually. In fact a group of University of Arizona astronomers had met in a Hogan on the campus of Navajo Community College with a Navajo medicine man, hundred year old Curly Moustache. As the group peered at maps of the Martian surface Mr. Moustache was asked to identify the best spots to land an exploratory vehicle, (noted by an official of the University of Arizona Arid Lands research center— an individual with two PhDs in Anthropology.)

Anthologist Clyde Klockholm's research on the "Skinwalkers" (Kluckhohn, Clyde.1933. BEYOND THE RAINBOW. Christopher Publishing House: Boston.), a book about traveling in Hopi and Navajo land) details that the Navajo believe Skinwalkers can be supernatural beings. Klockholm actually inspected Skinwalker ceremonial caves in the Lukachukai Mountains of the central part of the Navajo Reservation. The rituals of entrance into Navajo witchery of Skinwalking requires that a person consume flesh from a dead person's body – from all five orifices.

Among the Navajo people I have talked with over the years the belief ranges from those who go completely silent at the words and those who talk fluently about their existence – ranging from the supernatural to Navajo men dressed in costumes.

I often left the Greasewood residence at 3AM in order to arrive at Cibecue Community School before school began at 8AM. The campus was pitch dark at 3AM and I came out of the Greasewood residence with my father's .357 Magnum in my hand just to give me courage rather than with an expectation to use it on a Skinwalker. For the two years I came and went from Greasewood I scanned the nearby buttes and hills to assess the likely place for a Skinwalker cave. I only came up with some good guesses. I did learn that Greasewood was located in an area known to contain Skinwalker witchery.

Over the 30 years of my work on the Navajo Nation I heard a number of stories about Skinwalkers. More frequently, stories were relayed by non-Navajos who claimed to have had an interface with a Skinwalker. The common element in all these stories was that while driving at night they noticed something moving along outside and parallel to the highway. They always described what they saw as a manlike being with head covered in skins running at the same speed as their vehicle.

My associate Lynne D said that individuals passing late at night or inside the chapterbuilding complex saw a Skinwalker lurking at different times. That information cancelled any late night work that my associate Lynne or I did in the office of the Chapter House.

Details about skinwalkers is facinating. The Navajo believe that *yee naaldlooshii* (skinwalkers) are human beings who have gained supernatural power by breaking a cultural taboo. Specifically, a person is said to gain the power to become a *yee naaldlooshii* upon initiation into the Witchery Way. Both men and women can become *yee naaldlooshii* and therefore possibly Skinwalkers, but men are far more numerous. It is generally thought that only childless women can become witches.

Although it is most frequently seen as a coyote, wolf, owl, fox, or crow, the *yee naaldlooshii* is said to have the power to assume the form of any animal they choose depending on what kind of abilities they need. Witches use the form for expedient travel. They also may transform to escape from pursuers. Skinwalkers chant to curse instead of to heal.

Some Navajo also believe that Skinwalkers have the ability to steal the "skin" or body of a person, and that if you lock eyes with a Skinwalker, they can absorb themselves into your body. It is also said that Skinwalkers avoid the light and that their eyes glow like an animal when in human form.

A Skinwalker is usually described as naked, except for an animal skin. Some Navajos describe them as a mutated version of the animal in question. The skin may just be a mask, like those which are the only garment worn in the witches' song." (Chad Stambaugh. 2013. THE PARANORMAL DICTIONARY: A COMPLETE USERS GUIDE TO EVERYTHING PARANORMAL. Create Space, Amazon.)

RACISM

"Jerry, I'm tired of going into a room and feeling I have to apologize for being there." So declared Fred R to me during a handball game in the mid 1960's during graduate school days at the University of Illinois. Fred was an African Americans friend of mine working toward a doctorate at the University of Illinois. He was from North Carolina, had played college football and had already created a successful business of this own. He attained full professorship at New York University in an illustrious career. As I write he is a multi-millionaire.

I visited the Purdue University web site in hopes of getting some photographs of the campus to use in this book. I discovered a circumstance wherein a "Director of Diversity" had been fired for trying to put into action a policy to include more African Americans students and faculty at Purdue. How ironic but not surprising that seemed. Over fifty years had passed since, as a member of the faculty action group, I had supported in a 50 page policy document the principles and implementation plans "to put into action a policy to include more African American students and faculty at Purdue." I did not send the first few pages of the 1968 Faculty Action Committee "manifesto" to her as my fervor for doing so was waning. It may not be that valuable for her to realize how things don't seem to change. She probably already knew.

Gunner Myrdal, a Swedish anthropologist, in his book, "AN AMERICAN DILEMMA" states that, although America professes the principle of equality for all men in its founding documents, it violates such a principle with customs, culture, society and laws that treat African Americans and those of color as being less than their "white" counterparts. The excuses justifying vast forms of inequality vary in combinations of erroneous beliefs that Blacks are either unintelligent, or lazy, or immoral or dirty (black skin). The assumption is that equality is a way you treat people depending on whether they do or do not measure up to some arbitrary standard set by others. By insisting that the Black race is less than the Caucasian (white) race in desired attributes, they are tagged as undeserving and incapable of having the same rights of Caucasians to "life, liberty and the pursuit of happiness." All dark skinned people, including Native Americans, persons of Mongoloid Race and Latinos suffer from the same beliefs. Myrdal claimed that change could occur by exposing the inconsistency between America's founding codes and the realities of discrimination in our society. He also admitted that a cynical reaction could occur within the culture that would dim the possibility for equality. The force of rapid social change that has and is occurring over the past fifty years is frightening and frustrating for many Americans. There is a significant retreat back to the comfortable bias and prejudicial tenets of the past.

I am a "racist" like so many others who don't understand nor cop to the levels and degrees that exist for this attitude. Yet, Fred R was a dear friend, and I played on football teams in Winslow and Flagstaff closely bonding with my Black teammates. I worked in Gary, Purdue and Philadelphia on programs that created level playing fields, and I made over hundred calls and door-knocks during both of Obama's campaigns. I left the Catholic Church for 42 years because the local priest in West Lafayette refused to let a Black parishioner sing "Kumbayah." Still, I remain, in a sense, a racist. My second wife, Delphia, a member of the Kiowa Tribe of Oklahoma had skin almost as dark as the average dark skinned American if there is such a standard. Yet I am a racist. My son Jerrell retained some of the darkened pigmentation and looked like he had a perpetual suntan. Yet, I am still a racist.

One can be a "racist" and his or her persona can range in a spectrum from good to bad, from central to peripheral and from action to acquiescence. All racism means is that one is reacting in some way to a difference in skin color that is darker than Caucasian "white." Or, in the case of the African continent, people react to skin color that is lighter than black. There are quantitative and qualitative magnitudes of knowledge, emotions, attitudes and actions associated with race.

To be fair, when one says he or she is not a racist, they most likely mean that they do not apply the principles of justice, kindness, respect and support against people of color in favor of "whites." Discrimination against people of color is often shrouded by statements that they could have all the fruits of the American culture if only they would be more industrious (*pull themselves up by the bootstraps*), model the American ways and family values, clean themselves up and become informed and rational. The most cited epithet is "This is a free country and one can become and get anything he or she wants if they are willing to work for it." There is very little consideration of the long-term impact on African Americans caused by socio-cultural oppression, economic and job discrimination as well as the absence of quality education. It is like crippling a football player and requiring him to work his way into a starting position.

A recent Yale study revealed that individuals would reject any information, no matter if factual and based on research, if it conflicts with that of the group of which they are loyal member. The preponderance of research in anthropology and psychology concludes that there is little basic difference among the three races of Homo sapiens. Measured differences specified by advocates in support of the inferiority of Black and brown people have been shown to be faulty. I used a book written by Harvard professors in my advanced statistics class to point out the errors made on each step of their research. They floated a message that African Americans were not intelligent as their white counterparts.

I admit that I am a racist because race and color are the first things I notice when an individual or groups of people appear. It doesn't mean I have a negative reaction of fear, discomfiture or anger. I have been culturally engrained to notice differences and have a complexity of mindsets past and present that fire off in an instant. In the movie "GRAND CANYON," Danny Grover (Black) saved Kevin Kline (white) from a violent altercation with a Black gang. They bonded as friends and ultimately Kline suggested both families travel together on a trip to the Grand Canyon. An unhealthy silence ensued and Kline finally asked, "What is the matter?" Glover said, "But I and my family are Black." Kline replied, "Oh, I didn't notice." If only Martin Luther King's prediction would come true – that humans will "*judge a person by the quality of his character and not by the color of his skin.*"

I have been fortunate to have developed alternative attitudes to those prejudicial and discriminatory takes conditioned by my society and culture—particularly the media and especially by films. One bonds with football teammates in a lasting and caring manner, and in both my Winslow and Flagstaff football days I had Black teammates who were my captains and were as well All State champions. As a junior high student my heroes included a cadre of Blacks, Native Americans and Latinos. The small towns of Arizona were crucibles of democracy and friendships trumped any attempts to inculcate negative racist stances.

Winslow classmates related the time when, after a football game, a certain church group turned away Black teammates from a dance. The whole class exited, drove to the airport and used their car headlights to light the way for dancing. School integration is not only a requisite for justice but also an essential social-cultural tool to build character. For me the absence of irrational fear along with a trust learned in youth brought me, naively, at night, into the streets of Gary, South Chicago and Philadelphia. The cited church people, not alone in their past tradition, have changed for the better as have other entities. However, as I write the evil head of discrimination is again broiling.

I think the empathy gained from my troubles taught me to "walk in another person's moccasins." While visiting uncles in Houston one summer I foolishly made a point of using only "Colored Only" labeled fountains and toilets. I claim no special virtues as the concept of racial equality. But my life experiences and the kind of people that mentored me – including a wonderful father – saved me from acting out biased positions. I believe having Obama as our president has been stirred and is being sustained by the hateful racist attitudes of many Americans to the point where it has become open season on discrimination and violence against Black people. I believe I am obligated to counteract prejudice at every turn.

That empathy deep inside me, that gift due to "Suffering the Slings and Arrows of Outrageous Fortune," (from a soliloquy in the Nunnery Scene of William Shakespeare's play, HAMLET) brought poignant tears of joy when Obama's victory on the night of November 2, 2008 was announced.

THE NAVAJO CODE TALKERS

During my work on the Navajo Nation I became acquainted with many Navajo Code Talkers. I began to know these Code Talkers in a context different from their World War II connection. Later however, as I learned of their role in the Pacific Theatre I became more and more impressed with their skills and their contributions to the war effort. I quote from my own publication, "Shadows of the Past Over Route 66 – Arizona and New Mexico, Volume I:

"The Navajo Code Talk may have been the only unbreakable code in the history of warfare. It was so top secret that it was not declassified until 1968 – a time when the country's attitude toward war thwarted any public recognition of the significance of the Code Talk as a major weapon in the defeat of the Japanese. No Navajo Code Talker was awarded a Medal of Honor. No parades were held to recognize them.

In December of 1981, President Ronald Regan recognized the Navajo Code Talkers for their 'dedicated service, unique achievement, patriotism, resourcefulness and courage.' Through the efforts of then Senator Dennis DeConcini, April 14, 1983 was proclaimed as the first Navajo Code Talker Day.

The torturous climate of the battle area combined with the tenacity of the Japanese soldiers could well have combined to stop the essential U.S. capture of the Pacific Islands. Many believe that the Navajo Code Talkers tipped the balance, securing victory for the American forces. Major Howard Connor was to remark after the war that 'without the Navajo (Code Talkers), the marines would never have taken Iwo Jima,ß"(from Vol. I, Route 66 Chronicles).

When the movie Windtalkers, about the Code Talkers, was released in 2002 I got a call from 60 Minutes II about an issue involving the Code Talker's activities in the war theatre. I had an article in Passages West magazine about the Code Talkers which piece was replicated in my Route 66 book. The media must have found this story and named me as a resource regarding the true role of Code Talkers in the war scene. I had a chance to talk with a number of them – not in an interview format, but in the context of friendly and incidental conversations although in some cases these discussions were lengthy and quite detailed.

Carl Gorman, Sr. – "He was 90 and the oldest of the 400 Navajo code talkers who were proud to call themselves Washindon be *Akalh B-kosi-lai*, or, as the Japanese could never figure out, *United States Marines*. Carl was the father of celebrated Navajo artist R. C. Gorman of Taos, New Mexico. Mr. Gorman was himself a prominent artist who taught at the University of California at Davis before settling in a trailer-studio in Fort Defiance, Arizona, where he painted horses and other subjects."(New York Times, February 2,1998)

I was Director of Grant Management at Navajo Community College where Gorman was a resident teacher and artist. Mr. Gorman's conversation with me revealed that in the beginning he was used as a messenger crossing battlefields with vital information. The concept was that, if intercepted, the Japanese would not be able to debrief them for information, and the Army would treat them as expendable Native Americans. The significance of the Code Talker role shifted dramatically and they were soon infiltrating behind Japanese lines to radio the effectiveness of navel bombardment of enemy positions. King Mike, the father of a close friend, Richard Mike, related having nightmares years later because of the hand-to-hand combat he experienced behind enemy lines. He operated a radio to identify Japanese positions – the Japanese had set up a system of fake sites to confuse the Americans.

I felt that in order to do a valid report to 60 Minutes II I needed to effect my own research. I found a whole book of interviews of Code Talkers done by an Army officer who had been their leader. The interviews were conducted at a convocation in Window Rock. I found no evidence that Code Talkers operated under threat of death if it appeared they might be captured. I found it odd that the script of Carl Gorman, Sr. was cut so short. There was a hilarious reason for the brevity of Gorman's interview. He was asked what he did for rations when his group ran out of food on an island in the Pacific. He said, "I asked my men to give me their undies and I made soup" – a classic Gorman response.

Another story that Carl told me involved a situation on the same island when he and a buddy sat among the palm trees chatting and having a beer. Carl's friend commented that he was FBI – a full-blooded Italian. Carl said that he was also FBI – a full-blooded Indian. Their giggling was suddenly interrupted by an officer who shouted, "What do you mean you are FBI?!!" Carl and his buddy were grilled for two hours to determine if they were undercover FBI agents.

Sam Billison was one of the Code Talkers with whom I had the most contact. I first met Billison as the Chairman of the Board of the Navajo Teacher Education Development Program. I found him to be an incisive individual who asked penetrating questions and who held a non-nonsense attitude about my work. I have been fortunate to win trust and respect from Navajo people like Sam. He was the president of the Navajo Code Talker Association and was the voice of a Navajo Code Talker GI Joe. "Mt. Suribachi is secured" – his clear Navajo-accented English voice comes out of GI Joe followed by the Navajo version of the same sentence.

I wrote a number of proposals for Sam when he was the Director of the Navajo Academy in Farmington, New Mexico. He was a close friend of Dillon Platero and was the vice chairman candidate when Platero ran for Chairman of the Navajo Tribe. Billison was the western rep in the political partnership as Platero, being from Canoncito, an enclave near Albuquerque was at a disadvantage because the Canoncito Navajo had fought with the Spanish against the Western Navajo way back in time.

Sam called my house in Taos one day asking to talk with me. My wife at the time, Karen, said I wasn't there. Sam said "is this Gallup?" and Karen said, "No this is Taos." A confused Billison asked how I got to Taos from Gallup. His purpose for calling was that he was giving an address at a high school graduation the next day in Chinle and wanted a speech. I hurriedly created my usual epical narrative about the Navajo people and faxed it to Sam—"*After the Treaty of 1868 the Navajo people – yada, yada yada.*"

The uncommon courage manifested by Ted Draper during the Navajo Community College uproar demonstrated his spirit as a Navajo Code Talker. He stood up in opposition to the president of the community college – the cousin of the most powerful Native American in the United States, Peter McDonald. His behavior was doubly significant because of the sinister power McDonald possessed and the long standing custom of the Navajo to honor harmony and not rock the boat.

Ted Draper was also an artist and created numerous works – one, a notable depiction of the U.S. Marines dealing with Japanese mines on the beaches of the South Pacific.

MEDICINE PEOPLE AND MENTORS

ALFRED YAZZIE

I was befriended by Alfred W Yazzie who is known as the Head *Yeibichai* Dancer, or head *Fire Dancer*, of the Navajo within the *Nightway Ceremonies* of the Navajo.

The Nightway ceremony is a major curative ceremony that restores harmony invoking the *Yeis*, a special category of Holy People inclined to help the Navajo. A nine day ceremony, it is performed during the cold months when there is no chance of being hit by lightning and when the snakes are hibernating

Alfred was a veteran of the Korean War and told me about an episode wherein his company was fired upon with a rain of bullets. Everyone in his company was slain but him. He attributed his survival to his Defensive Way cultural role and membership. Many Navajos identify with what is known as the Beauty Way – "*in Beauty we walk.*" He related that his great grandfather, Solatso, was the first Navajo Chief of Police and had come into a Squaw Dance one night with a bear (*shush)* on his shoulders. Defensive Way people relate to and communicate with bears. Defensive Way people are protected from violence.

In my personal work with Robert P. I was asked to acquire a totem and I naturally turned to Alfred Yazzie. I asked him if he would grant me a totem, usually an animal. I invited him to Kayenta at the Holiday Inn for lunch. After a lengthy meal I sat there waiting for him to speak and he finally looked at me and said, "*Shushtso.*" Shushtso means "*Big Bear*" in Navajo. I realized that a Defensive Way powerful head of the Nightway Ceremony had just armed me with the persona of a grizzly bear. I became acquainted with a Northwestern University anthropology professor who had spent 17 years studying the "*Navajo Universe.*" I asked him what he thought of Navajo spirituality and healing ceremonies and he gave me the best answer, detailing the means of respect and reverence for Native Tradition – "Jerry, there are many realities." Though I felt I could not understand the power of *Shush* nor had I understood the great power the owls, (*sawpoh*), held over Kiowa people (signifying onset of death), by accepting the existence of their power I could let them help me, or empower me in the tests that I met. I have many times become a grizzly bear, actually evidencing protective actions. Many a time when semis have tailgated me I have turned into a grizzly and screamed at the top of my voice and have seen the semis back off.

When I was at Navajo Community College in the late 1970's, Alfred and I had lengthy conversations. He was the Chief of Police of the College. I have already alluded to his comments about the Rough Rock Community School and rumors of the misuse of funds. But his major concern was that non-Navajos did much of the writing about the Navajo culture and way of life. I promised him I would help him secure funds to 'record' the oral history of the Navajo people. I wrote a grant for $174,000 for a project to record that oral history. The volumes were published in 1984 with exquisite drawings and illustrations depicting critical periods and sites in Navajo history. (These volumes are currently listed on Amazon and Google books. The actual print files have unexpectedly disappeared.(NAVAJO ORAL TRADITION, 3 Volumes. 1984).

THE ENEMY WAY

"The Enemy Way, or *Ana'i Ndáá'* is one half of the major Navajo song ceremonial complexes, the other half being the Blessing Way. The Enemy Way is a traditional ceremony for countering the harmful effects of alien ghosts, or *chindi,* and has been performed for returning military personnel.

The Enemy Way ceremony involves the patient identifying (through chant, sand painting, and dance) with the powerful mythical figure Monster Slayer. The ceremony lasts three days, and on the second morning a mock battle is performed.

Associated with the Enemy Way is a Girl's Dance (sometimes called '*Squaw Dance*') to which marriageable young women invite young men. This derives from an aspect of the Monster Slayer myth, in which two captive girls are liberated. The Enemy Way ceremony is described in Tony Hillerman's novel "THE BLESSING WAY." (from Wikipedia, the free encyclopedia -THE ENEMY WAY)

LEAVING DELPHIA

In the spring of 1986 after I left CBQ I began to grow weary of my life with Delphia and the H family. My acceptance of two or three families and grandchildren bivouacked in our house began to wear thin. I enjoyed the powwow circuit up to a point until the late and long rides back to Arizona made me worry about the hazards of falling asleep at the wheel. Son Greg and stepson Charlie had already fallen asleep and gone off the road. In addition, Delphia had taken in two stepchildren orphaned by her brother's car accident death. Although the boy was very talented like his famous award-winning artist dad, he continued to do crazy things without Delphia holding him responsible for the consequences. He had for example ruined a brand new car by using a rag to plug the oil intake. Finally, when he broke a door off the hinges, I insisted he reattach it before he came into the house. Delphia and I had no mechanisms in place to mitigate our differences. One afternoon leaving Gallup, I just kept going down the off ramp road to the Greasewood BIA School (the family residence) and back onto I-40. I finally decided to stay on I-40 and drove south to Show Low to meet my alcoholic friends.

Susana

I knew a lady named Susana would be there. She was. She made a pass at me and I turned her down. It is one thing to desire and have an intimate interface with women one meets and another thing altogether to be with someone I love and understand – a person to whom one can commit. That is not to say that the latter relationship is any more virtuous than the former. My expectation that a significant other is going to supply all the needs one expects of a nurturing mother always ended in a disastrous exit. It was my nature to go out the back door if my partner at the time was failing to meet my idealistic, impossible expectations. The man who gets a sexual fix and then is on his way may in fact causes less damage than the one who stays and becomes an integral part of a family, as in my case the partner to a family matriarch, and then summarily exits without the slightest comment.

Sophie-Anaheim

In the autumn of 1985 I had some travel funds in the budget and made arrangements to attend a School Administrator's Conference in Anaheim, California. Of course I wasn't really interested in what the formal administrative regimens had to do with Cibecue. But, I knew Purdue buddy Ted Urich was going to attend the Conference and we could reunite and share the good old days. I had also been invited during the 1981 Flagstaff High Reunion by Sophie Bennet to dine someday with her in Santa Monica on the beach at her house. Once again I felt my chance to be with Sophie would finally happen. I had no other agenda but to see her again and talk about the past. I had no desire to bring up what I believed to be a Gatsby-like busted romance. To this day I do not want to broach the subject as I believe Sophie is totally innocent and certainly a non-participant in that dynamic – if it existed at all outside my fantasies. The major players, the mother and the priest, have passed away long ago. I learned much later during my Taos days, from former associates of the priesthood, that my vocation as a priest was not the only reason he wanted me back in the Gallup Diocese! (Ah hem).

I had left Phoenix Airport for Anaheim in a harried dynamic having been frustrated by Susana, who didn't wish to let me go. My ticket to LAX was only $35 round trip and I did not want to miss the plane. Once airborne I realized that I had left my address/phone number book in the front seat of the car. I didn't know Sophie's address in Santa Monica and thought I would go to information and call her once the

Anaheim Conference was over.

The morning of the day I was to meet Sophie for dinner I called for her number and was told it was unlisted. I began calling people in Flagstaff including her uncle John Bennet and my close friend, her cousin George Bennet. But no one had her number. I felt so bad and upon arriving home in Arizona I sent her a letter expressing my regret at missing the opportunity to see her. She wrote back and in so many words termed it one of those quirks of fate, and said she missed seeing me. She also said with some humor that it was "just like me" to not have her phone or address.

FLAGSTAFF REUNION 91

The Flagstaff Reunion of '91 was a time for the healing of any issues rooted in the dynamic of high school subculture. The spiritual gains that had been given me by my association with and the counseling by my alcoholic friends brought me to the point wherein I could no longer harbor resentments and prejudicial feelings toward a class-mate. "Don" had become in high school locked in my memory as a contentious "Moriarty" (from Sherlock Holmes) – one who projected what I thought to be the worst in the male persona – arrogance, insensitivity, dominance and misogyny. Maybe, as I was often told, my finger pointing should have also included a finger pointing back at me.

At the banquet when given the microphone to speak, I gave a short testimonial stating that I was an "alcoholic." Don approached me after the banquet to announce that he had two sons that were recovering alcoholics. We bonded immediately and he became a victim of my Lynch ancestry comedic episodes. The next day while standing with a group of my classmates I made a comment that "Don" was a "great quarterback."

"Why," retorted everyone, "was he a great passer?" I answered, "No." "Did he run and score a lot?" I said "No." I said "he just looked so good out there." Don could have doubled for Errol Flynn with his handsome features, wavy hair and excellent poise. Everyone laughed, especially his wife. Don knew that he was the recipient of my deep affection for him.

I repeated this episode each time I was in a group with Don in 2001, 2012, and re-cently at HALL OF FAME and HOMECOMING CELEBRATIONS. I had been gifted with the power to actually manifest some meaning behind the beatitudes that had become the focus of my morning meditation and a guide to my feelings, thinking and behavior. The power to change my attitude toward people was a gift that came from somewhere outside of me.

MARY LOU

Amiable Mary Lou

With a sad regret I look back at my dysfunctional relationships with women. I now understand how ill equipped I was to provide healthy and caring support for the women I tried to partner with for all those years. What seems so ironic is that "caring" was a core value in my soul.

One of the most poignant cases of tragic interface occurred with a lovely person in 1987. I had gone through Gary to a birthday party for my former Purdue University associate Bennie Mae Collins. From Gary I flew on the Montréal to a gathering of 70 thousand alcoholics from all over the world.

Later that summer I became highly energized and intensely optimistic by virtue of my participation in Hands Across America as well as the growing realization that I could truly attain the "happiness of my soul lifted above all circumstances." One Bob E., a speaker at a New Mexico State get together of alcoholics, shared how he had escaped the ghosts of the past into a new dimension of reality.

I went to my old established group of alcoholics in Sedona and saw a lovely blond lady (Mary Lou A.), a nurse at a local recovery center. I enticed her with my customary charm to accompany me to Phoenix, and the relationship accelerated from that point on. We later joined other alcoholic friends on a trip to Puerto Peñasco on the Sea of Cortez in Mexico. However, my disappointment in her failure to match the behavior I expected from a "mother" and the revelation of what I viewed as imperfections resulted in my usual rejection and abandonment. I did this twice, and after the last time I saw her I received a bitter and angry redress from her and her new boyfriend – a former detective from Los Angeles! I could not understand what she was so uptight about?! Certainly she should have realized that her being used by me was a noble contribution to my ongoing quest for the perfect mom. I have searched public records to locate one Mary Lou A. and found literally hundreds of women with that name. As I write, my next step is to send post cards asking "Are you the Mary Lou A. with whom I traveled to Puerto Peñasco? And if so, is there any way I can make up for my bad behavior?"

Learning "to care from the deepest part of me" (love) has been long in coming for me. Without "caring" I had little to give, even to myself. My distrust and rejection of women was conditioned by my own mother, who, God love her, did the best she could considering her tragic early years. Robert P. had stated, "Your mother was psychotic." I can't and don't use that as an excuse for my own transgressions.

IRAQI AT THE AMBASSADOR LOUNGE

The meetings of the ASCD Elementary Advisory Council offered excellent opportunities to negotiate romantic intrigue. One reason I have always been sensitive to the Iraqis in spite of that war was that I had an interaction with an Iraqi lady who must have been attached to their government. I was in Washington, D.C. hanging out at the Lounge in the Ambassador Hotel and I introduced myself to her, but rather than a passionate episode it turned out to be a comic scene characterized by neither of us understanding the language of the other. Last night watching "The Black Prince" about Saddam Hussein's son, I thought once again about the Iraqi lady – hoping the improbable that she was still alive, and murmuring a short prayer for her. In spite of Sigmund Freud's claim that sex trumps most all other motives, I want to believe that love for people will win out in the end, and that Francis of Assisi had the best recipe for joy.

BEAUTIFUL BLACK LADIES

Near the end of my alcoholic addiction, during my last year at Purdue I attended my last U.S. Department of Education workshop.

I stayed at the Brown Palace Hotel. The Hotel was configured like a ten story high donut with open air in the middle and a staircase winding up those ten stories. In the late 1800's, patrons rode their horses up the staircase causing quite a stir.

I had attended work sessions from 7 in the morning until 6 at night with an act-a-like Bennie Mae Collins and a Black lady named Rosemary Brooks. It always gave me great satisfaction when African Americans like Bennie Mae and Rosemary negated the prejudicial profile, faulting the concept that they are incompetent and lazy. In other countries these two women would have rose to positions equal to Margaret Thatcher of England or Angela Merkel of Germany.

I was deeply flattered when Rosemary Brooks showed up several years later as I gave a speech in Washington about OPEN EDUCATION and the 'development of one's belief that he or she can control their own destiny.' When I heard First Lady Michelle and President Obama state that they could accomplish anything if they believed in their own efforts, I could not help but think about Bennie Mae and Rosemary, wishing I could be with them face to face.

But, I did have an experience that might have occurred with either one of my Black friends. I was having coffee in a McDonald's attached to Sam's Club in Colorado

Springs. A young Black lady was sitting across the room, also enjoying a cup of coffee. We looked up at each other simultaneously and we both smiled. It was five days after Obama had been elected President of the United States. In the old days, Black people could be lynched in the South for giving direct eye contact to Whites. Now the light of justice had broken through the clouds and the beautiful personalities of African Americans could illuminate the rooms and our hearts. I had to hold back my tears that morning.

DOROTHY

My relationship with Susana, who was also a recovering alcoholic, had begun to fall apart. She had had a number of shock treatments at the Barrows Clinic in Phoenix and they had really rung her out. She suffered from bipolar depression. She had flown to northern Arizona with a former boyfriend but was now living with a gentleman friend in Glendale. Although she was a certified and practicing counselor, she had many past experiences and behaviors that were characteristic of nymphomania. I cannot contend that I wasn't taking advantage of her sexual obsession, but some of my commitment was basically codependent. I held on expecting that a healthy relationship would emerge but it never did, and things got worse.

My commitment to the Kayenta Township Project position required me to operate out of Flagstaff. As my mother and father had both passed away, their house on David Drive was essentially empty though it still contained some furniture and other items. I arranged timers inside the house, regulating the lights and the TV to suggest that the house was inhabited as protection against break-ins and robbery.

It felt strange to be alone in a house with all those happy memories. I painted the eves as I wanted the place well prepared for a sale. I held a yard sale and found that so often things of value go for only a small faction of their original cost.

During my days in Flagstaff I received a request from a Cibecue teacher to visit and shop in Flagstaff. The same weekend I was expecting Dorothy C to stay at the house I received a note from Diana S about joining a group at a local steakhouse, her phone number on the note. When I accepted her invitation with the stipulation that Dorothy C would join us, I never heard back from Diana. Dorothy and I went to the steakhouse but there was no group present.

We had dinner and went back to the house in Flagstaff. Dorothy consumed two glasses of some leftover wine and we retired for the night, she in what had been my father's room with its own bath and me in what had been my mother's room.

On awaking in the morning I walked past my father's room. The door was wide open and Dorothy C was propped against two pillows, covered only from the waist down. I shut the bedroom door. Later, I realized that most likely her exposure was an invitation to me but it went right over my naïve head. We had a bacon and eggs breakfast and as she went out the door on her way back to Pinetop she angrily stated, "I wasn't the only one that had the hots for you!"

I had been told by many women that the man is the aggressor. However, even considering my history I possessed few skills in enticing women, and for the most part that was not the first thing that came to my mind when entering a relationship.

I had stayed at Dorothy's house in Pinetop several times while back in the White Mountain area and there had never been an incident of intimacy generated either by Dorothy or me. We traveled from Arizona to Santa Fe once and stayed at the last room in the famous Loretta Inn. Our room had two second story balconies; the beds were pullouts from two couches. The walls featured beautiful painted Pueblo designs. We had breakfast on the balcony. There was no suggestive behavior by either of us. Later, an all day tour of northern Arizona ending in my staying at her house in Pinetop unraveled without incident. I was treating her as a friend and professional with no strategy on my part to do otherwise.

SUSANA-WINSLOW

By 1988 I had arrived at the point where I realized that my being happy, joyous and free was not dependent upon having a partner, a soul mate nor a mother as a compliment to my personality, or to act as "*the other half of me*" as phrased in Steve Wonder's song "*Angie.*" The serious tests of my acceptance of this newly born status of existence were two brief interfaces with my old partner in "mutual intimacy," Susana D. She was living in Winslow with a friend and I was asked to stay with them for a night while I had business there. I informed Susana that I was not interested in being intimate and that I did not need a lover or counselor, but simply a friend and supportive alcoholic. This had little or no effect on Susana as prior to retreating to separate rooms for the night she came for a "good night kiss" and pressed her body against me. I don't remember my words or body English except that they spelled a definite "no."

A month later Susana called from Winslow stating that she and her friend were coming to Flagstaff to "dance." I did go dancing with Susana, her friend and the friend's partner. Susana and I had separated from the other couple and agreed to meet at my motel at the end of the evening. Standing by the bed at the Roadway Inn in Flagstaff I remember wishing Susana a *bon voyage* back to Winslow. I did this with firmness absent of any sarcasm or put-downs.

Informing Robert P. of my independent achievement he retorted, "What is it with this celibacy!" His comment suggested that avoidance of enmeshment with a female did not mean abstinence from sex. My acceptance of his indirect counsel set me up for a twelve year "ship in port" in Taos.

DIANA

Prior to sailing into the 'Taos Port' I was attending alcoholic meetings wherein one Diana S's presence merged into my life resulting in attending group dinners, separate dates and finally an invitation to go to San Diego, sun bathe on the beaches and swim in the Pacific. I even suggested that we go as a group and include her son Abel. The day before our departure she said Abel would not be coming with us. We drove her Subaru to the Crystal Pier Motel high on a pier above the incoming waves from the Pacific – a perfect romantic setting to enjoy the first intimacy with Dorothy who would be my yearlong mate. I moved into her 1922 vintage house in Mountain Meadows south of Flagstaff, so comfy with its wood stove.

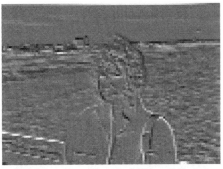

"Diana"—Crystal Pier Motel

I would spend the week in Kayenta and come to Flag for the weekend, attending dinners and watching movies in Mountain Meadows. Grateful for a place to live, I built a two hundred foot grape stake fence surrounding the back yard, digging twenty-post holes three feet deep. One day I worked in the rain covered with a poncho using a crow bar to break rock .

Later I also wired the 1920's house with a 220 watt service for her washer and dryer stackable combination. Notre Dame won the national championship in football that year. Daughter Maureen had moved from Oregon to Tucson and was attending the University of Arizona. Diana, son Abel, myself and son Jerrell took a trip to see the University of Arizona play Southern California. The first of several contentious episodes involving Abel occurred when he acted out his dislike of the football game and the dinner later at El Corral in north Tucson. Later during that same autumn of 1987, my daughter Mi Mi came from Tucson to Flagstaff for Thanksgiving with her current boyfriend.

The second sign of a growing relationship storm occurred in Las Vegas where Diana, I, her son and the daughter of a family friend, had traveled to stay at the Tropicana with its waterfall pouring into the swimming pool. Diana emphatically told Abel that the fireworks she had bought him could not be used until we returned to Flagstaff. Lounging poolside later the next morning, Diana suddenly remarked, "Where is

Abel?" Almost simultaneously two hotel detectives approached us to announce Abel's detention at a first floor room for igniting a smoke bomb in our tenth floor bathtub. The tenth floor alarm had been set off and we were told that if the general alarm sounded we would be guilty of a felony.

The growing incorrigibility of Abel along with the rather strange behavior of Diana during times of intimacy began to melt away my desire for a relationship. Things became even darker with an episode at Buster's Restaurant, in Flagstaff. Although I have never been able to relate to gay men even though I tried hard in the Conception Seminary days, I have always been accepting, empathetic and respectful toward them. Diana had been a close friend and business partner with a gay gentleman from San Francisco. It seemed that Mr. K. performed as the mentor and counselor for Diana in every aspect of life. Esteem and self-confidence issues tried my soul in the presence of the aggressive and self-assured Mr. K. I sensed some control and jealousy issues imminating from Mr. K. which I felt were uncalled for and unkind.

One evening during a dinner at Buster's Restaurant it became clear that the group was purposely dissing me, and that Diana was an accomplice in the scheme. Shame had been a powerful tool used by Diana. My trust and hope for our future and a possible marriage went out the window that night.

After her announcement that Mr. K. and his partner would be vacationing in Flagstaff, I told Diana I would at that time be giving a speech about Cibecue to an Indian Community School controlled conference in Albuquerque followed by a family get-together in Taos. That break was followed by an angry phone conversation a week later, interrupted and ended by the appearance of a drunk alcoholic bursting in my office in Kayenta. Our only communication for the past 30 years was eye contact at alcoholic group meetings and a letter of amends I sent to her in the 1990's.

Still, my relationship with Diana brought about a significant change in my life. Diana had done work on personal issues at the Meadows in Wickenburg, Arizona. The Meadows program featured state of the art attacks aimed at removing the causes and conditions of deep issues driving addiction and alcoholism. Pia Melody had identified the deep roots, an effective therapeutic scheme fostering mitigation in the causes and operation of dysfunctional behavior and the consequent reduction in codependency.

I dealt with many issues at two separate one-week sessions at the Meadows. The core issue was the presence of shame constraining my life from my earliest days. The fear of not being good enough, of someone discovering my imperfections was antennas to my psyche that ruled all my behavior. The pain of shame was to be avoided at all costs.

The Meadows identified the major source of my shame-based behavior as being from my mother's sexual abuse and the tragic dismissal from St. Anthony's third grade room by a Catholic nun of the Sisters of Loretta Order. I lost my voice for three days on two separate sessions at the Meadows due to unprincipled attacks on me. Ultimately, I felt the shame ball inside me shrink from a dark and dense basketball to a BB.

HOUSE IN TAOS

I traveled to Taos in September of 1988 to attend a festival get-together of sober alcoholics. Someone had brought a flyer about the event to a meeting in Kayenta in early August, and I thought at the time there was no better place to be than among the autumn leaves in Taos.

House in historic district of Taos

KAREN ANNE

Karen

The separation and apparent end to my relationship with Diana S had registered firmly in my mind, but not my heart. I was living in a trailer behind the Golden Sands Café with old *Bow and Arrow*, a non-neutered Wolf/Malamute with blond hair and beautiful blue eyes. I still left Kayenta on weekends to attend meetings in Flagstaff with my alcoholic friends. I would see Diana at these meetings, cognizant of my lingering obsession about her but helpless to accept the inevitable.

I was continuing therapy sessions with friend and psychologist, Robert P. He had transported me from the "in the hills" recovery status to the "mountain tops" of bolstered self-esteem and self-confidence. He took me deeper into the dark basement of shame and to the ghosts of the past who still fired their blue-black flames. I learned to use "back of the moon" retorts as a means of warding off putdown encounters in relationships and professional situations. Such putdowns would often destabilize my functioning, causing me to retreat defenselessly into silence or to plot means of escape to ease the pain of the moment. The first indicator of my evolvement out of these shame based dysfunctional episodes appeared the day I stopped Universality of Arizona colleague Albert S. dead in his tracks in the middle of one of his benign but devastating attacks on my character – my performance, motivations and my subordinate status in our cooperative efforts on the Navajo Nation. My children and family had the Flagstaff family house sold and in escrow when Albert suggested I should not sell the house but use the it as a basis of operation to establish and carry out a project addressing the problems of the Navajo families being relocated from Hopi lands to near areas. The delay in culminating the sale of the house caused the buyers to forego the escrow and the house lay unsold for another year, losing several thousand dollars in value.

My efforts with Robert P. and accomplishments during the Meadow sessions made me realize that my unsuccessful quest for someone to compliment my life was really a serious defect of my character.

I attended regular meetings with my alcoholic friends every Wednesday night at the Catholic Church in Kayenta. One night in 1988 someone mentioned an alcoholic festival in Taos. My habit of going to Taos and Santa Fe at least once a year drew me to attend.

The Festival was held at the Kachina Lodge with its distinctive round shaped coffee shop and pueblo-like rooms. As I perused the hospitality room I struck up a conversation with a bright eyed lady ten years younger than my 54 years. She was very attractive and had a sweet and easygoing personality. She seemed to practice all the principles I followed to assure that I would not get drunk again nor use any sort of mood altering chemicals.

Robert P. felt that my determination to maintain celibacy, while noble, really wasn't necessary. His opinion opened me up to a chance of intimacy in Taos among my alcoholic "people." Looking back now at myself in the late 1980's, I think I was weary of going back and forth across the four corners area.

I immediately bonded with Karen and we sealed a date to eat at the banquet scheduled for the coming evening at the Kachina Lodge center. The speaker that night was one Judith G., a wealthy heiress who lived north of Taos in a thick bosque of cottonwoods standing in a beautiful section of the Sangre de Cristo Mountains. For most 'hunters' she would have been serious game for someone ready for a new relationship. After all, Karen informed me that she ran a parking lot just south of the Taos plaza, worked as an artist who made teddy bears out of Pendleton blankets and was a very successful dealer in antiques. Taos was a gold mine for the marketing of antiques generated the property dissolution of wealthy residents and artists.

It seems rather foolish that I would have spent the night with Karen. I now know that the enchantment of Taos and it being "a port in the storm" – rather than any searing passion I had for Karen – pushed me into the decision to move in with her. She had lived in Taos for ten years, had once owned a house there and had had one in Wisconsin. She suggested we rent a nice place in the historic district of Taos just west of the PIaza. Karen's Thanksgiving dinner spread confirmed the excellence of her homemaking skills and sealed a long time commitment in our relationship, which relationship culminated in marriage in December of that year – 1988.

The following April we purchased a 1920's house in the Taos historic district two blocks west of the Plaza bordering the western perimeter of the old traditional residential quadrangle of early Taos.

The house had finished floors, with a beautifully tiled kitchen and bathrooms. An add-on room boasted a brick fireplace that we fashioned into a Kiva-like model a year later. The old place had a stonewall fence and small gate. I raised the wall to 6 feet to hide cars coming down the street. A fancy irregular wall was built across the back around a tree, creating a secluded and comfortable patio. Karen had been a wood stove vender and she purchased a Norwegian stove that warmed the whole house throughout the snowy northern New Mexico winters. It was *la dolce vita* for the early 1990's. I felt like Kit Carson venturing out west 300 some odd miles into the Navajo Nation on Sundays and coming back to my homeport in Taos every weekend.

There were so many places in Taos and in northern New Mexico to explore. Santa Fe was an hour away, the old plaza of Las Vegas was an hour to the southeast and nearby were such locales as Old Fort Union of the Santa Fe Trail as well as ancient Spanish towns like Mora. Taos reeked of Georgia O'Keefe types, and its architecture made one feel he was in fact living in an old pueblo.

My children, their families and the extended family on my mother's side came and went from Taos as well as Karen's brothers. Many a joyful Thanksgiving and Christmas were spent in that old house.

I supported Karen's one week session at the Meadows in Wickenburg, which allowed her to deal with some resolute issues. However, the repertoire of interrelationship skills I learned at the Meadows was never realized between Karen and I. My son Jerrell was the product of a totally different culture and society, and the Kiowa Tribe of Oklahoma emerged as a serious problem. Bitter conflicts arose over my son's presence in Taos and my support of him requiring frequent and extensive trips across the Navajo reservation and New Mexico to attend school sporting events. Karen's eventual refusal to allow Jerrell to come to Taos caused an angry and resentful standoff and eventual impasse. I suggested that we go to a "Couples Week" at the Meadows to resolve our conflicts, create a way to communicate and retain a loving relationship. Karen would not go to the Meadows and suggested we find a nearby counselor. We found a brilliant therapist right in Taos who had a reputation as a "Wise Man"– an extremely powerful resource for self-discovery and recovery. The emphasis on "self" was what the fates had designed for me as my work with "Dave S." took the final steps initiated by Robert P. for me to accept and take care of myself. Two jobs, one in Kayenta writing grants and the other at the Zuni Pueblo, enabled me to become financially and emotionally independent and to sever the relationship with Taos and Karen through divorce in 2004.

WINSLOW HIGH 2001 REUNION

I can't remember how I learned of a planned reunion of Winslow High School grads that summer of 2001. But, I was swimming in a new frame of life characterized by joy and freedom. I was totally fired up to go to the reunion as I felt I had "left my heart in" Winslow. The biggest sea change of my life had happened in Winslow in 1947- 48 precipitated by my football injury, the imminence of death and seven months in bed. I had gone from the heights of achievement to the depths of anguish. The grasp of newly achieved self-confidence and esteem had been snatched from my life and my horizon was dimmed with hopelessness and uncertainty. My departure away from Winslow to Flagstaff in May of 1948 held only sweet, haunting memories of those lost days in Winslow. Rolling on the Santa Fe train in 1952 on the way home for Christmas I peered out the window at the dark unlit silhouettes of the La Posada Hotel trying to reinvasion the football banquet, the dancing on the tennis court and standing in the snowfall awaiting the arrival of a sweet heart returning home from Barstow unaware that my Tucker Flat buddies were caught in a blizzard somewhere north of town.

Although never realized, reunions seemed to promise some reliving, some reigniting of fires long dormant. The mere illusion of any chance I had to recapture the poignant legacy of Winslow days thrilled me to the core. I did sense that my exuberance demanded caution. After all, the last time I was in Winslow I played a role as defensive halfback in the second and final humiliation of a Winslow Bulldog football team that season of 1950-51. My appearance at the field in Winslow was met with hateful glares and vicious tackles from my old buddies.

I had been attending Standing on the Corner Celebrations for several years and during the millennial 2000 all-school reunion of 800 alumni I had volunteered the back my pickup to haul members of the class of '51 during the parade.

My plan for the reunion the next year was to honor my old friends and classmates by sharing remembrances of what great people they were then, and how much they meant to me. What I did was bring my Toyota pickup full of firewood all the way from Taos to Winslow to provide a bonfire cookout and dance at the Ramada at Clear Creek – the old romantic swimming hole cherished and known by every kid in town.

I put up a sign at the registration table in the foyer of the La Posada Hotel inviting friends to Clear Creek for the cookout.

THE LA POSADA OF WINSLOW

Marie Coulter, architect and designer of the exquisite buildings at the Grand Canyon, claimed her favorite building was the La Posada, built in Winslow, Arizona in 1929. The cost of construction exceeded one million dollars. Since Winslow was surrounded by favored tourist destinations of the Southwest, the cost of the hotel was an easily justifiable extravagance. "The Resting Place" (English translation of La Posada) was a rendition of the great ranchos built by the Spanish dons in the 1700 and 1800's. It was built on eight acres and featured archways, great portals, tiled roofs, smooth pink plastered walls and wrought iron grills reminiscent of Spanish Mediterranean architecture. There were seventy guestrooms, five suites and a lunchroom designed with Spanish tile that seated 120 people. There was also a large dining room, as well as numerous corridors and lounges.

Walking into La Posada gave one the feeling of being in a great ranch house. Coulter had chosen rough-hewn pieces of furniture in combination with imported and rare furnishings and Navajo rugs for the floors in the rooms. Outside, there were horse stables, tennis courts and a sunken garden. The complex was considered a work of art, inside and out.

There were hand-hewn benches next to a two-hundred year old antique chest that had once hauled grain from Spain to the New World. Rare old Spanish plates and Chinese copper jars inside a primitive Mexican trastero (cupboard) – blue and white Chinese Chippendale jars in the lobby and a fine old samovar in the dining room – lampshades made from a cardinal's umbrella.

La Posada became a winter resort for wealthy Easterners, and an oasis in the hot Arizona summers of the 1930's and 1940's. One parched soul, after hours of viewing little but cactus and dry, cracked earth, described the entry into the La Posada lunchroom as "a sudden paradise." Travelers even changed their itinerary to stay a couple of nights after dining there.

Many celebrities crossed the portals of La Posada. Charles Lindbergh had a suite that is still there – the Lindbergh Suite is available for a one-night stay. John Wayne and Bing Crosby were guests, and Carol Lombard, the wife of Clark Gable, spent her last night at the hotel prior to her tragic death in a plane accident. My close friend and football team member, Arthur Rubi, was a bellboy at La Posada in the 1940s and carried baggage for Charles Lindbergh. I stood on the platform in front of the La Posada in 1945 when Harry Truman campaigned off the back of his special Pullman car. The whole town came out to see him.

Dances for teenagers were held on the tennis courts at La Posada in the mid-1940's. The scene remains vivid in my memory – green enameled lamp shades casting a dim light out over the courts … the moon shining bright … the balmy summer breeze of the Winslow night on the Little Colorado River Valley undulating with the rhythm of the music … *"It was only a paper moon, shining over a card board screen – but it wouldn't be make believe if you believed in me."* Pre-pubescence was over, along with World War II, and the world seemed like a magical, mysterious and wonderful paradise. It was easy then to believe in *"that old black magic called love."*

In December of 1947, the Winslow Bulldog football banquet was held at La Posada in Winslow. As always, the service and the food were exceptional, nothing better to be had in the entire state of Arizona.

Meandering through the halls of La Posada was a delightful, aesthetic experience. The hotel brought such beauty, such elegance to that small western town. It was pure enchantment, a different world – like walking through the set of a western movie. It was warm and lovely, it smelled of fresh rolls and roast beef and flowers and the magnificent pictures, sculptures and Navajo rugs were a feast for the eyes.

La Posada Court Dance

A huge yellow harvest moon hung over the empty tennis courts of the old La Posada Fred Harvey House in Winslow. The night sky was truly as buttermilk as it had been 50 years ago that July. The courts were enclosed on the perimeter by seven-foot walls of Moencopi sandstone, dotted periodically with small arched openings and barred with latillas. The old green shades of the now disconnected lights were spotted with rust and swayed in the winds of an oncoming western thunderstorm. Summer nights along the Little Colorado were balmy and fraught with a mysterious sense of promise. I shivered as the thrill of it all lit a spark somewhere deep in my soul, and the sweet scent of lilacs that bordered the court pushed me over the edge into a delicious reverie. *"The More I See You, the More I Want You … "* The voice of Dick Haymes lifted up from the record player at the southeast corner of the courtyard and I was back there again dressed in my Winslow tuxedo of Levis and white tee shirt. Wildroot Cream Oil had stiffened my crew cut, had returned to it a body that the sun at the pool drained out over the summer months. Darlene – La Posada – the trip to Tucker Spring during Christmas had been planned since Thanksgiving. Not a problem except that the internal juices of puberty began moving with the sound of Christmas music and romance had taken precedence over adventure during the holidays of 1944. Wanting to hang around the train stations at Fred Harvey's La Posada Hotel obsessed me. A classmate and current passion, Darlene, had gone to San Bernardino to see her dad and was supposed to be back before Christmas. I could not get that long dark hair and those shining eyes out of my mind. I absolutely could not wait to see her again. The scent of her perfume was in a sample bottle at the drug store and I'd sprayed some on my Levi jacket. I not only thought I loved Darlene, but I even liked her. *"Won't you tell her please to turn on some speed, Oh, how I need someone to watch over me."* Popular songs captured the essence of my emerging pubescent focus on living eternally with Darlene. I'd told Freddie and John I had to work at the drugstore but it was Darlene that had pulled me out of the winter expedition to Tucker Spring. Now I felt a deep guilt about letting my buddies down and once again was ashamed for being part of something that appeared totally stupid to an adult authority. I had ducked the trauma of trudging through a blizzard with friends Fredde and John.

LORRAINE 1947

"Every One Knows She's a Rambling Rose, A Beauty Growing Wild," truly depicted every aspect of Lorraine's persona. Sultry, coy, teasing, yet rich and mesmerizing were her ways. It was a Romeo and Juliet for me. Attempts by Lorraine and her family to "arrange" a union in the elementary grades had turned cold and died just when I fell in love with Lorraine – "My Sweet Lorraine" – as a temporary stand-in for the inaccessible Barbara. But scorn was the only daily bread I got from Lorraine. "A woman who's love is scorned will come back to put you down," I wrote in my log along with the corollary that you absolutely could not control with whom you might fall in love and when that might happen. It was all up to the mysterious forces of ro-

mance. Romance, *"viva la romance,"* was the cry of the Tucker Flat Gang during Junior High School days. Long nights in bedrolls next to the campfire were characterized by analyses of the relative qualities of the "goddesses" of Winslow and whether consent to letting a member of the Gang sit next to them in the Rialto qualified as some pseudo-eternal bonding and mutual eternal commitment. Lorraine moved off after high school and married a man in Michigan. She never came to a Winslow High School Reunion because of the turmoil of her life and the resulting divorce.

"She had the kind of affection that just winds around your heart. You better run for protection or she might upset your applecart." (from "Rambling Rose")
"Oh, our sweet Lorraine, where are you now," entered my mind traversing old

haunts.

I had said, "hello," to several of my old friends milling around the Reunion registration desk and was looking at the display of pictures of Coulter's projects in the Southwest when I thought I heard "Hi Lorraine!" Lorraine's existence was but a faint memory of a different time and place. My late night passage on the Grand Canyon Limited coming home for Christmas through the darkened depot and black silhouette of the La Posada suggested that

Winslow days had only been a dream and Lorraine had faded into oblivion long ago. "Wemo" (Welma) had told me that Lorraine moved to Michigan after high school and had been married and divorced from an alcoholic.

When I was a sophomore at Flagstaff High school, I followed my heart that still resided in Winslow and would actually attend the Winslow games and was even present in Prescott the day the Bulldogs defeated the Badgers for the first time in 20 years. I still wanted and felt a part of that intense energy of the Santa Fe town milieu along the Little Colorado River. Cruising with my old friend Freddie C in his four door Chevy we spied Lorraine. It was at a Bulldog game in September of 1948. She joined the cruise with me in the back seat and we did some "serious" sophomore necking. I was trying to make up for her total dismissal of me in front of her Winslow High hallway locker in 1947. Fifty three years had passed since September 25 of 1948 when I had said farewell to Lorraine. The song haunted me all the way home –

"Every one knows she's a rambling rose, she's a beauty growing wild – ."

"Hi, Lorraine." It seemed that my being recoiled into slow motion – I feared that reality was playing tricks on me. I was afraid to turn around and lose the absolute elation filling me from seeing empty space. There stood a well shaped 68 year old in a grey dress suit with smartly styled blonde hair. It was Lorraine.

I immediately walked up and started one of those unabashed conversations trying to hide my hyper and overwrought condition. I feigned civility and told Lorraine and her friend Carole C about the availability of "a sort of cook out" and bonfire at the Ramada at Clear Creek. "OK, sounds good Jerry, we'll get hot dogs and buns," Carole said. Lorraine said "I will bring some 'wine in a box.' "

Lorraine, Carole and whole carload of classmates came out to the Ramada just as the sun was setting. I built a fire and set up the DVD player with old 40's tunes – "*They say that falling in love is wonderful,*" (THE BEST OF DICK HAYMES.)

The fallowing Saturday night of the Reunion we sat by the fire in the La Posada and sang songs accompanied by Villarino's guitar. I rained all kinds of gestures on Lorraine, but she showed no particular interest in me and did not single me out for any tête-à-tête. As the events of the day closed at midnight sadness overtook me as I realized my reentry into the memories of Winslow Days could not last and would bear no lasting fruit. As I slowly moved up the stairway to my Gary Cooper Room, Carole and Lorraine commented on my mood – "You okay, Jerry? You look so sad." I sat for another hour on my bed listening to Dick Haymes and Rod Stewart's album of old tunes, tears rolling down my face.

The next morning after breakfast in the Turquoise Room everyone emerged from their rooms with their baggage and I stopped to say goodbye to Lorraine and she unexpectedly kissed me on the lips and quipped, "Why did I do that? I haven't kissed anyone in over 15 years!!!"

As the late morning sun warmed my back against the September chill I waved goodbye to Carole and Lorraine as they drove off toward the underpass that would take them south to Payson and on to Phoenix. What I thought was the end was not.

I received an email that the Reunion had been relished by everyone to the point that they wanted to schedule a "mini-Reunion" in 2003. Carole and Lorraine were to be the co-chairs. I began an email exchange with Lorraine with the onus (cover) that I would provide any technical assistance they would need – labels, programs, graphic charts and so forth. I injected as much personal comment and "life sharing" poignancy to my emails that I could without becoming too heavy. I did share my crush on Lorraine as my "queen" that landmark 1947 football season. I relived with her my consummation of the largest steak I ever ate playing Buddy Clark's "*Apple Blossom Wedding*" over and over again.

I made badges picturing a burning 'W' on them. I made a program with a "Goodbye Message" and charts with pictures. I made a "date" with Lorraine to sit with her at the banquet.

Wife Karen asked and I agreed that she should come to the 2003 reunion; I believe that I was trying to be fair and honest or I would have found an excuse "to leave her" in Taos. Nevertheless, I emailed Lorraine apologizing for complicating the chance to find time for us to share due to the appearance of Karen. The morning of the first day of the Reunion I called Lorraine who was in transit with Carole from Phoenix and told her I was in "the back booth of the Prairie Moon Bar" – the most infamous site in Winslow and all of northern Arizona.

Karen and I sat with Carole and Lorraine at the banquet in a rather strained atmosphere. Lorraine in her brazen honesty quipped in the middle of a conversation with Karen, "Well, he loved me first before you." Nothing of note happened that night and I retired with a detached resignation that this would be my last venture into my Bulldog fantasies of yesteryears.

The next morning a 5AM I took my standard Poodle "Zhin Zhin" (Navajo for Black Black) down into the Lobby where they offered the hotel's morning coffee. I got a cup and headed out the south door leading to the platform bordering the Santa Fe Railroad tracks. Lorraine was sitting on a stone bench near the Platform drinking a cup of coffee. "May I join you?" I asked. "Sure," she said. The sharing session went on for more than an hour interrupted by the tremendously powerful roll-byes of engines and long lines of freight cars. I was able to convey my deep love of Winslow and my friends and that Lorraine had always been the sweetheart I had lost. That connection and attraction I had tried to create over 50 years ago in the hallway at Winslow High had finally been turned on that morning of September of 2003. We parted with a pledge that we would find a time and place to get together to share the stories of our lives. By Thanksgiving I had separated from Karen and taken a job with the Zuni Pueblo south of Gallup, New Mexico.

Long ago and far away, I dreamed a dream one-day, And now that dream is here beside me!......................
..........Chills run up and down my spine, Aladdin's lamp is mine, The dream I dreamed was not denied me!
Just one look and then I knew, That all I longed for long ago, Was you!
(Jerome Kern, and lyrics by Ira Gershwin. 1944. Long Ago and Far Away. Movie, COVER GIRL.)

MARRIAGE TO LORRAINE

Lorraine and I agreed to meet in Santa Fe in February of 2005 at the Santa Fe Hotel. Once again in my life I was totally overtaken by intense infatuation, driven one more time by the expectation of finally attaining the state of nirvana that I felt had been denied me in some forgotten past. It was perfect exhilarating time and was followed by my trips to Michigan and Lorraine's trip to Zuni for a tour of Canyon de Chelly and the Navajo Rez.

That Apple Blossom Wedding—Finally

Things were getting dicey at the job in Zuni and the work ethic of the Pueblo began to go south. Lorraine and I decided to get married and I planned to move to Michigan although Dr. Francis Becenti and I had formed a business firm called SOARS – Sourcing of Assets and Resources (an innuendo that we would fly like an eagle). Becenti attended my wedding and became a dear friend who passed away fighting Parkinson's.

SOARS had signed a contract through Gary Nelson with the Kayenta Township to provide a state of the art description of the nine components of a municipal government as a guide to the expansion of the Township operations. I spent most of the contract money commuting from Michigan to Kayenta.

For one who loves to see distant mountains and red sandstone buttes, Michigan can seem very bleak and boring in spite of its water and trees. I had to get back to the West and I thought my proximity to the Navajo Nation would provide an easy market for what seemed to be an expanding business opportunity.

However, my refusal to side with the Kayenta Township Commission Chairman against Gary Nelson ended my chance to continue work with the Township.

Lorraine and I moved to Salida, Colorado in October of 2006. In preparation for the move to Colorado Lorraine rummaged her old footlocker of memorials and ran across her high school diary. I researched the date of our necking in Fredde's truck in September 25 of 1948. I asked her to look at that page in her diary and there it was—"I saw Jerry Knowles today and he looks really good after being sick so long." Lorraine could not record what really happened for fear her mother would find out.

SALIDA COLORADO

Having taken many trips to Salida, Colorado with Karen in her antique business operations, I felt that the beautiful mountain region would represent a compromise between my West and Lorraine's lakes and trees of Michigan.

We rented a house in Taos for February of 2006. During that month of February we traveled west to Gallup, Flagstaff and Colorado. I showcased Salida as a possible spot to resettle and Lorraine liked the idea. We moved to Salida in October of 2006.

Tenderfoot Mt.- Christmas Lights

BUSINESS SITE LEASE PROCESS

The township asked that I develop a position paper on the process they would use to create business site leases. Both the Tribe and the BIA refused to let the Township execute leases independently of clearance through their bureaucratic labyrinths. "Keep

your eye on the prize!!" The whole thrust of
Township existence was to cut red tape so as
to attract and establish businesses by timely
issuance of business site leases.

As the timeline march of the adjudication to
obtain the power to issue business site
leases, bitter wrangling arose by certain
business people (Watson's Blue Coffee Pot
Café and empty convenient store), by old
timer foes within the Chapter community,

Salida Circus

by certain Tribal councilmen and the Chair of the Economic Development Committee, one Leonard Platero. Many were drawn into the fray for political reasons.

Chapter meetings were attended by Navajo Tribal Councilmen and the Chair of the
Economic Development Committee; they were characterized by screaming and
yelling by foes wishing to compromise the very existence of the Township. Finally,
mass opposition to the Township being granted the power of business site leasing
morphed into critical mass. The end result was that ultimate and independent leasing
power was turned over to the Township.

For my part, we identified all the steps that the Tribe and the Bureau of Indian Affairs
had to execute, and we created a checklist that the Township would use to verify that
certain required conditions and tasks had been met prior to issuance of business site
leases. The creation of the authority and financing of the Township allowed the for-
mulation of a professional staff that could certify the completion of all necessary steps
to procure a lease. Any private, tribal or BIA entity could examine any lease issuance
procedure and react in a way common to municipalities across the land – appeal and
go to court with complaints, but don't slow the process in such a way as to discourage
economic development.

I was invited to and was present at the meeting wherein Councilman and Chairman of
the Economic Development Committee, Leonard Platero (from Cañoncito) signed the
document empowering the Township Commission to directly execute business site
leases. It took nearly 25 years to reach the original goal that energized the creation of
the Kayenta Township Government.

SOARS

After the inauguration of the Township manager, my direct work with the Township
ended. Two significant projects were accomplished under the name of the SOARS
Company – "Sourcing of Assets and Resources." SOARS was a consequence of my
partnering with one Dr. Francis Becenti. Dr. Becenti had a PhD from the University
of California and had been president of DQ University in California. I had known

Francis as a student rep on the NCC Board of Regents during the "revolution" to dispose President Attcity. He was a brilliant, most witty fellow and I loved him. (Francis passed away this year as I write from Parkinson's.) He was the head of Zuni Education at the time I was working in the Community Development Department.

SOARS was formed as a direct result of Township Manager Nelson's request for a proposal providing the township with a report identifying details of an upgraded township government, one comparable in operation to those advanced municipalities in states surrounding the Reservation.

Nelson wanted a functioning local government able to compete with any existing town in the Four Corners area. He wanted the Township to perform effectively and to pose as a capable institution that could in the future execute any municipal funds from the state of Arizona or the Federal government. Institutions within Indian Reservations are often denied services and funding under the onus that they are "sovereign nations." (As stated earlier, NCC limped along for many years, denied any funds from the state of Arizona). Though the Township's incorporation as a municipality under the state of Arizona might not be possible due to conflicts with both state and tribal legalities, if the Township "looked like a duck and walked like a duck" it could make a case for getting the same state and federal money being given to cities.

At the time of contract initiation from Nelson and the Township, I was living in Michigan with Lorraine.

I did most of the work on the contract from my office in Michigan, flying back and forth to Albuquerque and driving from there to Kayenta – an expensive process as most money went to travel. Chairman Mr. Y. of the Commission informed me unofficially that I could not use any of the contract money for travel. Of course I ignored his stipulation and received reimbursements without issue. Nelson was still the operational power of the Township. Mr. Y. exhibited the worst type of governance I had ever observed on the Navajo Nation.

Francis and I had originally decided to include former associate Lawrence as a third partner in SOARS. But, as our contract with the Township progressed, Lawrence began contacting the Township requesting funds be sent to him personally! The same old problem that deep sixed the consulting firm was about to emerge again. I called Nelson and told him to forward reimbursements directly to me. The rule was that reimbursement would go first to time and travel done by company members. Lawrence operated under the concept that any funds would be split equally regardless of time and travel. From that point on only Francis and I comprised the firm's officials.

In Michigan I researched a sample of municipalities in the Four Corners area to extract a model of common elements making up their structure. I found that most cities had nine distinct functions along with departments managing these functions.

I produced a lexicon detailing characteristics of each of the nine functions and submitted it as the product of our contract with the Township. The results of the study filled a three ring binder, six inches thick. Concepts of "smart growth" governing planning and zoning, integrated enforcement, judicial services and cutting edge practices in each of the nine areas were cited and explained.

SON JERRELL

LAST TIME JERRELL

Ironically, our presentation to the Commission recounting results of the study lasted several hours, with several Commissioners falling asleep. Nelson had already been removed as city manager and application of our study was unlikely, but we did a good job.

Irony cast a dark shadow over me, too, as it would be the last time I would see my son, Jerrell, alive. It was January 2006, and he presented me with a Christmas gift he had bought – a coffee service package with grinder, cup, beans and cookies. We had gone to an alcoholic group discussion that he had led. Delphia was the Kayenta Community School Director and lived in the BIA living quarters compound. I said goodbye to Jerrell and we embraced with the parting words, "I love you Jer." "I love you Dad." Jerrell died of a heart attack three weeks later on Super Bowl Sunday, February 6, 2006.

DEATH OF SON JERRELL

In our travels across country to spend February in Taos we cut across New Mexico from Tucumcari to Las Vegas and on to Taos. We stopped at a ghost town in central New Mexico in late January and I was peering through the window of an old abandoned schoolhouse when an explosive swishing sound appeared out of the eastern part of the roof. While I did not see what had come out of the roof I knew that it was an owl, a sinister taboo and dark omen for the Kiowa dimension of my past. It was unsettling for I had always been careful to avoid any contact or communication with owls as I knew the Kiowa people held the belief that interface with an owl was the forbearer of death

Sandia Mountain View

– the death of three people. Any fear that I might have had that February day I must have stuffed deep in my subconscious for I gave no further thought of it until Super Bowl Sunday.

I received a call from Kayenta. Stepdaughter Hattie E was crying on the phone and I couldn't make out the first part of her conversation and then, after she repeated again and again I realized that she was trying to tell me in couched sorrowful phases that son Jerrell had died that morning of a heart attack.

As I have mentioned I saw Jerrell on January 15, two weeks earlier, right after a meeting of alcoholics in Kayenta. Jerrell had been sober from alcohol and any drugs for several months and I was so happy to be with him and see Delphia H. "Hey Dad, come by the house. I have your Christmas present – " Jerrell caught me leaving the door at the Catholic Church. He gave me a coffee maker package with cup, beans, grinder and even cookies in a box covered with plastic to reveal the contents.

That last parting will remain forever in my heart. "I love you Dad." "I love you Jer-rell," I said as I hugged my son and saw him alive for the last time.

I sped as fast as I could from Taos, driving the Volvo and arriving in darkness at the BIA home in Kayenta. There was a fire going outside in front of the house and a group of the H family sitting around it. I went into the front room and held Delphia in my arms. She was dev-astated. As I think of it now, I appreciate the fact that the Kiowa people go

Jerrell Gravestone - Anadarko, OK

through a period intense grieving which acts as a healing process for the loss of loved ones. I had learned not to show nor have feelings. And all my life, I seemed to per-form well and kick into super action in the face of problems and trauma. Ironically, that probably served as the best support for the H family during the next two weeks of ceremonies in Kayenta and Jerrell's burial at the little Kiowa-Comanche cemetery outside of Anadarko. His grave is marked by a huge black head stone emblazoned with a buffalo, teepee, and RV on one side and a ceramic picture of him on the other side. My son and Jerrell's half brother, Gregory, accompanied me to Oklahoma and supported the H. family. Greg cruised at 80 mph, unaware that our rental car had steel mesh exposed on one of its tires.

Each year for four years after Jerrell's death a memorial pow wow was held in Kayenta that was a Kiowa custom. All the women of the H family had their hair cut short – another custom at the passing of a family member. Traditionally, in the old days, family members cut off a finger. I compiled a 15-minute DVD using 30 of Jerrell's photos spanning his life from infancy to the year of his death.

He was a star of the family punk band, the Horney Toads, and was a celebrity in the Four Corners area. The DJ from Farmington along with his brother Charlie offered a special tribute to him on the local radio station.

Beyond Catholicism

I have always felt that what happens outside of a church is more important than what happens in church. At the time of this writing I believe in a Higher Power of the universe, that universe representing mysteries far deeper and more complex than the often simplistic concepts found to one degree or another in religious dogma. Each spiritual ideology may have some valid connection to the mystery but they fail to grasp the reality of that eternal power. To me, for example, atheism is totally illogical. How can logic be applied to infinity and produce answers about the essence of the universe? I look at an ant sprinting across the hot cement surface of my patio and think that its complexity may be greater than all the material and energy in the Andromeda Galaxy. (We have no intelligent communication as yet from over 100 thousand other galaxies).

I believe that man has evolved intellectually (theologian Pierre Teilhard de Chardin "THE PHENOMENON OF MAN") to his highest point and his next steps are to protect, sustain, expand and create the institutions and ideologies that manifest the common values found at the core of all his spiritual domains. I have chosen the Sermon on the Mount and the Beatitudes as guides and goals to be followed. I do believe a man on the shores of Galilee outlined how to think and live in a manner productive to self and to all.

Without the trust, belief and hope generated by a reliance on what is shrouded from view, man depends on an intellectual prowess that nonetheless leaves him alone with fear and uncertainty, unable to answer questions about who he is, where he came from and where is he going. This fear and anxiety motivates man to find answers to these questions by joining and bonding with other human beings who, as a group, have supposedly defined and tenaciously adhere to certain precepts about unseen forces governing the universe. Having designated an ideology, members of a group subscribing to such tenants wish to reinforce their ideas by reaching out, hoping to convert others to join them and demonstrate their validity. A study by Yale University indicates that members of a group with a defined ideology accept only information that agrees with their thinking and reject contrary data and opinions. The acquiescence of members of a group to a set of ideas is used to affirm their legitimacy and "righteousness," thus empowering them to offer concrete answers to those ultimate questions and by doing so allay fears of the unknown." We have the truth," they proclaim.

I ceased to be a ritualized or even a practicing Catholic in the late 1960's. The local Catholic powers in West Lafayette and Lafayette, Indiana refused to let a Black parishioner sing "Kumbayah," a Black spiritual:

> *Someone need you, Lord, come by here*
> *Someone need you, Lord, come by here*
> *Someone need you, Lord, come by here*
> *Oh, Lord, come by here.*

This was at the height of my work in Gary, participating as I did in action groups aimed at enrolling more Blacks into Purdue. The wisdom of acting out my anger against the Church as an institution is questionable to me today as it left me searching for trust and hope from my political and professional compatriots. While my empathy for those in need was undimmed, and while I was motivated to choose paths that manifested such empathy the assurance garnered from a spiritual program based on religion was gone, generating great doubt in my mind that goodness prevails. I waxed cynical and rejected anything that looked like a superimposition from the "system" (the common clique term of the 60's).

The song about "riding a horse with no name … getting out of rain" would be all I had to guide me for 42 years. I know now that there will be "caring" in the world if I cared, and that by manifesting it I will in turn create it.

When I heard that song by America, "A Horse with No Name" I knew why I fell hard for alcohol –

That place of no pain where fear, distrust and frustration seemed to float away comforted me as I stared at those beautiful multi colored bottles on the shelves above the bar.

> *"I've been through the desert on a horse with no name*
> *It felt good to be out of the rain*
> *In the desert you can remember your name*
> *'Cause there ain't no one for to give you no pain"*
> (Bunnell, Dewey.1971. A Horse with No Name. America)

While working for the Zuni Pueblo south of Gallup I would come into town on Sunday mornings to meet with a group of my alcoholic friends for breakfast at a local Mexican restaurant. Of all things we gathered in what had been a posh bar with a red velvet décor. I arrived in Gallup very early and went to 8 o'clock mass at the Cathedral. The arched roof, statues and stained glass windows combined with the silence and the scent of incense were great stimulants for my mediation. I was back, and deep inside I recognized the peace I had enjoyed when in the minor basilica at Conception Abbey. I knew deep down that I had never left, and was never left alone. At my formal reentry into a partial concurrence about my life-long rituals, I went to confession with literally volumes of "sin reports" ready to dumb out. The session was very short. The penance was, "Kneel in front of the Crucifix and thank HIM for not giving up on you" which could not have been more apropos for my life at the time.

My friend and classmate from Flagstaff, Father Alfred T. who road the bus with me to Conception and who was by my side later on Grand Canyon Limited back and forth on holidays told me, "Jerry, you should have been a priest."

I said, "no Alfred T., I could have been a priest but not 'should' have been a priest." I believe today that attendance at mass in the Winslow football days got my Higher Power's attention which power imparted to me that I was a resource able to be used for all manner of His projects. I'll take that as a compliment.

"I love you, Bob. I love you, Tim. I love you, MiMi. I love you, Greg. I love you, Jerrell." I am so grateful I have been able to say this over and over again to my children. My father never said that to me. At the last dinner with my mother and father in-Flagstaff in 1985, my mother remarked, "Your dad loves you, and that is why he gave you the down vest from the Bean Company." I still wear the vest in winter; it's one of the few remaining things I have that my father gave me.

I learned growing up as an only child that a father's role can be indirect, and that the support one received was generated through many small actions. Rarely did my father lecture or correct me directly. His distress about my drinking problem was manifested by his 3,000 mile round trip to Purdue, his message of concern about my life. His conversion to Catholicism was his intercession to save me from glomerulonephritis and by virtue of his medical brilliance he saved my life by insisting that a white blood count be taken which averted a burst appendix. The innumerable examples of how he treated other people, his gentle respect for them instilled in me one of the core values of life. But, he was not a listener. Each time I tried to share my feelings he faded away, offering no response. I would lose the sense that he was actually there. Sometimes, he would even leave the room. I have attributed this predilection to some very dysfunctional and abusive grandfathers and other grand-people in his life.

On the other hand, my mother tried to replicate the modus operandi she employed to control her five younger brothers who were, to say the least, somewhat incorrigible. "I will beat you to within the inch of your life," was her favorite castigation at any serious misbehavior on my part. I now believe she had a great love for me but wielded the get tough attitude she had learned to use on her brothers. It was what she knew.

The experience with my parents equipped me with the belief that the first rule should be to show support and concern indirectly. Being with my children and doing things with them was a way to shape and support them, and the quality of what I expressed and what I did was far more relevant than the counsel I gave.

Unfortunately, because of the relative wealth of my parents, I acquiesced to their role in providing recreation and material things. My time and resources were limited by job perfectionism and relatively low income. After all, what could I give them that even came close to what the grandparents provided. I recall the great feeling of satisfaction I had the first Christmas away from Arizona in Libertyville. I had chosen for Tim and Bob one the popular little car sets that traveled remotely controlled on a winding track. My parents provided a large cash outlay of holiday and birthday gifts and paid the tab for Friday dinners and other festivities. Bob and Tim spent summers in Flagstaff, away from the alcoholic fray of my life. They lived like kings with boat trips on Lake Powel and treks to national parks throughout the Southwest. In my mind, the nurtured existence provided by the grandparents took me off the hook of responsibility. Bob and Tim made their first trip to Disneyland with my mother and father the summer I was bedridden, recovering from hepatitis.

One time in Lafayette, in a drunken rage I threw the kitchen table over a rail into the family room. I had also started tossing and breaking dishes and I put my fist through the wall. I hit Charlene and gave her a black eye. The children were so frightened they hid in the attic space on the third floor. Things got so extreme that my son Bob threatened me with a shotgun.

I coped well in the academic and creative dimensions of my life but was totally dependent upon my parents for street skills. I had traveled to Illinois to start graduate work with the idea that the family would enjoy living in Libertyville in Charlene's family home with her father Barney there as an anchor. In other words I relegated my family responsibilities to my father-in-law because of my insecurities about graduate school in the "big university." Barney left the house and moved in with his girlfriend down the street. Charlene was expecting the birth of Gregory and was rushed to the hospital one night while I was in Champaign scoping the Illinois campus. Tim and Bob spent the winter upstairs in Barney's house and experienced nights so cold their urine froze in the makeshift coffee can toilet.

My father and mother flew to Chicago and drove to Libertyville for son Gregory's baptism. They were flying in from O'Hare and as I was rushing to meet them, I was engulfed in dense fog – with the sun shining. Foolishly I followed the backlights of a semi into the airport complex and in spite of it all obviously survived.

One could debate the pros and cons of the impact moving around might have on my children's life and development. I knew of military brats and fellow classmates who never left Flagstaff, Arizona. Tim and Bob claim that their exposure to so many places has equipped them with a cosmopolitan point of view. They traveled to nearly all of the forty-eight states before finishing high school.

Life for them during graduate school days at Illinois was very stimulating what with the activities of a huge Big Ten University campus and a living area housing a United Nations population of playmates and friends. For Bob and Tim it was the beginning of summers their unaccompanied flights from Chicago to Phoenix and summers spent in Flagstaff with their grandparents.

The year in Scottsdale while teaching at ASU exposed them to the amusements of the metropolitan Phoenix area. Unfortunately, Bob contracted a disease called Valley Fever – a fungus infection of the lungs requiring him to stay in bed for several months. I believe those days in bed may have had the same effect on Bob as they did on me; he learned how to be alone, and cope.

While all four of the children continued to suffer the trials of living with an alcoholic they did receive an excellent education in West Lafayette, studying among classmates whose fathers for the most part were Purdue professors. All the children scored in the upper percentiles of achievement tests. Bob and Tim maintained a paper route and accompanied me to Purdue football games.

The children of my first marriage are such fine, accomplished humans. They have shown a lot of love for me, and I know that they care. I now realize though that they were shortchanged in many ways. Indirectly, they suffered from the persona and the antics of an alcoholic father. Too, they were often neglected due to my preoccupation with advancement driven by my attempts to overcome self-esteem and self-confidence issues. Of course if I had it to do again I would have done much more, been much different and would certainly have been a better father and husband.

There were a number of beliefs and attitudes I held during their young lives that accounted for my dysfunctional attributes as a parent. For one thing I subscribed to the notion that my father and mother could offer more to the children than I could. The times when I should have interceded, protected and led their development I was absent either mentally or physically and simply assumed that the grandparents would be there for them.

Leaving the warm and supportive environment that my parents provided in Flagstaff I moved the family to Libertyville to pursue graduate work at the University of Illinois. I had a long list of fears about Illinois. What if I failed? Could I handle the demands of a Big Ten University? I had contacted the Newman Club in Champaign in an attempt to find a "safe and supportive Catholic" place to live. I was operating under the assumption that Charlene's father, Barney, would be living with the family in Charlene's family home in Libertyville. Bottom line, I was abandoning my family to grandfather Barney and going on my own to Champaign. I realize now that I had a strange combination of both competencies and weaknesses. My existence as an only child forced me at times to disdain challenges and head out the back door. Once the family arrived in Libertyville and took possession of the house, Barney moved out to live around the corner with his girlfriend Bernice and their two children. Charlene was left alone to handle two small boys, infant Maureen and infant Gregory. Gregory was born during a scouting trip I had made to Champaign and almost had to be delivered in the back of a car.

Family life in Libertyville was bedlam on a number of levels. Bob and Tim slept upstairs in an unheated room during the freezing Illinois winter of 1964. They attended a Catholic school where their teachers emotionally abused them. Charlene was overwhelmed with taking care of the family and struggled to provide food and clothing for four children.

I came home each weekend in the Ford Thunderbird and later took the Milwaukee Road commuter to Chicago and then the Illinois Central to Champaign and back. I rationalized that weekend visits were enough to meet my responsibilities as a father. All my dysfunctional character defects spun out into a vortex during that first year of graduate school.

Christmas came as a big eye opener for me. It was the first time that I had been the main provider of Christmas gifts for my children and it made me feel great. Lamentably, the event produced but mild impact in lessening the abdication of my roles and responsibilities.

The family moved down to Champaign in 1965, taking student housing in a complex called Orchard Downs. We were jammed into a two bedroom apartment with no air conditioner. The boys were in one room and Maureen, Charlene and I in the other room. I have never come to know why Maureen would sit for hours, banging her body on the back of her bed.

The one positive factor about living in Champaign was that the children were exposed to other kids whose parents came from all over the world. It truly engendered an exploratory, ecumenical outlook into their lives, perspectives that continue to this day.

HEALTH OF CHILDREN

Jacquelyn—"We hardly knew ye."

Jacquelyn, the third born child, was named after her grandfather, Jack. We noticed that she might have a slight birthmark just above her nose, between her eyes. The doctor's report was tentative, and guarded. He said more tests would have to be done to determine the nature of the marking on her head.

Close examination revealed that she had a defective heart – she was missing a heart valve. Charlene and I were told we must watch her carefully, especially at night, and not let her cry. To carry this out required careful vigils in feeding and diaper changes.

At three months Jacquelyn began to express a little smile but still remained pallid and frail. The decision was made to take her to Children's Hospital in Chicago to assess and carry out corrective action to repair her heart.

At three o'clock in the morning a week later I heard a knock on the door at the house on Talkington Avenue. I still carried the paranoia of an empty house at night and answered the door with a pistol in my hand, my demeanor bringing yet more agitation into my mother's expression.

The Family— 1967

Jacquelyn passed away during a cardiac operation in Chicago. Still unable to express genuine, open emotion, I reacted classically that it was God's will and did not weep.

A funeral mass was held and I asked that a Gregorian Chant, the "Mass of the Angels," be sung. Burial was carried out at the Catholic Cemetery in Flagstaff.

TIMOTHY

Timothy Mark was my second born son, named for Apostle Saint Timothy. He was born just eleven months after the oldest son, Robert. In terms of body type Tim is more like his mother's family – thin, with dark hair.

Tim suffered or was privileged – whichever way one judges – to be bequeathed with the aspects of the sec-

Timothy

ond child in a large family.

Robert, being the first child, was the apple of his grandfather's eye. My father had a picture of Bob modified to look like an oil painting. Tim was a junior partner in his grandfather's adoration.

Tim started out early on with his life being threatened. He started sleeping for long hours and complained continuously of headaches. We took him to a pediatrician who said that the lengthy sleep periods were psychological. The headaches and sleep periods increased to the point where we took time to see Dr. Curran (a Long Islander), who turned out to be an excellent physician. After his early morning examination of Tim he directed us to immediately embark for Phoenix and the Barrows Neurological Clinic. A Dr. Green would be waiting to do brain surgery on Tim. Curran had diagnosed him as having a subdural hematoma – a blood clot under the brain, which would kill him if not attended to immediately.

The surgery was successful and Tim, with a shaved head, wore a helmet for several weeks to protect the healing cranium bone. We surmised that Tim hit the dashboard of the car when his grandfather had braked for a squirrel. We found out years later that his brother Bob had accidentally shut the car door on his head. There was a time when I feared that I might have forgotten shaking Tim for some reason such as a crying jag.

Some episodes one never forgets. I took Tim and Bob to the swimming pool at Arizona State campus. One day Tim ascended the high board tower to assumedly jump off into the water. I realized watching his body language on the board that he was going to dive. I yelled to him to wait, but he dived off and belly flopped into the water. It scared the bejesus out of me. But, he survived with a sore belly and a somewhat dampened trust of his Dad's protective abilities.

Tim has always been a whiz in using media. In Indiana it was his favorite pastime to make war movies. He and his friends dressed in combat-like fatigues and ran through the cornfields north of Bayberry Heights in West Lafayette. One time while simulating burning naval ships, the whole cornfield caught on fire requiring the presence of the fire department to put it out.

Tim has one of the keenest wits I have ever come across. He jabbed at the BS he found on social media to the point where he received death threats.

Tim studied and received a journalism degree from Northern Arizona University. As a student there he edited the University newspaper, The Lumberjack. He once printed an editorial that documented the University's prominent position in campus occurrence of felonies. The President of the University at the time was extremely conservative and chastised Tim for telling the truth. Tim published a letter to the editor as a junior in high school condemning the local school board for banning books in the high school library. He survived five years as the editor of the GALLUP INDEPENDENT, working for two very difficult (in fact psychotic) publishers.

Tim married a Navajo lady and has one child, Rachael. They divorced after a torrid relationship. Tim remarried a woman named Sharlotte and has had a long career as the head Counselor at Gallup High School.

Many a time Tim saved me from the perils caused by my naiveté and lack of streetwise discretion concerning normal life demands such as maintaining workable cars, having places to live and so on. And I stand ashamedly grateful to Tim for his everlasting care and remembrance of my holidays. I revel in his thoughtfulness.

BOB

Bob was the first-born and of course is the oldest. He was named after his Uncle Bob Amann, who was instrumental in bringing his mother to Arizona and NAU for college. Uncle Bob was an accessory in setting off dynamite in the center of the NAU campus blowing out dorm and classroom windows.

Bob

"Oh, by the way," Charlene told Dr. Young on the phone. "I lost my water yesterday." After taking Charlene to the hospital, Robert Christopher Knowles was born – amazingly, without complications. He immediately became the apple of his grandfather's eye.

In his early life in Flagstaff he attended what was then called "Nativity School," befriending daughters of prominent Flagstaff families and neighborhood children.

Bob retained a fine voice like his grandfather had. He sung in choirs at schools in New Jersey, Flagstaff and the Choir at the Naval Boot Camp in San Diego.

Right after high school Bob worked for local service stations and took classes at NAU. He joined the Navy in 1978 and I waved goodbye to him from the parking lot at NCC, (Navajo Community College). I saw his Camaro disappear over the hill from my viewpoint on the fifth floor of the Cultural Center at NCC. It was a sad and sinking feeling for I knew that he was facing a total sea change.

Greg, Maureen, Tim and I traveled to California to attend his graduation from Boot Camp. We stayed at a small hotel in La Jolla and Maureen ran down to the Pacific Ocean for her first interface with the sea.

Bob marched and sang with precision and beauty and the family celebrated his achievement with mother Charlene and grandparents at the famous Anthony's by the Sea.

Bob met and married a lady from the Philippines and two children-Christina and Christopher, generating his middle name, which came from my confirmation choice of St. Christopher.

Bob acquired a degree in business at the University of Arizona and then entered the Thunderbird School of Foreign Trade in Glendale, Arizona. Thunderbird grads were provided with the opportunity to move into significant corporate jobs. Bob began with Exxon Mobile Oil Company, shifted to his beloved San Francisco to work for Levi Strauss, culminating in the establishment of large plant in Warsaw Poland. He later served as the *Supply Chain Vice President* at Barnes and Noble, moving from San Francisco to Long Island, New York.

Bob is a staunch and loyal fan of the University of Arizona Wildcats—"Bear Down!!!"

MAUREEN

Maureen was named after St. Maur one of the two youths that St. Benedict of Monte Casino raised in the monastery. Her feistiness appeared when she pushed away hands trying to assist her during her first steps.

Maureen Anne

Once back in Flagstaff and Charlene and I had separated Maureen became more and more incorrigible. My tiny grip on a bit of maturity prompted me to suggest to Maureen that she would have to go to girls reformatory in Phoenix if she didn't straighten up!!? I was also afraid that the onset of being a teenager could involve sexual experimentation so I sent her to *Planned Parenthood*. My alcoholic counselor Rick criticized me for that. Miraculously though, it worked. Maureen ('MiMi' coined by brother Gregory's inability to pronounce Maureen) joined me in H family times but never really felt at home in that situation.

She graduated from High School and immediately went to Portland, Origin to live with a friend. Judy Collins song, *Living North Of San Francisco* always brought tears to my eyes in those days. When my parent's estate was divided it allowed MiMi to move to Tucson and study at the University of Arizona where she completed a degree in special education and took a position on the Navajo Reservation at Crown Point, New Mexico. Her twenty-five year devotion to special needs children qualifies her for sainthood.

Maureen married Bob Short while he was a teacher. He is now a Planner and administrator in the Coconino County offices. Maureen and Bob have a daughter and my granddaughter Aleah.

GREGORY KNOWLES

Gregory John Knowles was named after Pope Gregory John—the instigator of the second Vatican Counsel that brought about mass changes in the Catholic Church.

As noted earlier Gregory was born in a car on the way to the hospital in Libertyville, Illinois, my only child not born in Flagstaff.

Being the youngest child Gregory was most venerable to the shifting changes of locals and my personal and professional issues. Greg lived, traveled and was accepted into Delphia's H. family.

Experiencing difficulty adjusting to a nearly all-Navajo student body in Kayenta Gregory opted to go to Flagstaff High School under the guardianship of his grandparents who were local residents. However, they rejected his living with them and he spent his senior year living in a large rooming house with NAU students. One of his most poignant memories caused by a deeply and sad misbehavior on my part was to leave him on Christmas Eve waiting for me. I never showed up.

After graduation from high school Greg applied and was accepted at Arizona State University. Because of the extreme lack of support he received from me and others he ended up in the lower 50 percentile of his high school graduation class that would have disqualified him for admission to ASU. Fortunately, his grandmother was a tennis player and letter girl, being the member of the ASU Golden Alumni. Our appeal to the admission people enabled Greg to enter ASU. He joined a fraternity wherein he found "hots and a cot" because I had little or no funds to support him. Slowly recapturing the ability to own and express feelings, I would often leave ASU campus with tears in my eyes. His membership in ROTC became a stepping stone to a long and distinguished military career culminating in his promotion to a Lt. Colonel and culminating as a dangerous year in Iraq training that country's officers. I was there when he embarked and disembarked from Bagdad and both times I could not hold back the tsunami of my tears. He evolved into a fuel distribution specialist and now commands that top post in the US as a private citizen.

Greg married Birgette, a German national, now holding duel US-German citizenship. Son Kevin completed a distinguished career in succor and graduated from Tampa Bay University in 2013.

Both Bob and Tim came back to Arizona to Flagstaff High School in a category of their own – i.e., they were neither jock, hippie nor cowboy. They were more like new age kids, and had already published a national article in the Educational Leadership Journal.

Bob, as did Tim, worked several years at a local garage doing the normal service work. Bob attended NAU for two years and then joined the Navy and spent two years in the Philippines theatre.

DANCES WITH WOLVES FAMILY

Delphia had four children when we married in 1976—Hattie, Pasquirita, Charlie and Denise. Jerrell was the son of Delphia and I. I must say that they received my love, pride and attention for the ten-year span of my life with them and Delphia. Two other children became part of the family, Dino and Yanivia, when Delphia's brother and wife passed away. All of the children have manifested excellence in traditional Kiowa culture and in athletics and academics—Charlie becoming the Vice President of the Kiowa Tribe. Ironically in some way in deference to my own children that Delphia and I that took the family to Disneyland, San Diego and many other trips to North Dakota, midnight runs from powwows and Holidays in Oklahoma. Gregory was accepted as a member of Delphia's family. I was given unconditional affection and respect by all the Kiowa relatives and powwow people—I was gifted and initiated as a Gourd Dancer by Uncle Alfred pohlman. I love and think of them all many times.

SOPHIE-REUNION 2012

I had sent out announcements about the 2012 Flagstaff High School reunion to all my classmates. I was a co-chairman with Bill M who lived in Loveland. But, he was recovering from a recent kidney transplant and I made sure to do all I could to avoid placing too much pressure on him.

I received an email from Sophie B in California with an exciting note saying how glad she was to hear from me and how much she looked forward to the reunion. As I write I realize that there is little that can be jammed into a two-day interface with old acquaintances. But the gigantic, passionate fantasies that haunt the mind for so long expect some holy reunion of hearts, a meeting of soul mates. My intense conversation out on the patio sipping a glass of ginger ale and looking at the newspaper braggadocio clippings of the life of a classmate who had been the passionate former boy friend of Sophie's was so dense that it took me several seconds to recognize that the host and former cheerleader, Bobby Faye, was announcing the arrival of Sophie. As I turned to look at the side entryway into the living room I saw a lady with rather long dark hair, head veiled and slightly bowed, gliding slowly into the room.

I reveled at Sophie's presence and was riveted to her movements throughout the day, eagerly awaiting our chance to be alone with her.

The opportunity finally arose and I found myself sitting on the couch next to her with just the two of us in the room. Just when a substantive conversation had begun, someone popped down right beside her – a female classmate who insisted that she had waited years to talk with Sophie. Once again, in reality or fantasy or dream, my potential tryst with Sophie had once again been cancelled by the fates.

"Sophie, your daughter is on the phone and said she was coming to pick you up to take you back to Sedona." Sophie quietly went out of the room and my life again.

STEVE JOBS REAL CONTRIBUTION

Watching NBC's Brian Williams, (NBC, Brian Williams, YouTube 5/26/2006), replay of an early interview with the late Steve Jobs, one could easily miss the main point of what Steve said to Williams. NBC had noted Jobs' passing by comparing him to major figures who had lasting impact on the U.S. and the world, i.e., the likes of Edison and Ford. During the interview Williams twice challenged Jobs about whether or not he realized the impact that he had had on American culture, and, in fact, on the whole world. William's noted that Jobs had acquired enormous wealth and prestige through his inventions of the Apple personal computer, the iPod and iPhone, and the iPad. He asked several times if Jobs ever thought about Apple's far reaching impacts. Jobs responded twice with such unaffected responses that one might well have missed their significance amid Williams' musing on the attainment of power, wealth and prestige. Jobs told Williams that his driving passion was to create something useful, and, once done, to go on to create something else. Brian pressed on with the ritual comment that producing something in the U.S. culture must have had some payoff to the author in the form of increased power, money or visibility. Jobs' simple emphasis on creativity should be taken note of by all aspiring youth – that a college dropout revolutionized how we communicate and access information, and he did it in a garage, motivated by the mantra, "stay foolish and free."

"Creativity is just connecting things. When you ask creative people how they did something, they feel a little guilty because they didn't really do it, they just saw something. It seemed obvious to them after a while. That's because they were able to connect experiences they've had and synthesize new things," (Steve Jobs, COMMENCEMENT ADDRESS AT STANFORD UNIVERSITY, 2006).

A poignant addition to Job's notion of creativity is once again the quote of Bob Kennedy—*"There are those who look at things the way they are, and ask why... I dream of things that never were, and ask why not?"* (Robert F. Kennedy, 64th Us Attorney General. ROBERT KENNEDY IN HIS OWN WORDS: THE UNPUBLISHED RECOLLECTIONS OF THE KENNEDY YEARS. 1988. Bantam).

REWARDING AND DIFFICULT MOMENTS

There are times when I felt foolish, ashamed and angry eating a roast chicken dinner at the Golden Sands in Kayenta. It seemed as though the Township was a lark that allowed me to have a job and monthly salary without any productive end in site. I really didn't know how or what to do to find another job. The brief and unsuccessful interlude at NCC made me leery of any new endeavors within the Navajo Reservation. There were times when it took all I had to climb into my Toyota pickup in Taos late Sunday afternoons and head west on my trek to Kayenta. Thank God for the driving force of Al Bailey, Richard Mike, Jerry Gilmore and Lillian Smith. I certainly was not a "John Brown" of the Navajo Nation nor a key player in its developing dynamic, but I had been able to make a contribution based on the guidance of incredible Navajo individuals, as had been the case in Gary and Cibecue.

My point is that karma always provides some reward for decisions and efforts of intelligence and good will even though at the time it would seem that no one knows nor cares.

In 2010 when my significant other and I were visiting her daughter in Massachusetts we were invited to go to Boston for the day, guided by the daughter and two granddaughters. We viewed all the famous revolutionary sanctuaries along with the famous church bell tower of signal lights – 'one by day, two by night.'

We opted to head for Harvard University and while touring 'the square,' the John F. Kennedy School of Government complex came to mind. I asked a passerby its location and was pointed toward the northwest to an entire block of tall buildings.

The location of the Honoring Nations Project, an entity awarding recognition to Indian tribes for their remarkable and successful social and economic development efforts, was cited as being on the second floor of a nearby building.

"But she (the Director) is not here," the receptionist answered. Still, I took my group up the stairs and asked if Amy B., the director was there, "She is on maternity leave," one Ms. Old Coyote told me. "Who are you?" I said I was Dr. Knowles and connected to Kayenta Township. "Dr. Knowles"!!!!!!!!? Individuals literally came pouring from their office doors. I was abashed. Everyone gathered in the coffee room to hear my spiel about the Township Government.

I had to explain to my family that what had happened was really not "all about me." Native Americans are very gracious in the way they treat visitors; Ms. Old Coyote and the staff were trained to welcome with open arms any tribal visitors. Yet their accolades really had to go to those Kayenta Planning Board members who time and again went to Window Rock to lobby and support the Township, and especially to the Honorable Herbert Yazzie, Chief Justice of the Navajo Supreme Court. I had to insist to my family members that I did not stage a demonstration.

THE CENTENNIAL

On July 1, 2010 I presented my story celebrating the centennial anniversary of Kayenta. At this convocation I related details contained in this section about Kayenta Township and the trials and triumphs accompanying the birth and growth of the township. I received a call one week earlier to be a presenter at the Centennial Celebration and worked intensely to prepare an accurate, colorful account of the emergence of the Township. I was sent a copy of the program for the day, and was listed as a presenter.

When I arrived in Kayenta and appeared at the Rodeo Ground's big white tent I was handed a program and saw that it was totally different than the one I had received a week earlier. My name wasn't even on the agenda. Shackleton's mantra ringing in my mind, "Never for me the lowered banner ... never the last endeavor." I marched up to the head table where the podium and the presenters were and to the surprise of several

STAGE EIGHT—EGO INTEGRITY OVER DESPAIR (65 AND OVER)
Becoming older (65+ yrs.) as senior citizens, we tend to slow down our productivity, and explore life as a retired person. Accomplishments are contemplated and integrity develops if one is seen as leading a successful life.
If life is seen as unproductive, guilt felt about the past exists, or the feeling that life goals were not accomplished, dissatisfaction with life and despair develops, often leading to depression and hopelessness.
Success in this stage will lead to the virtue of wisdom. Wisdom enables looking back on life with a sense of closure and completeness, and also the acceptance of death without fear.

of them, sat down and waited. Obviously the control mechanisms in both the Township ruling junta and local politic were shifting. I had been bumped from the roster of presenters. I was gracefully received and lauded by the head table and spoke for nearly an hour lacing my comments with humous but kind comments about head table attendents and Kayenta leaders.

I was gratified by the success and achievement of the township and felt content about my role in its creation. It would be a lie to say that ego is not involved in one's participation in the achievement of excellence for I had written a Doctoral thesis with achievement as a subject. But, I also feel that a key force driving me most of my professional life has been the desire to create in the sense of Robert Kennedy's mantra, and with the force that drove Steve Jobs of Apple.

The Kayenta Township Government model, in addition to its highest honors award as a Native American Community, it also is cited in a Senate Subcommittee as a "model that is applicable and replicable for developing nations.

VIII—PASSAGES TO SHANGRI-LA

HUG YOUR DEMONS OR THEY WILL BITE YOU IN THE ....

The changes noted below as a result of the acquisition of a spiritual life and the resources to repair and heal defects and shortcomings of character have been accepted as guiding principles and ideals. Progress and not perfection characterizes my general status and daily realization of such attributes and not their conquest nor absolute attainment. Life is a journey and not a destination. I have at times been to MLK's mountaintop but found it hard to find, get there and stay. At the risk of appearing to generate hyperbole I have chronicled lexicon of the blessings and promises I more or less experienced in different degress. I have done this in respect to those many 'good angels' who have embraced my journey.

The 'fear of the pain of shame' had shadowed and crippled my journey down the road less traveled for half my life. Deep seated Shame drove and overwhelmingly constrained my feelings, thoughts and actions for over fifty years.

Toxic feelings of fear and loneliness about being abandoned with dreams of being in the dark and alone loomed in my soul.

Unsure personal worth and lack of self-confidence bequeathed by sexual abuse and the humiliation at St. Anthony's thwarted my knowing and acceptance of who I was.

Like many of my alcoholic buddies I have identified myself as being a child in an adult body. My immaturity problems triggered a widening list of adaptive habits. The addiction to alcohol seized my life, robbing me of normal development, and crippling me as a functioning person at the summit of my professional career. I adopted a serious set of issues – I felt either 'less than' or 'better than' depending on the situation; I had no protective boundaries and was therefore either totally open or totally closed to the outside world; I interpreted reality as being good or bad, with no gray. My response to the psychological whirlwind was to depend too much or to totally resist dependence on others. I had no sense of what I neither needed nor wanted, and my knee jerk reaction was aimed at super control of both myself and those around me.

My constant quest was to find a 'mothering' female and a trusting support group of like minds with whom I could feel safe. However, my well of cynicism got deeper and deeper as life's challenges and experiences became more intense and complex. The comfort of an avant-garde school environment and the joy it offered was wiped out during my first month at St. Anthony's. Modified sand lot football at St. Mary's in Albuquerque did produce a sense of group identity and belonging, but during the same period the taunting on the basketball court down on Stanford Avenue soon destroyed any sense of self worth derived from athleticism. However, Junior high basketball in Winslow and the antics of the Tucker Flat Gang forays into high desert hideouts created a bond with my preteen buddies that persists to this day. That 'Gang' was a diverse group of trailblazers, jokers and philosophers and became my 'only child' siblings. Eventually and many years later a ray of light broke through my fog of alcoholic delusion, to wit: "If I take a drink I cannot predict what will happen!" And with that revelation the long, disastrous, downward spiral of my existence propelled me toward a welcome and most pleasing end.

The odd crunching noise I heard the night of October, 1971 after running through a red light was my sideswiping of two cars. My father bailed me out of jail for the fourth DWI. Alone at the breakfast table the next morning I knew that I had utterly abandoned the person I thought I was. Reality finally broke through the dark clouds of delusion and denial, protective ego armor of 'arrogance and grandiosity' evaporated. I accepted that I could not take even a sip of alcohol and predict what I might do. Attempts to avoid alcohol after past traumas had all failed. I was helpless over use of booze and the deep abyss of its consequences. A scene from the movie, Days of Wine and Roses, had lain in the back of my mind for years. The character was me!! I reached out to some alcoholics who had overcome alcohol dependence and was amazed at what they told me about their shift from despair to cheerfulness; about their forward motion from unresolved problems to independence; and from serious personal deficits and dejected states of mind and body toward a freedom of body and soul. For the first time it appeared that there was an escape from the crippling effects of past failures. I had finally found my 'soul' group.

My sober friends were honest in sharing accounts of their horrible drinking experiences, about what intervened to stop its destructiveness and about how joy filled life was after they were able to truthfully analyze what was wrong with their character; after they made up for all the damage they had caused and were able, once and for all, to focus on the high side and not repeat serious misbehavior. Warrior Chief Crazy Horse of the Oglala Lakota Tribe claimed that humans were 'spirits living in a physical bodies.' I wanted to find my spirit. I sought to understand and find my own elements. First, I had to believe and then trust in some great universal power. Past abandoned tenets were not embraced, and totally new beliefs were formed from spiritual traditions, from philosophies of the wise, even from the nuances of astrphysics.— *"Many nights we prayed With no proof anyone could hear our hearts a hope for a song We barely understood…"*

My early practice of Catholicism was capped by two years of studying to be a priest in a Benedictine Monastery at Conception although even that venture could not provide a return of the trust I lost in those early years. Seven months in bed with a seemingly fatal disease and weekly visitations by Fr. X for my "confession" and the associated communion had messaged that I could hide, that I could be safe from the dark by becoming a priest. Withdrawing from Conception however left me with feelings of abandonment concerning my life's purposes and commitments. Fear of death, of being isolate in a casket drove me most of my days and that, along with a fear of the pain of shame combined to create a dismal perspective, one which I concealed with an almost theatrical show of humor and good will to hide my real feelings.

A short nonsexual affair with a girl named Sophie lifted me into the stratosphere of infatuation only to take me down from what I thought was a Gatsby-like boulevard to bliss. My shift to wife Charlene could have been a ricochet – but as I now realize, if I had owned any level of maturity I would have seen the deep blessing I was receiving. But, I was incapable of the loyalty, commitment and real love necessary to cement a life-long relationship. My four children were a great gift from that 20-year partnership but I have had to shoulder my great omissions as a father, for not being there for them, for not nurturing them when they needed me. Late in the game I did come to realize that love is eternal and not on a linear time line. Still, questions loomed large in my mind – how could I ever return to being happy, respected and useful once again? How could I rise out of such misery, such hopelessness?

Awash in my drunkenness, unaware of what other people thought, I was utterly oblivious to the downward spiraling of my reputation. Reverberations of my terrible conduct began to surface both during and after my recovery. I was told that my once-supported destiny to be a Department Chairman at the University of Illinois Chicago Circle Campus was trashed when my wild antics became known. Colleagues and faculty from the University of Illinois who had given me unqualified support would scowl when I entered conference rooms. The Dean of Illinois, Myron Atkins, refused to even meet with me years later as I passed through the campus. I received contemptuous glares from the top people in Education whom I had publicly dressed down at professional parties. During a visit to Purdue years later, a former colleague and onetime friendly faculty member, Dr. Pose L., walked out of his office when I came though the door and refused to even say hello. At the height of my arrogance I didn't even respond to a request to apply as a dean at Kent State University. I turned down an interview at NYU, embarrassing my Afro-American grad school friend, Dr. Fred R.

Most of my life was spent alone. Seven months in bed with the busted kidney and the success in coping with seclusion and threats of death reinforced my view that one could be alone even within a group and survive. As my professional career and my struggles therein became more intense, the loneliness reached such a critical mass that

I bordered on paranoia, roving about city streets and wandering hotels in search of any means of social comfort.

But being with a group of alcoholics, or even imagining being with them somewhere eased the fear and loneliness and relaxed every cell in my body and that association was transformed into an invisible power that I knew would "never leave me all alone with my troubles." Today, I am completely comfortable sitting alone of an early morning, or cruising by myself late at night down a road in the middle of nowhere.

In the movie " LONLEYHEARTS," a reporter fell for a lady he wrote to at the suggestion of his editor, and he set out to meet her in person. The lady opted to lie about the lack of intimacy with her husband due to an injury and conned the reporter into a one-night affair. The reporter, in shame for his drunkenness and his infidelity to his girl-friend, resigned, and at his departure the crippled husband showed up with a gun. His honest recounting about meeting her "unmet" needs caused the husband break down and drop his gun.

When one partner cheats, bitterness, disappointment and remorse pour in. When iden-tities don't fuse enough to create caring, loyalty, endurance and the creation of an in-terdependent relationship, the partnership is crushed like ice. Love begins when infatuation ends. Love addicts never find the perfect mother—rejecting and abandon-ing ideal after ideal. Sex addicts realize that one orgasm is too many and a thousand is not enough.

A minefield of toxic emotions will not allow access to joy – that being the holy grail of all wandering, wondering alcoholic souls. Liquor and other mood altering sub-stances taken in to provide artificial solace never worked for me, and in fact they transported me not to Shangri La but to a dark, bitter abyss of existence, one, seem-ingly, down a road of no return.

Unfortunately, many of my brothers and sisters have ended their lives due to their lack of hope of ever experiencing love in the vast forests of the alcoholic no man's land. I find it good once in awhile to watch "BAR FLY" with Mickey Rourke and Faye Dunaway, a film featuring the life of a creative writer frozen in the hopelessness of a tavern subculture. It gives me the shivers.

I have a temptation to rewrite the script with Rourke visited by a stranger, or even a guardian angel thereafter to be transported from a whirlpool of depression into spiri-tual sunshine. That is the magic of Hollywood – witness the astronaut (Rod Steiger) in "The Illustrated Man" finding a vessel on Venus to escape his drowning in an ever-lasting rain. I found a similar experience to be almost surreal, and life to be a dream from which you don't want to awaken. Still, the fear of disaster and failure had left me. The depressed air of "Barfly" was very far away.

Using a list of people, places and institutions I had harmed in some way associated with my drinking and my character deficits, I set out to make right any wrongs, to do whatever it might take to rectify the misery. The Navajo concept of amends is 'hozho'—returning a shattered entity back the way it was. Certain events in the past haunted me. I resisted making restitution in some cases with the excuse that the victim was just as much to blame as I. I wrote a letter to a local newspaper praising the work and the success of a University President whom I had railed against loudly in bars all over town. In one case, the act I had completed in the office of a university supervisor was so egregious that when I went to California to meet with him, seizing the opportunity to make amends, my probing of his memory indicated he had no recollection of the event. I stopped short as I felt revealing my behavior would do more harm than good. I approached all of my children with honest recalls and arranged to have my daughter spend a week in a facility where she could deal with issues caused by my failure to act, or for actual transgressions. Deep inside I felt there was a way out – but like many addicts, I did not want to give up the "feel good" resource.

At long last, the problem of booze was gone and I was able to reenter the world, able to live, give and produce for those around me. The virtues I saw in other recovering alcoholics, virtues I only dreamed of in the depths of despair were now part of my life. I have been able to create new attitudes concerning every dimension of existence – attitudes in direct opposition to the negative and dysfunctional. My mind's eye oversees my thinking, feelings and envisioned actions. Wherein in past times I acted out to damage people or even institutions, and certainly myself, I now concentrate on assisting and supporting to make up for a life of debasement.

My avoidance of direct communication and action slowly slipped away and has been replaced by self acceptance and self-confidence, by a profound sense of gratitude and the treasuring of myself. The deep fear constraining my focus in carrying out life's tasks was dispatched and replaced with the joyous expectation of being able to handle anything that came my way, (*Now we are not afraid Although we know there's much to fear*). One afternoon I sat atop the examination table of a urologist who informed me that there were lumps on my prostate gland. I was to return in week for x-rays and biopsy. I remember reacting with acceptance and trust that whatever there was to deal with, I would be taken care of.

I remember the morning when, after my last DWI arrest I languished in jail feeling that any optimism regarding my soul's journey had completely collapsed. I could not summon a state of good cheer. I knew that was an end but I realized as well that it was a beginning. I was about to reclaim the warmth of Jerome, the potency won in early maternal warring – the happiness of a soul rising above all storms. Dependency on things outside of self gave way to a stable reality deep down inside me. What was flighty and mercurial inside became solid and real, recast into a set of values that I could bank on again and again. The barren void that had characterized my perspective was dispelled and brilliant theatre lights illuminated my stage of existence.

I completed an accounting of all the times I had been angry, of all the times I had acted out that anger in and made a list of the resentments I harbored about all people, places and things – both currently and long standing. And when I was fifteen years sober, I identified healing procedures that could control and even extinguish major pools of animosity and resentment. Under the genius of a medical professional, a nurse who was multi-addicted created a powerful process to identify sources of crippling dysfunctions and the means to diminish and even remove their operation in one's life. At a professional institution employing this treatment I identified all the dimensions of my wrath – when, where, and by whom or how I came by such characteristics. A sizable portion of anger had accrued as a result of the conduct of my biological mother. I discovered that the feelings of inferiority and degradation resulting from her actions – done shamelessly by her – had deposited shame in me. I reduced both the shame and the anger by screaming at an invisible mother sitting in a chair in front of me. I lost my voice for three days screaming at that empty chair, raging about how angry I was and how I was now "giving her back the shame!" The cultural customs against 'blaming' parents or others is not the focus of shame and anger therapy. The focus is 'identifying and holding responsible' those individuals, institutions or situations that caused the damage and expressing feeling and confrontation to lessen or remove the original wounds.

Expressing confrontation and furor at the orgins of the shame actually decreased the black basketball- sized shame ball into a golf ball. Feelings of inferiority, of 'less than' and 'one down' occur very infrequently. I know now that there is nothing innately wrong with feelings, that they function as a key element in our persona and were posited in the evolutionary chain of growth to carry life forward. I was instructed that emotions have three dimensions – those that have been 'stuffed' in the basement, those that motivate one to 'act out' behavior and those that are actual gifts to 'sustain and protect' mental health. I realized at this juncture that most of my life I had been governed by the fear of the pain of shame when I was exposed to the faults and imperfections attendant to all human experience. *Self-confidence in and reliance on the validity of my own thinking and my own feelings have now become a major part of the gyrocompass of my soul.* Actions to change or judge my 'feelings and thinking' are unacceptable from the outside—but behavior is always open to outside judgment. And, I have come to know that what are perceived one-dimensionally as negatives can in reality be gifts. The *gift of anger* is 'strength to protect;' the *gift of fear* is the cultivating of 'wisdom' to avoid negative consequences; the gift of *loneliness* is inciting to 'reach out' to others to acquire the energy of the group; the gift of *shame* is owning error and the ability to 'correct mistakes' and misbehavior; and the *gift of guilt* is accepting opportunity to 'make restitution' for injuries done to people, places and institutions.

My toxic emotion of dread was stoked early in life by the extreme physical pain of a near burst of an infected appendix. The unbearable terror etched in my soul at three by "Uncle Gene's scary boo" and the episode of being confronted at a young age by a burglar crashing through a window out of a dark house expanded my fear exponentially. For years I was horrified at the thought of being alone in a house. I could not bear the darkness. Even today I leave lights on outside when I am alone. As a seventh grader I was left unattended for three nights at the family home in Winslow moving me to sleep with a loaded semiautomatic twenty two-caliber rifle. I was terrorized by imagined figures lurking outside the window in the back yard. Of a night a knock at the door at 3:00AM in the late '50's by my mother to announce the death of my daughter Jacquelyn was met by me with a 38-caliber revolver in my hand.

To mitigate the fear of darkness I was guided to go back into "a dark room" where the 'burglar lay in wait' and 'Uncle Gene ranged,' turn out the lights, confront the two perpetrators and overcome the darkness. After having done this, my insane phobia of the dark was reduced to a manageable level. It is strange that sleeping out in a yard or in the high desert caused me no anxiety whatsoever. Upon one occasion, a rattlesnake was coiled under the porch under which the Tucker Gang was sleeping. Silence and no movement saved the day as the snake slid out from the porch and into the depths of the canyon. The darkness out in the high desert posed no threat. Peace and comfort provided by a campfire always functioned to create complete security within the darkest night.

The attitudes I adopted from my experience in grad school through the university years – stances I took during civil rights and education reform – that had rendered me scornful and grandiose began to melt away. In my arrogance at believing I was smarter, more knowledgeable, more committed and even more virtuous than my colleagues at NAU in Flagstaff along with my egotistic drive to singlehandedly overhaul the educational system prompted me to become extremely angry one afternoon at a faculty meeting. I recall immediately retiring to a bar ironically called *Friar Tuck's*. The ill-advised decision to have five martinis, cruise the Ford station wagon with shades on at 9 at night ended in an accident scene and jail. I had run a red light and sideswiped two cars. A fatality could have meant life imprisonment. I am making amends for the malice by attending meetings in the 'Supermax' Federal Prison each week to support my incarcerated alcoholic friends.

Though I still have strong opinions I find that I can relinquish negative attitudes, substituting them instead with compassion and understanding. The transformation in my character has been ongoing, and profound in many ways. Many times the energy, motive and vision seem to come from outside of me. I have discovered a basis of understanding in identifying certain behaviors as obsessive-compulsive. I addressed my alcoholic friends with the notion that it is *"better to understand than be understood."* In several situations I have apologized for my behavior to gentlemen who had done grievous things to my family and me. My word to them was that I knew they were *'playing their best cards of the day'* and *'God bless.'*

Events that brought fear and anger are now met with thoughtful consideration, with a view to ameliorating a situation instead of burning the house down – a metaphor illustrated by the early days at Cibecue — like a Canterbury Pilgrim chopping through dense and dangerous jungles. Amidst the height of the chaos, mired in the confusion of administrating a community controlled school, of a morning I played Kiowa Gourd Dance songs so loud they shocked the double wide building. I would then rush down to the school ready to respond to the day's challenges, confident that everything would turn out well. My destructive mindsets, my detrimental thinking and actions are now monitored with regard to their impotency for creating joy, peace and freedom— '*…..although we know there's much to fear, we were moving mountains, long before we knew we could……'*

"Shut up,!!!" My counselor Dr. Robert P. suddenly shot at and startled me. "Look at yourself." I sat huddled, arms folded and literally shrinking in the chair. The discussion that followed used that 'crushed posture' to reveal my yet congenital low self worth and venerability to outside challenges. The uncovering of my strikingly poor self worth that had functioned in my persona most of my life was a very significant first step in recovery. Dr. P. armed me with the weapon of responding to 'put downs' by emitting 'back of the moon' comments. At a dismissal of a serious project I created for the Board Of Regents of Navajo Community College I responded to by stating "are each of you Regents legitimately elected?" The dense air of dismissal was blown away.

A key professional colleague armed with two Ph.D's in Anthropology had been habitually inventorying my feelings, thinking and bevaior. Although his motives seemed benigned, his comments always left me despondent and worthless. Of a day at the onset of one of his 'inventories' I asked him about a his family's medical emergency—effectively shifting the focus off of my character. The sea change in poor self worth toward healing and positive self identity had begun—then and in the future by deflecting and not resonating with unhealthy judgements.

The very nature of my experience led me away from self delusion, inspiring me instead to accept capabilities as tools given to serve my fellows. I shun going off the cliff of character self-deprivation and false humility which has posed a threat to some who, having inventoried and confessed to their defects, get stuck in the feeling that they are a composite and lasting example of those very defects – i.e., accepting the epithet, " I am a piece of crap."

I have been genuinely surprised again and again at my calm, frank, and open manner when facing conflictive, complex and confusing circumstances. Once and for all, my remorse over the past, my sad reveries are dead and I view with honesty the critical events of former times.

Avoidance of the return of self-will wherein the ego rules to 'be first, gets the most and must be one up' all the time, is governed by constant attention to the forces of 'our better angles' that guide us away from the dark side to the *sunshine of the spirit.*

The riddle surrounding all of us in recovery is that we confidently reached out and were able to access a power that is categorically indefinable but assuredly prescient in Einstein's mysterious universe—"*Many nights we prayed with no proof anyone could hear...*"— A continuous, conscious contact with this power is essential to maintain a sanguine outlook absent of degeneration into unsound motivations.

Having identified my dysfunctional thoughts, emotions and actions I set up a dashboard in my mind to monitor the surfacing of these old ideas and faults. By acknowledging them I can choose to block their fruition to influence my mind and behavior. By recognizing these dysfunctional attitudes I could generate opposite and positive thinking.

In the old days my Irish relatives of Trinidad, Colorado probably took the "pledge" – and probably drank again. Their death certificates state "pneumonia" as cause – likely a *code name* for alcoholism. I cannot remember the times I swore "never again" – but found myself drinking by sunset the next day. I have proclaimed that I was 'not going to drink' for over 45 years, since May 28th, 1972. Yet, I am sober and absent of any other mood altering chemicals. I find myself devoted to projecting tolerance, patience and good will in my personal relationships, even to the combative types. The core of my spirit now accepts others as intrinsically valuable human beings aside from any particular history or attributes of personality—its not about 'liking' but about caring.

I have since inhabited bars and been among imbibing partners without either the thought or the temptation to drink. I have followed Fr. Edmund's mantra from Conception – "*Do everything with full malice!*" I have done some bizarre things to escape tempting environments – once spitting coke all over a table when I recognized it was laced with whisky. The mantra posited to me by other alcoholics stating that I would "know intuitively" how to handle life's challenges I thought was BS, but today my experience continually confirms that somehow the formulas and paradigms for timing and action appear out of nowhere to guide me down the road. What used to be a premonition or the occasional inspiration has progressively become a consistent function of my mind.

I have been provided with the resources to search, find and deal with deep issues responsible for the cause and conditions that catalyzed and sustained my weaknesses, which weaknesses required alcohol to provide the counterfeit "feel good" state. The support of my alcoholic friends in helping me to accept once again a force greater than my solitary identity enabled me to access the power that sustained me through the dire straights of life's experiences, and that new sense of mastery enabled me to charge forward with confidence.

My drive down a lonely ice-covered hundred-mile road though the early morning darkness from Denehotso to Window Rock precipitated my first mental decision to turn over my destiny to an inviolable spirit I did not understand but knew existed. I am absolutely certain that the high-speed collision with a deer in the early '70's while traveling the continental divide out of Gallup was evidence of that protection. The front end of the vehicle, covered with manure and blood, was smashed and so was the driver side window pierced by the horns. I suffered only a small glass splinter in my thumb. The car was still mobile, and the next day my Navajo associates marveled at what they called much '*dethlil*' – *spirit power*. They did not know that as an alcoholic, (*toh dethill hostein),* I had a prime force protecting me all the time.

On the White Mountain Apache nation at Cibecue that same Power covered my back unconditionally, protecting me against harm. Facing off an Apache policeman when I refused to re-hire his son, walking alone to meet alcoholic allies through the pitch darkness of a night to the community center and maintaining my cool in the bedlam days of the startup of Cibecue school joyfully reaffirmed my reliance on a higher power. Titus M's threat with a pellet gun, Dilbert Q's threat to cut off my beard, the grim warning of a parent when a child was hospitalized with an eye wounded by a paper clip missal, the kindling of desert brush in an attempt to burn down the school—any one of which at another time would have been enough to insure my exit from Cibecue. I had no explanation as to how each dilemma was solved, how each issue was mitigated. It all seemed to come from nowhere, from a mysterious force but it certainly augured freedom from dysfunctional, counterproductive thinking and those dire consequences of past catastrophes.

I had indeed finally a force I could trust, that had provided 'a happiness of my soul that lifted me above all circumstances.' Whatever energy, light or power that exists beyond me now prevails as the dynamic that drives my life. Perhaps a spiritual being whispers in my ear – but in any case that power must be unleashed in order to accept the previously blocked and rejected positives. That spiritual force may always be indefinable. Paul Davies, an astrophysicist, in his book "THE MIND OF GOD" examines spiritual traditions under the microscope of modern physics. Rather than reject notions of unseen forces at work in the universe, he notes instead culminations in a randomly monotonous deposit of matter, patterns and forces created in a way opposite to what might be expected from the Big Bang that spawned the universe. Improbable events in my life do in fact confirm a reality beyond common perception. My alcoholic friends continually relate events of their lives, the chances of which are highly improbable. For example, men with interrupted schedules of time convening for a weekly breakfast walk out the door a nanosecond before interfacing with a missing member on the way to commit suicide. They stop him.

Contrary to some myths, it is believed that scientists are hard-nosed realists doubting any metaphysical ideas or phenomena. However, take the case of the University of Arizona astronomers sitting around a table with photomaps of Mars trying to decide where to land a probe. Who do they ask? Curly Mustache, a 100-year-old Navajo medicine man, placed his finger at a spot on one of the photos. *"How do you know?,"* the astronomers was asked, *"Because I have been there!"* Mr. Mustache responded. Navajo medicine people are known for being able to project entities out into the universe.

Astronomers, driven by Einsteirn's mysterious universe, search every culture and tradition for hypotheses concerning the nature of the physical universe. Renowned scientist and apologist for evolution theory, Paul Kammerer posited a theory of 'unseen reality.' He had a passion, and his passion was collecting *coincidences*. He published a book with the title THE LAW OF THE SERIES, (Kammerer, Paul. 1919. *Das Gesetz der Serie.* Deutsche Verlagsanstalt: Berlin, Germany).

His book was never translated into English. The book recounted some 100 anecdotes *of coincidences that had led him to formulate his theory of* 'seriality.' He postulated that *'all events are connected by waves of seriality – unknown forces causing what we would view as peaks, or groupings and coincidences.'* (Archive.org.)

It is true that my imagination has been fired, releasing me from care, boredom and worry. Life has become stimulating and exciting; sharing and giving to others is no longer hesitant, nor does it seem fruitless. Trappist Monk Thomas Merton's prayer became a magical tool to lift me out of toxic dread about my future and my security. When challenges present and the going gets rough, I pull out Merton's prayer and it begets calmness and peace.

Unfortunately, many practicing alcoholics, even while reaching the edge of oblivion, have been unable to accept and reach out for a power greater than themselves capable of lifting them out of their spin down into the abyss. Captured by personal beliefs or life experiences they shunned, then scorned the concept that any force outside themselves could transform them into functioning persons. Either the idea didn't seem logical or they could not find a path through traditional codes of religiosity of which some have bitter memories. Unfortunately, most of their lives succumbed to alcoholic addiction.

"Dear God, I have no idea where I am going. I do not see the road ahead of me. I cannot know for certain where it will end. Nor do I really know myself and the fact that I think that I am following your will does not mean that I am actually doing so. But I believe this: I believe that the desire to please you does in fact please you. I hope I have that desire in everything that I do. I hope I never do anything apart from that desire. And I know that if I do this you will lead me by the right road though I may know nothing about it at the time. Therefore, I will trust you always for though I may seem to be lost and in the shadow of death, I will not be afraid because I know you will never leave me to face my troubles all alone." (Thomas Merton.1948. THE SEVEN STORY MOUNTAIN. New York: Harcourt.)

Some of the greatest slaughters of humankind have been waged over conflicts about the nature and rules of devotion to different conceptions of God or gods. My theory has been that at the top of the evolutionary chain (Pierre Teilhard de Chardin, THE PHENOMENON OF MAN), humans, gifted with an intense intelligence are haunted by questions of *where they came from, where they are going and the meaning of life?* Often, the obsession to find answers to these questions, while based on no reason nor purpose, become driven by both the terror of earthly pain and everlasting agony. B.F. Skinner would suggest that any given event or concept that appears to answer these questions, when shared by two or more humans, becomes a obsession of faith. The commonly shared belief can drive an obsessive energy to defend and be used to proselyte and convert others to affirm its legitimacy. A study by Yale University indicated that members of such groups are impervious to any information inconsistent with their beliefs. Hence, we must not foreget certain historical examples— the tortuous Spanish Catholic inquisition of 1478, the genocides of the Nazis and the current Islamic State rationales for beheading and burning 'infidels' alive.

Having studied to be a priest I used Catholic theology to allay my terror about being left alone in pain—decaying in a casket for eternity. However, my abandonment of my faith in 1968 over the local St. Joe's pastor's preventing a Black gentleman from singing '*Kumbayah*' thrust me into a chasm of cynicism and dread. It caused me to be preoccupied with generating "care" to an extent that would prove that such a virtue could and did exist – a strange, twisted motivation for much of my outlandish behavior. The mistrust of traditional and institutional religious tenants yet functions in that regard for alcoholics, who often confuse rejected "religiosity" as the source of a belief in a *Power* greater than oneself. Unfortunately, some literature offered as guidance for the alcoholic, overtly laced with *Judeo-Christian* concepts, confirms suspicions of some about the source of *spiritualism*. And yet there are those alcoholics who reclaim religious ideas, but only after searching and finding their own *Higher Power*.

The folly of the human mind to either define or reject the existence of a *Higher Power* can be both horrendous and humorous. Einstein stated that A to B logic could not be used to bridge the intellectual chasm inclining toward acquisition of faith in metaphysical realities. "*Despite his categorical rejection of conventional religion,*" Brooke said that Einstein "*became angry when his views were appropriated by evangelists for atheism.*" He was offended by their lack of humility and once wrote, "*The eternal mystery of the world is its comprehensibility.*'"(THE GUARDIAN, United Kingdom.)

The very fact that the totality of our sense experiences is such that by means of thinking it can be put in order is a fact, which leaves us in awe and is an element we shall never understand. It is one of the great realizations of Immanuel Kant that the setting up of a real external world would be senseless without this comprehensibility. (Einstein, Albert.1936. PHYSICS AND REALITY– FOUND IN OUT OF MY LATER YEARS. Citadel Press.1956)

In time the more sinister realms of Catholicism were gone from my mind, more or less, and I thought of a *Higher Power* as being a caring and supportive force – quite a transformation from my prior and very bitter disappointments concerning my existence. It appeared that I might just be entering into an exotic, enchanting Shangri-la like reality.

Stripped long ago from the clouds of religiosity, I could feel the force of that Higher Power whilst wandering my less traveled path, following as I did a force that was with me during junkets veering off into unchartered waters. The seemingly and overwhelming complexity of trying to set up an impossible project on the Navajo; the onslaught of massive problems raining down upon the newly created community school at Cibecue; the rushing across the midnight empty campus of Navajo Community College hoping no shots would ring out; feeling like a sitting duck in the Navajo Tribal Council, waiting to stand at the podium to promote a new township government to a very critical and wise group of council delegates – in each case noxious emotions long discharged in the face of obstacles were quieted by a sense of clear purpose, by a lasting well-being, likely by improbable gifts from some other realm.

Where did such power come from? Many theorists accept a logic reducing all of reality into atomic particles (Reductionism). However, the notion of "purpose" is an unexplainable dimension of reductionism. (Davies, Paul.1992. THE MIND OF GOD: THE SCIENTIFIC BASIS FOR A RATIONAL WORLD. Simon and Shuster. New York).

Quantum physics suggests that myself and everything in the universe bear similarity to a misty heliographic fog. Crazy Horse of the Lakota people stated that we are but spirits living in human bodies. Soviet psychiatrists told an American investigator that souls exist outside of the body. I felt at times that I was a spirit rambling in a low energy realm. The near total improbability of various events recorded and shared by my fellow alcoholics has affirmed my belief in the existence and operation of a metaphysical sphere. I found I could accept a reality far too complex to be either defined or accepted by the many existing theologies that postulates its existence and nature. Early morning in Cottonwood, Arizona my spiritual father, Ed Aston, commanded I kneel each morning and pray that *God grant me the Trust—*

> "Many nights we prayed
> With no proof anyone could hear
> In our hearts a hope for a song
> We barely understood...."

The local circus performer moved a wheelbarrow over a tight wire for over 20 years. The Ring Director asked a local if he would get inside the wheelbarrel—'trust.'

I do not pretend nor claim to understand any detailed theological or metaphysical details about a Higher Power, but I can share a remarkable experience about addiction to tobacco. Some clean and sober addict friends claimed that nicotine was more addictive than alcohol, far more addictive even than heroin but I was told not to worry about quitting smoking until I had confidently separated from alcohol addiction. One August night in 1978, in Dennehotso, Arizona I launched a supplication into the starry night asking that *I never smoke again.* My fingers have not held a cigarette since, nor have I had an obsessive craving for nicotine. I fought physical withdrawal with orange juice, strong coffee, licorice (SenSen) and cold showers. Although this was a period of intense stress in my professional life I prevailed, having pledged not to smoke even if offered a cigarette before a firing squad. The removal of my nicotine obsession I consider a miracle. I have found no logical explanation for the banishment of that addiction – not self-hypnotism, not resolve nor a solemn vow. Some power greater than anything I knew liberated me from my smoking habit.

There are those who would argue the intuition to *choose the right road* comes from metaphysical sources, or from a healed mind returned to sanity. Every person has his or her own source of power – but in all cases it works if deferred to as the core of our consciousness. Such a gift would have been inconceivable to me camped on a barstool at 3AM in the Haunted House Tavern in Atlantic City. The repetitive litany of praying has been supplanted by my directing attention toward the unseen reality I know exists. My deference to that power provides me with a clear mind wherein my faculties can operate with assurance.

Shared, common peril is a key element in the cement that unites all of us sober alcoholics, a unity akin to the desperate gratitude of survivors of a Titanic-like shipwreck which supercedes the selfishness of the outside world. This was unknown to me the night I was dragged across an Indiana lawn screaming *"Doesn't anybody care?"* I screamed my abysmal chronic terror at facing the eternal loneliness and abandonment awaiting me and everyone else some day. Consider King Albert's take on life as he observed a bluebird flying out of an icy blizzard into a huge hall with a blazing fireplace and feast-decked tables: *"Fiat Lux—let there be light."*

I have spent the last 46 years enjoying the confirmation of a safe, secure place of the kind that I created with lifelong buddy Kenny behind a woodpile in 1930's Flagstaff, and in a secret hideout inside the garage in Winslow. I found *"There's always a place for me ..."* I have been in D.C. at midnight wherein a group of Black gentlemen refused to let me out into the city night and took me across town to a motel; I marveled at a group of pilgrims in an Episcopal church in Georgetown packed with military brass and one of the most powerful politicians in the U.S. I had *'come home to a place I had never been to before'* and knew that it was real. I found the same den of safety in a firehouse in McNary, Arizona and in a Community Center surrounded by beautiful Apache ladies dressed in traditional garb. Amid 70 thousand alcoholics in Montréal I had to shake thoughts from my head that I had somehow been *beamed up.* It was unquestionably Shangri la – with fine French restaurants.

My previous existence was crowded with pressures, seemingly impossible situations and bitter discord among colleagues and within institutions. Yet once free of alcoholism I found myself in a never-never land marked by an amplification of tranquility and caring for others. Never a week goes by that I am not reminded of scenes from the past wherein I had a negative impact. I recently made a commitment to apologize to the entire city of Gary, Indiana and to any of my former associates or students whom I adversely may have affronted 50 years ago. A special burst of positive energy was unleashed when I approached people I had offended and offered to mitigate any harm caused by my behavior. Forthwith, and free of deep-seated issues that bothered me, happiness almost overwhelmed me, reinforcing my commitment to seek out the offended and make amends. One phone call resulted in finding that the person had passed away. My last contact with that person was a repeat of the scene in the movie Up in Air wherein actor George Clooney, willing to give up bachelorhood, arrived at the door of actress Vera Farmiga in Chicago and was shocked to find her married, with children.

I have been blessed with a close confidant, an alcoholic mentor, who is known in his profession as a wise man – not unlike the sage in the movie Lost Horizon. His counsel provided me with a priceless mantra, "Don't Engage" – and today, I am learning to avoid obsessions and distractions. The litany of insane things I did while drinking seldom occur to me now and when they do, they are viewed with gentle amusement, no longer catching my 'hair on fire,' requiring massive and immediate extinguishment. My fresh perspective on harm done allows me to own my shame for the impact I had on others. Spirit accepts two concepts – that one's behavior can be abhorrent and that it defiles the original spirit given at birth. Navajo 'hozho' – being at one with and a part of the world around you – projects a design able to mend broken relations by being willing to do everything possible to restore things as they were. My fresh perspective admitting harm done allows me to be completely responsible to others

By applying principles learned from other alcoholics I have realized in this, my forty-sixth year without alcohol, an amazing transformation of personality. At my core I feel a meticulous sense of unqualified calmness and I note the absence of pernicious old terrors, particularly the *fear of the pain of shame*. I easily recount my experiences from before and after I quit drinking and find that this is useful to other alcoholics like me. What seemed at one time to be too abhorrent and disgusting to share has now become a resource able to benefit my friends. My background and the struggles of others are community property. Feelings of uselessness, of being no good have been altogether extinguished. The dark cynicism has been removed and empathy for others, once a key part of my being, has been returned to me. Past images of being lost, penniless, and out in the cold disappeared a long time ago. Situations that overpowered me and left me paralyzed and incapacitated I can now respond to appropriately with confidence and with success. For the first time since early childhood days I find myself contented and joyful, free from ghosts of the past and gloomy portents of the future. Sharing the bleak consequences of alcoholism has allowed me to closely bond to my alcoholic acquaintances.

During the final stage of my active alcoholism I engaged heavy props to cover, support and rationalize my addiction and the need to "feel good." After all I was at the citadel of educational reform and transformation. I was a revolutionary inside the university and in south Chicago. I entered unequipped to participate in the emerging sexual revolution of the 60's, albeit being as I fancied myself a card carrying member of the cultural revolution of those years. "Has anybody here seen my old friends Abraham, Martin and John?" I was like a combo of Rodney Dangerfield and Mr. Magoo within these urban adventures, and my props enabled me to justify the growing negative consequences of my drinking.

The transformation that I observed in other alcoholics – their peace, joy and freedom from the cares of life made me seek what it was they had discovered. At the end of my search I found that I had to take the classic step from the movie Indiana Jones wherein Harrison Ford, obeying a distant voice, stepped out over a chasm and, astonished, found that he was still held tight to terra firma. Of a dusky evening in Gallup, New Mexico a mentor of alcoholics suggested that I just open up and ask for that power, and I did so one night in Fort Defiance, Arizona (no pun intended). Very slowly over the next few months I directed my perplexities out into the universe with as much conviction and trust as I could muster. Things changed for the better, whether from outside intervention or my change in perception I do not know.

My passion and love for dogs I analyzed later in life. I truly believe it was like the burning torch used to symbolize some value or virtue that needs to be eternalized. The unconditional love of a dog in fact proved that very ideal of love and its existence and I thank you, Jippy, Sugar, Running, Saingoon, Bow and Arrow, Zhin Zhin, Nishoni and Yanivia! My most cherished movie, "BISCUIT EATER" demonstrated to me that it is easy to see how enough love can outclass a entire kennel of thoroughbreds. In the film, two Georgia boys ignore their racial differences to team up and befriend a feral bird dog who they train to participate and win in a fence-jumping contest (from Internet Movie Data Base, BISCUIT EATER). A dog's unconditional love and unshakeable devotion presents an ideal as to what relationships could be like, and should be like.

The empathy I acquired seems to have partially come from dogs, from their unconditional affection and loyalty as seen in the famous film, "LASSIE COME HOME." I would spend a whole day across town with my canine friend Jippy, slopping up his wags and licks as balm for my soul. When we moved to Denver the family Buick pulled out of Flagstaff abandoning Jippy on the lawn to an unknown fate. My memory of leaving him, my puzzlement at deserting him left with me a haunting sadness that reappears often in my mind.

Downing shots of Old Grand Dad and expecting bliss only to end up in box canyons of disaster characterizes my insanity and that of my alcoholic friends. One of the great minds of the twentieth century (Einstein) aptly defined craziness as *the act of doing the same thing all the time while expecting different results*. But once freed from the effects of alcohol, my mind began to function without being driven by the primitive emotions of fear, anger and ego. Eckhart Tolle's discourse on ego is very helpful in understanding the function of that archaic monster that endlessly cries out, "Gimmie! Gimmie! Gimmie!" Understanding that my spirit is separate and superior to my ego has been valuable in monitoring my thinking and my motivations. Ego is a center issue in the character of the alcoholic whose behavior is recurrently described as "self will run riot."

At the height of my dark journey the prayer of St. Francis was out of sight and out of mind for me. I thought the values and principles postulated therein were what duped me into a world wherein empathy – to understand rather than to be understood – was a con used by Machiavellians to control others, i.e., the "pie in the sky" posed by Karl Marx concerning the use of religion to control and quell resistance of the lower social classes. Today when my ego suggests "Illegitimi non carborundum" (don't let the bastards grind you down) I stop short and pray to St. Francis for the energy to practice his principles. It is a better road to follow but I do it more out of the motivation that acts of kindness and compassion create joy inside of one. Finding it now unnecessary to expend the enormous energy required to promote myself granted me the grace to care for and serve others.

Catholic theology postulates the existence of a "mystical body of Christ" in which all believers are spiritually united as brothers and sisters. Alcoholics believe that they are unified like shipwrecked survivors snatched from the icy North Atlantic. I have come to believe that the sum total of experience, that the strength and hope of each alcoholic exists in a pool that is shared by all. The vitality that sustains and drives this pool comes from caring about other alcoholics in a totally altruistic way. My alcoholic father Ed Aston defined love as "caring from the deepest part of a person about what happens to another." It is amazing that as of today I can think of being an old Winslow Bulldog out to 'kick someone's ass,' turn that scenario off and ponder instead what can I do to nurture and care for the very nemesis that has been bugging me. I did this yesterday and almost came to tears with gratitude when I realized how far I had come from the old days in being given the power to care rather than condemn.

"Light a candle and do not curse the darkness" begets a credible mantra. The soft touch of a hand, a humorous quip, a smile are agents capable of dispelling darkness, despair and misery. I accept that all humans function each day with the cards they hold in their hands and that we carry on with what we have and what we are, lifted up, hopefully, by our fellow man. My constant deferral to a power greater than myself has kept me from drinking all these years and I am grateful to those who shared with me the tremendous dividends they received by placing faith in an authority outside their own capabilities. The unimaginative dreams that used to medicate my mind have gone by the wayside and good things have been taking place ever since.

Spiritual guides traveling through the mountain passes of life have told us that dependence on the material – hoping to find happiness in places and possession of things – are dead end ventures. I was fortunate to be shown a way through those mountain paths, through the labyrinths of challenges and trials to ultimately arrive in sweet green valleys with my mind and body intact – knowing at last a state of contentment, peace and satisfaction after my lengthy sojourn on that long and winding road.

A strong sense of self awareness and confidence light up my being now. I place a high value on myself because of what has been given to me. There is a grand canyon of difference regarding the notions of humility – one connotes humiliation, stating that one is bad, worthless, no good and powerless – the other connotes that one has been blessed with life itself and is endowed with enormous opportunity and competence. The emphasis is on the "given" in that I did not create who I am and in fact, this concept still remains the great mystery whereof Einstein spoke. I find satisfaction in looking back on that trail, on seeing the things that I was allowed to generate because of my escape from the abyss of alcoholic dependency.

For after all, Shangri La can only be ours inside the mind, the spirit and the soul. As Joseph Baldwin proclaimed – l*ife is found in the inside*. All living things have purpose and value. I see each of those in my world as precious beings – pilgrims on their own passageway navigating their own mountain passes. The cold nosey touch and the shinning eyes of Yanavia, my Labradoddle, the steady affirming gaze of Nishoni, my Poodle, are symbolic of the peace and joy, the indescribable bounty within the hills and valleys of our lives.

As I write I am anticipating a journey to the minimum Federal Prison south of Tucson where I will share with my fellow alcoholics who are inmates. On Thursdays I go into the Supermax Federal Prison. Attendance at those alcoholic recovery meetings are always met with kudos of gratitude about how great it is for us "outsiders" to come into the prison. Little do they know that I go there to harvest the immense spiritual power being generated by men who are imprisoned! One such inmate declares that his hour in the group is the only hour of peace and freedom he experiences all week.

Though I am neither a ritually practicing Catholic nor could even be considered a

Christian, I study the Sermon on the Mount Beatitudes as principles and guides to my thinking and behavior.

Joy, peace and freedom have been irreplaceably bound to my being and will never go away. The eagle will fly over the storm without even a minute wavering of its wings. My soul has been lifted above all circumstance and will remain forever in Shangri La, where people and Labridoodles never grow old.

"Many nights we prayed
With no proof anyone could hear
In our hearts a hope for a song
We barely understood
Now we are not afraid
Although we know there's much to fear
We were moving mountains
Long before we knew we could,. . . "
(When You Believe by
Stephen Schwartz)

37216473R00183

Made in the USA
Columbia, SC
06 December 2018